W9-ABD-361

A Birdwatcher's Guide to the Eastern United States

by
Alice M. Geffen

Illustrated by Peter Hayman

BARRON'S/Woodbury, New York

To the memory of my father,
Joseph Geffen,
who taught me to love nature.

© Copyright 1978 by Barron's Educational Series, Inc.

All rights reserved.
No part of this book may be reproduced in any form, by
photostat, microfilm, xerography, or any other means, or
incorporated into any information retrieval system, elec-
tronic or mechanical, without the written permission of
the copyright owner.

All inquiries should be addressed to:
Barron's Educational Series, Inc.
113 Crossways Park Drive
Woodbury, New York 11797

Library of Congress Catalog Card No. 77-21436

Paper Edition
International Standard Book No. 0-8120-0774-3

Cloth Edition
International Standard Book No. 0-8120-5301-X

Library of Congress Cataloging in Publication Data
Geffen, Alice M.
   A birdwatcher's guide to the Eastern United States.

   Bibliography: p.
   Includes index.
   1. Bird watching—Northeastern States.   2. Bird
watching—Southern States.   3. Bird watching—
North Central States.   4. Birds—Northeastern
States.   5. Birds—Southern States.   6. Birds—
North Central States.   I. Title.
QL683.E27G43   598.2'073'0974   77-21436
ISBN 0-8120-0774-3

PRINTED IN THE UNITED STATES OF AMERICA

234567

Contents

THE NORTHEAST

THE SOUTHEAST

THE NORTH CENTRAL

Acknowledgements

I would like to thank the many people who assisted me in collecting and organizing the information included in this book. In particular, I would like to express my gratitude to the members of the various state departments of conservation, the National Park Service, and the Department of the Interior for supplying me with information on their services.

I am grateful to Lois Mauk of the Southeastern office of The Nature Conservancy for her assistance in preparing the section on the southeast; to Paula Jones of the Mid-Atlantic office of The Nature Conservancy for her help with Virginia and Maryland properties; and to Diane Snyder of the Long Island Nature Conservancy's office for her cooperation. Much of the information regarding Nature Conservancy properties is based on their *Preserve Directory* (1974).

In addition, I would like to thank John Gallegos, Richard Farrar, Charles Callison, Myron Swenson, James Bond, and the many people who answered my queries and encouraged me in this project. Furthermore, I appreciate the fine maps drawn by Mel Erickson for this book.

I owe a special thanks to May Swenson for taking me birding for the first time and to Carole Berglie for continuing to do so.

Introduction

This book is intended as a guide for the traveling birdwatcher. It covers those 26 states lying east of the Mississippi River and it subdivides this area into three regions: the northeast, the southeast, and the north central. Within each region, the states are arranged alphabetically. Each chapter (state) has an easy reference map, a general introduction, and descriptions of sanctuaries and preserves. These descriptions are followed by a section discussing, in brief, nature centers, Audubon sanctuaries, and Nature Conservancy preserves. At the end of each chapter there is also a listing of state parks. These parks, while not intended primarily as bird sanctuaries, are nevertheless generally rich in all forms of wildlife.

Descriptions of national parks, national forests, and national wildlife refuges are featured in the body of the text. Each write-up includes the full name of the sanctuary, address, and telephone number; traveling directions; hours of operation; available educational programs; a general description of the terrain; primary species sighted; nesting species; and the availability of a checklist. The descriptions of these areas are brief, but they provide all the essential information that a birdwatcher would need to judge whether a visit to a particular sanctuary would be rewarding. The information given for these sites is concerned primarily with the birdlife, although these areas may also be noted for other environmental highlights. When camping facilities are available, either at the site or nearby, this has been noted.

The traveling directions to the preserves are given using I (interstate), US (United States), SR (state route), and CR (county road) route numbers. Some sanctuaries charge a fee; others may have restricted hours or require a permit to visit. It is, therefore, advisable to make inquiries regarding these conditions before planning your trip and this is why whenever possible, a mailing address and telephone number have been included in addition to the traveling directions. When the postal address differs from the actual (street) address, this postal address is given second.

Sanctuaries, preserves, and refuges that are closed to the public are not discussed in this book. Also, since no two visits or visitors are ever the same, no attempt has been made to rate the places described in this guide.

The choice of birds included in each entry is highly arbitrary. In general, I have tried to pick those birds that are unusual or local to the area: for example, the Kirtland's Warbler, the Greater Prairie Chicken, the Anhinga, and the Fulvous Tree Duck are noted for the areas in which they are living. In a few instances real rarities are listed. Mostly, however, the birds mentioned are those that are rated by the local preserve as abundant, common, or uncommon. That is, the birds that you, the traveler, would have a good chance of seeing and for which you may have traveled to the region.

The bird names used in this book follow the A.O.U. checklist (Fifth edition plus supplements). Common and well-known names of subspecies are given in parentheses; for example, Yellow-rumped (Myrtle) Warbler. In general, the arrangement of orders and families follows Robbins, Bruun, and Zim, *Birds of North America*.

The names of local Audubon society chapters and other nature organizations are given at the end of the introduction for each chapter. For local and specific information regarding an area or help in locating a particularly rare bird, the reader is advised to consult *Operation Nature Guide*. This book is published annually by the Tacoma Audubon Society and is available from them for $3.95 (write: Nature Guide, 34915 4th Avenue South, Federal Way, Washington 98003). This book lists, state-by-state, volunteers who are willing to take visitors birdwatching and to direct them to local birdwatching spots. Nature centers, local Audubon societies, and rare bird alerts are also listed, as are special publications relating to state birds.

The bibliography is a good source of publications, including many limited circulation pamphlets and booklets from state governments and local nature groups. In addition there are listings of national birding organizations, as well as birding publications and journals. The index of birds cited in the text will help the reader to locate primary areas for spotting certain birds.

The Northeast

Connecticut

Delaware

Maine

Maryland and District
   of Columbia

Massachusetts

New Hampshire

New Jersey

New York

Pennsylvania

Rhode Island

Vermont

Virginia

West Virginia

Killdeer

CONNECTICUT

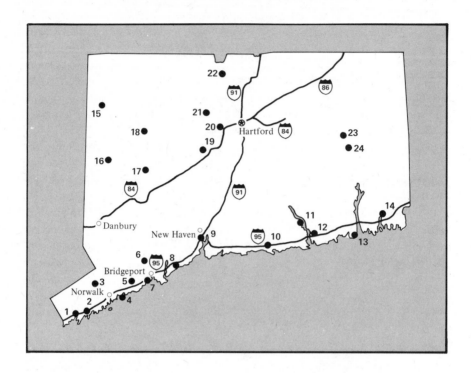

1. Audubon Center of Greenwich
   Bryam River Gorge/Wood Duck Swamp
2. Bartlett Arboretum
   Stamford Museum
3. New Canaan NC
4. Goose Island
5. Mid-Fairfield County Youth Museum
   Nature Center for Environmental
   Activities
6. Lucius Pond Ordway Preserve
7. Birdcraft Museum
   Connecticut Audubon Center
   Roy and Margot Larsen Audubon
   Sanctuary
8. George Treat Smith Bird Sanctuary
9. West Rock
10. Salt Meadow NWR

11. Turtle Creek
12. Lord's Cove
13. Connecticut Arboretum
    Thames Science Center
14. Denison Pequotsepos NC
15. Sharon Audubon Center
    Miles Wildlife Sanctuary
16. Eliot Pratt
17. Flanders NC
18. Litchfield NC
19. Harry C. Barnes Memorial NC
20. Shade Swamp Sanctuary
21. Environmental Centers
    Roaring Brook NC
22. Messenger Preserve
23. James L. Goodwin Forest
24. Rock Spring Wildlife Refuge

Connecticut is characterized by rolling hills and woodlands, freshwater lakes and rivers, saltwater marshes and inlets, and sandy beaches and estuaries. Although the number and variety of breeding birds on the Connecticut shore are limited, many species frequent the salt marshes near Westbrook *(Salt Meadow NWR)*, Old Lyme *(Great Island Wildlife Management Area)*, and Stonington *(Barn Island Wildlife Management Area)*. Here one can see rails, both the Sharp-tailed and Seaside Sparrows, and the Long- and Short-billed Marsh Wrens. The thickets along the Connecticut River (north of Hartford) are good places to look for the Connecticut Warbler, a species discovered over 175 years ago by Alexander Wilson.

Throughout Connecticut there are state wildlife management areas. Some, but not all, of these lands are open to hunting. It is suggested that birdwatchers confine their activities to Sundays during the hunting season (end of October through the end of December). These areas range in size from 150 to 800 acres. Habitats range from hardwood swamps to salt marshes to open water to uplands. For specific information regarding these areas, contact the Connecticut Department of Environmental Protection, State Office Building, Hartford 06115.

The Audubon Society in Connecticut is very active. Together with National Audubon, they operate sanctuaries in Sharon, Greenwich, and Fairfield. For additional information regarding birdwatching in Connecticut, the reader is advised to obtain a copy of *Places to Look for Birds,* available from: State of Connecticut, Department of Environmental Protection, State Office Building, Hartford 06115.

Audubon Center of Greenwich and Fairchild Wildflower Garden, 613 Riversville Road, Greenwich 06830; (203) 869-5272. The center is operated by the National Audubon Society. To reach the center, take Exit 28 (Round Hill) from the Merritt Parkway, turn right on Round Hill Road, and proceed 1½ miles to traffic circle, turn left at the circle, and continue for another 1½ miles to Riversville Road; the entrance is on the right. The center is open all year 9-5, closed on Sundays, Mondays, and holidays.

The center totals nearly 500 acres of open fields, wet meadows, mixed woodlands, and open water. Plantings to attract birds cover the area. A network of trails is maintained. In addition, a trailside museum and a bookstore are open. A variety of educational and interpretive programs is offered. There is also a wildflower garden. This area has a damp meadow, a small lily pond, and woodland. Among the 197 species of birds (87 nesting) seen here are: Green Heron, American Woodcock, Yellow- and Black-billed Cuckoos, Pileated Woodpecker, Cedar Waxwing, Philadelphia Vireo, and 14 species of warblers.

Salt Meadow National Wildlife Refuge. Administered by Ninigret NWR (in Rhode Island). The refuge is located on Old Clinton Road, a mile west of Westbrook, about halfway between New Haven and New London. Permits are required for use of the refuge and can be obtained from the refuge manager at

Ninigret. Camping is not permitted on the refuge; however, camping facilities are available at nearby state parks.

Salt Meadow Refuge was established in 1971 and now totals 177 acres. It consists of a variety of habitats ranging from upland hardwood forests to tidal salt marsh. The marshes receive heavy use from migrating shorebirds and waterfowl; the upland section provides food and shelter for American Woodcock, Ruffed Grouse, and many species of songbirds.

Sharon Audubon Center, Route 4, Sharon 06069; (203) 364-5820. The center is located 2 miles east of Sharon on SR 4. It is operated by the National Audubon Society. Admission is charged for non-NAS members. The center is open 9-5, Tuesday through Saturday; Sunday from 1-5; closed Mondays and holidays. A variety of educational and interpretive programs is regularly scheduled. Housed in the main building are a nature museum, a library, and a bookstore.

The 526-acre preserve consists of mixed hardwood forest, open fields, hardwood swamp, 2 large ponds, and streams. There are 11 miles of trails, an herb garden, a hummingbird garden, and several small wildflower gardens. The varied habitat supports diversified plant and animal communities. There have been 172 species of birds (16 nesting) recorded at the center. Among them are: Wood Duck, Green-winged Teal, Pintail, Ruffed Grouse, Cooper's Hawk, American Woodcock, Great Horned Owl, Common (Yellow-shafted) Flicker, Eastern Bluebird, Blue Jay, Scarlet Tanager, Common Redpoll, swallows, and warblers (including Lawrence's Warbler). A naturalist is on staff.

NATURE CENTERS

Throughout Connecticut there are many nature centers, arboretums, and bird sanctuaries. Most of these offer a variety of educational and interpretive programs. They can all be rewarding birdwatching places. These centers are described briefly below.

Bartlett Arboretum, 151 Brookdale Road, Stamford 06903; (203) 322-6971. The arboretum is operated by the University of Connecticut. This 62-acre park is characterized by evergreens, thickets, mixed hardwoods, a small pool, and a brook. Trails are maintained. The arboretum is open all year.

Birdcraft Museum, 314 Unquoa Road, Fairfield 06430; (203) 250-1063. The museum is operated by the Connecticut Audubon Society. It is a 5-acre preserve, open on weekends only throughout the year. Look for ducks and migratory passerines here.

Connecticut Arboretum, Quaker Hill, New London 06320. The arboretum is owned by Connecticut College. It is located off Williams Street, near SR 32. This 385-acre area consists of hardwood swamps, mixed deciduous forest, open water, and thickets. Trails are maintained; the arboretum is open all year. There have been 178 species of birds reported here. Among them are: Red-necked Grebe, Osprey, Broad-winged Hawk, Hooded Warbler, Wood Thrush, Blue-winged Warbler, and Rufous-sided Towhee.

Connecticut Audubon Center, 2325 Burr Street, Fairfield 06430; (203) 259-6305. The center is the headquarters for the Connecticut Audubon Society. There are 150 acres of mixed woodlands and open fields. Guided tours are available. Trails, some self-guiding, are maintained. The center is open all year, closed Mondays and holidays.

Denison Pequotsepos Nature Center, Pequotsepos Road, Mystic 06355; (203) 536-1216. The center totals 125 acres of mixed hardwood forest, open fields, hardwood swamp, and open water. A network of trails traverses the area. A collection of live avian predators is kept near the main building. There is also a nature museum. The center is open all year, closed on Mondays from 30 October to 30 April. Nesting species include: Ruffed Grouse, Hairy Woodpecker, Least Flycatcher, White-breasted Nuthatch, House Wren, Chestnut-sided Warbler, Hooded Warbler, and Northern (Baltimore) Oriole.

Eliot Prat Outdoor Education Center, Paper Mill Road, New Milford 06776; (203) 354-3665. The center totals 140 acres. A variety of educational and interpretive programs is available. Guided tours are offered. The center is open all year.

Environmental Centers, Inc., Gracey Road, Canton 06019; (203) 693-0263; also 950 Trout Brook Drive, West Hartford 06119; (203) 236-2961. The center totals 12 acres plus 100 acres in adjacent Werner State Forest. Trails, some self-guiding, are maintained. The center is open all year, closed on Mondays and holidays.

Flanders Nature Center, Flanders Road, Woodbury 06798; (203) 263-3711. The center totals 900 acres of mixed hardwoods, open brushy and hardwood swamps, and some open water. Of special interest are the Christmas tree farm and the maple sugaring operations. A trailside museum is maintained. There is a network of trails, some self-guiding. The center is open all year. There have been 119 species of birds reported here. Among them are: Wood Duck, Osprey, White-eyed Vireo, and Blue-winged Warbler.

George Treat Smith and Sarah Edward Hubbell Bird Sanctuary, Seaview Avenue, Milford 06460. The sanctuary is operated by the New Haven Bird Club and is open by appointment. For information, contact: Mr. Kevin Gunther, 1 Milford Point, Milford 06460. This is a good area for waterfowl, shorebirds, and marshbirds.

Harry C. Barnes Memorial Nature Center, 175 Shrub Road, Bristol 06010; (203) 589-6082. The center totals 70 acres. Trails, some self-guiding, are maintained. Guided tours are available. The center is open Tuesday through Sunday all year; it is closed on Mondays and during the month of January.

The James L. Goodwin Forest Conservation Center, Potter Road and Route 6, Box 100, R.R. 1, North Windham 06256; (203) 455-9534. The center is operated by the Connecticut Department of Environmental Protection. The center totals over 1800 acres (in the state forest of the same name) of open fields, hardwood swamps, and mixed woodlands. Trails are maintained; guided and self-guiding tours are available. The center is open all year, closed on Mondays and Tuesdays.

Litchfield Nature Center and Museum, Litchfield 06759; (203) 567-0015. This 400-acre center includes the White Memorial Foundation Sanctuary. Overnight facilities are available at the center. The diversified habitat types include open water, freshwater marsh, open fields, and mixed hardwood forests. There are guided and self-guiding tours available. Over 30 miles of trails and a wildflower garden are maintained. The center is open Tuesday through Saturday all year, Sundays from April to November; it is closed on Mondays and holidays. Among the many species of birds seen here are: Pied-billed Grebe, Blue-winged Teal, Canvasback, Ruddy Duck, Wood Duck, Virginia Rail, Barred Owl, Hairy Woodpecker, Wood Thrush, Veery, Blue-winged Warbler, Black-throated Blue Warbler, Bobolink, and Rose-breasted Grosbeak.

Mid-Fairfield County Youth Museum, Woodside Avenue, Westport 06880. This area totals 53 acres of mixed hardwoods, hardwood swamp, and open fields. Trails are maintained. A natural science library and a nature museum are located on the premises. This is a good area for warblers.

Miles Wildlife Sanctuary, West Cornwall Road, Sharon 06069; (203) 364-5302. The sanctuary is owned and staffed by the National Audubon Society. Arrangements to visit must be made in advance. The sanctuary totals 751 acres of mixed woodlands, marshes, and a lake. It is a nesting area for Hooded Mergansers, Mallards, Black Ducks, Wood Ducks, and Canada Geese.

The Nature Center for Environmental Activities, Inc., 10 Woodside Lane, P.O. Box 165, Westport 06880; (203) 227-7253. The center totals 53 acres. Guided tours are offered. Trails, some self-guiding, are maintained. A variety of educational and interpretive programs is offered. The center is open all year.

New Canaan Nature Center, 144 Oenoke Ridge, New Canaan 06840; (203) 966-9577. There are 4 separate areas that total 80 acres. The first area is the *Nature Center Museum.* This portion covers about 40 acres of lawns and woodlands; a trailside museum and a bookshop are located here. The second area is the *Bird Sanctuary and Nature Preserve.* This is owned by the Town of New Canaan and comprises 15 acres. A small pool, hardwood swamp, and wooded hillside characterize the area. The *Kelly Lowlands Sanctuary* is the third area and this is owned by the New Canaan Audubon Society. The *Kelly Upland Sanctuary* is the fourth area; it is also owned by New Canaan Audubon. This 12-acre sanctuary has mixed hardwoods, thickets, and open fields. All 4 areas have paths and/or trails. For additional information, contact the Nature Center itself (see above).

Roaring Brook Nature Center, Gracey Road, Canton 06019. The center totals 93 acres of mixed hardwoods, open fields, open marsh, ponds, and hardwood swamp. There is a trailside museum; trails are maintained. The center is open all year.

Roy and Margot Larsen Audubon Sanctuary, Burr Street, Fairfield 06430. This 160-acre sanctuary is characterized by mixed hardwood forest, hardwood swamp, open marsh, shallow ponds, and open fields. Trails are maintained.

Shade Swamp Sanctuary, Farmington 06032. The center is to the left and right of SR 6. This 500-acre sanctuary is characterized by open and brushy marshes, hardwood swamps, and mixed woodlands. Trails are maintained; the sanctuary is open all year. The Farmington River Watershed Association in Avon publishes a guidebook to the area.

Stamford Museum and Nature Center, 39 Scofieldtown Road, Stamford 06903; (203) 322-1646. The center totals 108 acres of mixed woodlands, thickets, and open fields. There are 3 miles of trails. The center adjoins the Bartlett Arboretum (see above), and is open all year.

The Thames Science Center, Inc., Gallows Lane, New London 06320; (203) 443-4295. The center covers 2 acres and has access to the Connecticut Arboretum (see above). The center also has use of the 42-acre Peace Sanctuary Nature Preserve as well as other areas. A variety of educational and interpretive programs is offered at the center. The center is open all year.

West Rock Nature Recreation Center, P.O. Box 2969, New Haven 06515; (203) 562-0151. The center is operated by New Haven Park and Recreation Commission. It totals 40 acres and is open all year.

NATURE CONSERVANCY PRESERVES

The Nature Conservancy owns and maintains 65 preserves in Connecticut totaling nearly 6800 acres. Most of these are located in the western half of the state and along the coast east of the Connecticut River. Fourteen of the preserves are in the Stamford area. Some of The Nature Conservancy's preserves adjoin state forests or wildlife management areas. All preserves are open to the public for hiking, photography, and birdwatching. Some of the preserves are briefly noted below. For permission to visit specific preserves and for further information about their preserves, contact: The Nature Conservancy, Connecticut Chapter, P.O. Box MMM, Wesleyan Station, Middletown 06457; (203) 344-0716.

Wood Duck

The Bryam River Gorge Preserve, in Greenwich. This preserve totals 120 acres of hardwood swamp with dogwood, red maple, and willow. Nearby is the *Wood Duck Swamp*, a 5-acre area that provides nesting habitat for Wood Ducks and a variety of woodpeckers.

Goose Island is a ½-acre island located off the coast of Saugatuck. It is a rocky nesting site for terns. The preserve is maintained by the Saugatuck Valley Audubon Society.

Lord's Cove Preserve, in Lyme, totals 76 acres and provides food and shelter for migratory waterfowl.

Lucius Pond Ordway Preserve (Devil's Den), in Weston. This 1471-acre tract is characterized by an oak-maple forest. Look for Canada Geese and other migratory birds.

The Messenger Preserve, in northeastern Connecticut, near Granby, is a typical Connecticut woodland. The 144-acre preserve provides habitat for deer, bobcat, black bear, and mink.

Rock Spring Wildlife Refuge, in Scotland, is 367 acres of mixed hardwood forest on hilly terrain. The refuge provides habitat for a wide variety of landbirds.

Turtle Creek Wildlife Sanctuary, in Essex, totals 89 acres and is located on the Connecticut River. It is characterized by marshlands and mixed woodlands.

STATE PARKS AND FORESTS

Birdwatching at Connecticut's state parks and forests is generally rewarding. However, as with parks in other states, these areas are not designed primarily as bird sanctuaries. They generally offer a variety of activities including camping, picnicking, hiking, and nature study. Following is a list of state parks and forests; those that are well known as good birdwatching places (or are near large bird sanctuaries) are marked with an asterisk (*). For further information about state parks in Connecticut, contact the Connecticut Department of Environmental Protection, State Office Building, Hartford 06115.

*Algonquin State Forest, Colebrook 06021; 2933 acres.
 American Legion, Winsted 06098.
 Bigelow Hollow, Union; day use only.
 Black Rock, Thomaston 06787.
 Bluff Point, Groton 06340; 275 acres.
 Burr Pond, Burrville.
 Campbell Falls, Norfolk 06058; 102 acres; day use only.
 Chatfield Hollow, Killingworth; 345 acres; day use only.
*Cockaponset State Forest, Haddam 06438; 2300 acres.
 Day Pond, Westchester; day use only.
 Dennis Hill, Norfolk 06058; day use only.
 Devils Hopyard, East Haddam 06423; 860 acres.
 Fort Shantok, Norwich 06360; day use only.
 Gay City, Manchester 06040; day use only.
 Gillette Castle, East Haddam 06423; 144 acres; day use only.
*Haddam Meadows, Haddam 06438; 143 acres; day use only.
*Hammonasset, Madison 06443; 918 acres.

*Harkness Memorial, Waterford 06385; 231 acres; day use only.

Hall Meadow, Torrington 06790; 690 acres.

Haystack Mountain, Norfolk 06058; 225 acres; day use only.

Hopeville Pond, Jewett City 06351.

*Housatonic State Forest, Sharon 06069; 5320 acres; day use only.

Housatonic Meadows, Cornwall Bridge 06754.

Humaston Brook, Thomaston 06787; day use only.

Hurd, Middletown 06457; day use only.

Indian Well, Derby 06418; day use only.

*James L. Goodwin State Forest, Hampton 06247; 1819 acres; day use only.

John A. Minetto, Torrington 06790; day use only.

Kent Falls, North Kent.

Kettletown, Southford.

Lake Waramaug, New Preston 06777.

Macedonia, Kent 06757; 2294 acres.

Mansfield Hollow, North Windham 06256; day use only.

Mashamoquet Brook, Abington 06230.

Mattatuck State Forest, Watertown 06795; 594 acres.

Meshomasic, Marlborough; day use only.

Millers Pond, Durham 06422; 261 acres.

Mohawk Mountain, West Goshen 06756; day use only.

Mohawk State Forest, Goshen 06756; 3245 acres; day use only.

*Mohegan State Forest, Scotland 06264; 371 acres.

Mount Tom, Woodville; day use only.

Nassahegan State Forest, Burlington; 1226 acres.

*Natchaug State Forest, Ashford; 10,827 acres; day use only.

Nathan Hale State Forest, Andover 06232.

Naugatuck State Forest, Naugatuck 06770; 2191 acres; day use only.

*Nehantic State Forest, Lyme; 1000 acres; day use only.

*Nipmuck State Forest, Union; day use only.

Nye Holman State Forest, Tolland 06084; 700 acres; day use only.

Old Furnace, Killingly; 101 acres; day use only.

Osborndale, Derby 06418; 350 acres; day use only.

*Pachaug State Forest: 4 areas totaling 23,000 acres; all near Jewett City; headquarters at Griswold area.

Paugassett State Forest, Newton 06470; 1900 acres; day use only.

Penwood, Bloomfield 06002; 787 acres; day use only.

*Peoples State Forest, Barkhamsted; 2954 acres; day use only.

Pootatuck State Forest, New Fairfield; 1066 acres.

Putnam Memorial, Bethel 06801; day use only.

Quaddick State Forest, Thompson 06277; day use only.

*Rocky Neck State Park, East Lyme 06333; 561 acres.
*Salmon River State Forest, Colchester 06415; 1840 acres; day use only.
 Shenipsit State Forest, Stafford 06075.
*Sherwood Island, Westport 06880; 218 acres; day use only.
*Sleeping Giant, Hamden; 1200 acres.
 Southford Falls, Southford; day use only.
 Squantz Pond, New Fairfield; day use only.
 Stoddard Hill, Norwich 06360; day use only.
 Stratton Brook, Simsbury 06070; day use only.
 Talcott Mountain, Bloomfield 06002; 401 acres; day use only.
 Tunxis State Forest, West Hartland 06091; 2300 acres; day use only.
 Wadsworth Falls, Middletown 06457; day use only.
 West Peak, Meridan 06450; day use only.
 Wharton Brook, Hamden; day use only.
*Wyantenock State Forest, Kent 06757; 301 acres.

Least Tern

DELAWARE

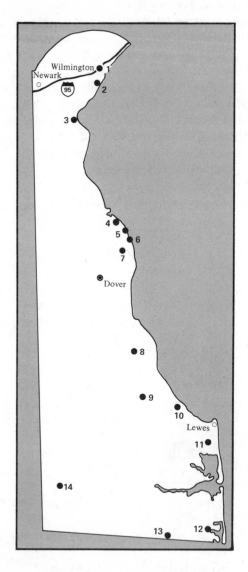

1. Wintherthur
2. Environmental Laboratory
3. Thousand Acre Marsh/
   Dragon Run Marsh
4. Woodland Beach
5. Port Mahon Access Area
6. Little Creek
7. Bombay Hook NWR

8. Milford, Neck
9. Silver Lake
10. Prime Hook NWR
11. Gordon Pond
12. Assawoman Wildlife Area
13. Great Cypress Swamp
14. Nanticoke Wildlife Area
    Tussock Pond

Delaware, the second smallest state in America, is nevertheless one of the best states for birdwatching. Delaware occupies slightly over one-third of the Delmarva Peninsula, home of the rare and endangered Delmarva Squirrel. Delaware's 96-mile length goes from rolling hills in the north to nearly sea level in the south. The beaches lie along the Atlantic Flyway and 2 large areas have been set aside as national wildlife refuges. The Delaware Dunes, a barrier beach fronting on the Atlantic Ocean, is also a protected area.

The state of Delaware maintains 40 fish and wildlife areas — these total about 25,000 acres. Most of them are good places for birdwatching, especially: *Woodland Beach*, 3664 acres near Bombay Hook NWR; *Port Mahon Access Area*, 23 acres near Bombay Hook NWR; *Little Creek*, 4000 acres near Port Mahon; *Silver Lake*, 34 acres near Milford; *Milford Neck*, 1370 acres near Thompsonville; *Gordon Pond*, 300 acres near Lewes; *Nanticoke Wildlife Area*, 1830 acres near Laurel; *Tussock Pond*, 15 acres near Laurel; and *Assawoman Wildlife Area*, 1450 acres near Bethany Beach. Camping is not permitted on these lands; however, state parks and/or private campgrounds are generally located nearby.

Other good places to go birdwatching include Thousand Acre Marsh and Dragon Run Marsh, both near Delaware City, and Great Cypress Swamp located on the Maryland border near Selbyville.

There have been 320 species of birds recorded in the Delaware Valley region (including some parts of New Jersey and Pennsylvania) plus 43 accidentals. Spring and fall waterfowl migrations are the most rewarding, although flycatchers, woodpeckers, vireos, and owls occur regularly in the woodland areas. In the summer, look for bitterns, ducks, rails, and other water- and shorebirds in the tidewater areas. Shorebird migrations reach their peak in early August; songbirds pass through Delaware in September and October; and waterfowl reach peak numbers in early November. Hawks, too, can be seen in October and November.

For further information about birdwatching in Delaware, contact: Delmarva Ornithological Society, Eastern Bird Banding, c/o Ms. Kathleen Klimkiewicz, 13117 Larchdale Road #2, Laurel, Maryland 20811 *or* the Delaware Valley Ornithological Club, Academy of Natural Sciences, Philadelphia, Pennsylvania 19100. The latter publishes "A Field List of the Birds of the Delaware Valley Region." There is also a rare bird alert for the area — the *Delaware Valley Birding Hotline*. The telephone number is: (215) 236-2473.

Bombay Hook National Wildlife Refuge, R.D. 1, Box 147, Smyrna 19977; (302) 653-9345. Bombay Hook Refuge is located near Dover. To reach the refuge, take SR 9 north from Dover for approximately 10 miles; watch for signs. Camping is not permitted at the refuge; however, facilities are available at nearby state parks. Prime Hook NWR is located about 30 miles to the south.

Bombay Hook NWR was established in 1937; it comprises 16,280 acres, of which about 10,500 are tidal marsh. The rest of the area includes 1200 acres of freshwater pools, brushy and timbered swamps, 1000 acres of croplands, and timbered and grassy uplands. The terrain of the refuge is flat — nearly all less than 10 feet above sea level. Bombay Hook is located along the Atlantic Flyway; look for the greatest numbers of waterfowl during March and November. Among the 261 species of birds (97 nesting) sighted here are: Mallard, Wood Duck, Common Goldeneye, Oldsquaw, Rough-legged Hawk, Least Bittern, Sora, Black-necked Stilt, Black-bellied Plover, Pectoral Sandpiper, Laughing Gull, Barred Owl, Eastern Wood Pewee, Purple Martin, Blue Jay, House Wren, Red-eyed Vireo, Chestnut-sided Warbler, Red-winged Blackbird, Indigo Bunting, Savannah Sparrow, Seaside Sparrow, and Lapland Longspur. Checklist available.

Prime Hook National Wildlife Refuge, R.D. #1, Box 195, Milton 19968; (302) 684-8419. The refuge is located north of Lewes. To reach it from Milton, take SR 16 (Broadkill Beach Road) east for about 10 miles. Camping is not permitted at the refuge; however, camping facilities are available at nearby Redden State Forest and Ellendale State Forest. Recreational facilities at Prime Hook include canoeing (over 15 miles of streams and ditches), fishing, boating, and hiking. There are also several roads open to automobile traffic.

Prime Hook NWR was established in 1963 primarily to preserve coastal wetlands. It is located on the Delaware Bay. The refuge totals 10,700 acres: 7300 acres of marsh and water, 1200 acres of brush and timber, and 2100 acres of croplands and pasture. Management programs on the refuge include producing supplemental waterfowl food. Shorebirds and waterfowl can be easily observed from the shaded interior of a car, which acts as a blind. Resident mammals at Prime Hook NWR include white-tailed deer, red fox, and striped skunk. Prime Hook is another in the chain of national wildlife refuges that parallel the Atlantic Flyway. Among the many birds that can be seen here are: Snow Goose, Gadwall, Ruddy Duck, Marsh Hawk, Bobwhite, Great Blue Heron, Black-crowned Night Heron, Sora, American Avocet, Black-bellied Plover, Willet, Dunlin, Western Sandpiper, Laughing Gull, Black Tern, Common (Yellow-shafted) Flicker, Red-bellied Woodpecker, Eastern Phoebe, Barn Swallow, Carolina Chickadee, Brown Creeper, Long- and Short-billed Marsh Wrens, Wood Thrush, Water Pipit, Black-and-white Warbler, Kentucky Warbler, American Redstart, Bobolink, Scarlet Tanager, Indigo Bunting, and Sharp-tailed Sparrow.

NATURE CENTERS

In addition to the refuges described in the previous pages, there are some gardens and nature centers in Delaware that can prove to be rewarding birdfinding areas.

Environmental Laboratory, Gunning Bedford Middle School, Delaware City 19706; (302) 834-4528. The laboratory covers 165 acres. A variety of educational and interpretive programs is offered. Guided tours are available by appointment; trails are maintained. The laboratory is open all year.

Winterthur Museum and Gardens. The museum is located in Wilmington. The extensive gardens are open all year 10-4; they are closed on Mondays. An admission fee is charged.

STATE PARKS AND FORESTS

Delaware state parks and forests offer a variety of recreational activities. Most offer camping in addition to interpretive programs, guided and self-guiding nature tours, picnicking, canoeing, and swimming. Several of the parks have nature centers. Those parks that are particularly well known for birdwatching opportunities are marked with an asterisk (*). For additional information regarding Delaware state park and forests, contact: Delaware Natural Resources and Environmental Control, State Capitol, Dover 19901; (302) 678-4431 *or* Delaware State Visitors Service, 630 State College Road, Dover 19901.

Blackbird State Forest, Blackbird 19977.
*Brandywine Creek, P.O. Box 3782, Wilmington 19702; 430 acres; day use only; nature center.
*Cape Henlopen, Lewes 19958; (302) 645-8983; 2700 acres; nature center.
*Delaware Seashore, P.O. Box 850, Route 2, Rehoboth Beach 19971; (302) 277-2800; 2000 acres.
*Ellendale State Forest, Ellendale 19968.
Fort Delaware, Pea Patch Island, Delaware City 19706; 160 acres; day use only.
*Holts Landing, P.O. Box 76, Millville 19967; (302) 539-9060; 33 acres; day use only.
Killens Pond, Route 1, Box 198A, Felton 19943; 560 acres; day use only.
*Lums Pond, Route 71, Kirkwood 19708; (302) 834-4559; 1100 acres.
*Redden State Forest, Redden 19968.
*Trap Pond, Box 331, Route 2, Laurel 19956; 960 acres.
Walter S. Carpenter, Jr., Route 896, Newark 19711; 430 acres; day use only.

MAINE

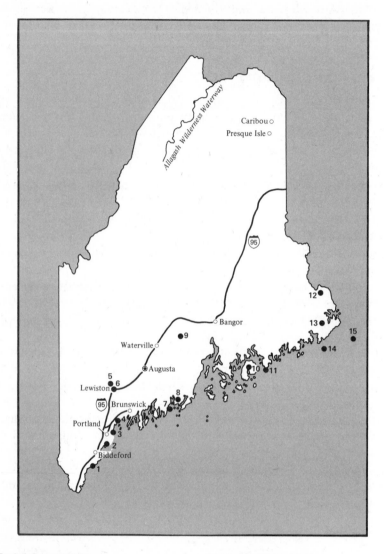

Allagash Wilderness Waterway

Caribou ○
Presque Isle ○

95

12 ●

Bangor ○

13 ●

15 ●

Waterville ○   9 ●

Augusta ⊕   10 ● 11

5   8 ●
Lewiston ● 6   7 ●
95 Brunswick ○
Portland ○ 4
3
2
○ Biddeford
1

14 ●

1. Rachel Carson NWR
2. P. W. Sprague Memorial Sanctuary
   Scarborough Marsh NC
3. Pond Island NWR
4. Mast Landing Sanctuary
5. Maine Conservation School
6. Thorncrag Bird Sanctuary
7. Franklin Island NWR
8. Todd Wildlife Sanctuary
9. Carleton Pond Waterfowl Production
   Area

10. Acadia National Park
11. Petit Manan NWR
12. Moosehorn NWR
13. Moosehorn NWR
14. Machias Seal Island
15. Grand Manan Island (Canada)
    Kent Island (Canada)
16. Allagash Wilderness Waterway

Birdwatching in Maine — from its rocky coast to the Allagash Wilderness Waterway — is rewarding. The northern coastal regions and the many islands that dot the bays and harbors are habitat for a wide variety of seabirds not found in states further south. The best time for seabirds is from the middle of May to the middle of June. Places such as Matinicus Island (ferry from Rockland) and Monhegan Island (ferry from Port Clyde) are good for Leach's Storm-Petrels, Common Eiders, Black Guillemots, ducks, gulls, terns, thrushes, and warblers. On the trip over, look for shearwaters, Gannets, and Northern Phalaropes. Shorebirds and marshbirds can be seen in large numbers around Prouts Neck and the Scarborough salt marshes south of Portland; look for turnstones, plovers, sandpipers, egrets, loons, gulls, and ducks.

Further south, in Biddeford Pool, shorebirds are also abundant. They regularly visit the mud flats of this tidal bay. Look for Marbled and Hudsonian Godwits, Whimbrels, Willets, Red Knots, plovers, dowitchers, and other shorebirds. Roseate, Common, and Arctic Terns are also quite common. In Portland, landbirds — particularly warblers — are frequently seen in Baxter's Woods and in the Evergreen Cemetery. The best time for them is during spring migration (the first 2 weeks of May).

Just north of Bath is Merrymeeting Bay — where the Kennebec and Androscoggin rivers meet. During April, this is a resting place for impressive numbers of ducks and geese; look for Red-breasted Mergansers, Ring-necked Ducks, Common Goldeneyes, Pintails, Greater Scaups, and Snow and Canada Geese.

Puffins can also be seen in Maine. A good place to go is Machias Seal Island, off the Maine coast, in Canada. It can be reached by boat from Cutler (Maine) or from Grand Manan Island (New Brunswick). Also in Canadian possession are 2 islands in the Bay of Fundy (known for its 50-foot tides) that are noteworthy birdwatching spots: Grand Manan and Kent. Grand Manan can be reached by ferry from Blacks Harbor (NB); Kent can be reached from Grand Manan. For information about ferry service to Grand Manan, write to: Coastal Transport, Ltd., P.O. Box 26, Saint John, New Brunswick. The Bowdoin Scientific Station (operated by Bowdoin College) is on Kent Island. The station has facilities for scientists wishing to conduct research in ornithology. Visitors are also welcome. For information, write Director, Bowdoin Scientific Station, Department of Biology, Bowdoin College, Brunswick 04011. (In summer, write to: Kent Island, Grand Manan, New Brunswick.) Nesting birds on Kent Island include Common Eiders, Leach's Storm-Petrels, Black Guillemots, Boreal Chickadees, Blackpoll Warblers, and Golden-crowned Kinglets.

The Department of Inland Fisheries and Game manages over 23,000 acres of wilderness that are divided into 19 wildlife management areas. Although public use is restricted on some areas or during certain seasons, these areas are public property and are available for many uses including hiking, fishing, cross-country skiing, photography, and birdwatching. The Scarborough Wildlife Management

Area, which includes the Scarborough Marsh Nature Center; the Steve Powell Area, near Merrymeeting Bay in Perkins Township; and the Madawaska Area, in Palmyra are just 3 of these areas. Management emphasis at many of these areas is on waterfowl nesting and migratory bird resting and feeding.

For further information about birdwatching in Maine, contact the Maine Audubon Society, Old Route 1, Falmouth 04105; (207) 781-2330. The society publishes a book — *Enjoying Maine Birds* — which is helpful; they also issue a checklist of Maine birds. Other information about birdwatching, conservation, camping, and wildlife in Maine can be obtained from the Maine Forest Service, or the Maine Department of Inland Fisheries and Game, or the Maine State Park and Recreation Commission — all are at: State Office Building, Augusta 04330.

Acadia National Park, R.F.D. #1, Box, Bar Harbor 04069. Acadia National Park is located on Mount Desert Island just outside of Bar Harbor, about 20 miles south of Ellsworth. (The park includes other areas as well, such as Isle-au-Haut and the Schoodic Peninsula.) To reach park headquarters, take SR 3 south from Ellsworth toward Bar Harbor; headquarters are about a mile south of Hulls Cove. Public facilities at Acadia include camping, picnicking, boating, hiking, swimming, and various interpretive and naturalist programs.

The diverse habitat — from ocean to rocky cliffs to spruce forest — provides food and shelter for a wide variety of plant and animal life. The Atlantic Ocean dominates the park: it creates tidepools and erodes cliffs, and its fogs permeate the woodlands.

There have been 315 species of birds (140 nesting) recorded at Acadia. Among those seen here during the summer months are: Common Loon, Sooty Shearwater, Greater Shearwater, Manx Shearwater, Leach's Storm-Petrel, Wilson's Storm-Petrel, Ring-necked Duck, Common Eider, Goshawk, Marsh Hawk, Bald Eagle; American Bittern, Virginia Rail, Killdeer, Purple Sandpiper (rare in summer), Arctic Tern, Roseate Tern, Black Guillemot, Great Horned Owl, Pileated Woodpecker, Yellow-bellied Flycatcher, Cliff Swallow, Gray Jay, Boreal Chickadee, Short-billed Marsh Wren, Eastern Bluebird, Cedar Waxwing, Black-throated Blue Warbler, Black-throated Green Warbler, Bobolink, Rose-breasted Grosbeak, White-winged Crossbill, and Sharp-tailed Sparrow. Transient and winter visitors include Barrow's Goldeneye, Oldsquaw, Harlequin Duck, Hudsonian Godwit, Red Phalarope, Pomarine Jaeger, Black-legged Kittiwake, Sabine's Gull, Razorbill, Common Murre, Thick-billed Murre, Common Puffin, Dovekie, Hawk Owl, Snowy Owl, and Hoary Redpoll. Checklist available.

Carleton Pond Waterfowl Production Area. Administered by Moosehorn NWR. Carleton Pond is located 6 miles south of Detroit (about 35 miles southwest of Bangor) on SR 220. It was established in 1966 to preserve 1068 acres of nesting habitat for ducks and geese. The area is open for birdwatching, nature study, and photography during daylight hours. Black Ducks, Ring-necked Ducks, and Canada Geese are among the birds found here.

Franklin Island National Wildlife Refuge. Administered by Moosehorn NWR. This 12-acre rocky island became a refuge in 1973 when it was acquired from the Coast Guard. Franklin Island is located in Muscongus Bay, south of Friendship (about 15 miles southwest of Rockland). The refuge is open to the public from 1 August to 31 March. Access is by boat only. Camping is not permitted on the refuge. The island is largely forested with white spruce. Among the nesting birds are Leach's Storm-Petrel, Common Terns, Common Eiders, and various passerine birds. Osprey also nest, and the island has potential as a site for Bald Eagle nesting.

Moosehorn National Wildlife Refuge, Box X, Calais 04619; (207) 454-3521. To reach the refuge from Calais, take US 1 south for 6 miles; turn south on Charlotte Road and watch for signs. Camping is not permitted at the refuge; however, facilities are available at nearby state parks and private campgrounds. A fee may be charged for entry into parts of the refuge. Facilities include a visitors' center, a self-guiding auto tour through the heart of the refuge, and hiking trails.

Moosehorn was established in 1937 as one of a chain of migratory bird refuges extending from Maine to Florida. The refuge consists of 2 units — the Baring Unit (16,065 acres) and the Edmunds Unit (6600 acres). Baring is partially bounded by the St. Croix River and is crossed by US 1; it is on the Canadian border, near Calais. Edmunds is on Cobscook Bay, slightly to the south, near Dennysville. Refuge headquarters are located on the Baring Unit. Moosehorn is primarily an upland area. Deer, black bear, and moose roam the refuge. At the Edmunds Unit, one may see the harbor seal and the Atlantic harbor porpoise.

Moosehorn is managed chiefly to increase habitat for the American Woodcook and for waterfowl. The average summer Woodcock population is 1100 birds. In early spring, the unusual mating performance of the Woodcock may be observed in clearings. The forests, small freshwater marshes, numerous streams, and rocky shorelines provide a diversified habitat that is reflected by the wide variety of birds to be seen at Moosehorn. There have been 207 species of birds (137 nesting) observed here. Among them are: Red-throated Loon, Great Cormorant, Green- and Blue-winged Teals, Bufflehead, Ring-necked Duck, American Kestrel (Sparrow Hawk), Ruffed Grouse, Killdeer, Upland Sandpiper (Plover), Arctic Tern, Great Horned Owl, Whip-poor-will, Black-backed Three-toed Woodpecker, Yellow-bellied Sapsucker, Eastern Kingbird, Red-breasted Nuthatch, Short-billed Marsh Wren, Red-eyed Vireo, Nashville Warbler, Black-throated Green Warbler, Chestnut-sided Warbler, Northern Waterthrush, Bobolink, Evening Grosbeak, Red Crossbill, Common Redpoll, and Vesper Sparrow. Checklist available.

Petit Manan National Wildlife Refuge. Administered by Moosehorn NWR. Petit Manan is a 9-acre island located off the coast, south of Milbridge (about 50 miles southeast of Ellsworth). At low tide it joins to Green Island, which is managed by the state. Camping is not permitted at the refuge; however, facilities are available at nearby Acadia National Park. Both Petit Manan and Green islands provide nesting sites for Common Eiders, Laughing Gulls, Arctic Terns, and other seabirds. The area is also a resting spot for large numbers of Black Ducks, Ospreys, Green Herons, American Bitterns, Black-bellied Plovers, Whimbrels, and Ruddy Turnstones.

Pond Island National Wildlife Refuge. Administered by Parker River NWR (in Massachusetts). Pond Island is a 10-acre treeless island located near Popham Beach, 16 miles northeast of Portland. The refuge was established in 1973. Camping is not permitted on the island.

Pond Island is vegetated with mixed grasses, dune grass, bayberry, blueberry, poison ivy, and roses. It furnishes ideal nesting habitat for Common Eiders. In addition, it is a refuge for Leach's Storm-Petrels, geese, gulls, terns, and various passerines such as the Sharp-tailed and Seaside Sparrows. The refuge is not open to the public during the nesting season (1 March to 31 July). However, nature study, birdwatching, and photographic opportunities are available to the public throughout the rest of the year during daylight hours.

Rachel Carson National Wildlife Refuge. Administered by Parker River NWR (in Massachusetts). Rachel Carson Refuge is located in York and Cumberland counties, along the coast, south of Biddeford. When acquisition is complete, the refuge will total approximately 4000 acres of coastal marsh — about 96 percent of the land being acquired is wetland, the remaining is upland. Management emphasis will be on preservation of the salt marsh. Shorebirds, wading birds, migratory waterfowl, gulls, terns, and a wide variety of songbirds use the area.

Seal Island National Wildlife Refuge. Administered by Moosehorn NWR. The island is located 25 miles off the coast of Maine. Direct access is limited owing to landing difficulty. The island is a center for breeding Common Eiders and provides habitat for other migratory birds. For information about and assistance in visiting Seal Island, contact the refuge manager at Moosehorn.

NATURE CENTERS

In addition to the federally owned parks and refuges described in the previous pages, there are several nature centers and Audubon sanctuaries that can also prove to be rewarding birdfinding places. These are briefly discussed below.

Guy Van Duyn Wildlife Refuge. The refuge is maintained by the Mid-coast Audubon Society. It covers 20 acres and is open to the public by prior arrangement only. A naturalist is on staff.

Maine Conservation School, Freeman-Waterhouse Conservation Campus, Bryant Pond 04219; (207) 289-2515. The school is located northwest of Lewiston. It is operated by the University of Maine, the State Department of

Educational and Cultural Services, and the Conservation Education Foundation of Maine. A wide range of educational and interpretive programs is offered; there are guided and self-guiding tours. This 200-acre center is open everyday from May to October.

Common Loon

Mast Landing Sanctuary. The sanctuary is located near Freeport. From Freeport, take US 1 north to Mast Landing Road, turn right (east), and continue for 9½ miles to the sanctuary entrance. Mast Landing is a 150-acre preserve situated on a freshwater stream near the Harraseeket River. There are open fields, evergreen forests, apple orchards, and salt marshes. The sanctuary is open all year; there are self-guiding nature trails. A variety of interpretive programs is offered. Shorebirds, Ruffed Grouse, American Woodcock, and warblers can be seen here.

P. W. Sprague Memorial Sanctuary. The sanctuary is owned by the National Audubon Society. It is located within the limits of the town of Saco and covers about 30 acres on Stratton and Bluff islands. The islands are a nesting and roosting area for various shorebirds. The sanctuary is maintained by the Prout's Neck Audubon Society. Although the sanctuary is open to the public — during daylight hours — no transportation is provided.

Scarborough Marsh Nature Center, Pine Point Road, Route 9, Scarborough 04074; in summer, (207) 883-5100; in winter, (207) 774-8281. The center is located just outside of Portland and is operated by the Maine Audubon Society in cooperation with the Maine Department of Inland Fisheries and Game. The center totals 2000 acres and a full range of educational and interpretive programs is offered. Guided and self-guiding tours are available. The center is open every day from May 1 to September 30. Among the many species of birds seen here are: Pintail, Northern Shoveler, Willet, Glossy Ibis, Glaucous Gull, Black-bellied Plover, and many other species of waterbirds and waterfowl.

Thorncrag Bird Sanctuary, Lewiston 04240. The sanctuary is owned and maintained by the Stanton Bird Club. It is located north of Lewiston; take US 202 north to Montello Street, go into Montello Heights, and proceed to the sanctuary. Thorncrag covers over 200 acres of mixed woodlands, a meadow, and a small marsh; a large brook winds through the area. There is a network of trails. Landbirds breed here. Look for flycatchers, thrushes, sparrows, and warblers.

Todd Wildlife Sanctuary, Keene Neck Road, Medomak 04551; (207) 529-5148. The sanctuary is operated and owned by the National Audubon Society. This 345-acre sanctuary is the site of the Audubon Workshop of Maine which offers summer ecology courses for adults. It is in upper Muscongous Bay, east of Damariscotta and includes all of Hog Island plus some acreage on the mainland. A visitors' center is operated on the mainland portion of the sanctuary during July and August. It is best to arange visits in advance. Look for Osprey, Hermit Thrush, Northern Parula, and Black-throated Green Warbler.

NATURE CONSERVANCY PRESERVES

The Maine Chapter of The Nature Conservancy owns 55 preserves totaling over 7800 acres. Many of these are excellent birdwatching places, especially those along the coast. A few are known nesting sites for Osprey, others are feeding and resting grounds for many species of sea- and shorebirds. Several of these preserves have been grouped together to form the Rachel Carson Maine Seacoast; they are marked with an asterisk (*). Conservancy preserves are managed by volunteer stewardship committees; and only those preserves that are open to the public are listed here. For specific information contact: Maine

Chapter, TNC, Manchester 04351; (207) 622-3101. (Because of space limitations, these preserves are not shown on the map.)

Appleton Bog, Appleton; 84 acres; supports one of the northernmost stands of Atlantic white cedar; located off SR 105, west of Appleton Ridge Road.

*Barred Island, Sunset; a 5-acre wooded, rocky island off Goose Cove on the west side of Deer Isle; feeding ground for shorebirds.

*Basket Island, Cumberland; 9 acres of mixed hardwoods and conifers on a rocky island; located off the town landing in Falmouth Foreside.

*Bass Rock Preserve, Round Pond; 12 acres of seacoast consisting of rocky cliffs spotted with white pine; take SR 32 at Round Pond Center, then north on Back Shore Road for a mile.

*Big Garden Island, Vinalhaven; an 18-acre wooded, rocky island in Hurricane Sound, off Vinalhaven, with small beach and cove.

*Big White Island, Vinalhaven; a 20-acre wooded, rocky island in Hurricane Sound.

*Bradbury Island, Deer Isle; 46 acres; forested granite ledges with undergrowth of mosses and ferns, some marshy area; nesting ground for Osprey; reached by boat from Blastow's Cove on Little Deer Island.

Butler Preserve, Kennebunk; 6 acres of woodland fronting the Kennebunk River; located off Old Port Road in Kennebunk.

*Crockett Cove Woods, Stonington; 100 acres of high, wooded ground with glacial boulders, swamps, and moss-covered ledges; borders Crockett Cove on the west side of Deer Isle.

Crystal Bog, Crystal/Sherman; nearly 3800 acres; an untouched northern sphagnum bog supporting at least 10 species of orchids; a registered national natural landmark; located 3 miles southeast of Patten.

Damariscove Island, Boothbay; 209 acres; mostly open island with rugged coast and a small lake; located off Linekin Neck.

*Doughty Island, Harpswell; 2-acre island; nesting site for Osprey; to reach it, go south, by boat, from Princess Point Road.

Doughty Point, Harpswell; 40 acres of salt marsh and mixed forest; south from Princess Point Road.

Douglas Mountain, Sebago; 150 acres, views of White Mountains (New Hampshire) and Sebago Lake; mixed woodlands; located 1¼ miles southeast of Sebago, take SR 107 and Douglas Hill Road.

Dyer's Neck, Jefferson; 50 acres; peninsula of mixed conifer forest dropping off to ponds and marshlands on either side; located on Dyer Long Pond.

Eustis Preserve, Georgetown; 43 acres of wooded land with long shoreline, noted for stand of rare pines; located at Five Islands in Georgetown.

Fernald's Neck, Lincolnville (near Camden); 285 acres of hardwood and evergreen forest on scenic peninsula jutting into Lake Megunticook.

*Flint Island, Harrington; 134-acre, rock-bound island in Marraguagus Bay; has undisturbed spruce-fir forest and fossil formations.

*Harkness Grant, Rockport; 5 acres of woods — consisting mostly of white pine, hemlock, red oak, and American chestnut — fronting on a coastal stream; to reach the preserve, take US 1 to the west side of Spruce Street, just north of Maple.

The Hermitage; about 20 miles northeast of Dover; 35 acres; large grove of white pines on a bluff overlooking the west branch of the Pleasant River; moose and beaver are resident; located 17 miles northwest of SR 11 from Brownville Junction and Katahdin Iron Works.

*Heron Islands, Phippsburg; 3 rocky islands comprising 5 acres off the coast near Boothbay Harbor; nesting sites for Double-crested Cormorants and Greater Black-backed Gulls. Transient shorebirds include Black-bellied Plover, Ruddy Turnstone, and Whimbrel.

Indian and Fowl Meadow, Anson; 32 acres; 2 wooded islands with floodplain forest of mixed trees; in Kennebec River at Anson, north of Waterville.

*Ketterlinus Preserve, Tremont; 20 acres; spruce- and fir-covered sample of rock-bound coast; located off SR 102 in Tremont.

Lane's Island, Vinalhaven; 79 acres of rolling moors and wild, rocky coast; cover of blueberry and bayberry; feeding and resting ground for land- and seabirds; located just outside the town of Vinalhaven.

*LaVerna Preserve, Round Pond; 119 acres; rocky coastal area covered by a dense stand of fir and spruce; located on Muscongus Bay.

Marshall Preserve, Arundel; 181 acres; mixed woodlands with some swampy areas including ½-mile frontage on the Kennebunk River; located on River Road beyond Goff Brook.

Meadow Mountain, Warren; 282 acres; densely wooded mountainside bordered by a stream; to reach it, take Beechwood Road from Thomaston until it becomes Mountain Road.

Mill Creek, Falmouth; 20 acres of woodland and salt marsh on Mill Creek; located northwest of SR 88 on the north side of Mill Creek in Falmouth.

*Mill Cove, South Portland; 30 acres of tidal flats and some marsh; resting area for shorebirds; located on the northeast side of Ocean Street going into Mill Cove.

*Montsweag Preserve, Woolwich; 45 acres; open field with mixed hardwoods and conifers, land slopes to a saltwater marsh and estuary; located off Montsweag Road in Woolwich.

Mullen Woods, Newport; 115 acres of mixed forest composed of hemlock, white pine, balsam, fir, and hardwoods; located south of SR 22.

Osborne Finch Preserve, Waldoboro; 11 acres characterized by coastal spruce and white pines; located on the west side of the Medomak River on Dutch Neck.

Plummer Point, South Bristol; 70-acre wooded peninsula located on the Damariscotta River.

*Redin's Island, Cape Porpoise; 6-acre island covered with brush, grassland, and marsh; located 100 yards from the mainland, east of Cape Porpoise.

Ritchey Preserve, Portland; 60 acres; high, wooded ledge terminating in a sheer rock bluff on Cushing Island; located on the northeast side of Cushing Island from Whitehead to Rock Quarry.

*Round Island, Stonington; 36 acres; wooded area with rocky ledges on the shoreline; located in Merchant Row.

Sabra Creeper Hill, Stow; 12 acres; 2 marshy areas at a remote outlet of Kezar Lake; located near the New Hampshire border in Stow, off SR 113.

St. Clair Tract, Northport; 240 acres of swampland and upland fir-spruce forest; located off Knights Pond Road in Northport.

*Salt Pond, Bristol; 78-acre mixed forest, mostly white pine and red oak, on eastern shore of Muscongus Bay; located off SR 32 in Round Pond.

Seboeis River Gorge; near Baxter State Park; 673 acres including over 9 miles on Wild River Gorge; located toward Shin Pond from Patten.

Sheep Island, Little Deer Isle; 5 acres of coastal habitat; bird nesting area; located just beyond Blastow Cove in Little Deer Isle.

Simonton Corner Quarry, Rockport; 11 acres of rolling coastal countryside with water-filled old lime quarries; located 2½ miles north of US 1 at Rockport.

*Smith Island, Vinalhaven; 12-acre open island in Isle au Haut Bay; rookery; located on the east side off Barley Hill.

*Stave Island Preserve, Gouldsboro; 132 acres, wooded, mostly spruce and fir; nesting site for the Bald Eagle; located on Stave Island.

Step Falls, Newry; 23 acres; stream with rapids, waterfalls, and glacial boulders, bordered by white pine forest; located off SR 26 in Newry.

Stone Island, Machiasport; a 60-acre, very rugged island off Point of Maine; spruce forest; nesting site for Great Blue Herons and Ospreys.

Sucker Brook, Lovell; 21 acres of marsh and woods bordering Moose Pond; to reach the preserve from Fryeburg, take SR 5 for 5 miles to SR 113, then turn right, continue for ½ mile to Gray Farm, left for 1000 feet, then right for 3½ miles to dead end.

*Turtle Island, Winter Harbor; 140 acres of rocky shoreline, natural cove, and mature spruce and fir forest; located off the end of Winter Harbor at Grindstone Neck.

Vaughn's Island, Kennebunkport; 48 acres; grassy low-lying areas and uplands with mixed hardwood forest; located straight out from the Sahmut Inn.

*Wreck Island, Stonington; a 70-acre, rocky, spruce-covered island located in Merchant Row.

Wolfe Preserve, Perry; 5 acres on Passamaquoddy Bay; scenic, open area overlooking the bay.

STATE PARKS AND FORESTS

Maine has an extensive system of state parks. Most of these offer camping in addition to many other recreational facilities, such as boating, swimming, and nature study. The parks are only open from May to October, with a few exceptions. For additional information, contact: Maine Department of Conservation, Bureau of Parks and Recreation, State Office Building, Augusta 04333, or the Maine Campsites-Maine Forest Service, at the same address. Some of Maine's parks are well known as birdwatching spots; these are marked with an asterisk (*).

*Allagash Wilderness Waterway; 200,000 acres; north of Baxter State Park. If a canoe trip is planned, contact the Department of Conservation, Bureau of Parks and Recreation at the above address. There are many campsites located along this vast wilderness waterway.

Aroostook, Presque Isle 04769.

*Baxter, Millinocket 04462; 200,000 acres.

Bradbury Mountain, Pownal 04069.

Camden Hills, Camden 04843.

Cobscook Bay, Dennysville 04628.

*Crescent Beach, Cape Elizabeth 04107; day use only.

*Damariscotta Lake, Jefferson 04348; day use only.

Fort Point, Stockton Springs 04981; day use only.

Grafton Notch, Grafton; day use only; Appalachian Trail crosses park.

*Holbrook Island Sanctuary, Brooksville 04617; day use only.

Lake St. George, Liberty 04949

Lamoine, Lamoine.

Lily Bay (Moosehead Lake), Greenville 04441.
Moose Point, Searsport 04974; day use only.
Mount Blue, Weld 04285.
Peacock Beach, Richmond 04357; day use only.
Peaks-Kenny, Dover-Foxcroft 04426; day use only.
*Popham Beach, Phippsburg 04562; day use only.
 Quoddy Head, Lubec 04652; day use only.
 Rangeley Lake, Rangeley 04970.
*Reid, Georgetown 04548; 792 acres; day use only.
*Sebago Lake, Naples 04055.
*Two Lights, Cape Elizabeth 04107; day use only.
*Warren Island, Isleboro 04848; access by boat only.
*Wolf Neck, Freeport 04032; day use only.

Barn Swallow

MARYLAND and DISTRICT OF COLUMBIA

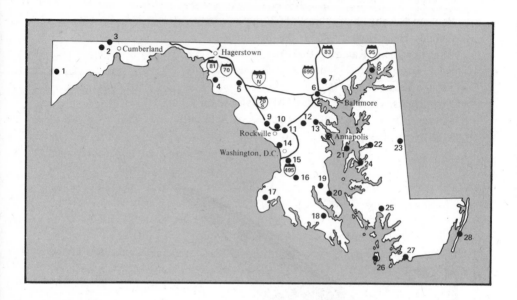

1. Garrett County Resource Center
2. Carey Run Wildlife Sanctuary
3. Finzel Swamp
4. Chesapeake and Ohio Canal National Historic Park
5. Monocacy Natural Resource Area
6. Clyburn Wildflower Preserve
   Soldier's Delight Natural Environment Area
7. Catoctin Mountain Park
8. Susquehanna NWR
9. Meadowside NC
10. Brookside NC
11. Greenbelt Park
12. Patuxent Wildlife Research Center
13. Severn Run Natural Environment Area
14. Rock Creek Park
    Theodore Roosevelt Island
15. Clearwater NC
16. Mattawoman Natural Environment Area
17. Nanjemoy Marsh Sanctuary
18. Chancellor's Point
19. Battle Creek Cypress Swamp
20. Hellen Creek Hemlock Preserve
21. Eastern Neck NWR
22. Mill Creek Wildlife Sanctuary
23. Pelot Sanctuary
24. Hambleton Island
25. Blackwater NWR
26. Martin NWR
27. Irish Grove Sanctuary
28. Asseteague Island National Seashore

Although Maryland stretches from the Allegheny Mountains to the Atlantic Ocean, its outstanding feature is its coastline — several hundred miles along the Chesapeake Bay. The Bay's adjoining tidal marshes and estuaries make it the focal point for huge numbers of migrating waterfowl. Owing to Maryland's geographical position in relation to the ranges of birds with northern and southern affinities, rare and interesting combinations of northern and southern breeding species are found in the state. Few states can exceed Maryland's record of 28 species of regularly nesting warblers.

Maryland lies on the Atlantic Flyway and, as such, is criss-crossed by a maze of migration routes. All parts of the state are good for passerine birds; fall hawk flights can be seen along all the ridges. Falcons and Ospreys predominate on coastal routes; Whistling Swans, ducks, and geese follow the Susquehanna; and Ring-billed Gulls use the Potomac River as their flyway.

The state maintains several thousand acres of land as wildlife management areas and/or natural environment areas. These are generally good for birdwatching, however they are subject to certain restrictions, depending on the time of year. It is advisable to inquire in advance. Contact: Maryland Park Service, Tawes State Office Building, Annapolis 21401; (301) 267-5761.

For further information about birdwatching in Maryland, contact: Maryland Ornithological Society, Clyburn Mansion, 4915 Greenspring Avenue, Baltimore 21209; (301) 377-8462. For up-to-date telephone information, call *Voice of the Naturalist* (rare bird alert): (301) 652-3295; in Washington, D.C., call (202) 652-3295.

Assateague Island National Seashore, Route 2, Box 294, Berlin 21811; (301) 641-1441. Assateague can be reached from Ocean City via US 50 (west) and SR 611 (south). From points north and south, take US 113 to Berlin, then east on SR 376 to SR 611; turn south on SR 611 and continue to Assateague. Camping facilities are available.

Most of the Virginia portion of Assateague Island is occupied by Chincoteague National Wildlife Refuge. At Assateague, interpretive activities, including conducted walks, are regularly scheduled from Memorial Day through Labor Day. Rangers are on duty.

Among the many species of birds seen at Assateague are: Red-throated Loon, Horned Grebe, Surf Scoter, Red-breasted Merganser, Oldsquaw, Common Goldeneye, Clapper Rail, American Oystercatcher, Black-bellied Plover, Ruddy Turnstone, Whimbrel, Willet, Bonaparte's Gull, Brown Creeper, Hermit Thrush, Ruby- and Golden-crowned Kinglets, Yellow-bellied Flycatcher, Common Yellowthroat, Black-and-white Warbler, and Snow Bunting. In the winter, the Maryland Ornithological Society organizes pelagic trips to Baltimore Canyon (60 miles offshore). On these trips it is possible to observe jaegers, Gannets, and Black-legged Kittiwakes. For additional information about birdwatching, see entry for Chincoteague NWR (Virginia chapter).

Blackwater National Wildlife Refuge, Route 1, Box 121, Cambridge 21613; (301) 228-2677. Blackwater is located 12 miles south of Cambridge. To reach the refuge, take SR 16 south to Church Creek, then SR 335 to the refuge. Camping is not permitted at Blackwater. The nearest state campground is at Martinak State Park, near Denton, about 35 miles northeast.

Blackwater was established in 1932 as a refuge for migratory waterfowl. Its 12,890 acres include rich, tidal marsh; freshwater ponds; mixed woodlands; and a small amount of cropland. Programs designed specifically for waterfowl include: limited planting of crops, construction of freshwater ponds, and management of the brackish marsh. Two of our endangered species receive special attention — the Delmarva Peninsula Fox Squirrel and the Bald Eagle. Among the recreational opportunities offered are woodland walking trails, an observation tower, a 2½-mile scenic drive, and a wildlife interpretive center (closed from 1 June to 31 August). There is also a picnic area. The refuge is located along the Atlantic Flyway; the best times for birdwatching are during spring and fall migration. Although most waterfowl migrate north in the spring, some remain at Blackwater through the summer. Among the 250 species of birds (102 nesting) sighted at the refuge are: Brant, American Wigeon, Common Goldeneye, Red-tailed Hawk, Peregrine Falcon, Bald Eagle, Little Blue Heron, American Bittern, Common Gallinule, Greater Yellowlegs, Black Tern, Black-billed Cuckoo, Barred Owl, Belted Kingfisher, Red-bellied Woodpecker, Eastern Wood Pewee, Blue Jay, Short-billed Marsh Wren, Mockingbird, Golden-crowned Kinglet, Worm-eating Warbler, Northern Parula, Hooded Warbler, Boat-tailed Grackle, Cardinal, and Henslow's Sparrow. Checklist available.

Carey Run Wildlife Sanctuary. Owned by the Maryland Ornithological Society. Contact: Ms. C. Gordon Taylor, 75 Broadway, Frostburg 21532; (301) 689-6791. Carey Run is located in northwestern Maryland, about a 3-hour trip from Baltimore. To reach the sanctuary from Frostburg, take US 48 west to SR 546 (Finzel Road), turn right and continue to Beall School Road, turn south (left) and follow this road to dead end; keep bearing right to gate behind schoolhouse. Accommodations are available at the sanctuary by reservation only.

Carey Run totals 162 acres and is essentially the valley of 2 small streams: Carey Run and Hefner Run. Because of this, the terrain is relatively rugged. About 55 acres are fields — some mowed, some planted with shrubs attractive to wildlife. There are also some stands of pine and cut-over deciduous forests. Winter birdwatching is not spectacular here; spring, summer, and fall are much better. About 150 species of birds have been sighted at Carey Run. Among them are: Ruffed Grouse, Turkey, Black-capped Chickadee, Bewick's Wren, Veery, Black-throated Blue Warbler, Golden-winged Warbler, and Vesper Sparrow.

Catoctin Mountain Park, Thurmont 21788; (301) 824-2574. Catoctin, a national park, borders on Cunningham Falls, a state park. Catoctin can be reached by going northeast from Baltimore on US 70 to Frederick; then north to Thurmont on US 15; then west into the park on SR 77. Camping, interpretive programs, scenic drives, self-guiding trails, and 25 miles of hiking trails are available. There is a trailside museum.

Catoctin Mountain Park was established in 1954 and comprises nearly 5800 acres. The original recreational demonstration area has been permitted to develop toward an eastern hardwood climax forest. Among the 150 species of birds (75 breeding, 23 permanent residents) sighted here are: Ruffed Grouse, American Kestrel (Sparrow Hawk), Yellow-billed Cuckoo, Great Horned Owl, Great Crested Flycatcher, Tufted Titmouse, Bewick's Wren, Wood Thrush, Black-throated Green Warbler, Worm-eating Warbler, Ovenbird, and Vesper Sparrow. Checklist available.

Chesapeake and Ohio Canal National Historic Park, Box 158, Sharpsburg 21781; (301) 432-5124; for information about the lower section of the park (from Georgetown to Seneca), phone Great Falls Tavern: (301) 299-3613. The park runs from Washington, D.C., northwest for 180 miles to Cumberland (Maryland). Public facilities include camping, conducted walks and interpretive programs, horseback riding, picnicking, boating and canoeing, and hiking and bicycling. There are 14 park service ramps that provide public access to the river. Hiking and biking are done along the canal towpath, on an elevated trail that follows the entire length of the canal. Portions of the towpath are impassable during wet periods; some sections may become flooded or washed out after heavy rains. It is advisable to check conditions in advance.

The C & O Canal Park offers many opportunities for nature study and birdwatching. There are 117 species of birds common to the Allegheny (northwest) region of the park. Among these are: Pied-billed Grebe, Wood Duck, Bufflehead, Common Goldeneye, Sharp-shinned Hawk, Cooper's Hawk, Osprey, Turkey, Green Heron, Great (Common) Egret, Yellow-billed Cuckoo, Screech Owl, Whip-poor-will, Belted Kingfisher, Pileated Woodpecker, Yellow-bellied Sapsucker, Great Crested Flycatcher, Purple Martin, Carolina Chickadee, Brown Creeper, Winter Wren, Wood Thrush, Blue-gray Gnat-catcher, Cedar Waxwing, Loggerhead Shrike, Warbling Vireo, Prothonotary Warbler, Worm-eating Warbler, Cerulean Warbler, Ovenbird, Eastern Meadow-lark, Northern (Baltimore) Oriole, Scarlet Tanager, and Chipping Sparrow. Checklist available.

Eastern Neck National Wildlife Refuge, Route 2, Box 225, Rock Hall 21661; (301) 639-7415. Eastern Neck NWR is located between Baltimore and Dover (Delaware), on the eastern side of the Chesapeake Bay. To reach the refuge, take SR 445 south from Rock Hall to Eastern Neck. Camping is not permitted at the refuge; however, facilities are available at nearby Tuckahoe State Forest.

The 2285-acre refuge was established in 1962 and is a major feeding and resting place for migratory waterfowl. Eastern Neck is located at the meeting of river and bay; its marshes, coves, and ponds have made it a natural home for waterfowl through the years. The diversity of habitat — including sand beaches, open fields, shoal waters, marshes, swamps, hedgerows, and woodlands — provides for a wide variety of birdlife. The endangered (and rare) Delmarva Peninsula Fox Squirrel can be easily observed on the refuge. Nearly 10 miles of roads and trails are open to the public. Among the 243 species of birds sighted at Eastern Neck (153 actually *on* the refuge; 103 nesting locally) are: Double-crested Cormorant, Wood Duck, Canvasback, Bald Eagle, Bobwhite, Killdeer, Forster's Tern, Screech Owl, Chimney Swift, Belted Kingfisher, Eastern Kingbird, Eastern Phoebe, Purple Martin, Brown Creeper, Carolina Wren, Gray Catbird, Hermit Thrush, Ruby-crowned Kinglet, White-eyed Vireo, Nashville Warbler, Chestnut-sided Warbler, Orchard Oriole, Indigo Bunting, and Grasshopper Sparrow. Checklist available.

Greenbelt Park, Greenbelt 20770. Greenbelt Park is located 12 miles north of Washington, D. C. From the Capitol Beltway (I-495) take Exit 28 at Kenilworth Avenue (SR 201); proceed south toward Bladensburg and follow the signs into the park. From the Baltimore-Washington Parkway, exit at Greenbelt Road (SR 193) and proceed to the park. Public facilities at Greenbelt Park include camping, picnicking, 3 self-guiding nature trails, and nearly 12 miles of hiking trails. In addition, various interpretive programs are offered.

Greenbelt Park is an 1100-acre woodland in a rapidly expanding metropolitan area; it is a refuge for plant and animal life. In the spring there are impressive displays of azalea, laurel, and dogwood; summer brings ferns and wildflowers; fall colors are as vivid as can be found in the region. Abandoned farmland, marshes, streams, and forest all combine to support a varied wildlife community. Red fox, deer, and raccoon find food and shelter here as do many species of birds. Among the birds likely to be seen at Greenbelt Park are: Pied-billed Grebe, Wood Duck, Red-shouldered Hawk, Bobwhite, Clapper Rail, Killdeer, American Woodcock, Mourning Dove, Barn Owl, Common Nighthawk, Red-bellied Woodpecker, Hairy Woodpecker, Yellow-bellied Sapsucker, Least Flycatcher, Purple Martin, Blue Jay, House Wren, Gray Catbird, White-eyed Vireo, Tennessee Warbler, Northern Parula, Black-throated Green Warbler, Prairie Warbler, Northern Waterthrush, Mourning Warbler (rare), American Redstart, Blue Grosbeak, Rufous-sided Towhee, and Bachman's Sparrow (rare).

Irish Grove Wildlife Sanctuary. Owned by the Maryland Ornithological Society. Contact: Mr. Sam Cimino, 704 Parkway Circle, Salisbury 21801; (301) 749-7852. Irish Grove is about a 3-hour drive from Baltimore; it is located near Crisfield, just outside of Marion. In Marion, turn southeast on SR 357 to Quindocqua Road, bear right on to Rumbly Point Road, and proceed to sanctuary entrance. Accommodations are available at the sanctuary — by reservation only. Birding is best here in the winter and spring. About 80 to 90 species winter here, including various species of waterfowl, hawks, and owls. Insects abound during the summer months (June through September). Visitors are advised to bring protective clothing, head nets, and several cans of insect repellent and salves. The sanctuary is about 70 percent marshland interspersed with tidal streams. There are several fresh- and saltwater ponds, which are surrounded by pine woods, and about 25 acres of open fields. Several trails traverse the property and there is an observation deck on Round Pond Road. Tidal canoeing is possible. There have been 225 species of birds recorded here. Among these are: Osprey, Green Heron, Great Blue Heron, Clapper Rail, Willet, Barn Owl, Long- and Short-billed Marsh Wrens, Brown-headed Nuthatch, Pine Warbler, Seaside Sparrow, and Sharp-tailed Sparrow.

Martin National Wildlife Refuge, Ewell, Smith Island 21824. The refuge is managed by Blackwater NWR. Martin was established in 1954. It comprises over 4400 acres and is located approximately 10 miles offshore, making it one of the more remote islands in the Chesapeake Bay. The island is mostly made up of tidal bays and salt marsh. In addition to the wide variety of waterfowl that winters here, Martin also supports several wading bird rookeries and a large population of nesting Ospreys.

Mill Creek Wildlife Sanctuary. Owned by the Maryland Ornithological Society. Contact: Mr. Robert Sharp II, Doncaster; (301) 822-2324. Mill Creek is on the Chesapeake Bay near the town of Wye Mills. It is about a 1½-hour drive from Baltimore. To reach the sanctuary from Wye Mills, take SR 662 south to the entrance.

Mill Creek Sanctuary comprises 155 acres; it is wild and hilly. The uplands are mostly beech-oak forest and there is a small field along the road. The swampy area around the creek, which bisects the property, is mostly red maple and sycamore. Three trails are maintained and are well marked for easy hiking. There have been 150 species of birds reported at Mill Creek. Among them are: Acadian Flycatcher, Rough-winged Swallow, Winter Wren, Ruby-crowned Kinglet, Hermit Thrush, Yellow-throated Warbler, Hooded Warbler, Prothonotary Warbler, Kentucky Warbler, Blue Grosbeak, and Summer Tanager. Around the swampy areas, various species of ducks may also be seen. Spring is the best time for birdwatching at Mill Creek.

Patuxent Wildlife Research Center, Laurel Bowie Road, Laurel 20810; (301) 776-4880. The center is operated by the United States Fish and Wildlife Service and covers 4500 acres along the Patuxent River. It is open to the public on weekdays from 8-4:30. The center is located on SR 197, 2 miles southeast of the Baltimore-Washington Parkway.

A broad variety of programs to study and protect migratory birds is conducted here. The best-known project is the endangered species program and its star is the Whooping Crane — there are 19 at Patuxent. Studies are also done on the effect of toxic substances on eagles' eggs. The center comprises meadow, oak forest, and marshlands. Resident birds include Canvasbacks, Black-crowned Night Herons, Bald Eagles, kestrels, owls, and Red-winged Blackbirds.

Pelot Sanctuary. Owned by Maryland Ornithological Society. Contact: Mr. A. J. Fletcher, Garland Lake Road, Denton 21629; (301) 479-1529. The sanctuary is located near Greensboro, about a 2-hour drive from Baltimore. To reach the sanctuary from Greensboro, take SR 313 north for 1 mile, then turn east onto Red Bridges Road for ½ mile to Choptank River; continue to the sanctuary.

Pelot Sanctuary totals approximately 60 acres of deciduous swamp forest. Look for ducks, owls, flycatchers, thrushes, vireos warblers, and sparrows.

Rock Creek Park, Washington, D.C. For information about the park, contact: Park Manager, Rock Creek Nature Center, 1100 Ohio Drive SW, Washington 20242; for information about the park in Maryland, contact: Maryland-National Capital Park and Planning Commission, 8787 Georgetown Avenue, Silver Spring 20907; (301) 589-1480. As is the case with other parks in large cities, Rock Creek Park is not always safe. It is inadvisable to visit the park alone and to wander too far from main paths.

Rock Creek Park is a woodland area of about 1750 acres in Washington, D.C. The park offers a wide range of activities including interpretive programs, guided and self-guiding nature tours, hiking, picnicking, and a variety of sports. There are about 15 miles of hiking trails. Because of pollution, the creek itself contains very little life — a few fish, including some eels, swim in Rock Creek. Most of the mammals common to the park are nocturnal including opossum, fox, raccoon, weasel, and muskrat. There have been about 145 species of birds reported in Rock Creek Park. Among them are: Ring-necked Duck, Wood Duck, Red-tailed Hawk, Rough-legged Hawk, Green Heron, Great Black-backed Gull, Great Horned Owl, Common Nighthawk, Belted Kingfisher, Pileated Woodpecker, Blue-gray Gnatcatcher, Hermit Thrush, Red-eyed Vireo, Golden-winged Warbler, Swainson's Warbler, Hooded Warbler, Ovenbird, Rusty Blackbird, Rose-breasted Grosbeak, Indigo Bunting, Red Crossbill, and Vesper Sparrow. Checklist available.

Susquehanna National Wildlife Refuge. Administered by Blackwater NWR. The refuge consists of a 4-acre island in the mouth of the Susquehanna River plus 13,365 acres of open water in the Chesapeake Bay. The island is located off the coast near Perryville. For information regarding visits to the refuge, contact the refuge manager at Blackwater.

Susquehanna was established in 1939, primarily as a refuge for Whistling Swans, Canvasbacks, Redheads, Ruddy Ducks, and Ring-necked Ducks. In addition one can see large numbers of Pintails and Common Goldeneyes. Other birds seen here include: Horned Grebe, American Wigeon, Lesser Scaup, and American Coot.

Theodore Roosevelt Island, Washington, D.C. Contact: Park Superintendent, George Washington Memorial Parkway, Turkey Run Park, McLean

22101. The island is located in the Potomac River in Washington, D.C., and is accessible from the Virginia shore by footbridge.

It was established as a wilderness area in 1932 and covers 88 acres of swamp, marsh, and upland forest. There are nearly 3 miles of foot trails that traverse the island and give the visitor an excellent opportunity to observe wildlife. The marsh areas are characterized by cattails, arrowhead, and pickerelweed; the swamp environment is created by willow, ash, and maple trees that root on the mudflats; the higher, central spine of the island forms the upland forest which is dominated by oak, elm, red maple, and tulip trees. Among the birds likely to be seen on the island are: Wood Duck, Belted Kingfisher, Downy Woodpecker, Carolina Chickadee, Long- and Short-billed Marsh Wrens, Wood Thrush, and Red-winged Blackbird.

NATURE CENTERS

In addition to the refuges, preserves, and parks described in the foregoing pages, there are several nature centers, natural environment areas, and sanctuaries located throughout the state. These centers often can be rewarding birding places. They are described briefly below.

Brookside Nature Center, 1400 Glenallan Avenue, Wheaton 20901; (301) 946-9071. The center is operated by the Maryland-National Capital Park and Planning Commission. It covers 500 acres and features a farm. Guided tours are offered; trails, some self-guiding, are maintained. The center is open all year, closed on Mondays.

Chancellor's Point, St. Marys City (near Lexington Park). The preserve is maintained by the St. Marys City Commission, St. Marys City 20686. It totals 66 acres of woods and open land on a bluff overlooking the St. Marys River. The lagoon serves as a bird refuge. Also in the same area is the St. Marys River Park — 450 acres of mixed hardwoods and conifers on the St. Marys River. The park is maintained by the state.

Clearwater Nature Center, Route 1, Box 325, Clinton 20735; (301) 297-4575. The center is operated by the Maryland-National Capital Park and Planning Commission. It covers 73 acres. A variety of educational and interpretive programs is offered. Guided tours are available, trails, some self-guiding, are maintained. The center is open all year.

Clyburn Wildflower Preserve and Garden Center, 4915 Greenspring Avenue, Baltimore 21209; (301) 542-3109. The center is operated by the Bureau of Parks of Baltimore City and the Clyburn Wildflower Preserve, Inc. The preserve totals 70 acres located within a 176-acre park. Guided tours are offered; trails, some self-guiding, are maintained. The center is open all year. It also serves as headquarters for the Maryland Ornithological Society.

Garrett County Resource Center, P. O. Box 73, Oakland 21550; (301) 334-9417. The center is operated by the Garrett County Board of Education. It covers 100 acres and features a planetarium. A variety of educational and interpretive programs is offered. Guided tours are available. The center is open all year, Monday through Friday.

Mattawoman Natural Environment Area. The area is owned and maintained by the state. It covers 9435 acres and is located south of Washington, D.C., near Mattawoman, adjacent to Cedarville State Forest.

Meadowside Nature Center, 5100 Muncaster Mill Road, Rockville 20902. The center is operated by the Maryland-National Capital Park and Planning Commission. It covers 250 acres. A variety of educational and interpretive programs is offered. The center is open all year, closed on Mondays and legal holidays.

Monocacy Natural Resource Area. The area is owned and managed by the state. It is located south of Frederick, along SR 85. The area consists of a hardwood forest along the Monocacy River.

Nanjemoy Marsh Sanctuary. The sanctuary is owned by the National Audubon Society, and maintained by the Southern Maryland Audubon Society. Contact: Dr. George B. Wilmot, 401 Amherst Road, Bryans Road 20616; (301) 748-2552. The sanctuary is open by appointment only. This is a 58-acre area consisting of marshland and is located south and east of SR 6 near the town of Nanjemoy. It serves as a feeding ground for a large heronry that is located nearby. Bald Eagles, also nesting nearby, use the area too.

Severn Run Natural Environment Area. The area is owned and maintained by the state. It totals 1618 acres and is located south of Baltimore, adjacent to Severn Run State Park.

Soldier's Delight Natural Environment Area. The area is owned and maintained by the state. It is located 7 miles from Baltimore, west of the Beltway off Liberty Road (SR 26). The area is due north of Liberty Road and intersected by Deer Park and Ward Chapel roads. It totals 2076 acres. Guided tours are offered; trails, some self-guiding, are maintained. Birds seen here include Turkey Vulture, Downy Woodpecker, Blue Jay, Tufted Titmouse, Black-capped Chickadee, and Prairie Warbler among others.

In addition to those areas described above, the state maintains other natural environment areas: *Morgan Run,* 1500 acres in Carroll County; *South Mountain,* 18,386 acres in Frederick and Washington counties; and *Zekiah Swamp,* 5000 acres in Prince George County. Also, the Chesapeake Audubon Society maintains an unnamed 121-acre sanctuary that is open by prior arrangement.

NATURE CONSERVANCY PRESERVES

The Nature Conservancy maintains several preserves in Maryland. These are described below. Additional Nature Conservancy lands have been deeded either to the state or to the federal government for inclusion in state parks or wildlife refuges. Most of the preserves listed below are open with permission only. It is advisable to arrange visits in advance by contacting the preserve manager.

Battle Creek Cypress Swamp. Contact: Dr. Hayward Hamilton, U. S. Atomic Energy Commission, Division of Environmental and Biomedical Research, 19021 Cott Field Court, Gaithersburg 20760; (202) 973-4156. The 100-acre preserve is a national natural landmark and is open to the public. To reach the preserve from Annapolis, take SR 2 south to Prince Frederick, turn west (right) on SR 506, and continue for about 2 miles to the wooded bridge, which is in the middle of the swamp area. The parking area is west of the bridge. This is one of the northernmost cypress swamps in the country. During the spring, waves of warblers pass through Battle Creek Cypress Swamp. Other birds seen here include: Wood Duck, American Woodcock, Cooper's Hawk, Marsh Hawk, Pileated Woodpecker, White-breasted Nuthatch, Mockingbird, and Rufous-sided Towhee.

Finzel Swamp. Contact: Dr. Melvin L. Brown, Professor of Biology, Frostburg State College, Frostburg 21532; (301) 689-4355. This 285-acre preserve is located in northwestern Maryland. From Cumberland, take SR 40 west to Frostburg, turn north (right) on SR 546, and proceed to the preserve. The preserve is open by prior arrangement only. The area known as Finzel Swamp is a unique northern bog in a southern latitude. Some species of plants found here are found as far north as the Arctic Circle. It is one of the southernmost places where the tamarack (larch) grows. Hundreds of different ferns and wildflowers thrive here. Among the many birds to be seen at Finzel Swamp are: Wood Duck, Killdeer, Long-eared Owl, Pileated Woodpecker, Brown Creeper, Brown Thrasher, Golden- and Ruby-crowned Kinglets, Rose-breasted Grosbeak, and White-crowned Sparrow.

Hambleton Island. Contact: Dr. Edgar Garbisch, Environmental Concern, Inc., P. O. Box P, St. Michaels 21663; (301) 745-9620. The preserve is open by prior arrangement only. To reach Hambleton Island, take US 50 east from Annapolis across the Chesapeake Bay and into Easton, then turn west on SR 33 and go to St. Michaels, turn left on Chew Avenue and proceed to town dock. The Environmental Concern building is on the left. This 25-acre island is located in the Chesapeake Bay. The island is forested with pine and cedar. The surrounding shoal flats serve as a feeding area for ducks during the winter. Osprey nest in the trees along the shore.

Hellen Creek Hemlock Preserve. Contact: Dr. Hayward Hamilton, U. S. Atomic Energy Commission, Division of Environmental and Biomedical Research, 19021 Cott Field Court, Gaithersburg 20760; (202) 973-4156. This 21-acre preserve is open with permission only. It is located near Battle Creek Cypress Swamp. To reach the preserve, take SR 2 to Lusby, turn south on SR 266 (Sollers Wharf Road), and go for 2 miles, past St. John's Church on the right, then turn left; proceed for 2½ miles, turn left again, and go for ¾ mile to Hellen Creek. Hellen Creek Preserve is covered with a notable stand of eastern hemlock which grows close to the edge of the tidal marsh. Look for owls, woodpeckers, and warblers.

STATE PARKS AND FORESTS

There are many state parks and forests in Maryland — from the Appalachian region to the coastal plain. Most of them have camping facilities, nature trails, campfire programs, and a variety of other recreational activities. Those that in addition are good spots for birdwatching are marked with an asterisk (*). For additional information about Maryland state parks and forests, contact: Maryland Park Service, Tawes State Office Building, Annapolis 21401. The park service also administers the state-owned natural environment areas.

*Assateague, Route 2, Box 293, Berlin 21811; (301) 641-2120; 700 acres.
 Big Run, Route 2, Grantsville 21536; (301) 895-5453; 300 acres.
*Calvert Cliffs, Lusby 20657; 982 acres; day use only.
 Casselman, Grantsville 21536; 4 acres; day use only.
*Cedarville, Route 4, Box 133, Brandywine 20613; (301) 881-1622; 340 acres.
 Cedarville State Forest, Brandywine 20613; 3232 acres; day use only.
*Cunningham Falls, Route 1, Thrumont 21788; (301) 271-2495; 5000 acres; day
 use only.
*Dan's Mountain, Lonaconing 21539; 479 acres; day use only.
*Deep Creek Lake, Route 2, Swanton 21561; (301) 387-5563; 1800 acres.
 Deer Creek (Rocks Area), Jarrettsville 21084; (301) 557-7994; 683 acres; day
 use only.
*Doncaster State Forest, Doncaster; 1485 acres; day use only.
*Elk Neck, Route 2, Northeast 21901; (301) 287-5333; 1575 acres.
*Elk Neck State Forest, Northeast 21901; 2742 acres.
 Fort Frederick, P. O. Box 1, Big Pool 21711; (301) 842-2504; 360 acres.
 Fort Tonoloway, Hancock 21750; 26 acres; day use only.
 Gambrill, Route 8, Frederick 21701; (301) 473-8360; 1136 acres.
 Gathland, Box 374, Burkittsville 21718; (301) 371-6630; 135 acres; day use
 only.
 Greenbrier, Route 2, Boonsboro 21718; (301) 739-7877; 1139 acres; day use
 only; Appalachian Trail crosses park.
*Green Ridge State Forest, Hancock 21750; 26,535 acres.

*Gunpowder, Kingsville 21087; 9827 acres; day use only.

*Herrington Manor, Route 1, Oakland 21550; (301) 334-9180; 365 acres; day use only.

*Janes Island, Route 1, Box 4, Crisfield 21818; (301) 968-1565; 2874 acres; access by boat.

Jonas Green, Annapolis 21400; 5 acres; day use only.

Martinak State Park, Deep Shore Road, Denton 21629; (301) 479-1619; 99 acres.

Mattapeake, Mattapeake; 20 acres; day use only.

*Milburn Landing, Route 1, Pocomoke City 21851; (301) 957-3353; 370 acres.

New Germany, Route 2, Grantsville 21536; (301) 895-5453; 243 acres.

*Patapsco, 1100 Hilton Avenue, Baltimore 21228; (301) 747-6602; 7820 acres.

*Pocomoke State Forest, Pocomoke City 21851; 11,506 acres; day use only.

*Point Lookout, Scotland 20687; (301) 872-5688; 513 acres.

Potomac State Forest, Oakland 21550; 12,390 acres.

Rocky Gap, Route 2, Box 167, Flintstone 21530; (301) 724-3735; day use only.

*Sandy Point, Route 2, Box 137, Annapolis 21401; (301) 757-1841; 813 acres; day use only.

*Savage River State Forest, Frostburg 21532; 52,251 acres.

Seneca, 11990 Clopper, Gaithersburg 20760; (301) 924-2127; 2611 acres; day use only.

*Shad Landing, Route 1, Snow Hill 21863; (301) 632-2566; 545 acres.

Smallwood, Box 25, Rison 20861; (301) 743-7613; 333 acres; day use only.

*Susquehanna, 801 Stafford Road, Havre de Grace 21078; (301) 939-0643; 1193 acres; day use only.

*Swallow Falls, Route 1, Oakland 21550; (301) 334-9180; 257 acres.

Swallow Falls State Forest, Oakland 21550; 6933 acres.

Seth State Forest, Easton 21601.

Tuckahoe State Forest, Queen Anne 21657.

*Washington Monument, Route 1, Box 147, Middletown 21768; (301) 432-8065; 104 acres; Appalachian Trail crosses park.

Wicomico State Forest, Pittsville 21850; 1110 acres; day use only.

Wye Oak, Wye Mills 21679; 29 acres; day use only.

MASSACHUSETTS

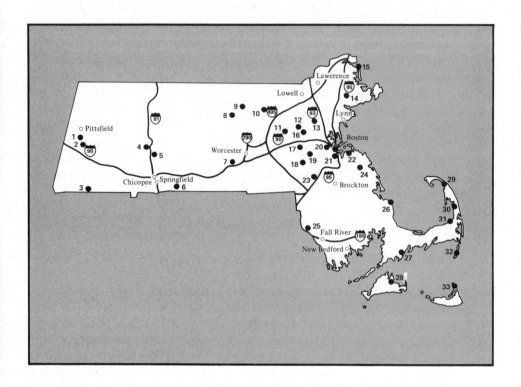

1. Pleasant Valley Wildlife Sanctuary
2. Bullard Woods Preserve
3. Bartholomew's Cobble
4. Arcadia Nature Center
5. Mount Tom State Reservation
6. Laughing Brook
7. Buck Hill
8. Cook's Canyon/Wildwood
9. Wachusett Meadows Wildlife Sanctuary
10. Oxbow NWR
11. Environmental Education Center
12. Great Meadows NWR
13. Drumlin Farms
14. Ipswich River
    Crane Wildlife Refuge
15. Parker River NWR
16. Walden Pond
17. Broadmoor/Little Pond

18. Stony Brook NC
19. Hale Reservation
20. Arnold Arboretum
21. Blue Hills
22. Great Esker Park
    World's End Reservation
23. Moose Hill Wildlife Sanctuary
24. Southshore Natural Science Center
25. Caratunk Wildlife Refuge
26. Manomet Bird Observatory
27. Ashmet
28. Felix Neck Wildlife Sanctuary
29. Cape Cod National Seashore
30. Wellfleet Bay Wildlife Sanctuary
31. Cape Cod Museum of Natural History
32. Monomoy NWR
33. Nantucket NWR

Massachusetts — from the Berkshires to Cape Cod — has diversified habitats that provide food and shelter for an incredible variety of birds. In 1975, 343 species of birds were recorded. Cape Cod, Nantucket, Martha's Vineyard, and the Elizabeth Islands — all are situated along the Atlantic Flyway and are excellent places for observing shorebirds, marshbirds, and seabirds — at all seasons of the year. The woodlands are host to waves of warblers in May. Even the suburbs are good for birdwatching. Ludlow Griscom, the late, well-known American ornithologist, recorded 180 species from his yard in Cambridge. Bird populations shift and change, and whereas 20 years ago the Snowy Egret and Tufted Titmouse were rarities in Massachusetts, today they are more common. The Snowy Egret nests on the offshore islands and the Tufted Titmouse is a regular breeding bird throughout the state.

There are 31 state wildlife management areas located throughout Massachusetts. These areas range in size from 200 to 4000 acres. There are upland areas, abandoned fields interspersed with thickets, wooded areas, and marshy areas. Various recreational activities, including nature study, are encouraged on these lands.

Other good birdwatching places in Massachusetts include the Elizabeth Islands in Buzzards Bay. These can be reached by boat from New Bedford. Harlequin Ducks, Razorbills, Dovekies, Black Guillemots, Gannets and other seabirds can be seen at Martha's Vineyard in the winter.

The Massachusetts Audubon Society is very active. In addition to the sanctuaries that they own and staff, they sponsor various birdwatching trips. They issue a birder's kit, which includes pamphlets on "Where to Watch Birds in Massachusetts," a checklist of Massachusetts birds, and a booklet entitled "An Introduction to Massachusetts Birds." They also staff *Voice of Audubon,* which is the rare bird alert for Massachusetts. The eastern number is (617) 259-8805; *Western Voice of Audubon* is (413) 566-3590. They were the first to start this service — over 20 years ago. *Voice of Audubon* provides up-to-the-minute phone information on what is being seen in the state. In the spring of 1978, eastern *Voice of Audubon* was supplying birdfinders with information about a Eurasian curlew being seen on Martha's Vineyard. For further information about birdwatcing in Massachusetts, contact the Massachusetts Audubon Society, South Great Road, Lincoln 01773; (617) 259-9500.

Arcadia Nature Center and Wildlife Sanctuary, Easthampton 01027; (413) 584-3009. To reach the sanctuary from I-91, take Exit 18 south to US 5, follow US 5 south for nearly 1½ miles to East Street, take the first right across the oxbow, then continue just over a mile to Fort Hill Road, the first right; take Fort Hill Road to sanctuary entrance. The sanctuary is owned and staffed by the Massachusetts Audubon Society. It comprises 560 acres of woodland, meadow, and marsh, and borders on an old oxbow of the Connecticut River. A full range of educational and interpretive programs is offered. Guided and self-guiding tours are available. Arcadia is open to the public all year. Over 200 species of birds (70 nesting) have been seen here. Among them are: Wood Duck, American Kestrel (Sparrow Hawk), Screech Owl, and Northern Waterthrush.

Arcadia Sanctuary also administers a smaller sanctuary — *High Ledges*. Arrangements to visit it must be made in advance. It comprises 400 acres of northern hardwood forest, upland swamps, and a stream. It is located off Patten Road in Shelburne. Nesting birds include Dark-eyed Juncos and various warblers. There is also a large beaver pond. A map of the area is available at Arcadia Nature Center.

Bartholomew's Cobble, Ashley Falls 01222. The preserve is managed by the Trustees of Reservations, 224 Adams Street, Milton 02186. A parking (admission) fee is charged. To reach the cobble from Great Barrington, take SR-7 south to intersection with 7A, turn right on 7A (toward Ashley Falls), and follow signs to Bartholomew's Cobble. Trails are maintained, and a naturalist is on staff.

This 170-acre area is a natural rock garden. Trees, ferns, and wildflowers grow on rocky outcrops — called cobbles — which are more than 500 million years old. Such unexpected birds as: Golden Eagle, Snowy Egret, Black-backed Three-toed Woodpecker, Blue-gray Gnatcatcher, and Summer Tanager have been seen here. Many other, more common species are observed regularly. Look for warblers and other passerines.

Cape Cod National Seashore, South Wellfleet 02663. There are 4 major areas of the national seashore: Province Lands, Pilgrim Heights, Nauset, and Marconi Station. The latter houses the headquarters. All areas have interpretive exhibits, nature trails, and beaches. There are no camping facilities at the Seashore; however, there is a large state-owned campground nearby and there are 3 private campgrounds located within the park's boundaries.

Cape Cod National Seashore was established in 1961; and will, when acquisition is complete, total 27,000 acres of land. Cape Cod is located on the Atlantic Flyway. Its forests, tidal flats, fresh- and saltwater marshes, ponds, swamps, and dunes are refuge for hundreds of thousands of birds. Monomoy NWR is located just off the southern end of the Nauset Beach area.

Common summer birds of the Cape Cod National Seashore include: Wilson's Storm-Petrel, Black Duck, Marsh Hawk, Black-crowned Night Heron, Green Heron, Piping Plover, Black-bellied Plover, Whimbrel, Ruddy Turnstone, White-rumped Sandpiper, Dunlin, Short-billed Dowitcher, Red Knot, Ring-billed Gull, Roseate Tern, Arctic Tern, Great Horned Owl, Yellow- and Black-billed Cuckoos, Downy Woodpecker, Tree Swallow, Gray Catbird, Hermit Thrush, Cedar Waxwing, Pine Warbler, Prairie Warbler, and Chipping Sparrow. Checklist available.

Caratunk Wildlife Refuge, Brown Avenue, Seekonk 07221. The refuge is owned by the Caratunk Wildlife Trust and is managed by the Audubon Society of Rhode Island. Seekonk is just across the border from Providence (Rhode Island); use SR 114A. This 159-acre refuge includes mixed woodlands, ponds, old fields, and croplands. There are demonstration food plantings for wildlife. Trails are maintained. Among the many birds to be seen here are: Red-shouldered Hawk, American Woodcock, Common (Yellow-shafted) Flicker, Eastern Kingbird, Black-capped Chickadee, Brown Creeper, Gray Catbird, and a variety of warblers and finches.

Cooks Canyon/Wildwood Nature Center, South Street, P. O. Box 638, Barre 01005; (617) 355-4064. The center is located about 20 miles northwest of Worcester, in Barre. From Barre Common, take South Street for ½ mile south to reach the center. The sanctuary is owned and operated by the Masschusetts Audubon Society. High school, college, and teacher training programs are offered. Interpretive programs and walks are regularly scheduled. Wildwood Nature Center comprises 40 acres of mixed woodlands, pine plantation, pond, and brook. Trails are maintained. The center is open all year.

Cook's Canyon also administers 2 smaller sanctuaries. Arrangements to visit them must be made in advance. They are as follows: *Burncoat Pond* — 125 acres of laurel and red oak forest with a brook, located on the Spencer-Leicester town line; and *Rutland Brook* — 98 acres of woodlands that include ponds, brook, marsh, and a beaver colony, located in Petersham off SR 32.

Drumlin Farm Educational Center and Wildlife Sanctuary, South Great Road, Lincoln 01773; (617) 259-9005. The center is located on SR 117, 4½ miles west of the overpass over SR 128 (I-95), or just over ½ mile east of the intersection of SR 117 and SR 126. Drumlin Farm is owned and operated by the Massachusetts Audubon Society; it is also their headquarters. The sanctuary totals 220 acres of pasture, fields, woodland, and ponds. A variety of educational and interpretive programs is offered; an educational farm is operated; and a network of trails is maintained. There are also guided tours. The center is open all year; closed on Mondays (except those Mondays that are holidays). Nesting birds at the sanctuary include Barn Swallow, Gray Catbird, Scarlet Tanager, and Indigo Bunting.

Drumlin Farm Center also administers several smaller sanctuaries. Arrangements to visit them must be made in advance. They are as follows: *Fairhaven* — 20 acres of wood-rimmed salt marsh bordering Shaw's Cove; *Great Neck* — 35 acres of woodlands in Wareham, located at the end of Mayflower Road; *Hemlock Pond* — 15 acres rimming a pond and brook, has population of rare freshwater "jellyfish," located in Weston, off Newton Street; *Little Pine Island* — 2¾-acre island, Osprey nesting site, located north of Great Island in the east branch of the Westport River; *Norwell Property* — 13 acres of salt marsh, located off River Street in Norwell; *Rendezvous Lane Salt Marsh* — 14 acres, mostly salt marsh, located in Barnstable on Rendezvous Lane; *Thick Thicket* — 7½ acres of upland adjacent to Sippewisset Marsh; and *Weld Pond* — 12 acres of woodlands, located in Dedham, near the Dedham School.

Felix Neck Wildlife Sanctuary, located on Martha's Vineyard. Mailing address: Felix Neck Wildlife Trust, Box 494, Vineyard Haven 02568; (617) 627-4850. To reach the sanctuary, take a ferry from Woods Hole to Vineyard Haven; the sanctuary is 4 miles southeast on Edgartown Road, on the left side. The 200-acre sanctuary is owned by the Massachusetts Audubon Society; the interpretive programs are operated by the Felix Neck Wildlife Trust, Inc. Trails are maintained; there are also photography blinds and a visitors' center. The sanctuary is open all year.

More than 100 species of birds have been recorded on or near the ponds and marshes of Felix Neck. Among them are: Red-throated Loon, Brant, Pintail, Mallard, Black Duck, American Wigeon, Redhead, Sharp-shinned Hawk, Yellow-crowned Night Heron, Glossy Ibis, Common Gallinule, Ruddy Turnstone, Whimbrel, Red Knot, Wilson's Phalarope, Laughing Gull, and Eastern Bluebird.

Great Meadows National Wildlife Refuge, 191 Sudbury Road, Concord 01742; (617) 369-5518. Great Meadows is located 20 miles west of Boston; it is divided into 2 refuge areas, one on either side of SR 126. Refuge headquarters are on Sudbury Road, just south of the center of Concord. Camping is not permitted on the refuge.

Established in 1944, Great Meadows NWR will comprise 4000 acres when acquisition is complete; it now totals just over 3000 acres. Hiking trails, observation towers, and blinds are among the facilities available. Ornithologists consider Great Meadows Refuge to be one of the finest inland birding areas in Massachusetts. The diverse habitat of open water, marsh, and upland is attractive to many species of birds. There have been 214 species (90 nesting) recorded at the refuge. Among them are: Pied-billed Grebe, Gadwall, Wood Duck, Greater and Lesser Scaups, Sharp-shinned Hawk, Wilson's Phalarope, Ring-billed Gull, Mourning Dove, Great Horned Owl, Common (Yellow-shafted) Flicker, Least Flycatcher, Red- and White-breasted Nuthatches, Hermit Thrush, Northern Shrike, Solitary Vireo, Nashville Warbler, Blue-winged Warbler (rare), Chestnut-sided Warbler, Wilson's Warbler, Rusty Blackbird, Evening Gros-beak, Common Redpoll, and Sharp-tailed Sparrow. Checklist available.

Ipswich River Nature Center and Wildlife Sanctuary, Perkins Row, Topsfield 01983; (617) 887-2241. To reach the center, from US 1, turn east on SR 97 at the lights; Perkins Row is the first left; the sanctuary entrance is a mile further, on the right. It is located about 15 miles south of Parker River NWR. The center is owned and staffed by the Massachusetts Audubon Society; it is open all year, closed on Mondays.

The sanctuary comprises over 2500 acres of woods, fields, swamp, and river. There are 19 miles of trails, an observation tower, and waterfowl impoundments. At the center, various educational and interpretive programs are offered; a library is also maintained. There have been 221 species of birds (94 nesting) at the sanctuary. Among them are: Wood Duck, Cooper's Hawk, Red-tailed Hawk, Marsh Hawk, American Bittern, Yellow- and Black-billed Cuckoos, Whip-poor-will, Black-and-white Warbler, Golden-winged Warbler, Black-throated Green Warbler, Canada Warbler, and Blackburnian Warbler.

Ipswich River Sanctuary also administers several smaller sanctuaries. Arrangements to visit them must be made in advance. They are as follows: *Norman's Woe Sanctuary*, 26 acres on Hesperus Avenue in Glocester; the *Hardy Property*, 6 acres of woods lying within Boxford State Forest; *Lynnfield Marsh*, 75 acres of swampland in the Great Swamp area between Wakefield and Lynnfield north of SR 128; and *Straitsmouth Island*, a 33-acre rocky island off Rockport, resting area for gulls.

Monomoy National Wildlife Refuge. Administered by Great Meadows NWR. Monomoy is located off Cape Cod, about 90 miles from Boston. Refuge headquarters, staffed during the summer months, is located on Morris Island in Chatham; use SR 28. The refuge is accessible by boat only. Boats are for hire in and around Chatham. *Caution is advised, for winds and riptides make the 1-mile crossing dangerous.* Camping is not permitted at the refuge.

Monomoy Refuge was established in 1970. The island is a coastal barrier beach about 8 miles long and up to 1½ miles wide. It is a typical barrier beach island of salt- and freshwater marshes, sand dunes, freshwater ponds, and sparse dune vegetation. Located on the Atlantic Flyway, Monomoy has long been renowned as a shorebird area. The Hudsonian Godwit frequents the island during fall migration. Among the 252 species of birds sighted (29 nesting) are: Cory's Shearwater, Gannet, Black Duck, Green-winged Teal, Harlequin Duck (rare), Common Eider, King Eider (rare), White-winged Scoter, Sharp-shinned Hawk, Black-crowned Night Heron, Clapper Rail, Semipalmated Plover, Black-bellied Plover, Semipalmated Sandpiper, Sanderling, Whimbrel, Red Knot, Northern Phalarope, Hudsonian Godwit, Parasitic Jaeger, Great Black-backed Gull, Arctic Tern, Black-billed Cuckoo, Short-eared Owl, Yellow-bellied Flycatcher (rare), Brown Creeper, Long-billed Marsh Wren, Water Pipit, Philadelphia Vireo (rare), Northern Parula, Palm Warbler, Connecticut Warbler (rare), Rose-breasted Grosbeak, Seaside Sparrow, and Lapland Longspur. Checklist available.

Moose Hill Wildlife Sanctuary, 300 Moose Hill Street, Sharon 02067; (617) 784-5691. To reach the sanctuary from Sharon, go west on SR 27 to Moose Hill Street, take Moose Hill Street for 1½ miles; or, from the intersection of SR 1 and SR 27, take SR 27 east to the first right (less than ½ mile), which is Moose Hill Street. This 227-acre sanctuary is owned and staffed by the

Massachusetts Audubon Society. A natural history day camp is operated; other interpretive and educational programs are offered. Nearly 10 miles of trails are maintained. The sanctuary is open all year. The habitat consists primarily of hills, woods, meadows, and marshes. Over 100 species of birds are regularly seen here. In the woodlands one is likely to find: Cooper's Hawk, Ruffed Grouse, American Woodcock, Hermit Thrush, Veery, Solitary Vireo, Ovenbird, Black-throated Green Warbler, Chestnut-sided Warbler, American Redstart, and a variety of sparrows.

Nantucket National Wildlife Refuge. Under management of Ninigret NWR (in Rhode Island). The refuge is administered under a cooperative agreement with the town of Nantucket. Established in 1973, Nantucket Refuge comprises 40 acres. It is located on the northernmost tip of Nantucket Island, about 25 miles south of Cape Cod. Public access is by boat or on foot from the main part of the island. Access to Nantucket Island is by (summer) ferry from Falmouth or Hyannis. The refuge is on the Atlantic Flyway, just south of Monomoy NWR, and provides feeding and resting grounds for migrating waterfowl especially sea ducks, Black Ducks, and Canada Geese. Also seen on Nantucket are Black-crowned Night Herons, Short-eared Owls, and Savannah Sparrows. For information about visiting the refuge, contact the refuge manager at Ninigret NWR.

Oxbow National Wildlife Refuge. Administered by Great Meadows NWR. This 622-acre refuge was established in 1974. It is located 40 miles west of Boston in Harvard. The refuge is composed mainly of marshland that is fed by the Nashua River. There are numerous trails which provide opportunities for hiking, nature study, and birdwatching. Look for ducks, herons, swallows, and warblers. There are several state wildlife management areas in the vicinity.

Parker River National Wildlife Refuge, Northern Boulevard, Plum Island, Newburyport 01950; (617) 465-5753. Parker River is located about 35 miles north of Boston on Plum Island, which is 3 miles east of Newburyport. Camping is not permitted at the refuge; however, facilities are available at nearby Salisbury Beach State Reservation. Because of massive public visitation (from May to September), the refuge often closes to prevent overcrowding. The number of vehicles allowed to enter the refuge is determined by the number of available parking spaces (there are 15 parking lots). Be prepared to be turned away after 9 AM on busy summer weekends.

Parker River was established in 1942. The refuge's 4650 acres include 1000 acres of sand dunes, over 3200 acres of salt marsh and tidal waters, 272 acres of freshwater marsh, and 91 acres of upland. There are 6 miles of ocean beach. Peak concentrations of up to 25,000 ducks and over 6000 Canada Geese occur during spring and fall migrations.

There are many trails, observation towers, and blinds. Especially noteworthy is the 2-mile Hellcat Swamp Nature Trail at parking lot #9. The trail goes through several types of habitat — beach, freshwater swamp, dunes, saltwater marsh, and freshwater marsh. Many species of birds can be found here. There have been 268 species of birds (61 nesting) identified on the refuge. Among these are: Red-throated Loon, Gannet, Double-crested Cormorant, Canada Goose, Blue Goose, Blue-winged Teal, Greater Scaup, Common Eider, Surf Scoter, Red-breasted Merganser, Marsh Hawk, American Coot, Killdeer, Greater Yellowlegs, Dunlin, Sanderling, Black-legged Kittiwake, Common Tern, Roseate Tern, Black Skimmer, Razorbill, Thick-billed Murre, Dovekie, Snowy Owl (winter), Barn Swallow, Brown Thrasher; Ruby-crowned Kinglet, Wilson's Warbler, Hooded Warbler (rare), Mourning Warbler, Common Yellow-throat, Rufous-sided Towhee, and Sharp-tailed Sparrow. Checklist available.

Pleasant Valley Wildlife Sanctuary, Lenox 01240; (413) 637-0320. To reach the sanctuary from Lenox, take Main Street to Undermountain Road; go a mile to Reservoir Road, turn right; then a mile further, bearing right, to the entrance. Pleasant Valley Sanctuary is owned and staffed by the Massachusetts Audubon Society. The sanctuary comprises 680 acres of freshwater marsh, ponds, mixed woodlands, and open fields. There is a trailside museum (not always open). A variety of educational and interpretive programs are offered. Ten miles of trails (self-guiding) are maintained. A beaver colony has constructed dams and ponds in the swamp. There have been 180 species of birds (60 nesting) recorded at Pleasant Valley. Among these are: Green Heron, Barred Owl, Pileated Woodpecker, Tree Swallow, Veery, Solitary Vireo, Nashville Warbler, Golden-winged Warbler, Canada Warbler, Louisiana Waterthrush, Indigo Bunting, and Scarlet Tanager.

Wachusett Meadows Wildlife Sanctuary, Goodnow Road, P. O. Box 268, Princeton 01541; (617) 464-2712. Princeton is about 15 miles north of Worcester. To reach the sanctuary from the center of Princeton, take SR 62 west for nearly a mile to Goodnow Road; the sanctuary is a mile further on Goodnow Road. The Massachusetts Audubon Society owns and staffs Wachusett Meadows Sanctuary.

This 907-acre sanctuary contains a 100-acre marsh, upland forest, and meadows. There is a boardwalk that goes over the swamp. A network of trails is maintained. Educational and interpretive programs are offered. Among the many birds seen here are: Goshawk, Cliff Swallow, Eastern Bluebird, Canada Warbler, Bobolink, and Rose-breasted Grosbeak.

Wellfleet Bay Wildlife Sanctuary, West Road, P. O. Box 236, South Wellfleet 03663; (617) 349-2615. The sanctuary is on Cape Cod; the entrance is on the western side of SR 6, immediately north of the Eastham-Wellfleet town line. The sanctuary is owned and operated by the Massachusetts Audubon Society. Wellfleet Bay Sanctuary comprises 700 acres of salt marsh, tidal inlets, sandy beach, pine woods, fields, and brooks. Educational and interpretive programs are offered; 4 miles of trails are maintained — 1 trail is self-guiding.

Among the 258 species of birds seen here are: Common Eider, Surf Scoter, Clapper Rail, Piping Plover, and Pine Warbler. In addition, many other seabirds, marshbirds, and shorebirds are to be found here. For additional information, see the entries for Cape Cod National Seashore and Monomoy NWR — both of these areas are located near the sanctuary.

Wellfleet Bay Sanctuary also administers several smaller sanctuaries. Arrangements to visit them must be made in advance. They are as follows: *Dead Neck/Sampson's Island* — a tidal seabird nesting area at Osterville; *Maraspin Creek* — 10 acres of salt marsh and tidal creek, on the bay side of Cape Cod, near Millway; *Momonoy Lighthouse Research Station* — 2 acres within borders of Monomoy NWR; *Outermost House* — site of Henry Beston's book, 41 acres of dune and beach within Cape Cod National Seashore on Nauset Beach, Eastham (the house no longer stands); *Pepper Lot* — 2 acres of woods and thickets off Cedar Street in Chatham; *Popponesset Sandspit* — a sandspit in Barnstable; and *Tern Island* — 10 acres of tidal sandspit located off Chatham fish pier.

NATURE CENTERS

In addition to those preserves, refuges, and sanctuaries discussed above, there are many nature centers, arboretums, and smaller parks located throughout Massachusetts. Most of these areas are good birding places. They are described, in brief, below.

Arnold Arboretum, The Arborway, Jamaica Plain 02130. The arboretum was begun as a tree farm for Harvard University over 100 years ago. It now has over 6000 varieties of trees and shrubs. It is located in southwestern Boston, off US 1. The arboretum covers 265 acres. There have been 154 species of birds (23 nesting) sighted here. Among them are: Swainson's Thrush, Cape May Warbler, and Song Sparrow.

Ashumet, Ashmet Road, East Falmouth 02536; (617) 563-6390. To reach the sanctuary from North Falmouth, at the intersection of SR 28 and SR 151, take SR 151 east for 4 miles; Ashumet is on the north side of SR 151. The sanctuary is owned and staffed by the Massachusetts Audubon Society. The sanctuary covers 45 acres; trails are maintained. There are 65 varieties of holly; a collection of rhododendron and azaleas; an herb garden; and the unusual fall-flowering Franklinia at Ashumet. The sanctuary is located on the southwestern end of Cape Cod; bird life will be similar to that of Monomoy NWR, which is located nearby.

Blue Hills Trailside Museum, 1904 Canton Avenue, Milton 02186; (617) 333-0690. The center is operated by the Society for the Metropolitan District Commission in cooperation with the Massachusetts Audubon Society. The sanctuary totals 5700 acres and offers guided tours, lectures, and interpretive programs. It is open all year; closed on Mondays and major holidays.

Broadmoor/Little Pond, 79 South Street, South Natick 01760; (617) 655-2296. To reach the center from South Natick, go west on SR 16 for about a mile to South Street, then turn left, and continue for ½ mile to the sanctuary. The sanctuary is owned and staffed by the Massachusetts Audubon Society. It comprises 538 acres of woodland, ponds, fields, and marshes. Trails are maintained. The sanctuary is open all year.

Buck Hill Conservation and Education Center, McCormick Road, Spencer 01562; (617) 829-5663. The center is operated by Worcester County Conservation District. Overnight facilities are available. Interpretive and educational programs are offered. The center totals 300 acres; trails are maintained. The center is open all year.

Bullard Woods Preserve. Located in Lenox, on Hawthorne Street, across from Tanglewood. The 25-acre preserve is made up of mixed woodlands and open fields near Lake Mahkeenac (Stockbridge Bowl). There is a trail. The preserve is open during daylight hours.

Cape Cod Museum of Natural History, Route 6A, Brewster 02631; (617) 896-3867. The museum is on Cape Cod, near the national seashore. The center totals 60 acres; interpretive programs are offered. Trails are maintained. The museum is open all year; closed on Mondays and Fridays from October to May. Look for waterfowl and shorebirds here.

Crane Wildlife Refuge, Ipswich. The refuge totals 1352 acres of meadows, mixed woodlands, beach, and salt marsh. It provides habitat for many animals especially the white-tailed deer. A self-guiding trail is maintained. The refuge is owned and staffed by the Trustees of Reservations.

Environmental Education Center at Elbanobscot, Weir Hill Road, Sudbury 01776; (617) 443-9931. The center is operated by the Elbanobscot Foundation, Inc. It totals 80 acres and offers educational programs and teacher training. The center is open all year.

Great Esker Park, 402 Essex Street, Weymouth 02188; (617) 337-9224. The park is operated by the Weymouth Parks Department. Great Esker Park totals 138 acres of mixed woodlands and marshes. Trails and a museum are maintained. Courses in marine biology are taught here. The park is open from June through August.

Hale Reservation, 80 Carby Street, Westwood 02090; (617) 326-0163. A variety of educational and interpretive programs is offered at this 1000-acre center. Trails are maintained. The center is open all year.

Laughing Brook Education Center and Wildlife Sanctuary, 789 Main Street, Hampden 01036; (413) 566-3571. To reach the center from the Massachusetts Turnpike (I-90), take Exit 8, follow signs to Monson, then turn sharp right at High Street, continue for nearly 7 miles to Hampden, bearing left as indicated. Laughing Brook is the former home of famous author Thornton Burgess. This 84-acre sanctuary is owned and operated by the Massachusetts Audubon Society. A variety of educational and interpretive programs and guided tours is offered at the center. Trails are maintained. *Western Voice of Audubon* — (413) 566-3590 — is located here. The center is open all year, closed Mondays and holidays. Among the 90 species of birds seen here are: Wood Duck, Cooper's Hawk, Screech Owl, Eastern Bluebird, Blue-winged Warbler, and Rose-breasted Grosbeak.

Manomet Bird Observatory, off Point Road, P.O. Box O, Manomet 02345; (617) 224-3559. This 18-acre center is open all year, closed on weekends. An internship in ornithology is offered here. Interpretive and educational programs are available; guided tours only are offered. Appointments are advised. Bird banding, observation, and research are major programs at the observatory.

Mount Tom Reservation, Holyoke. This state-owned reservation encompasses over 1600 acres of mixed woodlands near the Connecticut River. To reach Mount Tom take US 5 north from Holyoke for 4 miles to Smith's Ferry, turn left into the reservation. Look for Goshawk, Cooper's Hawk, Sharp-shinned Hawk, Pileated Woodpecker, Magnolia Warbler, Black-throated Blue Warbler, and Louisiana Waterthrush.

Southshore Natural Science Center, Inc., Jacobs Lane, Norwell 02061; (617) 659-2559. The center covers 21 acres and offers a variety of educational and interpretive programs. It is open all year; closed on weekends.

Stony Brook Nature Center, North Street, Norfolk 02056; (617) 528-3140. Norfolk is about 30 miles south of Boston. To reach the center from Norfolk, take SR 115 south for one mile to North Street, turn on North Street, and proceed to the center. This 100-acre sanctuary is operated by the Massachusetts Audubon Society. It borders the 200-acre Bristol-Blake State Reservation, which includes ponds, woods, fields, and a boardwalk over a marsh. A variety of educational and interpretive programs is offered at Stony Brook Nature Center. Trails are maintained. The center is open all year.

Walden Pond State Reservation. Walden is located 1½ miles south of Concord, off SR 126. It is a large pond surrounded by woods. The area is open all year. The site of Thoreau's cabin is well marked (the cabin is gone). Look for flycatchers, thrushes, vireos, and warblers.

World's End Reservation, Hingham. This 250-acre peninsula consists of open fields and mixed woodlands. World's End is owned and maintained by the Trustees of Reservations.

STATE PARKS AND FORESTS

There are 26 state campgrounds and 64 state day use areas located throughout Massachusetts. In addition there are several state reservations. With a few exceptions, only those parks and forests that allow camping are listed below. Campgrounds are assigned on a first-come, first-serve basis; no reservations are accepted. For additional information regarding camping in Massachusetts, contact: Massachusetts Department of Natural Resources, Division of Forests and Parks, 100 Cambridge Street, Boston 02202. A wide variety of recreational facilities are available at all state parks and forests. Those parks which are well known as birdwatching areas are marked with an asterisk (*).

Beartown State Forest, Monterey 01245.
Clarksburg State Park, Clarksburg.
D. A. R. State Forest, Goshen 01032.
*Demarest Lloyd Park, Dartmouth 02714; 221 acres; day use only.
Erving State Forest, Erving 01344
Granville State Forest, Granville 01034.
*Greylock Mountain State Reservation, Adams 01220.
Harold Parker State Forest, North Reading 01864.
Horseneck Beach State Reservation, Westport 02790.
Lake Dennison State Park, Winchendon 01475.
Massasoit State Park, Taunton 02780.
Mohawk Trail State Forest, Charlemont 01339.
Myles Standish State Forest, South Carver 02566.
October Mountain State Forest, Lee 01238.
Otter River State Forest, Winchendon 01475.
Pearl Hill State Park, Townsend 01469.
Pittsfield State Forest, Pittsfield 01201.
R. C. Nickerson State Forest Park, Brewster 02631.
Salisbury Beach State Reservation, Salisbury Park 02122.
Savoy Mountain-Florida State Forest, Florida 02124.
Scusset Beach State Reservation, Bourne 02166.
Shawme Crowell State Forest, Sandwich 02563.
Tolland Otis State Forest, Otis 01253.
Wells State Park, Sturbridge 01566.
Willard Brook State Forest, Ashby 01431.
Wompatuck State Reservation, Hingham 02043.

NEW HAMPSHIRE

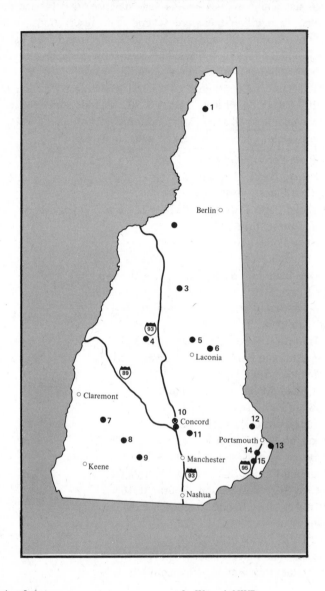

1. Connecticut Lakes
2. Pondicherry Wildlife Refuge
3. White Mountain National Forest
4. Paradise Point
5. John and Anna Porter Wildlife Sanctuary
6. Lake Winnipesaukee
7. Ashuelot Great Blue Heron Sanctuary
8. DePierrefeu-Willard Pond Sanctuary
9. Wapack NWR
10. Audubon House
11. Bear Brook Nature Center
12. Bellamy River Sanctuary
13. Odiorne Point Nature Center
14. Hampton Saltmarshes
15. George Burrows Brookside Sanctuary

New Hampshire is a land of impressive mountains, thick forests, and swift rivers. From the Flume in the White Mountains to the tidal marshes near Portsmouth there is great diversity. This diversity is reflected in the variety of wildlife that is to be found in the state. About 300 species of birds occur regularly in New Hampshire.

The northcentral part of the state is dominated by the White Mountains through which the Appalachian Trail passes. Most of the state is forested; and there are several large lakes, the largest being Lake Winnipesaukee. Migrating waterfowl can be seen along the beaches south of Portsmouth; migrating passerines can be seen along the Connecticut River (Vermont border) during spring and fall — warbler waves can be impressive. The northernmost part of the state, near the Canadian border, is a good place to see such birds as Spruce Grouse, Saw-whet Owl, Gray Jay, Northern Raven, Black-backed Three-toed Woodpecker, Northern Three-toed Woodpecker, Boreal Chickadee, and White-winged Crossbill. The dense spruce and fir forests are broken by a series of small lakes known as the "Connecticut Lakes."

The Fish and Game Department maintains 52 wildlife management areas scattered throughout the state. Fifteen of these are upland areas; the rest are bogs, swamps, and marshlands. These areas range in size from 10 to 8800 acres. Many of them are co-owned by the state and federal governments, some remain in private hands, others are owned by the Fish and Game Department. Most of these areas are good for birdwatching as they provide both open water and sheltered places. Waterfowl management is given priority at many areas; management programs include impoundments and flooding. For further information regarding these areas, contact the State of New Hampshire, Fish and Game Department, Box 2003, 34 Bridge Street, Concord 03301.

Additional information about birdwatching in New Hampshire can be obtained by contacting the Audubon Society of New Hampshire, 3 Silk Farm Road, Concord 03301; (603) 224-9909.

Wapack National Wildlife Refuge. Administered by Parker River NWR (in Massachusetts). Wapack is located 3 miles northeast of Peterborough, off SR 136 (about 50 miles northwest of Parker River NWR). Camping is not permitted at the refuge; however facilities are available at nearby Monadnock and Greenfield state parks.

The refuge totals over 700 acres of the Pack Monadnock Mountains. It was established in 1972, and is the first NWR in New Hampshire. The terrain consists of bogs and swamps, ledges and cliffs, mountain peaks, and hardwoods and pine groves. There is a 3-mile nature trail. Ideal nesting conditions exist for many species of migratory birds such as Winter Wren, Swainson's Thrush, Magnolia Warbler, Tree Sparrow, and White-throated Sparrow. Other birds sighted include American Woodcock, Ruffed Grouse, Red-tailed Hawk, Belted Kingfisher, Pine Siskin, Canada Warbler, Red Crossbill, and Pine Grosbeak.

White Mountain National Forest, Laconia 03246. The 727,000-acre Forest (part of which is in Maine) is located in the central part of the state between Laconia and Berlin. To reach the Forest, use US 2, US 3, US 202, and SR 16. As in most national forests, there are camping facilities. Other public recreational facilities include boating, swimming, and hiking. There are also 8 ski areas. Interpretive trails are located at 4 of the recreation sites. The 650 miles of streams and 39 lakes and ponds provide opportunities for fishing. There are scenic drives through famous notches and along mountain highways.

Wildlife management is being carried out at White Mountain National Forest by providing as many different types of habitat as possible. White-tailed deer, black bear, snowshoe hare, moose, beaver, otter, bobcat, and mink are some of the animals that live here.

The Flume, Old Man of the Mountains, and Lost River Gorge are all located here — off US 3 near Lincoln. Both this area and the area near Waterville Valley (to the southwest) are good for birdwatching. Among the many species of birds that are to be seen here are: Canada Goose, Black Duck, Mallard, Hooded Merganser, Wood Duck, Spruce Grouse, Ruffed Grouse, Broad-winged Hawk, Osprey, Great Blue Heron, American Woodcock, Black-backed Three-toed Woodpecker, Northern Three-toed Woodpecker, Yellow-bellied Sapsucker, Red-headed Woodpecker, Barn Owl, Eastern Bluebird, Least Flycatcher, Philadelphia Vireo, House Wren, Wood Thrush, Veery, Ruby-throated Hummingbird, Nashville Warbler, Magnolia Warbler, Mourning Warbler, Pine Grosbeak, and Evening Grosbeak.

AUDUBON SANCTUARIES

The Audubon Society of New Hampshire operates 11 sanctuaries located throughout the state. They are described below; for additional information, contact them at their headquarters, Audubon House, listed below.

Ashuelot Great Blue Heron Sanctuary, Washington 03280. This 23-acre sanctuary is the site of a heronry. In order to protect the area as a nesting site, it is open only by special permission. Contact the New Hampshire Audubon Society.

Audubon House, Audubon Society of New Hampshire, 3 Silk Farm Road, Concord 03301; (603) 224-9909. Headquarters for the society. A variety of educational and interpretive programs is offered; guided and self-guiding trails are available. The 16-acre center is open to the public on weekdays. Among the birds seen here are: Yellow-billed Cuckoo, Eastern Wood Pewee, House Wren, Veery, Chestnut-sided Warbler, Ovenbird, Scarlet Tanager, and Indigo Bunting.

Bear Brook Nature Center, Bear Brook State Park, Route 1, Suncook 03275; (603) 485-3782, mailing address is c/o Audubon Society of New Hampshire (see above). The center is open during the summer. A wide range of educational and interpretive programs is offered; exhibits are on display at the center; guided tours are offered and self-guiding nature trails are maintained.

Northern Oriole

Bellamy River Sanctuary, Dover 03820. This sanctuary is characterized by a mixture of tidal creeks and mixed woodlands. There are fine views of the Bellamy River as it enters Great Bay. Self-guiding nature trails interlace the area.

DePierrefeu-Willard Pond Sanctuary, Antrim 03440. This 600-acre sanctuary is located at Willard Pond, just outside of Antrim. A naturalist is on staff.

George Burrows Brookside Sanctuary, South Hampton. This 20-acre sanctuary is composed of mixed woodlands and wetlands. The variety of habitat supports a diverse wildlife community.

Hampton Saltmarshes, Hampton-Seabrook. Located near Hampton Beach State Park, this sanctuary now totals 200 acres. This estuary is one of the finest salt marsh areas in the state. Acquisition is not yet complete. In the harbor, look for: Piping Plover, Ruddy Turnstone, Red Knot, Dunlin, gulls, and terns. In the marshes, look for: herons, egrets, and Short-eared Owls. The pond behind the beach is good for migrating waterfowl.

John and Anna Porter Wildlife Sanctuary (Camp Kabeyun), Alton Bay, Lake Winnepesaukee 03810. this preserve is a camp during the summer; the rest of the year it is maintained as a wildlife sanctuary. The sanctuary totals 100 acres on Lake Winnepesaukee, the largest lake in New Hampshire.

Odiorne Point Nature Center, Rye 03870. This center is located in the 136-acre Odiorne Point State Park. A variety of educational and interpretive programs is offered. The coastal area is a good place to see shorebirds, marshbirds, and waterfowl.

Paradise Point, Newfound Lake, East Hebron 03232; (603) 744-3516. This 43-acre refuge consists of mixed woodlands and 3000 feet of shoreline. Guided tours are offered; self-guiding nature trails are available to the public year round. The nature center is open from June to September.

Pondicherry Wildlife Refuge, Whitefield 03598. The refuge covers over 200 acres and contains 2 ponds. The ponds are bordered by tamarack-spruce bogs. Pondicherry is a registered national natural landmark. Among the birds seen here during the summer are: American Bittern, Green-winged Teal, Wood Duck, Yellow-bellied Flycatcher, Gray Jay, Boreal Chickadee, Wilson's Warbler, and Rusty Blackbird.

STATE PARKS AND FORESTS

In addition to the White Mountain National Forest, which covers most of central New Hampshire, there are many state parks and forests. These offer a wide range of recreational facilities, including camping (at most parks), picnicking, swimming, hiking, and nature study. Those parks that are also good birdwatching places are marked with an asterisk (*). For additional information write: New Hampshire Division of Economic Development, Concord 03301.

*Bear Brook, Allenstown; 9300 acres; Audubon Society Nature Center.
  Cardigan, Orange; day use only.
  Clough, Weare 03281; day use only.
*Coleman, Stewartstown 03576.
*Crawford Notch, Crawford House 03577; within White Mountain NF; traversed
    by Appalachian Trail; of special interest are the scenic waterfalls: the Flume,
    Silver Cascades, and Arethusa Falls.
  Echo Lake, Conway 03818; within White Mountain NF; day use only.
  Ellacoya, Gilford; day use only.

Forest Lake, Dalton; day use only.

*Franconia Notch, Franconia and Lincoln 03580; 6440 acres; within White Mountain NF; traversed by Appalachian Trail; of special interest is the Old Man of the Mountains.

Greenfield, Greenfield 03047; 351 acres.

*Hampton Beach State Park, Hampton 03842; includes Hampton State Beach.

*Kingston, Kingston 03848; 44 acres.

Milan Hill, Milan 03588; adjoining White Mountain NF.

*Miller, Peterborough 03458; day use only.

Monadnock, Jaffrey 03452.

Moose Brook, Gorham 03581; adjoining White Mountain NF.

*Mt. Sunapee, Newbury 03255.

*Odiorne Point, Rye 03870; 136 acres; Audubon Society Nature Center.

Otter Brooke, Keene 03431; day use only.

Pawtuckaway, Bottingham.

*Pillsbury, Washington 03280; primitive camping only, wilderness area.

*Rhododendron, Fitzwilliam 03447; day use only; over 16 acres of wild *Rhododendron maximum.*

Rollins, Warner 03278; day use only.

*Rye Harbor, Rye 03870; day use only.

Silver Lake, Hollis 03049; day use only.

Waldleigh, Sutton; day use only.

Wallis Sands, Rye 03870; day use only.

Weeks, Lancaster 03584.

Wellington, Bristol 03222; day use only.

Wentworth, Wolfeboro 03894.

White Lake, Tamworth 03886.

*Winslow, Wilmot 03286; day use only.

In addition, there are 4 historic sites and 8 wayside picnic areas — all day use only areas.

NEW JERSEY

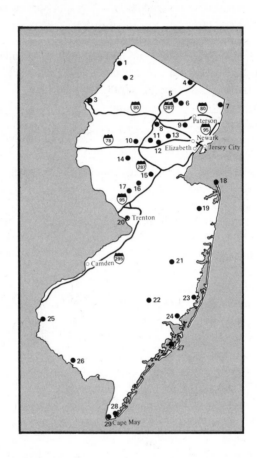

1. Thunder Mountain Education Center
2. New Jersey School of Conservation
   Stepping Stone Environmental Center
3. Delaware Water Gap
4. Campgaw Mountain Reservation
5. Lucine Lorrimer Sanctuary
6. Bergen County Wildlife Center
7. { Englewood Nature Association
     Palisades Interstate Park
     Palisades Nature Association
     Tenafly NC
8. Troy Meadows
9. Montclair Hawk Lookout Sanctuary
10. Scherman Wildlife Sanctuary
11. Great Swamp NWR Center
12. Trailside Nature and Science Center
13. Cora Hartshorn Arboretum
14. Somerset County Environmental Center

15. Boy Scouts Conservation Center
    William Hutcheson Memorial Forest
16. Herrontown Woods
17. Newland Research Reserve
18. Gateway NRA/Sandy Hook Unit
19. Monmouth County Park System
20. John Roebling Memorial Park
21. Conservation and Environmental Center
22. Batsto NC
23. Barnegat NWR
24. Tuckerton Meadows
25. Killcohook NWR
    Supawna Meadows NWR
26. Cohansey Natural Area
27. Brigantine NWR
28. Wetlands Institute
29. Cape May Point

New Jersey has a long coastline that parallels the Altantic Flyway. As such, the birdwatcher is treated to spectacular displays of waterfowl — especially during spring and fall migrations. Although densely populated, over half of the state's land is in farms and forests. Northern New Jersey is hilly and wooded, while the southern half of the state has extensive sandy plains. In the central interior are the famous Pine Barrens — a sparsely inhabited country characterized by flatlands, low hills covered with pitch pines, meandering streams bordered by hardwoods, and white cedar swamps. Except for its 50-mile northern border, New Jersey is surrounded by water: the Delaware River and Delaware Bay on the west and south, the Atlantic Ocean on the southeast, and the Hudson River on the northeast.

The hawk migrations (best seen at Hawk Mountain in Pennsylvania) can be seen in northwestern New Jersey near Bound Brook, while the waterbird migrations are best viewed from the NWRs and on the barrier islands along the eastern coast.

Special birding areas in New Jersey include Cape May Point; the rookery at Stone Harbor (near Cape May); the cattail marsh called Troy meadows (near Troy Hills); the area known as Cohansey Natural Area near Cohansey Creek on the Delaware Bay (near Sea Breeze and Fortescue): Salem Marshes and Mannington Meadow (north of Salem, near Killcohook NWR) and the Tuckerton Meadows located between Little Egg Harbor and Great Bay (near Tuckerton).

The *New York Rare Bird Alert* also provides information for northern New Jersey: (212) 832-6523; the *Delaware Valley Birding Hotline:* (215) 236-2473 provides information for southwestern New Jersey. For further information about birdwatching in New Jersey, contact: New Jersey Audubon Society, 790 Ewing Avenue, Franklin Lakes 07417; (201) 891-1211. They maintain sanctuaries as well as a wildlife research unit, and are most helpful. There is also a book — *The Birds of New Jersey,* by Charles Leck — that can prove useful to the birdwatcher.

Barnegat National Wildlife Refuge. Administered by Brigantine NWR. The refuge is located in the southern end of Barnegat Bay, between Manahawkin and Barnegat, 2 miles east of US 9. To reach the refuge from Brigantine refuge, take US 9 north for about 20 miles. Camping is not permitted at the refuge; however, facilities are available at nearby state forests.

Barnegat was established in 1967 and totals over 5000 acres. It is still largely in the developmental stage as a refuge. Primary species include waterfowl, marshbirds, and shorebirds.

Brigantine National Wildlife Refuge, Great Creek Road, P. O. Box 72, Oceanville 08231; (609) 652-1665. Brigantine is on the Atlantic coast about 11 miles north of Atlantic City. To reach the refuge from Atlantic City, take US 30 east to US 9, then take US 9 north to Oceanville. Camping is not permitted at the refuge; however, facilities are available at nearby Bass River State Forest.

Brigantine was established in 1939. It comprises over 20,000 acres, consisting primarily of cordgrass-saltgrass tidal marsh interspersed with tidal bays and channels. Along the western portion of the refuge are the upland brush and wooded areas. Since Brigantine is on the Atlantic Flyway, birding opportunities reach their zenith during spring and fall migrations. There are observation towers, wildlife trails, an auto-tour route, and an information center. Among the 269 species of birds (111 nesting) identified on the refuge are: Mute Swan, Black Duck, Redhead, Bufflehead, White-winged Scoter, Common Scoter, Osprey, Merlin (Pigeon Hawk), Great Blue Heron, Glossy Ibis, Clapper Rail, American Oystercatcher, Ruddy Turnstone, Willet, Dunlin, Sanderling, Great Black-backed Gull, Forster's Tern, Long-eared Owl, Downy Woodpecker, Great Crested Flycatcher, Tufted Titmouse, Hermit Thrush, Black-and-white Warbler, Blackpoll Warbler, American Goldfinch, Dark-eyed (Slate-colored) Junco, and Field Sparrow. Checklist available.

Delaware Water Gap National Recreation Area, I-80, Columbia 07832. The Delaware Water Gap Area is located along the New Jersey-Pennsylvania border and was established as a national recreation area in 1965 in order to preserve a large portion of the Delaware River. The Area now totals 70,000 acres, but acquisition is not yet complete. Visitors are asked to respect the rights of property owners. Hiking, canoeing, swimming, and fishing are enjoyed by the people who use the Area. There are camping facilities at nearby state parks. The Delaware Water Gap Area provides many activities: there are guided and self-guiding tours, scenic drives and overlooks, reconstructed farms and villages, crafts cooperatives, and an environmental education center. Campfire and outdoor skills programs are offered during the summer. Hikers should be aware of poisonous snakes in the area: copperheads and timber rattlesnakes.

The mountains, river and streams, fields, and forests of the Delaware Water Gap Area provide habitat for a wide variety of birds. Among the 256 species sighted in this area are: Red-throated Loon (rare), Mute Swan, Brant, Snow Goose, Pintail, Wood Duck, Canvasback, Bufflehead, Goshawk, Sharp-shinned Hawk, Cooper's Hawk, Golden Eagle, Peregrine Falcon (rare), Ring-necked Pheasant, Great Blue Heron, Snowy Egret, American Bittern, Common Snipe, Black-billed Cuckoo, Screech Owl, Belted Kingfisher, Pileated Woodpecker, Red-headed Woodpecker, Least Flycatcher, Winter Wren, Brown Thrasher, Eastern Bluebird, Water Pipit, Northern Shrike (rare), Philadelphia Vireo, Golden-winged Warbler, Blue-winged Warbler, Black-throated Green Warbler, Black-throated Blue Warbler, Northern Parula, Cerulean Warbler, Mourning Warbler (rare), Wilson's Warbler, Bobolink, Scarlet Tanager, Indigo Bunting, White-winged Crossbill (rare), Henslow's Sparrow (rare), and Snow Bunting. Checklist available.

Gateway National Recreation Area, Sandy Hook Unit, P. O. Box 437, Highlands 07732; (201) 872-0115. Sandy Hook is located east of Perth Amboy and north of Long Branch. It is a spit of land that divides the Atlantic Ocean from Sandy Hook Bay, and lies directly south of Brooklyn (New York). To reach the Area, take SR 36 north from Long Branch for about 7 miles.

The Sandy Hook Unit consists of beaches, dunes, salt marsh, freshwater ponds, and a holly forest. A network of trails through these various habitats is maintained. Exhibits are on display at the visitors' center. Among the 267 species of birds that have been seen here are: Osprey (nesting), Great Blue Heron, Clapper Rail, Great Horned Owl, Whip-poor-will, Wood Thrush, Northern Parula, Rufous-sided Towhee, and Song Sparrow. Sandy Hook is situated along the Atlantic Flyway; look for migrating waterfowl and shorebirds.

Great Swamp National Wildlife Refuge, Pleasant Plains Road, R.D. 1, Box 148, Basking Ridge 07920; (201) 647-1222. The refuge is located 7 miles south of Morristown, near Basking Ridge. To reach the refuge from Basking Ridge, take Maple Avenue north to Madisonville Road, go east to Pleasant Plains road; watch for signs. Camping is not allowed at the refuge.

Great Swamp Refuge was established in 1960. Its 5800 acres of upland timber, hardwood swamp, brush, pasture, croplands, and marsh and water provide a diverse habitat for a great number of birds. A mile-long boardwalk, blinds, and interpretive displays are offered at the Wildlife Observation Center. Among the 205 species of birds (96 nesting) seen at the refuge are: Canvasback, Goshawk, Bobwhite, Ring-necked Pheasant, Green Heron, Common Gallinule, American Coot. Solitary Sandpiper, Barred Owl, Red-bellied Woodpecker, Eastern Kingbird, Willow (Traill's) Flycatcher, Black-capped Chickadee, Long-billed Marsh Wren, Yellow Warbler, Brown-headed Cowbird, Evening Grosbeak, and Tree Sparrow. Checklist available.

Killcohook National Wildlife Refuge. Administered by Brigantine NWR. Killcohook was established in 1934 and totals over 1000 acres. Killcohook is located on the Delaware River, 5 miles northwest of Salem. For information about visiting the refuge, contact the refuge manager at Brigantine NWR.

Among the birds seen here in autumn are: Mallard, Black Duck, Pintail, Northern Shoveler, Red-winged Blackbird, and Common Grackle.

Palisades Interstate Park. This park is located in both New Jersey and New York. It is operated by the Palisades Interstate Park Commission. The New Jersey offices are located at Alpine 07620. The section of the park that falls in New Jersey totals 2500 acres and extends along the Hudson River for 13 miles. Facilities include boating, fishing, hiking, picnicking, and nature study. For more information, see entry in New York chapter (page 76).

Supawna Meadows National Wildlife Reffuge. Administered by Brigantine NWR. This refuge is located about 3 miles northwest of Salem, near Killcohook NWR. At present, the refuge totals over 700 acres; when acquisition is complete, Supawna will total nearly 4000 acres. For further information about the refuge, contact the refuge manager at Brigantine NWR.

Wetlands Institute, Stone Harbor Boulevard, Stone Harbor 08247; (609) 368-1211. To reach the Institute, take exit 10 east off the Garden State Parkway over Stone Harbor Boulevard to the town of Stone Harbor. Three miles from the parkway, just before crossing the Intracoastal Waterway, is the entrance. The Institute owns over 30 acres of marsh and, in addition, has the use of 5000 acres of adjacent marshland that is owned by the state. From the observation tower one can see shorebirds, gulls, and terns.

Nearby is the *Stone Harbor Bird Sanctuary* located on Ocean Drive between 111th and 117th Streets, near the southern end of town. There is a heronry here. Among the nesting birds are Green Herons, Louisiana Herons, Black-crowned Night Herons, Common Egrets, Snowy Egrets, and Glossy Ibises.

NATURE CENTERS

In addition to the state and federal properties described in the previous pages, there are many nature centers, arboretums, sanctuaries, and environmental education centers located throughout the state. Many of these centers are good birdwatching places. They are described briefly below.

Batsto Nature Center, Batsto R.D. 1, Hammonton 08037. A variety of educational and interpretive programs is offered. Guided tours are available by appointment. The center is open from April to November. It is located in Wharton State Forest in the Pine Barrens. There have been 84 species of nesting birds identified here. Among them are: Broad-winged Hawk, Green Heron, American Woodcock, Prothonotary Warbler, and Eastern Meadowlark. Other birds seen in the Barrens include: Cooper's Hawk, Great Horned Owl, Whip-poor-will, Yellow-billed Cuckoo, White-breasted Nuthatch, Chestnut-sided Warbler, Northern Parula, Eastern Bluebird, Indigo Bunting, Cedar Waxwing, and Red Crossbill.

Bergen County Wildlife Center, Crescent Avenue West, Wyckoff 07481; (201) 891-5571. The center is operated by Bergen County Park Commission; it covers 81 acres. There are guided tours available. Trails, some self-guiding, are maintained. The center is open all year, closed on holidays.

Boy Scouts of America Conservation Education Center, Routes 1 and 230, North Brunswick 08902; (201) 249-6000. The center covers 20 acres. Guided tours are offered. Trails are maintained. The center is open all year, closed on major holidays.

Campgaw Mountain Reservation, 17 Fike Road, Mahwah 07430; (201) 216-7804. The area is operated by Bergen County Park Commission; it covers 1400 acres: Guided and self-guiding tours are available; a variety of educational and interpretive programs is offered. The reservation is open from April through November.

Conservation and Environmental Studies Center, Inc. (Browns Mills), Box 2229, Whitesbog 08015; (609) 893-9151. The center covers 3000 acres. A variety of educational and interpretive programs is offered. It is open all year, closed on school holidays.

Cora Hartshorn Arboretum, 324 Forest Drive South, Short Hills 07078; (201) 376-3587. The arboretum is operated by Millburn Township and Cora Hartshorn Arboretum and Bird Sanctuary. The 17-acre area is open all year. Guided tours are offered; trails are maintained.

Englewood Nature Association, Englewood 07631; (201) 567-1800. The preserve covers 75 acres; it is open all year. Guided tours are offered and self-guiding trails are maintained.

Great Swamp Outdoor Education Center, 247 Southern Boulevard, Chatham 07928; (201) 635-6629. The center is operated by the Morris County Park Commission. The center totals 40 acres plus the use of adjoining Great Swamp NWR. Guided tours are available. Trails, some self-guiding, are maintained. A variety of educational and interpretive programs is offered. The center is open every day from September through June.

Herrontown Woods, Snowden Lane, Princeton; postal address: Mercer County Park Commission, 640 South Broad Street, Trenton 08611; (609) 989-8000; ext. 533. The preserve totals 134 acres. Guided and self-guiding tours are available. It is open all year.

John A. Roebling Memorial Park, Trenton. The park comprises 300 acres of mixed woodlands, open meadow, marsh, and a lake. Among the nearly 200 species of birds seen here are: Green Heron, Least Bittern, Wood Duck, Barred Owl, Virginia Rail, Purple Martin, Yellow Warbler, and Rose-breasted Grosbeak.

Lucine L. Lorrimer Sanctuary, 790 Ewing Avenue, Franklin Lakes 07417; (201) 891-1211. The sanctuary is operated by the New Jersey Audubon Society. It covers 14 acres. A variety of educational and interpretive programs is offered. A network of trails and a nature museum are maintained. The sanctuary is open all year; closed on Sundays, Mondays, major holidays, and during Christmas week.

Montclair Hawk Lookout Sanctuary, Crestmont Road, Montclair 07042. The sanctuary is owned and operated by the New Jersey Audubon Society. To reach the sanctuary take Valley Road north, then turn north again on Upper Montclair Avenue, make a left on Bradford Avenue, then a right on Edgecliff Road. Go to the top of the hill and park at the corner of Crestmont Road; proceed to the top on foot. The sanctuary is on the crest of First Watchung Mountain. The best time for birding here is during the fall migration. Look for: Sharp-shinned, Broad-winged, Red-tailed, Cooper's, American Kestrel, Osprey, and Marsh Hawk. Merlins and Peregrine Falcons are seen rarely.

Monmouth County Park System, Box 326, Newman Springs Road, Lincroft 07738; (201) 842-4000. The park is operated by the Monmouth County Board of Recreation Commissioners. It covers 2100 acres; there is an arboretum. Guided tours are offered. Trails are maintained. The park is open all year.

New Jersey School of Conservation, Box 272, Branchville 07826; (201) 948-4646. The school is operated by Montclair State College (Upper Montclair). There are 240 acres plus use of an additional 25,000 acres of state lands. A variety of educational and interpretive programs is offered. The school is open all year; closed on certain holidays and during school vacations.

Newland Research Reserve, P.O. Box 171, Titus Mill Road, Pennington 08534; (609) 737-3735. The reserve is operated by Stony Brook-Millstone Watersheds Association. It covers 400 acres; trails are maintained. Guided tours are available. The reserve is open all year.

Palisades Nature Association, Greenbrook Sanctuary, Box 155, Alpine 07620; (201) 768-1360. The sanctuary adjoins Palisades Interstate Park; it covers 165 acres, and is open all year. Trails are maintained.

Scherman Wildlife Sanctuary and Nature Interpretation Center, Hardscrabble Road, P. O. Box 693, Bernardsville 07924; (201) 766-5787. The sanctuary is operated by the New Jersey Audubon Society and covers 120 acres of mixed woodlands with a stream. Guided tours are available. A variety of educational and interpretive programs is offered. Trails, some self-guiding, are maintained. The sanctuary is open all year; closed on Sundays, Mondays, major holidays, and during Christmas week. There have been 120 species of birds (60 nesting) observed here.

Somerset County Environmental Education Center, Long Stirling Road; postal address: Box 837, Somerville 08876; (201) 722-1200. The center is operated by Somerset County Park Commission. It covers 400 acres and in addition has the use of 2000 acres of county-owned park lands. A variety of educational and interpretive programs is offered at the center. The center is open all year.

Stepping Stone Environmental Education Center, R.D. 2, Box 270, Branchville 07826; (201) 948-3141. The center is operated by Carteret Board of Education; it covers 28 acres. The center is open all year; closed on school holidays and most weekends.

Tenafly Nature Center, Box 422, Tenafly 07870; (201) 568-6093. The center covers 50 acres. Guided and self-guiding tours are available. It is open all year.

Thunder Mountain Education Center, Layton 07851; (201) 948-6767. The center is operated by Newton Board of Education; it totals 237 acres. Guided tours are available; there is a working farm. The center is open all year; closed on weekends and school holidays.

Trailside Nature and Science Center, Coles Avenue and New Providence Road, Mountainside 07092; (201) 232-5930. The center is operated by Union County Park Commission. It is located in the Watchung Reservation, a 2000-acre area. Guided tours are offered; trails, some self-guiding, are maintained. There is a planetarium. Interpretive exhibits are on display at the trailside museum. The center is open all year; closed on Fridays. Look for migrating hawks in the fall.

William L. Hutcheson Memorial Forest, Somerset County. The preserve is operated by Rutgers University (New Brunswick 08903) with a reverter to The Nature Conservancy. It consists of 150 acres of old fields and hardwood forest with intermittent streams. Look for Bobwhite, Eastern Meadowlark, Water Pipit, Horned Lark, Indigo Bunting, Grasshopper Sparrow, and Chipping Sparrow.

Snowy Egret

STATE PARKS AND FORESTS

New Jersey has a large number of state parks and forests, most of which offer camping in addition to a variety of other recreational facilities. Although nature study (including birdwatching) is encouraged, it is not the prime focus of these parks, which are designed as multiple use areas. Those parks and forests that are well known as good birdwatching spots are marked with an asterisk (*). For further information contact: State of New Jersey, Department of Environmental Protection, Bureau of Parks, Trenton 08625.

Allaire, Box 220, Farmingdale 07727; (201) 938-2371; 2425 acres.

Bass River State Forest, New Gretna 08224; (609) 296-2554; 9100 acres.

Belleplain State Forest, R. D. 2, Woodbine 08271; (609) 861-2404; 11,223 acres.

Bulls Island Recreation Area, R. D. 2, Box 417, Stockton 08559; (609) 397-2949; 80 acres.

*Cape May Point, Box 107, Cape May Point 08202; 190 acres; day use only.

Cheesquake, Mataway 07747; (201) 566-2161; 1001 acres.

Hacklebarney, R. R. 2, Long Valley 07853; 569 acres.

*High Point, R. R. #4, Box 287, Sussex 07461; (201) 875-4800; 12,686 acres.

*Island Beach, Seaside Park 08752; 3002 acres; day use only.

Jenny Jump State Forest, Box 150, Hope 07844; (201) 459-4366; 1118 acres.

Lebanon State Forest, New Lisbon 08064; (609) 726-1191; 27,304 acres.

Parvin, R. D. 1, Elmer 08318; (609) 692-7039; 1125 acres.

Penn State Forest, c/o Bass River State Forest (see above); 3366 acres; day use only.

Rancocas, Box 69, Rancocas 08073; 1057 acres; day use only.

Ringwood, R. D. Box 1304, Ringwood 07456; 3112 acres.

Round Valley Recreation, c/o Spruce Run Recreation Area (see below); 4003 acres.

Spruce Run Recreation Area, Box 289--A, Van Syckles Road, Clinton 08809; (201) 6990; 1863 acres.

Stephens-Saxton Falls, Hackettstown 07840; (201) 852-3790; 222 acres.

*Stokes State Forest, R. R. 2, Box 260, Branchville 07826; (201) 948-3821; 14,869 acres.

Swartswood, R. R. 5, Box 548, Newton 07860; (201) 383-5230; 1253 acres.

Vorhees, R. D., Glen Gardner 08826; (201) 638-6969; 485 acres.

Washington Crossing, R. R. 1, Box 337, Titusville 08560; 795 acres.

Wawayanda, Box 198, Highland Lakes 07422; 9020 acres.

Wharton State Forest, Batsto, R. D. 1, Hammonton 08037; (609) 561-0024; 99,639 acres.

Worthington State Forest, c/o Jenny Jump State Park (see above); 5830 acres; Appalachian Trail crosses the Forest.

In addition, there are 2 undeveloped (except for hiking trails) state forests in northern New Jersey: *Abram S. Hewitt Forest* — 1890 acres, located near Hewitt; and *Norvin Green State Forest* — 2296 acres, located near Macopin. There are also several undeveloped state parks that have not been listed here. Neither are many of the state parks and historical sites that are designed for day use only.

New Jersey also has several "natural areas." Most of these are still in the stage of acquisition, such as *Cohansey Natural Area* — a 12,400-acre salt marsh tract located in Cumberland County (southern New Jersey). For information about Cohansey and other areas in this program, contact: Director, Division of Parks and Forestry, Department of Environmental Protection, Box 1420, Trenton 08625.

Canada Geese

NEW YORK

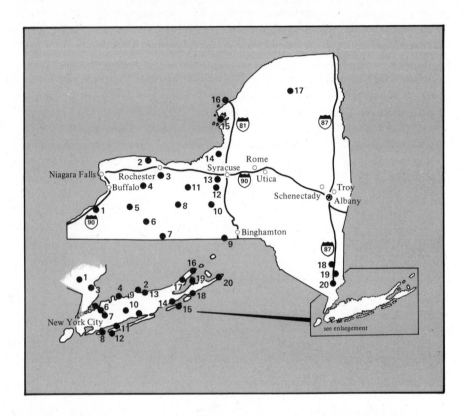

No other state in the east has such diverse birdwatching areas as New York. From Niagara Falls to the Adirondack Mountains to Montauk Point — nearly every bird seen in the eastern United States can be seen somewhere in New York. Principal migration routes in New York are along Lake Ontario and up the Hudson River; New York City and Long Island are situated along the Atlantic Flyway. The high, coniferous forests of the Adirondacks provide habitat for the Boreal Chickadee; the Magnolia Warbler can be seen in westcentral New York swamps; and at Orient Point, Oldsquaws winter over.

Orient Point, at the northeastern tip of Long Island is a very rewarding birdfinding place. It is excellent for wintering waterfowl. Most of the tip is a state park. In the winter, look for King Eider, Common Goldeneye, Oldsquaw, Harlequin Duck, and Snowy Owl (rare); in the summer, Osprey, Piping Plover, Least Tern, and Horned Lark can be seen. *Montauk Point,* at the easternmost end of Long Island (the south fork) is one of the best birdwatching places in the entire state. Most of the tip is a state park, some is a county park. In the winter, look for Common Loon, Red-throated Loon, King Eider, Common Eider, Red-breasted Merganser, Great Cormorant, Gannet, Bonaparte's Gull, and other ducks, gulls, and wintering waterfowl. All along the south shore beaches in this area (especially the Moriches and Shinnecock Inlets), the birdwatching is always rewarding. Sometimes a pelagic bird, such as a shearwater, storm-petrel, or jaeger, can be seen. Pelagic trips, generally sponsored by a local Audubon chapter, leave from Montauk.

New York City, too, is good for birdwatching. In *Manhattan,* the best place to go is Central Park. Unfortunately the park is not always safe, and the visitor is advised to use caution when going there. It is best not to go alone and not to stray too far from the paths and roadways. Central Park covers 862 acres of open meadows, woodlands, and thickets. The most rewarding birdwatching area is known as the Ramble. This is located between 72 and 79 Streets on the western side of the park. There have been about 260 species of birds identified in Central Park. Among them are: Wood Thrush, Blue-gray Gnatcatcher, and 29 species of warblers — including Kentucky, Mourning, Black-and-White, Prairie, and Bay-breasted. Other parks in Manhattan can be good birding places, depending upon the time of day and year. They include: Battery Park, Madison Square Park, and Fort Tryon Park. In *Brooklyn,* the best place for birdwatching is Prospect Park and the adjacent Brooklyn Botanic Garden. Over 230 species of birds have been recorded here. In the *Bronx,* Van Cortlandt Park (1130 acres) and the Bronx Botanical Gardens and Park are both very good places. At Van Cortlandt, look for wrens, flycatchers, and vireos; the swampy areas are good for spring warblers. The Bronx Park (700 acres) has aviaries, a wonderful zoo, and extensive botanical gardens. Look for owls, thrushes, and warblers. Pelham Bay Park, located on Long Island Sound, is the largest park in the Bronx. It is an area of meadows, salt marsh, woodlands, and bay front. Although a good place all year round, winter can be most rewarding here. Look for Black Duck,

Canvasback, Common Goldeneye, Red-breasted Merganser, and other water-fowl. Owls also winter here. On *Staten Island*'s eastern shore is Great Kills Park. In the winter, many seabirds can be seen here. Look for loons, grebes, gulls, and owls. Oakwood Beach, just north of the park, is good for shorebirds in spring and fall. In *Queens,* good places to look for birds include Cunningham Park, Forest Park, Alley Pond Park and Alley Creek, Oakland Lake Park, and Jacob Riis Park. The latter park is on the south shore of Rockaway Peninsula, just south of Jamaica Bay Wildlife Refuge (see page 80). It is best in spring and fall. Look for Philadelphia Vireo, Connecticut Warbler, Orange-crowned Warbler, and Blue Grosbeak among others.

In addition to the many state parks and forests, New York maintains over 3½ million acres of public lands as game management areas. While these are intended primarily for hunting and fishing, they can also be good birdwatching places. Most of the areas have some restrictions; some are closed during certain periods of the year. It is best to make arrangements in advance if you wish to visit these areas. For information regarding these game management areas, contact: Department of Environmental Conservation, 50 Wolf Road, Albany 12201; (518) 457-5745.

Several counties, notably Suffolk County in eastern Long Island, maintain systems of parks. These parks are intended for the use of county residents. The Suffolk County park system includes 44 parks totaling nearly 17,000 acres. Several of these parks are maintained as bird sanctuaries. Many local Audubon chapters take trips to them. For additional information regarding Suffolk County Parks, contact: Suffolk County Department of Parks, P. O. Box 144, Montauk Highway, West Sayville 11796, (516) 567-1700.

There are many ponds, lakes, marshes, beaches, reservoirs, back roads, fields, and forests that are well known locally as good birdwatching places. They are not discussed below. For localized information consult: *Enjoying Birds in Upstate New York; Enjoying Birds Around New York City;* and *Short Walks on Long Island.* The visitor to the New York City area can also call the *New York Rare Bird Alert:* (212) 832-6523. A tape, made daily, will give up-to-the-minute information on what to see, where, and how to get there. A recent call proved profitable: 2 Peregrine Falcons were in Manhattan; and on North Line Island, near Wantaugh, there were 700 Red Knots, 30 Western Sandpipers, 9 Hudsonian Godwits, and a score of other shorebirds. The *New York Rare Bird Alert* is sponsored by the Linnean Society of New York and the National Audubon Society. The Linnean Society of New York has its offices at the American Museum of Natural History, Central Park West at 79 Street, New York City. (The office of the John Burroughs Memorial Association is also at the museum. His home, Slabsides, is located near Esopus — the trails are always open, the house only once a year.) For rare bird information in the Albany area, call: (581) 377-9600. The Buffalo area is covered by *Dial-A-Bird:* (716) 896-1271.

Because there are so many birdwatching places in New York, the state has been divided into 2 areas: upstate New York and New York City and environs.

Upstate New York

Adirondack Forest Preserve. For information, contact: Director, Division of Lands and Forests, Department of Environmental Conservation, 50 Wolf Road, Albany 12201. The law states that "the Forest Preserve . . . shall be forever kept as wild forest lands." Although much of the land within the preserve boundaries is privately owned, within the 2 million acres protected by the AFP there are 15 wilderness areas that total 1 million acres. In addition, there are canoe areas, primitive areas, wild forests, and other protected areas. Throughout the preserve there are thousands of miles of trails; hundreds of streams, ponds, and marshes; and multiple opportunities for the birdwatcher and nature enthusiast. One of the better-known trails traversing the preserve is the 133-mile Northville-Lake Placid Trail. The Department of Environmental Conservation issues trail leaflets for the routes in each major region. In addition, there are many Adirondack Guides — each one intimately knows a small area of the preserve. Lake George (and the Lake George Islands) falls within the park boundaries as do other famous lakes: Placid, Saranac, Schroon, and Sacandaga.

Birdwatching throughout the Adirondacks is rewarding — especially in the less popular and less crowded areas. For example, just outside of Lake Placid, the area of the *Chubb River* is a good place for birds that are common to northern coniferous forests. Look for Black-backed Three-toed Woodpecker, Boreal Chickadee, Winter Wren, Golden-crowned Kinglet, Red-breasted Nuthatch, Swainson's Thrush, and Northern Parula. Near Lake Placid in the area around *Heart Lake* look for Great Horned Owl, Veery, and Indigo Bunting. Higher up, such as on *Mount McIntyre,* one can see Pileated Woodpecker, Boreal Chickadee, and Nashville Warbler. Closer to Schroon Lake (south of Lake Placid) is *Elk Lake*. In the summer here, the birdwatcher can see Common Loon, Hooded Merganser, Sharp-shinned Hawk, Barred Owl, Pileated Woodpecker, White-winged Crossbill, and probably 20 species of warblers. The islands in *Lake George* provide habitat for Ring-billed Gull, Yellow-rumped (Myrtle) Warbler, Cedar Waxwing, and Song Sparrow.

Baltimore Woods, Marcellus 13108. The preserve is owned by The Nature Conservancy. To reach the preserve from Syracuse, take SR 175 west to Marcellus, turn south on SR 174 (Bishop Hill Road), and proceed for about 1½ miles to the parking area.

This 124-acre preserve consists of rolling glacial hills, open meadows, a forest, and a small quarry. There is also a cattail marsh. The forest is characterized by mixed hardwoods and giant hemlock and supports many wildflowers and ferns — notably the early yellow violet and fragile maidenhair fern. Although trails exist through Baltimore Woods, widespread use of the area has not been encouraged. Among the many species of birds that can be seen here are: Red-tailed Hawk, Great Horned Owl, Pileated Woodpecker, Red-bellied Woodpecker, Hooded Warbler Canada Warbler, Cerulean Warbler, Mourning Warbler, Blue-winged Warbler, Golden-winged Warbler, Blackburnian Warbler, Scarlet Tanager, and Northern (Baltimore) Oriole.

Bentley Woods, Victor 14564. The preserve is owned by The Nature Conservancy. Bentley Woods is located 18 miles south of Rochester, off Log Cabin Road. To reach the preserve, the visitor must cross private property. For further information, contact the preserve manager. Permission to cross the property must be obtained from the owner: Gilbert Holtz, 366 Log Cabin Road, Victor 14564; (716) 924-3495.

This 23-acre preserve consists of woodlands and a spring-fed bog. The lowland supports pine, hemlock, and hardwoods; flowers such as hepatica, marsh marigold, and trillium; and a wide assortment of ferns, mosses, and mushrooms. There are no trails in the lowland area; it is suggested that summer visitors wear boots and bring insect repellent. Among the 66 species of birds that have been identified at Bentley Woods are: Great Horned Owl, Pileated Woodpecker, Downy Woodpecker, Red-headed Woodpecker, Great Crested Flycatcher, Yellow-throated Vireo, Tennessee Warbler, Blue-winged Warbler, Cape May Warbler, and Indigo Bunting.

Canadaway Creek Nature Sanctuary, Dunkirk 14048. The sanctuary is owned by The Nature Conservancy. To reach Canadaway Creek from Dunkirk, take SR 5 (West Lake Road) south to the sanctuary entrance; there is also an entrance on Temple Road (off SR 5). The sanctuary comprises 30 acres of typical stream and lakeshore habitat. Visitors are advised to wear boots. The sanctuary is a major stopover for migrating birds. Among the 140 species of birds recorded here are: Black-crowned Night Heron, Wood Duck, Hooded Merganser, Red Phalarope, Willet, Caspian Tern, Tufted Titmouse, and Common Redpoll.

Constitution Island Marsh Sanctuary, R. F. D. #1, Route 9D, Garrison 10524; (914) 265-3119. The sanctuary is located in Garrison. Visiting is limited and arrangements must be made in advance by contacting the warden at the above address. The 267-acre sanctuary is owned by New York State and managed by the National Audubon Society. A warden-biologist is on duty.

The sanctuary is a tidal marsh on the eastern shore of the Hudson River. Over 100 species of birds have been seen here. Among them are: Wood Duck, Broad-winged Hawk, Golden Eagle, American Kestrel (Sparrow Hawk), Great Blue Heron, Green Heron, Killdeer, Greater Yellowlegs, Screech Owl, Common Nighthawk, Yellow-bellied Sapsucker, Eastern Wood Pewee, Winter Wren, Long-billed Marsh Wren, Black-throated Green Warbler, Chestnut-sided Warbler, Canada Warbler, and Swamp Sparrow.

Cornell Laboratory of Ornithology. See Sapsucker Woods Sanctuary.

Deer Lick Sanctuary, Persia. The preserve is owned by The Nature Conservancy. To reach Deer Lick from Gowanda, turn east at the bridge over Main Street onto Water Street (parallel and south of the creek); continue to Broadway (SR 4), which is just beyond a railroad crossing; then turn right up the hill to Point Peter Road, and proceed about a mile to the sanctuary. Deer Lick covers 400 acres and consists of woodlands, abandoned fields, and open meadow. It also includes Deer Lick Falls. There are 4 trails through the preserve. Among the many birds to be seen here are: Red-tailed Hawk, Red-shouldered Hawk, Pileated Woodpecker, Great Horned Owl, Scarlet Tanager, flycatchers, warblers, and sparrows.

Durand-Eastman Park. The park is located northeast of Rochester on Lake Ontario. To reach the park from Rochester, take I-490 (Eastern Expressway) east to SR 47 (Sea Breeze Expressway), and follow signs to the park. This park, covering nearly 800 acres, has a varied habitat consisting of 3 ponds with marshlands, rolling terrain with extensive tree plantations, and a mile-long sand and rock beach. Look for loons, grebes, and diving ducks during the spring and fall. Hawks are common during April, and warblers (as many as 22 species) pass through on migration. Cedar Waxwings, White-winged Crossbills, and Purple Finches can be seen in the orchard area in winter.

El Dorado Beach Preserve, Ellisburg 13636. The preserve is owned by the Nature Conservancy. To reach the preserve, take SR 3 north from Pulaski, pass Southwick Beach State Park, and continue for about 4 more miles to Stony Creek Road, turn left and go for about a mile to Grandjean Road, turn left again, and proceed to the entrance and parking area.

This 250-acre preserve is a low, sandy peninsula with a section of rocky shoreline. It is best known for shorebirds, and the best time to visit the sanctuary is during migration. Fall shorebirds appear the first week in July; peak numbers have arrived by late August or early September. By October, the number and variety slack off, but the opportunity for rarer species such as Red Phalarope and Purple Sandpiper continues through November. The visitor is advised to wear boots and a raincoat. Look for Little Blue Heron, Green Heron, Ruddy Turnstone, Semipalmated Plover, Sanderling, and Short-billed Dowitcher. The hedgerow behind the shoreline is good for sparrows; and the woods further away from the shore are good for warblers and other landbirds.

Eldridge Wilderness, Ithaca 14850. The preserve is owned by The Nature Conservancy. Eldridge Wilderness is located on South Hill, above Ithaca, at the southern end of Cayuga Lake. To reach the preserve from Ithaca, take Coddington Road south to Troy Road, continue on Troy Road for about 2½ miles to the preserve.

The area is generally wooded and there is a small gorge on the southeast border that has small waterfalls and cascades. The main trail circles the preserve;

there are side trails that go into the central portion. Since portions of the trail may be wet, it is advisable to wear boots. Among the 113 species of birds seen here are: Ruffed Grouse, American Woodcock, Screech Owl, Barred Owl, Great Horned Owl, Black-billed Cuckoo, Hermit Thrush, Carolina Wren, Eastern Bluebird, and 24 species of warblers, including the Prairie Warbler which is rare for this area.

Helen Jahn Memorial Area (Derby Hill), Mexico/Richland 13114. The area is owned by The Nature Conservancy and operated by the Onondaga Audubon Society. To reach the preserve from Mexico, take SR 3 north for about 4 miles to SR 104B, turn left; go for about ½ mile to Sage Creek Drive, turn right and proceed to Derby Hill. Park at the north end of Sage Creek Drive; then walk up the hill to the top of the ridge and along the bluff.

Derby Hill is a north-south ridge on the edge of Lake Ontario and is well known for impressive hawk migrations. Migration at Derby Hill begins in early March with Red-tailed Hawks, Red-shouldered Hawks, and Goshawks; they are followed by the Broad-winged Hawks. Migration is essentially over by the end of May. The best time to visit the preserve is when there is a south wind. This spot is also good for migrant waterfowl in the fall, especially when the wind is from the northwest.

Highvista, Scott. The preserve is owned by The Nature Conservancy. To reach Highvista from Cortland, take SR 41 north to Vincent Hill Road (which is at the Onondaga-Cortland county line), then turn left on Vincent Hill Road, and proceed to the preserve.

This 137-acre preserve overlooks Skaneateles Lake, one of the most beautiful of the Finger Lakes. Most of Highvista is woodlands, the rest is abandoned fields. There are also streams, springs, and a small marsh area. Among the usual hardwoods are flowering dogwood, tulip, and oak — more typical of lower elevations. There are no trails yet; be prepared to bushwack. Look for woodpeckers, flycatchers, warblers, and other typical woodland birds.

Ironsides Island, Alexandria. The preserve is owned by The Nature Conservancy. The island is located in the St. Lawrence River; access is by boat only. Written permission to visit the island must be secured in advance from the preserve director: George Maxwell, R. D. 3, Oswego 13126; (315) 342-0021; or the assistant manager: James Parker, R. D. 1, Redwood 13676; (315) 482-3137. A good departure point is Kring Point State Park, located 1½ miles south of Ironsides.

This 20-acre island is one of the Thousand Islands; it is largely wooded — mostly white pine and oak. Ironsides gets its name from its 30- to 40-foot vertical cliffs that are covered with rust-colored lichen. The island was purchased primarily to preserve its large Great Blue Heron colony. Over 200 nests have been counted on a 3-acre section of the island. Among the other birds nesting on

Ironsides are: Mallard, Great Horned Owl, Black-capped Chickadee, Warbling Vireo, Yellow Warbler, Northern (Baltimore) Oriole, and Rough-winged Swallow.

Iroquois National Wildlife Refuge, R. F. D. 1, Basom 14013; (716) 948-5445. Iroquois is located between Buffalo and Rochester, near Batavia. Refuge headquarters are on SR 63, 8 miles north of Oakfield and 7 miles south of Medina. Use New York State Thruway exit 48 or 48-A. Camping is not permitted on the refuge; however, facilities are available at nearby state parks.

Iroquois was established in 1958 to provide a refuge for waterfowl. The refuge totals nearly 11,000 acres of wet meadow, swamp, marsh, pasture, and cropland. There are overlooks, hiking trails, and auto trails. Birdwatching is best from March through November. Among the 211 species of birds (97 nesting) recorded at Iroquois are: Pied-billed Grebe, Pintail, Hooded Merganser, Red-shouldered Hawk, American Bittern, Common Snipe, Black Tern, Screech Owl, Belted Kingfisher, Downy Woodpecker, Red-breasted Nuthatch, Gray Catbird, Warbling Vireo, Yellow-rumped (Myrtle) Warbler, American Redstart, Northern (Baltimore) Oriole, and Vesper Sparrow. Checklist available.

Manitoga (Dragon Rock), Garrison 10524. The preserve is owned by The Nature Conservancy; an admission fee is charged. The preserve is open from 15 April to 15 October. Guided tours are available. This 80-acre wooded sanctuary was once an abandoned quarry. Now ferns, laurel, hemlock, and dogwood characterize Manitoga. There are 4 miles of trails that ramble past pools and streams, through wooded areas, and across open meadows. Look for Hermit Thrush, Gray Catbird, Indigo Bunting, warblers, and other woodland birds.

Montezuma National Wildlife Refuge, R. D. 1, Box 1411, Seneca Falls 13148; (315) 568-5987. The refuge is located on US 20, about 4 miles east of Seneca Falls. Camping is not permitted on the refuge. Facilities are available at nearby state parks.

Established in 1937, Montezuma Refuge contains 6334 acres of widely diversified habitat — from upland hardwoods to extensive marshes. There are 2 observation towers, a picnic area, a 5-mile self-guiding automobile trail (around the main pool), and a 3-mile hiking trail. A naturalist is on duty. Among the 236 species of birds (110 nesting) recorded at Montezuma are: Canada Goose, Wood Duck, Ruddy Duck, Red-tailed Hawk, Marsh Hawk, Sora, Virginia Rail, Whimbrel, Dunlin, Barn Owl, Pileated Woodpecker, Tree Swallow, Brown Creeper, Veery, Warbling Vireo, Nashville Warbler, Chestnut-sided Warbler, Indigo Bunting, and Snow Bunting. Checklist available.

Moss Lake Nature Sanctuary, Caneadea. The sanctuary is owned by The Nature Conservancy. To reach Moss Lake from Houghton, take SR 19 south for about 2½ miles to Sandhill Road, turn right; the sanctuary is located just south of the intersection.

The 8-acre sanctuary is about a mile from the Genesee River and contains a 15-acre bog situated in a kettle hole surrounded by glacial debris. There are trails; and a boardwalk has been constructed over the sphagnum mat. In addition to the birds to be seen here, there are many rare and beautiful wildflowers. Special dates include: April for trailing arbutus; May for bog laurel and wood azalea; June for the pitcher plant and stemless lady's slipper; and August for the golden horned bladderwort. Among the birds seen here are: Pied-billed Grebe, Horned Grebe, Canvasback, Redhead, Marsh Hawk, Osprey, Great Blue Heron, Green Heron, Greater Yellowlegs, Yellow-bellied Flycatcher, Swainson's Thrush, and 17 species of warblers.

Palisades Interstate Park, Palisades Interstate Park Commission, Bear Mountain State Park, Bear Mountain 10911; (914) 786-2701. The Bear Mountain-Harriman State Park section of Palisades Interstate Park totals nearly 50,000 acres. There are trails; a trailside museum — which furnishes up-to-date birding information; and many recreational activities — including camping, hiking, and canoeing.

The extensive woodlands, lakes, mountainous areas, and streams all combine to provide a diverse habitat. As a result, the park supports a wide variety of plant and animal life. Among the many species of birds to be seen here are: Broad-winged Hawk, Pileated Woodpecker, Common (Yellow-shafted) Flicker, Tufted Titmouse, House Wren, Canada Warbler, Black-throated Blue Warbler, Worm-eating Warbler, Pine Siskin, and Rose-breasted Grosbeak.

At the *Tallman Mountains* section of the park, just north of the New Jersey border, look for Soras, Virginia Rails, and passerines in the freshwater marshes. *Rockland Lake* has migrant waterfowl; *Stony Point* is good for ducks and owls; and at *Iona Island,* bitterns, rails, herons, gulls, and terns can be seen.

Riemen Woods, Enfield. The preserve is owned by The Nature Conservancy. Riemen Woods is located between Robert Treman State Park and the Connecticut Hill Game Management Area. To reach the preserve from Ithaca, take SR 13 south to Enfield Falls Road (CR 327), turn right and go for about 5 miles to Trumbull Corners Road, turn left, go for ½ mile to Porter Hill Road, turn left again and continue for about a mile to the preserve.

This 37-acre preserve is characterized by a mixed conifer forest. Among the birds nesting at Riemen Woods are Ruffed Grouse and Ovenbirds. In addition, look for Goshawk, Red-breasted Nuthatch, woodpeckers, flycatchers, thrushes, and warblers (especially Canada, Prairie, and Black-throated Green).

Rock City Park, Rock City. The park is located near Allegany State Park, about a mile from the Pennsylvania border. From Olean, take SR 16 south to Rock City. Among the birds to be found here are: Hermit Thrush, Swainson's Thrush, Tufted Titmouse, Cardinal, and at least 8 species of warblers: Magnolia, Hooded, Canada, Black-throated Blue, Black-throated Green, Blackburnian, Mourning, and Blue-winged.

Sapsucker Woods Sanctuary, Ithaca 14850. The Cornell Laboratory of Ornithology is located 6 miles northeast of Ithaca. Drive north on SR 13, turn right on Warren Road, then left on Hanshaw Road, and left again on Sapsucker Woods Road; proceed to the entrance. This 180-acre sanctuary is maintained by Cornell University. The habitat is a moist woodland — consisting mostly of birches, beech, maples, and hemlocks — with ponds. The laboratory is on a 10-acre pond at the north end of the sanctuary. Here are exhibits, feeders, and observation points. Trails through the sanctuary are wet in spring and winter. Among the many species of birds seen here are: Black Duck, Pintail, Hooded Merganser, Ruffed Grouse, Barred Owl, Red-shouldered Hawk, Pileated Woodpecker, Yellow-bellied Sapsucker, Brown Creeper, Northern Waterthrush, Scarlet Tanager, Canada Warbler, and Ruby-crowned Kinglet.

Cornell University owns several preserves in and around Ithaca. *Ringwood Nature Preserve* is located 5 miles east of Ithaca, on Ringwood Road, off SR 13. It is a typical hardwood forest with small wooded swamps, characterized by oak, beech, and yellow birch. Look for Ruffed Grouse, thrushes, cireos, and warblers.

Cornell Plantations Test Gardens and Mitchell Woods are located east of Ithaca along SR 392 (Forest Home Drive). An extensive wildflower garden is featured. The area is traversed by a system of trails and paths. Birdwatching is best here in the spring. Look for vireos, warblers, and sparrows. In summer, Northern (Baltimore) Orioles can be seen; in winter, Brown Thrashers, Gray Catbirds, and White-winged and Red Crossbills are to be found.

Beebe Lake is located on the north side of the Cornell University campus. Since parking is restricted, a visitor may park at the Plantations (see above) and walk to Beebe Lake. In the wooded areas around the lake look for thrushes, vireos, and warblers; on the lake, look for Pied-billed Grebes and migrant waterfowl.

Also on the campus is *Cascadilla Gorge*. This area is on the south edge of the campus; parking is on College or Oak avenues. Enter the gorge from their junction. The network of paths makes birdwatching easy. Look for wrens, thrushes, and warblers.

On the east side of the Cornell campus, just off Judd Falls Road, are the *Fishery Laboratory Grounds*. Keep to the road. This is a good place to see Green Herons, Solitary and Spotted Sandpipers, Cedar Waxwings, Palm Warblers, Mourning Warblers, and flycatchers, wrens, and sparrows. The habitat is characterized by small ponds, deciduous woods and thickets, and a rocky stream.

About 20 miles southwest of Ithaca is the *Arnot Forest*. This 4000-acre forest is managed by Cornell. To reach it, take SR 13 south to Newfield, then CR 132 and CR 13. The Forest is open during daylight hours from 1 May to the end of the fall hunting season. Look for thrushes, vireos, and warblers in springtime; in summer look for Ruffed Grouse, Broad-winged Hawk, Barred Owl, Hermit Thrush, and warblers.

On the eastern side of Cayuga Lake is the *McLean Bog Preserve*. The preserve is owned by Cornell but is surrounded by privately owned farm land. It is located nearly ½ mile west of SR 13 on Sweetland Road, northeast of Dryden. Access to the preserve is across open fields on the north side of Sweetland Road. Visitors are requested to stay on the trail. The preserve is well known as an orchid and fern area and its rare plants include pitcher plant, golden club, labrador tea, and bog rosemary. Among the birds seen here are Mallard, Ruffed Grouse, American Woodcock, Pileated Woodpecker, Great Crested Flycatcher, and Swamp Sparrow.

For additional information about birdwatching in the Cayuga Lake basin, consult: *Birding in the Cayuga Lake Basin* (see the bibliography). It is an excellent book and gives traveling directions, habitat, and birds sighted for 76 sites around Cayuga Lake.

Stewart Park, Ithaca. Stewart Park is a municipal park located on Cayuga Lake. To reach the park, drive north on SR 13 and watch for the turnoff sign to the park on the southeast shore. The park is largely wooded. Look for Yellow-billed Cuckoo, Pileated Woodpecker, Tufted Titmouse, Cerulean Warbler, Indigo Bunting, and Rose-breasted Grosbeak.

Near the lake is a small pond — the Louis Agassiz Fuertes Waterfowl Sanctuary. Around this area look for Ring-necked Duck, Redhead, Canvasback, Bufflehead, grebes, loons, and other waterfowl.

Thompson Pond, Pine Plains. The pond is owned by The Nature Conservancy. For further information, contact the Eastern Regional office. To reach Thompson Pond, take Lake Road from Pine Plains.

The preserve totals over 300 acres. Thompson Pond is a shallow glacial pond surrounded by marsh and swamp. Cattails and waterlilies are abundant. Look for ducks, thrushes, Blue-winged Warblers, Golden-winged Warblers, and Louisiana Waterthrushes. The area around Pine Plains, that is, other ponds and abandoned fields in the vicinity, are also good birdwatching places. Be aware of private property rights and no trespassing signs.

West Hill Nature Preserve, Naples 14512. The preserve is owned by The Nature Conservancy. West Hill is located between High Tor Wildlife Management Area and the Cumming Nature Center. To reach the preserve from Naples, take County Road north for about 4 miles to Sermon Road, turn right, and proceed for about 2 miles to the preserve.

This 313-acre preserve is located on a hill bordering Canandaigua Lake. It is mostly wooded with abandoned fields. Foot trails follow old farm lanes through the woods. There have been 125 species of birds identified at West Hill. These include 10 species of hawks and falcons, 20 species of warblers, and 12 species of sparrows.

Whitney Point Reservoir Recreation Area. The area is owned by the state of New York. Whitney Point is located near Binghamton; the area is a mile north of the town of Whitney Point, off SR 26. This 4200-acre recreation area is on the Otselic River at Whitney Point Lake. The area is excellent for waterbirds and waterfowl from late March through early May. There have been 165 species of birds recorded in this area. Among these are: Common Loon, Double-crested Cormorant, Red-necked Grebe, Horned Grebe, Whistling Swan, 23 species of ducks, Osprey, Bald Eagle, Rough-legged Hawk, Marsh Hawk, Great (Common) Egret, Common Tern, Black Tern, Great Horned Owl, Short-eared Owl, Northern Shrike, Loggerhead Shrike, and many passerines.

New York City and Environs

Amagansett National Wildlife Refuge. Administrated by Target Rock NWR. Established in 1968, this refuge consists of 36 acres including over 1300 feet of barrier beach. The refuge is located 4 miles east of East Hampton, just off the Montauk Highway (SR 27), along Bluff Road. Public access is allowed along the shore; a special-use permit is required for entrance into the fragile dunes. Look for waterbirds and shorebirds.

Conscience Point National Wildlife Refuge. Administered by Target Rock NWR. This refuge was established in 1971 and totals 60 acres. It is located near Setauket on the north shore of Long Island. The area consists of open fields, woodlands, meadows, and about 15 acres of brackish marsh. Look for Buffleheads and other wintering waterfowl.

Croton Point Park, Croton-on-Hudson 10520. The park is located near Van Cortland Manor. From Ossining, take US 9 north to Harmon, turn left on Croton Point Avenue, and proceed to the park. The park juts out into the Hudson River and is a good place for birdwatching. Portions of the park are wooded; there are also fields, marshy areas, and a pine grove. Look for Red-necked Grebes, hawks, gulls, owls, and passerines.

Fire Island National Seashore, P. O. Box 229, Patchogue 11772. Fire Island is located south of Long Island. Access is by boat only except at the western end (Robert Moses State Park) and the eastern end (Smith Point County Park) of the island. These 2 parks are accessible by bridge. There are no roads on Fire Island. Some of the land within the boundaries of the national seashore is privately owned. Visitors are asked to respect the rights of private owners. There are campsites at the Seashore that are available by reservation only; write at least one month in advance.

Fire Island is a narrow sandbar extending for 32 miles on the Atlantic shore. Black gum, juneberry, beach plum, wild rose, and vines of poison ivy and wild grape are characteristic of the vegetation. The plant communities are very important to the island — they alone hold the sand against erosion by water and wind. Wildlife abounds at Fire Island. The Seashore is located along the Atlantic

Flyway; its protected waters hold rafts of waterfowl during migration periods in spring and fall. Common and Least Terns nest here. Among the birds most likely to be seen at Fire island are: Horned Grebe, White-winged Scoter, Black Duck, Brant, Marsh Hawk, Green Heron, Snowy Egret, Piping Plover, Ruddy Turnstone, Greater Yellowlegs, Spotted Sandpiper, Sanderling, Great Black-backed Gull, Black Skimmer, Common (Yellow-shafted) Flicker, Downy Woodpecker, Tree Swallow, Brown Thrasher, Ovenbird, Northern Parula, American Redstart, and Tree Sparrow.

Garvies Point Preserve, Barry Drive, Glen Cove 11542; (516) 292-4205. The preserve is owned and operated by Nassau County. Garvies Point is located at the northern tip of Hempstead Harbor in Glen Cove. To reach the preserve, use Garvies Point Road. There is a nature museum at the preserve (closed Mondays). A network of trails, all self-guiding, is maintained. A variety of educational and interpretive programs is offered.

This 72-acre preserve consists of open fields, woodlands, cliffs, beaches, and a pond. Among the many species of birds seen here are: Ring-necked Pheasant, Common (Yellow-shafted) Flicker, Brown Thrasher, Mockingbird, Philadelphia Vireo, Blackpoll Warbler, and Evening Grosbeak. From the cliffs and beaches ducks, gulls, and migrating waterfowl can be seen.

Jamaica Bay Wildlife Refuge. A unit of Gateway National Recreation Area, Floyd Bennett Field, Brooklyn 11234. To reach the refuge, take the Belt Parkway or Woodhaven Boulevard to Cross Bay Boulevard, turn south and continue to the refuge entrance, which is on the right.

Jamaica Bay Refuge was established in 1953 by the city of New York. In 1974 the refuge became a part of the Gateway National Recreation Area. Jamaica Bay Refuge comprises 9000 acres of marsh and water; it is situated along the Atlantic Flyway. The bays and inlets, dunes and marshes, thickets and grassy hassocks, and small beaches provide habitat for a wide variety of animal life. There have been 312 species of birds (65 nesting) recorded at the refuge. Among these are: Red-throated Loon (rare), Horned Grebe, Eared Grebe (rare), Snow Goose, Gadwall, Pintail, Shoveler, Redhead, Canvasback, Common Goldeneye, Oldsquaw, King Eider (rare), Ruddy Duck, Marsh Hawk, Peregrine Falcon (rare), Great Blue Heron, Louisiana Heron, Glossy Ibis, Clapper Rail, American Oystercatcher, American Golden Plover, Ruddy Turnstone, Whimbrel, Willet, White-rumped Sandpiper, Stilt Sandpiper, Marbled Godwit (rare), Wilson's Phalarope, Iceland Gull (rare), Forster's Tern, Black Skimmer, Snowy Owl (rare), Short-eared Owl, Least Flycatcher, Horned Lark, Tree Swallow, Red-breasted Nuthatch, Long-billed Marsh Wren, Hermit Thrush, Blue-gray Gnatcatcher, Cedar Waxwing, Philadelphia Vireo, Blue-winged Warbler, Nashville Warbler, Northern Parula, Yellow Warbler, Black-throated Blue Warbler, Bay-breasted Warbler, Wilson's Warbler, Yellow-headed Blackbird (rare), Scarlet Tanager, Rose-breasted Grosbeak, Dickcissel, Pine Siskin, Sharp-tailed Sparrow, Dark-eyed Junco, Lapland Longspur, and Snow Bunting.

John F. Kennedy Memorial Wildlife Sanctuary. Department of Public Works, Town Hall, Oyster Bay 11771; (516) 922-5800; ext. 271. A permit is required (available at no charge) to use the sanctuary. Address inquires to the above address. To reach the sanctuary, take the Long Island Expressway (US 495) to Meadowbrook Parkway; take Meadowbrook Parkway south to Jones Beach. The sanctuary is located between Jones Beach parking field #9 and the Tobay Beach parking lot. Enter at Tobay Beach and make an immediate left; proceed to sanctuary parking area.

JFK Sanctuary was established in 1959. It is a 500-acre stretch of dunes and salt marsh with a large brackish pond that is very attractive to birds. there are trails, blinds, and an observation tower. Among the many species of birds that are to be seen here are: Back Duck, Gadwall, American Wigeon, Great Blue Heron, Snowy Egret, Glossy Ibis, Marbled Godwit, Willet, Clapper Rail, Piping Plover, Least Tern, Black Skimmer, Short-eared Owl, Blue-winged Warbler, Northern Parula, Yellow Warbler, and Rufous-sided Towhee.

Kalers Pond Nature Center, Chet Swezey Road, East Moriches 11940. The Center is operated by the Moriches Bay Audubon Society (Box 802, Center Moriches 11934). To reach the center, take Montauk Highway (SR 27A) to Chet Swezey Road, turn north, and proceed a few hundred yards to the entrance. There is a nature museum that is open 10-4, Wednesday through Sunday. The preserve consists of mixed woodlands, open fields, and a pond. There is a self-guiding trail that winds through the preserve. Among the many birds to be seen here are Wood Thrush, Blue Jay, American Robin, Cardinal, and a variety of warblers.

Marshlands Park. Department of Parks, Recreation, and Conservation, Westchester County, County Office Building, White Plains 10601. Marshlands is a 120-acre sanctuary located on US 1 (Boston Post Road) in Rye. To reach it from New York City, take I-95 north to Exit 11 (Rye/Playland); take Playland Parkway ½ mile east to US 1, then turn south on US 1, and continue for about 1½ miles. A naturalist is on duty and may be reached at (914) 682-2626.

The park is made up of open grasslands, deep woodlands, and tidal marshes. There are interpretive trails (including a special trail for blind visitors), overlooks, and a visitors' center that houses exhibits pertaining to the natural life of the area. this unique area on Long Island Sound is a feeding and nesting site for many shorebirds. There have been 255 species of birds observed at Marshlands. Among them are: Canada Goose, Snowy Egret, American Bittern, Killdeer, Virginia Rail, Black-bellied Plover, Semipalmated Plover, Solitary Sandpiper, Great Black-backed Gull, Least Tern, Eastern Kingbird, Barn Swallow, Rough-winged Swallow, Chimney Swift, House Wren, Yellow Warbler, Chestnut-sided Warbler, Indigo Bunting, Bobolink, Red-winged Blackbird, and Sharp-tailed Sparrow.

Mianus River Gorge Preserve, Bedford 10506. The preserve is owned by The Nature Conservancy and operated by the Mianus River Gorge Committee, 151 Brookdale Road, Stamford (Connecticut) 06903. To reach the preserve from Bedford, take Round Ridge Road for about a mile to Long Ridge Road, turn right, continue for about ½ mile, then turn right again on Millers Mill Road, and directly left on Mianus River Road; proceed to the preserve.

The Mianus River cuts a deep ravine through a mixed hardwood forest which has a mature stand of hemlock. The preserve totals 337 acres. A network of trails is maintained. Look for owls, thrushes, Louisiana Waterthrush, and other warblers here.

Morton National Wildlife Refuge, Noyack Road, Sag Harbor 11963. Administered by Target Rock NWR. The refuge is located on the north side of Noyack Road, about 5 miles west of Sag Harbor. Morton Refuge consists of 187 acres; it serves as a resting area for waterfowl and shorebirds. There is an upland portion of 70 acres and a narrow peninsula, known as Jessup's Neck, of 110 acres. Sandy, gravelly, and rocky beaches fringe the peninsula, and the wooded bluffs of the neck overlook a small brackish pond. There is a 2-mile trail to the north tip of Jessup's Neck. Among the 221 species of birds (53 nesting) recorded at the refuge are: Black Duck, Osprey, Bobwhite, American Bittern, Black-bellied Plover, Roseate Tern, Black-billed Cuckoo, White-eyed Vireo, Ovenbird, Chestnut-sided Warbler, Bobolink, Scarlet Tanager, Savannah Sparrow, and Snow Bunting. Checklist available.

Muttontown Forest Preserve, East Norwich. The preserve is operated by Nassau County. Muttontown Preserve is located off SR 25A near the intersection of SR 106. From Glen Cove, take SR 107 south to Cedar Swamp Road, bear left, continue to 25A, turn east (left); proceed to Muttontown Lane (about 3 miles) turn right.

This large preserve on the north shore of Long Island is comprised of open fields, mixed hardwood forests, ponds, and marshy areas. There is a nature center near the parking lot. A variety of educational and interpretive programs is offered. The park is traversed by a network of bridle paths and trails. Among the many species of birds to be seen here are: Goshawk, American Woodcock, Black-billed Cuckoo, Great Horned Owl, Common (Yellow-shafted) Flicker, House Wren, Wood Thrush, Gray Catbird, Common Yellowthroat, Nashville Warbler, Blue-winged Warbler, Eastern Meadowlark, Rose-breasted Grosbeak, Indigo Bunting, and Field Sparrow.

Charles B. Church Wildlife Refuge (Shu Swamp), Mill Neck. The sanctuary is open 9-5 all year; a small parking area is located on the property (there is no parking allowed on any of the roads in Mill Neck at any time). To reach Shu Swamp from Glen Cove, take Forest Avenue to Buckram Road, which becomes Oyster Bay Road, continue to Frost Mill Road, turn left, go for about a mile, at intersection bear left, continue for about 1½ miles; the sanctuary is on the left just before the Mill Neck railroad station.

This preserve, although small, has a diverse habitat — including upland hardwood forest, brackish and freshwater ponds and marshes, and a stream. The forested areas are full of magnificent stands of tulip trees — some over 150 years old and more than 100 feet tall. Shu Swamp provides ideal habitat for a large number of birds. Among those likely to be seen here are: Mute Swan, Whistling Swan, Canada Goose (nesting) Wood Duck (nesting) Snowy Egret, Yellow-crowned Night Heron, Common Snipe, Yellow-bellied Sapsucker, Common (Yellow-shafted) Flicker, Hermit Thrush, Brown Thrasher, Black-throated Green Warbler, Yellow Warbler, Yellow-rumped (Myrtle) Warbler, Rusty Blackbird, Red-winged Blackbird, Common Redpoll, and Purple Finch.

Just north of Shu Swamp (continuing on Frost Mill Road to Cleft Road, and turning left) is *Beaver Dam*. Part of this area is an NWR, and there is no parking on the causeway that crosses Beaver Lake; but birdwatching here is quite good. Look for: Brant, Canada Goose, Mute Swan, Whistling Swan, Common Goldeneye, Canvasback, Bufflehead, Gadwall, American Wigeon, Snowy Egret, and Yellow-crowned Night Heron.

Oyster Bay National Wildlife Refuge. Administered by Target Rock NWR. Established in 1968, this refuge comprises significant portions of the marsh and open bay areas of Mill Neck Creek, Oyster Bay, and Cold Spring Harbor. This 3117-acre refuge is of special value in the protection of migratory birds. Access to the refuge is limited. For further information, contact the refuge manager at Target Rock NWR.

Playland Lake, Rye Playland Park, Rye 10480. After the summer crowds have left, this park becomes a good spot for birdwatching. From October on through the winter, one can see Horned Grebe, Greater Scaup, Common Goldeneye, Bufflehead, Oldsquaw, Red-tailed Hawk, and Rough-legged Hawk. In spring, look for Osprey. To reach the park, take I-95 (New England Thruway) north from New York City to exit for Rye; go to Playland Parkway and follow signs to the park.

Near Playland is the *Rye City Park,* a woodland sanctuary of 15 acres. It is located across the street from the Episcopal Church on US 1 (Boston Post Road). Look for Black-capped Chickadee. Tufted Titmouse, Yellow-breasted Chat, and Rose-breasted Grosbeak.

Quogue Wildlife Refuge, Quogue 11959. The refuge is located north of the railroad tracks, above the village of Quogue. To reach the refuge, take Exit 64S (CR 104) off of the Montauk Highway, go south for two miles to Old Country Road, then turn right on Old Country Road and continue for ½ mile; parking is on the left.

The 1500-acre refuge is characterized by pine-oak woods, pine barrens, freshwater bog, and a pond. Many species of waterfowl winter here. Look for Canada Goose, Hooded Merganser, Mallard, Green Heron, Hermit Thrush, and various passerines.

Smith Point County Park. This park is the eastern part of Fire Island National Seashore. To reach the park from Long Island, take Sunrise Highway (SR 27) to Floyd Parkway (SR 46, also known as Suffolk Boulevard). Go south, across the causeway (toll) to the parking area. The park is about 4½ miles long, leading to Moriches Inlet. This is a good place for waterfowl, shorebirds, and waterbirds. Terns and Black Skimmers nest here. Also look for Whimbrels, Willets, Hudsonian Godwits, Piping Plovers, Black-bellied Plovers, and American Oystercatchers.

Tackapausha Preserve, Washington Avenue, Seaford 11783. The preserve is operated by Nassau County. To reach Tackapausha, take Sunrise Highway (SR 27) to Seaford, turn south on Washington Avenue, proceed for about 5 blocks to the museum and parking lot. A variety of interpretive and educational programs is offered at the preserve.

The 80-acre preserve has a wildlife sanctuary, forest, pond, and brackish marsh. There is a network of nature trails. There have been nearly 200 species of birds recorded at Tackapausha Preserve. Look for ducks, egrets, herons, woodpeckers, thrushes, vireos, and warblers.

Target Rock National Wildlife Refuge, Target Rock Road, Lloyd Neck, Huntington 11743; (516) 271-2409. Entrance is by permit only; the refuge is open all year during daylight hours. To obtain a permit, write (or call) the refuge manager at the above address. Target Rock is located near Huntington. To reach the refuge, take West Neck Road north from SR 25A (in Huntington) for 8 miles. The road terminates at the refuge. There are parking facilities; a network of trails is maintained.

Target Rock, a former 80-acre estate, is exposed to both Huntington Harbor and Long Island Sound. Despite its size, its diverse habitats — including brushlands, native hardwoods, a brackish pond, and 2000 feet of tidal shoreline — provide food and shelter for a wide variety of birds. The 2 formal gardens, of azaleas and rhododendrons, are in bloom at the time of warbler migration making this area highly attractive during the third week of May. Among the 191 species of birds (48 nesting) seen here are: Bufflehead, Red-breasted Merganser, Ring-necked Pheasant, Common (Yellow-shafted) Flicker, Bank Swallow, Mockingbird, Wood Thrush, Red-eyed Vireo, Blackburnian Warbler, Blue-winged Warbler, Northern Parula, American Redstart, Northern (Baltimore) Oriole, and Rose-breasted Grosbeak. Checklist available.

Ward Poundridge Reservation, Cross River 10601; (914) 763-3993. The park is operated by Westchester Department of Parks, Recreation, and Conservation. There is a trailside museum. A variety of educational and interpretive programs is offered. A wildflower garden lies along a small stream behind the museum. Trails are maintained. Primitive (no tents) camping is allowed.

This 4500-acre park is largely wooded, although there are open fields, streams, and marsh areas. The park is open all year; the museum is closed Mondays and Tuesdays. Among the 151 species of birds to be seen here are: Black-billed Cuckoo, Common (Yellow-shafted) Flicker, Cedar Waxwing, Winter Wren, Tufted Titmouse, Yellow-rumped (Myrtle) Warbler, Northern (Baltimore) Oriole, Evening Grosbeak, Pine Siskin, and Cardinal.

Wertheim National Wildlife Refuge. Administered by Target Rock NWR. This 1937-acre refuge was established in 1947. It is located in Brookhaven. The Carmen River, recognized as a state scenic river, passes through the refuge. Wertheim Refuge consists mainly of brackish marsh, salt marsh, fresh meadows, and uplands. The area is valuable as habitat for waterfowl and shorebirds, and contains one of the last natural esturine environments on Long Island. Among the many birds to be seen here are: Black Duck, Mallard, American Wigeon, Green-winged Teal, Rough-legged Hawk, Marsh Hawk, Least Bittern, American Coot, and Clapper Rail.

NATURE CENTERS

There are many nature centers, arboretums, and small parks and preserves located throughout New York. Most of them have trails and exhibits and offer a variety of educational and interpretive programs. Many of them also have classes for schoolchildren as well as for college students and teachers. The first part of this listing covers those centers in the western and central portions of the state (that is, west of Utica); the second part will cover the centers in the eastern portion of the state; the third part will describe the centers in Westchester, New York City, and Long Island. Owing to lack of space, these centers are not shown on the map.

WESTERN AND CENTRAL NEW YORK

Allenberg Bog. The sanctuary is operated by Buffalo Audubon Society; it totals 318 acres. The area is open by prior arrangement. The sanctuary is located between New Albion and Napoli. To reach the refuge, take SR 353 north to Little Valley, then turn left on SR 242 to Napoli, then turn north on the road to New Albion. The trails at the refuge are difficult to follow, a map with detailed directions is available from the Buffalo Museum of Science, Humboldt Park, Buffalo 14200. Nesting birds include Winter Wren, Brown Creeper, Hermit Thrush, Veery, and Northern Waterthrush.

Beaver Lake Nature Center, 8477 East Mud Lake Road, Baldwinsville 13027; (315) 638-1223. The center is operated by Onondaga County; it covers 500 acres. Guided and self-guiding tours are available. The center is open all year, closed Sundays and Mondays.

Beaver Meadow Wildlife Refuge. The refuge is operated by Buffalo Audubon Society and totals 250 acres. There is a beaver pond and wet woodlands. Permission to visit the sanctuary must be secured in advance. The refuge is located 35 miles southeast of Buffalo. To reach it from SR 78 in Java, turn east on Welch Road and continue for 2½ miles to the refuge. Look for Hooded Merganser, Wood Duck, Veery, Northern Waterthrush, Hooded Warbler, Mourning Warbler, and Scarlet Tanager.

Bentley Wildlife Sanctuary. The sanctuary is operated by Jamestown Audubon Society; it totals 35 acres. Arrangements to visit the sanctuary must be made in advance.

Burgeson Wildlife Sanctuary. The sanctuary is operated by Jamestown Audubon Society; it totals 185 acres. Arrangements to visit the sanctuary must be made in advance.

Cumming Nature Center, R.D. 3, Naples 14512. The center is operated by the Rochester Museum of Science. It is located 6 miles north of Naples on Gulick Road. The center totals 800 acres.

Highland Park. To reach the park from Rochester, go south for 3 miles on South Avenue to Reservoir Avenue; turn left into the park. This 108-acre park has trails and an arboretum. It is best known for spring and fall warbler migrations. Over 500 varieties of lilac bloom here, peaking in mid-May.

Laboratory of Ornithology, Cornell University, 159 Sapsucker Woods Road, Ithaca 14850; (607) 256-5056. The sanctuary totals 250 acres; guided and self-guiding tours are available; the center is open all year (see page 77).

Minna Anthony Common Nature Center, Alexandria Bay 13607; (315) 482-2479. The center is operated by Thousand Islands State Park Commission; it totals 600 acres. Guided and self-guiding tours are available; the center is open all year.

Mendon Ponds Park, Clover Street at Pond Road, Rochester 14472; (716) 334-3780. The park is operated by Monroe County Department of Parks. It covers 2400 acres. Guided and self-guiding tours are available; the park is open all year, closed Mondays.

Reed Road Swamp, Rochester. The swamp is owned and maintained by the Genesee Ornithological Society. It is located South of Rochester. Take SR 383, turn right on Ballantyne Road, then left onto Reed Road; proceed to the swamp. One road and several trails are maintained. Among the birds seen here are: Yellow- and Black-billed Cuckoos, Pileated Woodpecker, Red-headed Woodpeckers, Veery, Blue-gray Gnatcatcher, Scarlet Tanager, and many warblers.

Rogers Environmental Education Center, Route #80, Sherburne 13460; (607) 674-2861. The center is operated by New York Department of Environmental Conservation. The center covers 550 acres; guided and self-guiding tours are available. The center is open all year, closed on weekends.

The Roost. The sanctuary is operated by Jamestown Audubon Society and covers 30 acres. It is open to the public.

Sonnenberg Gardens. The gardens are located near Canandiagua and cover 50 acres. They are open every day 9-5 from May to October. An admission fee is charged.

William P. Alexander Sanctuary, Gowanda. The 130-acre sanctuary is owned and maintained by the Nature Sanctuary Society of Western New York. It is located between Gowanda and Springville. Among the many birds nesting here are: Great Horned Owl, Pileated Woodpecker, Solitary Vireo, Black-throated Green Warbler, Canada Warbler, and American Redstart.

EASTERN NEW YORK

Bear Mountain Trailside Museums, Bear Mountain State Park, Bear Mountain 10911; (914) 786-2701. The museums are operated by Palisades Interstate Park. There are 4 museum buildings and sections with live animals. Self-guiding trails are maintained. The museums are open all year.

Capitaland Natural Science Center (Tivoli Lakes Nature Study Sanctuary), Philip Livingston Junior High School, Northern Boulevard, Albany 12206; (518) 472-8860. The center is operated by the Albany Board of Education and the Capitaland Natural Science Center. It totals 82 acres; guided and self-guiding tours are available. The center is open all year.

Five Rivers Environmental Education Center, Game Farm Road, Delmar 12054; (518) 457-6096. The center is operated by the New York State Department of Environmental Conservation. It covers 260 acres and is open all year. Guided and self-guiding tours are available.

Lakeside Outdoor Education Center, Lakeside School, South Main Street, Spring Valley 10977; (914) 356-7032. The center is operated by the Edwin Gould Foundation, Edwin Gould Services for Children. The center totals 150 acres; guided and self-guiding tours are available. It is open all year; closed on weekends.

Museum of the Hudson Highlands, The Boulevard, Cornwall-on-Hudson 12520; (914) 534-2320. The museum is operated by the Village of Cornwall and the Cornwall Neighborhood Museum Association, Inc. Guided and self-guiding tours are offered. The center covers 60 acres and is open all year; closed on Fridays and holidays.

Stony Kill Environmental Education Center. For information, contact: New York State Department of Environmental Conservation, Division of Educational Services, Albany 12201.

Teatown Lake Reservation, Spring Valley Road, Ossining 10562; (914) 762-2912. The center is operated by the Brooklyn Botanic Garden. It totals 306 acres and is open all year; closed on Mondays. Guided and self-guiding tours are available. Look for waterfowl.

WESTCHESTER, NEW YORK CITY, AND LONG ISLAND

Arthur W. Butler Memorial Sanctuary, Chestnut Ridge Road, Mt. Kisco 10549. The sanctuary is across the street from Westmoreland Sanctuary (see below). It is owned by The Nature Conservancy. The sanctuary covers over 350 acres of swamp, stream, meadow, and upland hardwood forest. There have been 123 species of birds sighted here. Among them are: Eastern Wood Pewee, Philadelphia Vireo, Cape May Warbler, Pine Grosbeak, Eastern Meadowlark, and Rufous-sided Towhee.

Bailey Arboretum, Feeks Lane, Locust Valley, Long Island 11560; (516) 676-4497. The arboretum is open all year, closed on Mondays. It comprises 42 acres of mixed woodlands, lawns, and a pond. Look for Canada Geese, Wood Ducks, and Black-crowned Night Herons among other birds. Trails are maintained. An admission fee is charged.

Bayard Cutting Arboretum, Montauk Highway (SR 27A), Box 66, Oakdale, Long Island 11769; (516) 581-1002. The arboretum is operated by the Long Island State Parks Commission. It covers 690 acres and is open Wednesday through Sunday (and on holidays) from 15 March to 1 November, and on weekends and holidays from 1 November to 1 December.

Clark Memorial Gardens, Albertson, Long Island 11507. The gardens are owned by the Brooklyn Botanic Garden. The entrance is next to the Albertson railroad station. The gardens cover 12 acres. They are open from 12:30-4:30, from April to October. An admission fee is charged.

High Rock Park Conservation Center, Nevada Avenue, Staten Island 10306; (212) 987-6276. The center is operated by the Staten Island Institute of Arts and Sciences. It covers 72 acres and is open all year. Trails are maintained. Look for Screech Owl, American Goldfinch, woodpeckers, and sparrows.

Massapequa Preserve, Massapequa, Long Island 11758. The preserve entrance is on Clark Boulevard, parking is on Lake Shore Drive. This long, narrow preserve is sandwiched between Southern State Parkway and Sunrise

Highway. It consists of a stream, weedy ponds, and wooded areas. There are trails along the stream and into the woods. The wetlands are good for ducks.

Oceanside Marine Nature Study Area, Slice Drive, Oceanside, Long Island 11572; (516) 766-1580. The Marine Study Area is located at the foot of Slice Drive. From Rockville Centre, take Oceanside Road south; turn east on Waukena Avenue, then south on Park Avenue, continue to Slice Drive. The area is open 9-5 Tuesday-Saturday from April to October. A network of trails traverses the 52-acre area — from salt marsh to sand dunes to ponds. There have been 165 species of birds observed here. Among them are: Green- and Blue-winged Teal, Black Skimmer, Cooper's Hawk, Short-eared Owl, Veery, Nashville Warbler, Bobolink, Red Crossbill, and White-crowned Sparrow.

Planting Fields Arboretum, Planting Fields Road, Oyster Bay, Long Island 11771; (516) 922-9200. The arboretum is operated by the Long Island State Parks Commission. To reach Planting Fields from Glen Cove, take SR 107 south to Cedar Swamp Road, bear left, continue to Chicken Valley Road, turn left, continue to Planting Fields Road, turn right and proceed to entrance. Planting Fields is open daily 10-5; an admission fee is charged. This 400-acre former estate has many gardens and greenhouses. There are also trails through woods and across open fields. A variety of educational and interpretive programs is offered. Look for woodpeckers, thrushes, warblers, and finches.

Wave Hill Center for Environmental Studies, 675 West 252 Street, Bronx 10471; (212) 549-2055. The entrance is at West 249 Street and Independence Avenue. The center covers 28 acres. Trails are maintained. There are formal gardens, an herb garden, and greenhouses. The center is open every day from April to October. A variety of educational programs is offered.

Weinberg Nature Center, 455 Mamaroneck Road, Scarsdale 10583; (914) 723-4784. The center is operated by the Village of Scarsdale. It covers 12 acres; there is a museum. The center is open all year, closed on Fridays.

Westbury Gardens, Old Westbury Road, Old Westbury, Long Island. The gardens are open 10-5, Wednesday through Sunday. An admission fee is charged.

Westmoreland Sanctuary, Inc., Chestnut Ridge Road, Mt. Kisco 10549; (914) 666-8488. To reach the sanctuary from Bedford, go south on SR 22 to Chestnut Ridge Road, turn right, and proceed to the sanctuary. The Arthur Butler Sanctuary is located across the street. Westmoreland covers 280 acres of mixed woodlands and open fields. Trails are maintained and there is a museum that is open 9-5, Wednesday through Sunday. The sanctuary itself is open every day. A variety of educational and interpretive programs, including bird banding, is offered. Among the many birds seen here are: American Woodcock, Downy Woodpecker, Black-capped Chickadee, Wood Thrush, and a variety of warblers.

William T. Davis Wildlife Refuge, Travis Avenue, New Springville, Staten Island 10312; (212) 727-1135. The refuge is operated by the Staten Island Museum and the New York City Department of Parks, Recreation, and Cultural Affairs. The refuge totals 260 acres; guided and self-guiding tours are available. It is open every day from 15 September to 15 November and from 1 April to 1 July.

AUDUBON SANCTUARIES

Throughout New York there are a number of Audubon sanctuaries — some are owned and/or maintained by local chapters, others by National Audubon. The first group listed consists of sanctuaries located in Westchester County; they are maintained by the Saw Mill River Audubon Society, Pleasantville 10570; (914) 769-7340. The second group listed consists of sanctuaries owned by the National Audubon Society.

SAW MILL RIVER AUDUBON SOCIETY SANCTUARIES

Brinton Brook, Rt. 9A, Croton-on-Hudson. The sanctuary is located north of Croton-on-Hudson, on old US 9 (Albany Post Road); turn east off the highway at the small sign "Brinton Brook," and continue to the parking area (about ¼ mile). The sanctuary totals 129 acres of upland hardwoods with a pond, an orchard, and a small ravine. There is a wide variety of plants including dogwood, mountain laurel, trillium, violets, and fringed gentians. The varied habitat provides shelter and food for many species of birds. They include herons, ducks, American Woodcock, Ruffed Grouse, woodpeckers, and warblers.

Cameron-Murtfeldt Sanctuary, Kipp Street, Chappaqua. To reach the sanctuary take Douglas Street from its intersection with Quaker Street (SR 120); take the first right off Douglas Street, which is Kipp Street. The sanctuary totals 6 acres which are in 2 separate plots; it is primarily a wetland area. There is a short trail on the west section only.

Chernik Sanctuary, Beech Hill Road, Mt. Pleasant. To reach the sanctuary from Pleasantville, take SR 117 west, cross over the Taconic Parkway; just before SR 117 becomes divided, make a sharp right onto Beech Hill Road; take Beech Hill Road to Briarwood Lane, past Briarwood, park on the right across the street from the Chernick sign. The sanctuary totals 6 acres; the trail is usually wet.

Choate, Millwood Road, New Castle. To reach the sanctuary from Mt. Kisco, take SR 133 (Millwood Road) west for ½ mile to Crow Hill Road; park just west of Crow Hill Road on SR 133, walk to sanctuary. Choate totals 25 acres of mixed woodland and open fields; a trail is maintained.

Gedney Brook, Woodmill Road, New Castle; (914)-769-6414. To reach the sanctuary, continue on SR 133 past Choate Sanctuary and past Seven Bridges

Road intersection; Woodmill Road is about a mile further. The sanctuary is off a stub road at the right near the end of Woodmill Road. The sanctuary totals 24 acres. There are many trails, some self-guiding.

Hass Sanctuary, Tripp Street, New Castle. To reach the sanctuary take SR 128 from either Armonk or Mt. Kisco, look for Sheather Road, which is about 2 miles north of the New Castle-North Castle line (near Mt. Kisco). Take Sheather Road to the first right, which is Tripp Street; the sanctuary is on the left less than ½ mile further. Trails are maintained through this 7½-acre area.

Pinecliff Sanctuary, Pinecliff Road, Chappaqua. To reach the sanctuary take Quaker Street (SR 120) north to Pinecliff Road; the sanctuary entrance is at a dead-end turnaround off Pinecliff, between private homes. The sanctuary totals 7 acres; a trail is maintained.

Thurber Sanctuary, Ossining. To reach the sanctuary, take the Briarcliff-Peekskill Parkway (SR 9A/100) to the exit for SR 133. The 6-acre sanctuary is a wetland; there are no trails. Check with Saw Mill River Audubon Society before visiting the sanctuary.

NATIONAL AUDUBON SOCIETY SANCTUARIES

Graf Audubon Sanctuary, Furnace Dock Road, Croton-on-Hudson 10520. The sanctuary is maintained by the Saw Mill River Audubon Society (see above). Permission to visit the sanctuary must be secured in advance. This 33-acre sanctuary adjoins a county park that protects a large area along the river. The sanctuary is heavily wooded and includes an exceptionally fine stand of tulip trees.

Palmer Lewis Sanctuary, Bedford. Maintained by the Bedford Audubon Society; contact: Linda Shoumatoff, R.D. 2, Route 200, Katonah 10536; (914) 232-8349. The sanctuary covers 24 acres of mixed woodlands and open fields. There is a nesting program for Eastern Bluebirds at the sanctuary.

Ruth Walgreen Franklin and Winifred Fels Audubon Sanctuaries, North Salem. Maintained by Bedford Audubon Society (see above). The 2 adjoining sanctuaries total 181 acres of woodlands. There are trails. The extensive areas of ferns, wildflowers, and berry-producing shrubs attract large numbers of songbirds.

Theodore Roosevelt Sanctuary, P. O. Box 5, Oyster Bay 11771; (516) 922-3200. Operated by four Long Island Audubon chapters. This 10-acre wooded sanctuary is located on the north shore of Long Island, just east of the village of Oyster Bay. From Oyster Bay, take Cove Road east for about 2 miles; the sanctuary is on the right. A variety of educational and interpretive programs, including bird banding, is offered. A nature museum and a network of trails are maintained. Among the many birds that can be seen here are: Black-capped Chickadee, Tufted Titmouse, and a variety of thrushes, warblers, and finches.

NATURE CONSERVANCY PRESERVES

The Nature Conservancy is especially active in New York State. Below is a listing of their preserves in eastern New York; following that is information about their Long Island preserves. For additional information about TNC preserves in this area, contact: Eastern New York Chapter, The Nature Conservancy, P. O. Box 22, Altamont 12009. Additional information regarding preserves in central and western New York can be obtained from: Central New York Chapter, The Nature Conservancy, Box 175, Ithaca 14850. Some of the preserves that have limited access, or are very small or which require special permission to visit, are not listed.

EASTERN NEW YORK

Andrew J. Whitbeck Memorial Grove, New Scotland. This area is located near *Five Rivers Environmental Center* (see above). From New Scotland, take SR 85 west for a mile to a dirt road that is just past the railroad overpass; park on the dirt road and walk into the grove. This area comprises 26 acres and consists of 2 woodlots separated by a meadow. Look for woodpeckers and warblers.

Amy LeMaire Woods (Central Park Natural Area), Schenectady. The preserve adjoins Central Park. It is located off SR 7. There are nearly 16 acres of woods.

Barberville Falls, Poestenkill. The preserve is not always open. Contact the chairperson at the chapter office (see above). The preserve totals 123 acres and includes a 110-foot waterfall. There is a steep gorge with hemlocks and mixed hardwoods.

Bear Swamp, Westerlo. To reach the preserve from Westerlo, take SR 401 southwest to SR 404, turn right, and proceed into the swamp. This living museum features a wooded swamp; the road divides the swamp into Great Bear and Little Bear. Look for Goshawk, Pileated Woodpecker, Red-winged Blackbird, and warblers.

Christman Sanctuary. To reach the preserve from Duanesburg, take SR 7 west to Weaver Road, turn left, then left again on Schoharie Turnpike; proceed to small parking area. The sanctuary comprises 97 acres and includes the Bozenkill Falls. There is a self-guiding trail.

Emanuel and Frances Freund Wildlife Sanctuary, Old Chatham. To reach the preserve from Old Chatham, take Pitt Road; park along Pitt Road. This 57-acre sanctuary adjoins the *Wilson M. Powell Wildlife Sanctuary*, which is maintained by the Alan Devoe Bird Club. This club also maintains the Freund Sanctuary. The Powell Sanctuary covers 103 acres of woodlands. There are about 3 miles of trails. Over 250 species of birds have been sighted here. Look for Wood Duck, Golden-winged Warbler, Blue-winged Warbler, woodpeckers, flycatchers, and various passerine birds.

Emmons Pond Bog, West Davenport. The preserve is located south of Oneonta. To reach it, take SR 23 southeast to South Side Road, then turn right on Swart Hollow Road (unpaved), then left on White Hill Road, and continue to the preserve. Emmons Pond totals 150 acres of swamp forest, bog, abandoned pasture, and upland hardwoods. There are trails and a boardwalk. Visitors are requested to stay on them; this is a fragile habitat.

Everton Falls Preserve, Santa Clara. The preserve is located between St. Regis Falls and Duane Center. This 530-acre area is on the border of the Adirondack Forest Preserve (see page 71). The dominant conifer is balsam fir; on the slopes, hardwoods prevail. The St. Regis River, which traverses the preserve, is canoeable for a 10-mile stretch. Look for deer and beaver in addition to woodland birds.

Hannacroix Ravine, Berne and New Scotland. To reach the preserve, take SR 443 from Berne to Clarksville, turn right on Cass Hill Road, and continue for just over 2 miles to the preserve. There are no marked trails, but there is an abandoned logging road. The 123-acre preserve stretches along both sides of the Hannacroix Creek.

Kenrose Sanctuary, Berne. To reach the sanctuary, take SR 9 south from West Berne to Bridge Road, park along the road. The 360-acre preserve is mostly wooded. There are marked trails.

Limestone Rise Preserve, Knox. To reach the preserve, take SR 146 west from Altamont for six miles. This 31-acre preserve is of special geologic interest. Walk carefully through the preserve, especially if there is snow on the ground or if it is covered with autumn leaves. Birdwatching is good here, especially across the road in the swamp and open fields beyond the wooded preserve.

Lisha Kill Natural Area, Niskayuna. To reach the preserve from Schenectady, take SR 7 east to Rosendale Road, turn left, and continue to Lisha Kill. The sanctuary covers 108 acres of woodland. The Lisha Kill as well as tributary streams traverse the area. The preserve is often closed in early spring. Look for warblers and finches.

Lordsland Conservancy, Roseboom. To reach the preserve from Roseboom, take SR 165 to Gage Road, turn left on Gage Road, and proceed to the sanctuary. Lordsland comprises 78 acres of abandoned farmland, stream, and swamp. In the uplands look for Ruffed Grouse, Rose-breasted Grosbeak, Indigo Bunting, thrushes, woodpeckers, nuthatches, warblers, swallows, and finches. In the swampy areas, look for Gray Catbirds, wrens, flycatchers, and warblers.

Mildred Denton Wildlife and Bird Sanctuary, Greenwich. To reach the sanctuary from Schuylerville, take US 4 northeast, crossing the Hudson river, and continue to River Road; turn left on River Road and proceed to the Denton home; park there. The sanctuary covers 370 acres of open land, ponds, and woodlands. There are no formal trails; and the area near the river tends to be wet in the spring. Look for Great Blue Heron, Little Blue Heron, and ducks.

Mineral Spring Falls Preserve, Cornwall. The preserve totals 115 acres of woodland. There are no parking facilities. Contact the preserve director: Paul Jeheber, Box 251, Cornwall-on-Hudson 12520; (914) 534-7965; he will assist you in making arrangements.

Moccasin Kill Sanctuary, Rotterdam. The sanctuary is located on Crawford Road, near Gregg Road, about 2 miles from Exit 26 on the New York State Thruway (I-90). The sanctuary totals 50 acres and is completely covered with second-growth forest. Beware of poison ivy. Look for Pileated Woodpeckers here.

Stewart Preserve, Nassau and Sand Lake. To reach the preserve from Rensselaer, take SR 43/66 southeast to Methodist Farm Road, turn right, continue for less than a mile to Steward Lane, turn left, and continue to the preserve. The preserve covers 123 acres of abandoned farmlands, woodlands, and swamp.

Moonbeams Sanctuary, Wallkill. To reach the sanctuary, take Exit 118 from SR 17 (the Quickway), then take CR 76 to Prosperous Valley Road, turn left and continue for about 2 miles, crossing abandoned railroad tracks. The preserve totals 150 acres of woodlands and meadows, stream and swamp. There are informal trails. Look for Eastern Meadowlark, Eastern Bluebird, Bobolink, hawks, flycatchers, swallows, and migrating waterbirds such as herons.

Ten Mile Creek Conservancy, Rensselaerville. To reach the preserve from Rensselaerville, take Hale Road south for just over a mile. The sanctuary covers 111 acres of overgrown fields and mixed woodlands on the west side of Ten Mile Creek. This area is near the *Huyck Preserve* (not owned by TNC), which is just north of Rensselaerville; it totals 1200 acres, and there is a resident biologist. The land is forested and there are 2 lakes.

Virginia Viney Smiley Preserve (formerly Bonticou Conservancy), Rosendale. To reach the preserve from New Paltz, take SR 299 through New Paltz, cross the creek, and take the first right (Springtown Road), then make first left on Mt. Rest Road; continue to Mossy Brook Road, turn right, then right again on Mountain Road; park on Mountain Road. The preserve totals 243 acres and contains table rocks and ice caves. There have been 54 nesting species of birds recorded here. Look for American Woodcock, Black-backed Three-toed Woodpecker, Mockingbird, flycatchers, warblers, and sparrows.

Waitecliff, Altamont. For information about visiting the preserve, contact the chapter office (see above). The preserve totals 73 acres of steep, wooded lands. The Red-tailed Hawk nests here. The preserve is closed from April to June.

Wellborn Woods Conservancy, Providence. To reach the preserve from Saratoga Springs, take SR 29 west to Mosherville, turn north (right) on Barkersville Road (SR 16) and continue to Glenwild Road, then turn left on Center Line Road, and go on to Dixon Road (unpaved); park here and walk into the preserve on Dixon Road. Wellborn Woods is bordered on the north by the Adirondack Forest Preserve (see page 71). It totals 98 acres of woodlands and is crossed by Evan's Creek. Plant and animal life thrive in this varied habitat. Look for Belted Kingfisher, Great Crested Flycatcher, warblers, and sparrows.

West Branch Nature Preserve, Hamden. To reach the preserve from Oneonta, take SR 28 south to Delhi, then turn right on SR 10 to Hamden, and continue to the preserve. Park at the end of the dirt road. The preserve comprises 446 acres — mostly wooded. Look for Pileated Woodpeckers here.

LONG ISLAND

As of 1973, The Nature Conservancy owned over 60 preserves on Long Island. Acquisition of lands continues. Many of these preserves are small — some even less than an acre, others total 70 acres or more. Most of these properties are either near one another or near larger state- or county-owned lands. Although intended to preserve and conserve wildlife, these preserves are not bird sanctuaries. However, many local nature study groups (including local Audubon chapters) do make trips to them, and have found them to be rewarding birdfinding places. Some of the preserves are briefly described below. For additional information about Nature Conservancy preserves, contact: Long Island Chapter, The Nature Conservancy, Box 72, Cold Spring Harbor 11724; (516) 367-3225; or South Fork-Shelter Island Chapter, P. O. Box JJJJ, East Hampton 11937; (516) 267-3748.

Blydenburgh Sanctuary, Smithtown (Suffolk). This 27-acre preserve is located off Landing Avenue. It consists of mixed hardwoods and a marsh along the Nissequogue River. Among the birds seen here are: Eastern Bluebird, Cedar Waxwing, and Brown Creeper. Trails traverse the area.

Butler-Huntington Woods Preserve, Nissequogue (Suffolk). This 66-acre preserve is located near the town of St. James and is accessible from Old Mill Road in the village of Nissequogue. It consists of mixed woodlands; laurel dominates the understory. There is a network of marked trails. Among the birds seen here are: Wood Thrush, Brown Thrasher, Eastern Wood Pewee, Scarlet Tanager, Rufous-sided Towhee, and Dark-eyed Junco.

Daniel R. Davis Sanctuary, Coram (Suffolk). This 58-acre preserve is located off Mt. Sinai Road. It is a breeding ground for the Hermit Thrush. Trailing arbutus and lady's slipper are among the 155 flowering plants to be found here. A network of trails is maintained.

David Weld Sanctuary, Nissequogue (Suffolk). This 83-acre preserve extends from Boney Lane north to Long Island Sound. It consists of mixed woodlands, cliffs, and a tidal marsh. Breeding birds include: Yellow-crowned Night Heron, Red-eyed Vireo, and Carolina Wren. Among the other birds seen here are: Ring-necked Pheasant, American Woodcock, Bobwhite, Yellow-breasted Chat, and Blue-winged Warbler.

Fox Hollow Preserve, Laurel Hollow (Nassau). This 26-acre preserve is located off White Oak Tree Road, on the south side of SR 25A. The preserve is made up of a mature oak forest with dense stands of white pine. Breeding birds include Broad-winged Hawk and Great Horned Owl. Other birds seen here are: Red-bellied Woodpecker, Tufted Titmouse, and Cardinal.

Husing Pond Preserve, Mattituck (Suffolk). This 19-acre sanctuary consists of a spring-fed pond, stream, field, and upland. It is located on the north fork of Long Island, off Great Peconic Bay Boulevard, across from the Mattituck Yacht Club. Birds sighted here include: American Woodcock, Common Snipe, Black Duck, Wood Duck, and Mallard.

Meadow Beach Preserve, Nassau Point (Suffolk). The preserve is located east of Cutchogue and can be reached by walking from Nassau Point Park (where parking is available). Meadow Beach is a 15-acre salt marsh with a barrier beach. Of special interest are the shore birds which use this area during spring and fall migration. Look for Black-crowned Night Heron, Great Blue Heron, Snowy Egret, Piping Plover, terns, and ducks.

Oaces Sanctuary, East Norwich (Nassau). This 26-acre preserve consists of mixed woodlands and is noted for its fine stand of American chestnut. It should be approached through the development that is known as The Hollows on the south side of SR 25A, just east of the intersection with SR 106. Look for warblers.

St. John's Pond Preserve, Cold Spring Harbor (Nassau). This preserve is located behind St. John's Church, on the south side of SR 25A. It is adjacent to the New York State fish hatchery. Parking is available in the church's upper lot. The preserve consists of a pond, swampy area, mixed hardwoods and thickets. Nodding trillium, trailing arbutus, and lady's slipper are among the many wildflowers to be found here. Among the birds seen here are: Green Heron, Wood Duck, Mute Swan, Great Crested Flycatcher, Prothonotary Warbler, Northern Waterthrush, Canada Warbler, Scarlet Tanager, and Northern (Baltimore) Oriole.

Wading River Marsh Preserve, Wading River (Suffolk). This 55-acre preserve consists mostly of wetlands with some wooded areas and open fields. It is located off Sound Road; entrance to the sanctuary is via the Kempf driveway. Visitors are asked to remain on the trails.

STATE PARKS AND FORESTS

There are numerous state parks and forest recreation areas located throughout New York State. Most of them offer camping in addition to a variety of other recreational facilities. The following listing is arranged by region; each region administers the parks in its area. Those parks and recreation areas that are well known as birdwatching places are preceded by an asterisk (*). State historic sites are not listed. For further information about parks in New York State, contact: Parks and Recreation Department, Albany 12223; (518) 474-0456. For specific information, contact the individual park or its regional park commission.

ALLEGANY STATE PARK COMMISSION, SALAMANCA 14779; (716) 354-2535

*Allegany, Salamanca 14779; (716) 354-2535.
Cuba Reservation, Cuba 14727; (716) 968-1166.
Lake Erie, Dunkirk 14048; (716) 792-9214.
Long Point on Lake Chautauqua, Maple Springs 14756; (716) 386-2106.

CAPITAL DISTRICT STATE PARK COMMISSION, BOX 398, SARATOGA SPRINGS 12866; (518) 584-8520

Cherry Plain Area, Stephentown 12168; (518) 733-5400.
Grafton Lakes, Grafton 12082; (518) 279-9697.
*John Boyd Thacher, Altamont 12009; (518) 872-1237.
Moreau Lake, Glens Falls 12801; (518) 793-0511.
Thompson's Lake, Altamont 12009; (518) 872-1674.
Toe Path Mountain, Middleburgh 12122; (518) 827-4711.

CENTRAL NEW YORK STATE PARKS COMMISSION, CLARK RESERVATION, JAMESVILLE 13078; (315) 469-6911.

Battle Island, Fulton 13069; (315) 593-1935.
Bowman Lake, Oxford 13830; (607) 334-2718.
*Chenango Valley, Chenango Forks 13746; (607) 648-5251.
Chittenango Falls, Cazenovia 13035; (315) 655-9620.
Clark Reservation, Syracuse 13200; (315) 492-1590.
Delta Lake, Rome 13440; (315) 337-4670.
Gilbert Lake, New Lisbon 13415; (607) 432-2114.
Glimmerglass, Springfield Center 13468; (607) 547-8662
Green Lakes, Fayetteville 13066; (315) 637-6111.
Pixley Falls, Boonville 13309; (315) 942-4713.
*Selkirk Shores, Pulaski 13142; (315) 298-5737.
*Verona Beach, Verona Beach 13162; (315) 762-4463.

FINGER LAKES STATE PARK COMMISSION, TAUGHANNOCK FALLS STATE PARK, R.D. 3, TRUMANSBURG 04886; (607) 387-7041

*Buttermilk Falls, Ithaca 14850; (607) 273-5761.
*Cayuga Lake, Seneca Falls 13148; (315) 568-5163.
 Chimney Bluffs, Wolcott 14590; (315) 594-8251.
 Fair Haven Beach, Fair Haven 13064; (315) 947-5205.
 Fillmore Glen, Moravia 13118; (315) 497-0130.
 Harriet Hollister Spencer Recreation Area, Tabors Corners; (716) 987-8111.
 Keuka Lake, Penn Yan 14527; (315) 536-3666.
*Long Point, Aurora 13026; (315) 497-0130.
 Newtown Battlefield Reservation, Elmira 4901; (607) 732-1096.
*Robert H. Treman, Ithaca 14850; (607) 273-3440.
 Sampson, Ovid 14521; (315) 6392.
 Seneca Lake, Geneva 14456; (315) 789-2331.
 Stony Brook, Dansville 14437; (716) 987-8111.
*Taughannock Falls, Trumansburg 04886; (607) 387-6739.
 Watkins Glen, Watkins Glen 14891; (607) 535-4511.
*Whitney Point Reservoir Recreation Area, Whitney Point 13862.

GENESEE STATE PARK COMMISSION, CASTILE 14427; (716) 493-2611

*Braddock Bay, Manitou Beach; (716) 964-2462.
 Darien Lakes, Darien Center 14040; (716) 493-2611.
 Hamlin Beach, Hamlin 14464; (716) 964-2462.
 Lakeside Beach, Albion 14411; (716) 964-2462.
*Letchworth, Mount Morris 14510; (716) 493-2611.
 Silver Lake, Silver Springs 14550; (716) 493-2611.

LONG ISLAND STATE PARK COMMISSION, BELMONT LAKE STATE PARK, BABYLON 11702; (516) 669-1000

*Bayard Cutting Arboretum, Islip 11751; (516) 581-1002.
 Belmont Lake, Babylon 11702; (516) 667-5055.
 Bethpage, Bethpage 11714; (516) 249-0700.
*Captree, Bay Shore 11706; (516) 669-0449.
*Caumsett, Lloyd Neck, Huntington 11743.
 Connetquot River, Oakdale 11769.
 Hecksher, East Islip 11730; (516) 581-2100.
 Hempstead Lake, Hempstead 11550; (516) 766-1029.
 Hither Hills, Montauk 11954; (516) 668-2461.
*Jones Beach, Wantagh 11793; (516) 785-1600.
*Montauk Point, Montauk 11954; (516) 668-2461.
*Nissequogue River, Smithtown 11787.

*Orient Beach, Orient 11957; (516) 323-2440.
*Planting Fields Arboretum, Oyster Bay 11771; (516) 922-9200.
*Robert Moses, Fire Island; (516) 669-0449.
 Sunken Meadow, Kings Park 11754; (516) 269-4333.
 Valley Stream, Valley Stream 11580; (516) 825-4128.
 Wildwood, Wading River 11792; (516) 929-4314.

NIAGARA FRONTIER STATE PARK COMMISSION, PROSPECT PARK, NIAGARA FALLS 14303; (716) 285-8251

 Beaver Island, Grand Island 14072; (716) 773-3271.
 Big Six Mile Creek Marina, Grand Island 14072; (716) 773-3270.
 Buckhorn Island, Grand Island 14072; (716) 773-7600.
 Devils Hole, Niagara Falls 14300; (716) 285-8251.
 Evangola, Angola 14006; (716) 549-1802.
 Fort Niagara, Youngstown; (716) 745-7273.
 Four Mile Creek, Youngstown; (716) 745-7273.
 Golden Hill, Barker 14012; (716) 795-3885.
 Joseph Davis, Lewiston 14092; (716) 754-4596.
 Niagara Reservation, Niagara Falls 14300; (716) 285-8251.
 Reservoir, Niagara Falls 14300; (716) 285-8251.
 Whirlpool, Niagara Falls 14300; (716) 285-8251.
 Wilson-Tuscarora, Wilson 14172; (716) 751-6231.

PALISADES INTERSTATE PARK COMMISSION, BEAR MOUNTAIN STATE PARK, BEAR MOUNTAIN 10911; (914) 786-2701

*Bear Mountain, Bear Mountain 10911; (914) 786-2701.
*Harriman, Willow Grove; (914) 786-2701.
*High Tor, Mount Ivy; (914) 786-2701.
 Nyack Beach, Nyack 10960; (914) 786-2701.
 Palisades State Park-New Jersey, Alpine, New Jersey; (201) 268-1360.
*Rockland Lake, Congers 10920; (914) 786-2701.
*Stony Point Reservation, Stony Point 10980; (914) 786-2701.
*Tallman Mountain, Sparkill 10976; (914) 786-2701.

SARATOGA SPRINGS COMMISSION, ADMINISTRATION BUILDING, SARATOGA SPRINGS 12866; (518) 584-2000

 Saratoga Spa, Saratoga Springs 12866; (518) 584-2000.

TACONIC STATE PARK COMMISSION, STAATSBURG 12580; (914) 889-4100

*Clarence Fahnstock Memorial, Cold Spring 10516; (914) 225-7207.
 Clermont, Tivoli 12583; (518) 537-4240.

Hudson Highlands, Beacon 12508; (914) 225-7207.

James Baird, Billings 12510; (914) 452-1489.

Lake Taghkanic, Ancram 12502; (518) 851-3631.

Margaret Lewis Norrie, Hyde Park 12538; (914) 889-4527.

Mohansic, Yorktown Heights 10598; (914) 245-4434.

Ogden and Ruth Livingston Mills Memorial, Staatsburg 12580; (914) 889-4646.

Taconic/Rudd Pond Area, Millerton 12546; (914) 789-3059.

Taconic/Copake Falls Area, Copake Falls 12517; (518) 329-3993.

Canvasback

THOUSAND ISLANDS STATE PARK COMMISSION, KEEWAYDIN STATE PARK, ALEXANDRIA BAY 13607; (315) 482-2593

Ausable Point, Valcour; (315) 561-7080.
Burnham Point, Cape Vincent 13618; (315) 654-2522.
Canoe-Picnic Point, Grindstone Island, Clayton 13624; (315) 482-2593.
Cedar Island, Chippewa Bay 13623; (315) 482-2593.
Cedar Point, Clayton 13624; (315) 654-2522.
Coles Creek, Waddington 13694; (315) 388-5336.
Cumberland Bay, Plattsburgh 12901; (315) 583-5240.
DeWolf Point, Alexandria Bay 13607; (315) 482-9144.
Eel Weir, Ogdensburg 13669; (315) 393-1138.
Grass Point, Fishers Landing 13641; (315) 686-5093.
Higley Flow, Colton 13625; (315) 265-7255.
Jacques Cartier, Morristown 13664; (315) 375-8980.
Kewaydin, Alexandria Bay 13607; (315) 482-2625.
*Kring Point, Chippewa Bay 13623; (315) 482-2444.
Long Point, Three Mile Bay 13693; (315) 649-5258.
Macomb Reservation, Schuyler Falls 12985; (518) 643-9952.
Mary Island, Chippewa Bay 13623; (315) 482-2593.
Robert Moses, Massena 13662; (315) 769-8663.
St. Lawrence, Morristown 13664; (315) 393-1977.
Southwick Beach, Woodville 13698; (315) 846-5338.
Valcour Island, Valcour; (518) 563-0820.
Waterson Point, Alexandria Bay 13607; (315) 482-9144.
Wellesley Island, Alexandria Bay 13607; (315) 482-9652.
Westcott Beach, Sackets Harbor 13685; (315) 938-5080.
Whetstone Gulf, Lowville 13367; (315) 376-6630.

In addition to the above-mentioned parks, there are many forest recreation areas and state campgrounds located mainly in the Catskills and Adirondacks. For information about these areas, contact the Department of Environmental Conservation, Albany 12201.

PENNSYLVANIA

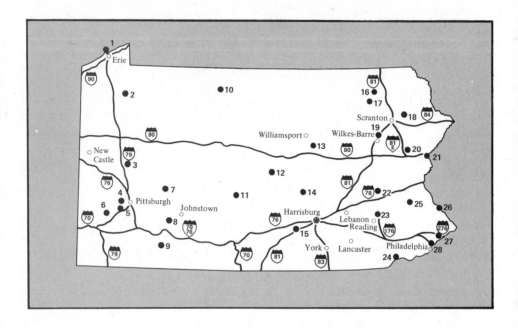

1. Presque Isle State Park
2. Erie NWR
3. Jennings Nature Reserve
4. Todd Sanctuary
5. Schenley Park
6. Wildflower Reserve
7. Lodge Nature Trail
8. Powdermill Nature Reserve
9. Bear Run Nature Reserve
10. Allegheny National Forest
11. Stone Valley Recreation Area
12. Penns Valley Area Land Resource Laboratory
13. Montour Preserve
14. Middle Creek
15. F. J. Reineman Wildlife Sanctuary
16. Salt Springs State Park
17. Woodburne Forest and Wildlife Sanctuary
18. Lacawac Sanctuary
19. Kirby Park Environmental Education Center

20. Tannersville-Cranberry Bog
21. Delaware Water Gap
22. Hawk Mountain Sanctuary
23. Reading Nature Museum
24. Longwood Gardens
25. Lake Towhee Outdoor Laboratory
26. Bowmans Hill State Wildflower Preserve
27. { Silver Lake Outdoor Education Center
Audubon Wildlife Sanctuary
Briar Bush NC
Churchville Outdoor Education Center
Conservatory Environmental Education Center
Crosswicks NC
28. { Curtis Arboretum
Four Mills Nature Reserve
John Tyler Arboretum
Morris Arboretum
Penllyn Natural Area
Schuylkill Valley NC
Tinicum National Environmental Center

Pennsylvania is a mountainous state: the Bald Eagle Mountains, the Jacks Mountains, the Tuscarora Mountains, the Blue Mountains, and of course the Allegheny Mountains. The Appalachian Trail roughly parallels the Blue Mountains from Harrisburg to Stroudsburg. Pennsylvania also has an extensive network of creeks, rivers, and small mountain streams. Near Philadelphia, on the Delaware River, are freshwater marshes, now being preserved through the Tinicum National Environmental Center. Diagonally opposite, in Erie (on Lake Erie) is Presque Isle State Park — an area of lagoons, marshes, and sand dunes. Many waterbirds breed at Presque Isle. However, the dominant ornithological event in the state is the fantastic hawk migration. At Hawk Mountain Sanctuary along the Kittatinny Ridge (in the eastern part of the state) the birdwatcher can see literally thousands of hawks in a single day.

The Pennsylvania Game Commission (P. O. Box 1567, Harrisburg 17120) maintains several thousand acres as wildlife management areas. Although the primary purpose of these areas is to serve the hunter and fisherman, many of them also prove to be good birdwatching places. Most notable is *Middle Creek* (located in Middle Creek near Middleburg), where 229 species of birds (108 nesting) have been recorded, including: Horned Grebe, Barnacle Goose (rare), Goshawk, Bald Eagle, Glossy Ibis, Northern Phalarope (rare), Philadelphia Vireo, Blue-winged Warbler, Mourning Warbler, Connecticut Warbler, Scarlet Tanager, and Common Redpoll. For additional information regarding these management areas — including traveling directions; restrictions to visiting, if any; and birdlists — contact the Game Commission at the address above.

In addition to the places described in the following pages, several large areas in Pennsylvania can be very rewarding for the birdwatcher. Among them are: the Allegheny River area around Sharpsburg; the Beaver Run Reservoir near Slickville; Donegal Lake near Donegal, Fox Chapel, just outside of Pittsburgh; Harrison Hills County Park, also outside of Pittsburgh; Lake Oneida near Butler; North Park, 15 miles from Pittsburgh (yearly average of 150 species); the area around Geneva; the Shenango Reservoir outside of Mercer; Stoughton Lake and Boswell Marsh in Somerset County near Jenners; and the Conejohela Flats near Columbia.

The Audubon Society of Western Pennsylvania publishes a helpful guide entitled: *Where to Find Birds in Western Pennsylvania*. It describes these areas in greater detail. The book can be obtained by writing to the society at: 24 Woodland Road, Sewickley 15143. For up-to-date information about birds and birding in the Philadelphia area, call the *Delaware Valley Birding Hotline* — (215) 236-2473.

Allegheny National Forest, Warren 16365. The Forest is located in northwestern Pennsylvania near Warren and Bradford. To reach Allegheny Forest from Warren, take SR 59 east and/or US 6 south; from Bradford, take US 219 south. A wide range of recreational activities is offered at Allegheny including camping, swimming, fishing, and hiking.

Allegheny National Forest encompasses 495,000 acres of virgin timber, 260 miles of trout streams, 85 miles of rivers, 32 lakes, and the Allegheny Reservoir. This all combines to provide food and shelter for a wide variety of wildlife, including many species of birds. There are 132 breeding birds in Allegheny Forest as well as 63 migrants and winter visitors. Among the breeding species are: Wood Duck, Marsh Hawk, Turkey, Least Bittern, Great Horned Owl, Yellow-bellied Sapsucker, Tree Swallow, Tufted Titmouse, White-breasted Nuthatch, Winter Wren, Black-throated Blue Warbler, Blackburnian Warbler, Eastern Meadowlark, and Chipping Sparrow. Migrants include: Horned Grebe, Ruddy Duck, Olive-sided Flycatcher, Bay-breasted Warbler, and Lincoln's Sparrow; winter visitors include: Common Goldeneye, Common Redpoll, Lapland Longspur, and Snow Bunting. Checklist available.

Delaware Water Gap National Recreation Area. For information, see entry in New Jersey chapter (page 60).

Erie National Wildlife Refuge, R. D. 2, Box 191, Guys Mills 16327; (814) 789-3585. The refuge is located about 14 miles east of Meadville in northwestern Pennsylvania. To reach the refuge from Meadville, take SR 27 east, then turn north on SR 198, and proceed to refuge headquarters. Camping is not permitted at the refuge; however facilities are available at nearby state parks and forests.

Erie NWR was established in 1959, and now totals over 5000 acres of diversified habitat — from ponds to upland forests. Facilities include the Beaver Run Nature Trail, Pool 9 Overlook, and a network of gravel roads which are open to public travel. Erie is a haven for migratory birds. There have been 223 species of birds (77 nesting) sighted at Erie. Among them are: Common Loon, Whistling Swan, Pintail, Hooded Merganser, Osprey, Ring-necked Pheasant, Black-crowned Night Heron, Least Sandpiper, American Woodcock, Black Tern, Mourning Dove, Screech Owl, Ruby-throated Hummingbird, Great Crested Flycatcher, Purple Martin, Short- and Long-billed Marsh Wrens, Veery, Cedar Waxwing, Blue-winged Warbler, Yellow Warbler, Palm Warbler, Northern Waterthrush, American Redstart, Bobolink, Savannah Sparrow, and Vesper Sparrow. Checklist available.

Hawk Mountain Sanctuary, Route 2, Kempton 19529; (215) 756-3431. To reach the sanctuary from Hamburg, take SR 61 north for about 4 miles to SR 895, turn north (right) on SR 895, and proceed to the sanctuary entrance. Camping facilities are available at nearby Hickory Run State Park.

Hawk Mountain — the 2110-acre sanctuary on a spur of the Kittatinny Ridge — was the first sanctuary for raptors. Until the sanctuary was established in 1934, hundreds of hawks were slaughtered daily as they migrated along the thermals to their wintering grounds. Now, thanks to pioneers like Maurice Bronn and the Emergency Conservation Committee of New York City, these diurnal birds of prey are protected.

The fall migration of the thousands of hawks which pass over this spot is a never-to-be-forgotten thrill for the birdwatcher. Fourteen kinds of hawks are regularly seen at Hawk Mountain, including Ospreys, Bald Eagles, Sharp-shinned Hawks, and Cooper's Hawks. About half the number of passing hawks are Broad-winged Hawks — one year, over 11,000 Broad-winged Hawks were counted. The birdwatcher must bear in mind that all flights are subject to weather conditions in New England. However, the Broad-winged Hawks start as early as the third week in August. Peak migrations are usually in September and early October. According to the sanctuary's records, "big days" can be anywhere between the 11 and 24 of September — depending on the wind.

For further information about Hawk Mountain Sanctuary — its fascinating history and its equally fascinating present — the reader is referred to Maurice Broun's *Hawks Aloft: The Story of Hawk Mountain* and Michael Harwood's *The View from Hawk Mountain.*

Powdermill Nature Reserve, Carnegie Museum, Rector 15677; (215) 593-2221; also Caverley Lodge, Ligonier 15658; (215) 593-7821. The reserve is owned and operated by the Carnegie Museum as a research station. To reach the reserve from Ligonier, take US 30 east for 2 miles, then turn south (right) on SR 381; continue for 6 miles. There is a parking lot next to the headquarters building. A trailside museum is open weekends from April through October. The reserve is located near an experimental state agricultural farm.

Powdermill Reserve totals 1800 acres of mixed woodlands, old fields, meadowlands, small ponds, and a cattail marsh. There have been over 200 species of birds observed here. They include: Green Heron, Broad-winged Hawk, American Woodcock, Barred Owl, Pileated Woodpecker, Acadian Flycatcher, Carolina Wren, Wood Thrush, Blue-gray Gnatcatcher, Solitary Vireo, Northern Parula, Cerulean Warbler, Mourning Warbler, Hooded Warbler, Scarlet Tanager, and American Goldfinch.

NATURE CENTERS

In addition to the places described in greater detail in the previous pages, there are many privately or state-owned sanctuaries, preserves, and nature centers located throughout Pennsylvania. They are all good birdwatching places. At many of them a variety of educational and interpretive programs is offered. These centers are briefly discussed below.

Audubon Wildlife Sanctuary, Mill Grove, Audubon; (215) 666-5593. The sanctuary is located in Audubon, near Valley Forge Historical Park. Past the park, turn left on Audubon Road to the main entrance on Pawling Road. There is a museum with Audubon memorabilia; trails are maintained. A variety of interpretive programs is offered. The 120-acre sanctuary is open all year. Among the birds seen here are: Chimney Swift, Common (Yellow-shafted) Flicker,

Eastern Phoebe, House Wren, Brown Thrasher, Eastern Bluebird, and Northern (Baltimore) Oriole.

Bear Run Nature Reserve, R. D. 1, Box 97, Mill Run 15464; (412) 329-4743. The preserve is operated by the Western Pennsylvania Conservancy. It covers 1500 acres. Guided tours are available. The center is open from 1 March to 15 December, closed on Mondays and holidays.

Briar Bush Nature Center, 1212 Edge Hill Road, Abington 19001. The center is operated by the Township of Abington. It covers 20 acres; guided tours are available by appointment. Trails are maintained. A variety of educational and interpretive programs is offered. The center is open all year.

Bowmans Hill State Wildflower Preserve, Washington Crossing State Park, Washington Crossing 18977; (215) 862-2924. The preserve covers 100 acres. Guided tours are offered; trails, some self-guiding, are maintained. The preserve is open during daylight hours all year; closed on Election Day and other holidays. There have been 144 species of birds seen here. Among them are: Broad-winged Hawk, Hairy Woodpecker, Eastern Wood Pewee, Barn Swallow, Hermit Thrush, Warbling Vireo, and 34 species of warblers.

Churchville Outdoor Education Center, 501 Churchville Lane, Southampton 18966; (215) 357-4005. The center is operated by Bucks County Department of Parks and Recreation and totals 50 acres. Guided and self-guiding tours are available. There have been over 200 species of birds recorded at the center. It is open all year; closed on Mondays, Tuesdays, and major holidays.

Conservancy Environmental Education Center, Ridley Creek State Park, Sycamore Mills Road, Media 19063; (215) 566-9133. The center is operated by Tri-County Conservancy of the Brandywine, Inc. It covers 2500 acres and is open weekdays, closed on school holidays and for the month of August. A variety of educational and interpretive programs is offered at the center.

Crosswicks Nature Center. The center is operated by Wyncote Bird Club, P.O. Box 2, Wyncote 19095; it is owned by the National Audubon Society. This is a 16-acre area. A variety of educational and interpretive programs is offered. Trails are maintained. The center is open all year. It is located at Crosswicks and Delene Roads, Jenkintown.

Curtis Arboretum. The arboretum is located off Church Road, near Wyncote. It is open all year.

F. J. Reineman Wildlife Sanctuary. For information, contact: C. John Ralph, Department of Biology, Dickinson College, Carlisle 17013.

Four Mills Nature Reserve, Morris Road, Ambler 19002; (215) 656-0267. The preserve is operated by Natural Lands Trust, Inc. It covers

50 acres along Wissahickon Creek. Guided tours are available; trails, some self-guiding, are maintained. The preserve is open all year; the museum is open by appointment.

Jennings Nature Reserve, R. D. #1, Box 281, Slippery Rock 16057; (412) 794-6011. The preserve is operated by Slippery Rock State College. It covers 383 acres. Guided tours are available; trails are maintained. A variety of educational and interpretive programs is offered. The center is open every day from February to December; in December and January it is open on weekends only.

John J. Tyler Arboretum, 515 Painter Road, Lima 19060; (215) 566-5431. The arboretum covers 711 acres. Guided tours are offered; self-guiding trails are maintained. The arboretum is open all year. Over 150 species of birds (80 nesting) have been observed here. Among them are: Green Heron, Wood Duck, Great Horned Owl, Eastern Bluebird, Winter Wren, Hermit Thrush, Worm-eating Warbler, Cerulean Warbler, and Purple Finch.

Kirby Park Environmental Education Center and Trailwood Nature Environmental Education Center. The centers are operated by the city of Wilkes-Barre. For further information, contact: Executive Director, Recreation Board of the City of Wilkes-Barre, 701 South Main Street, Wilkes-Barre 18702.

Lake Towhee Outdoor Laboratory, Saw Mill Road, Applebachsville. The center is operated by Bucks County Department of Parks and Recreation. It covers 507 acres. Guided tours are available by appointment. Trails, some self-guiding, are maintained. A variety of educational and interpretive programs is offered. The center is open all year.

Lodge Nature Trail, University Lodge, Indiana University of Pennsylvania, Indiana 15701; (412) 465-8150. The center is operated by the University's Student Cooperative Association. It covers 300 acres. Guided tours are available. Trails, some self-guiding, are maintained. The center is open all year.

Longwood Gardens, Kennett Square 19348; (215) 388-6741. The gardens are located west of Philadelphia on US 1, in Kennett Square. There are extensive formal gardens and conservatories. They are open every day, 9-6; an admission fee is charged. There have been nearly 200 species of birds identified here; among them are: Canada Goose, Turkey Vulture, American Kestrel (Sparrow Hawk), Killdeer, Downy Woodpecker, Mockingbird, Eastern Bluebird, Golden-crowned Kinglet, Cape May Warbler, Northern (Baltimore) Oriole, Scarlet Tanager, Indigo Bunting, and Song Sparrow.

Montour Preserve, R. D. 1, Turbotville 17772; (717) 437-3131. The preserve is operated by the Pennsylvania Power and Light Company. It covers 1000 acres. Guided tours are available; trails, some self-guiding, are maintained. The preserve is open all year.

Morris Arboretum, (215) 242-3399. The arboretum is located on Stenton Avenue, off Germantown Avenue, near the College of Chestnut Hill (in Philadelphia). It is open all year.

Penllyn Natural Area, Wissahickon Valley Watershed Association, 473 Bethlehem Pike, Fort Washington 19034; (215) 646-8866. The center covers 18 acres and is open all year. Trails are maintained.

Penns Valley Area Land Resource Laboratory, R.D. 2, Spring Mills 16875; (814) 422-8854. The laboratory covers 30 acres. It is open by appointment only.

Reading Nature Museum and Trails, c/o Bureau of Recreation, City Hall, Reading 19601; (215) 373-5111; ext. 201. The center covers 30 acres next to 1700 acres of city-owned land. Guided tours are offered; trails are maintained. A variety of educational and interpretive programs is offered. The center is open every day from June through September. Among the 106 species of birds seen here are: Broad-winged Hawk, Green Heron, Screech Owl, Ruby-throated Hummingbird, Eastern Phoebe, White-breasted Nuthatch, and Blue-winged Warbler.

Schenley Park Nature Museum, Schenley Park, Pittsburgh 15201; (412) 681-2272. The museum is operated by the Pittsburgh Department of Parks and Recreation. The park covers 440 acres and is open all year. Trails are maintained.

Schuylkill Valley Nature Center, Hagy's Mill Road, Philadelphia 19128; (215) 482-7300. The center covers 360 acres of woods, fields, and ponds. Guided tours and a variety of educational and interpretive programs are offered. Headquarters are staffed; there is a library. Trails are maintained. The center is open all year; closed on holidays.

Silver Lake Outdoor Education Center, Bath Road, Bristol 19007; (215) 785-1177. The center is operated by Bucks County Department of Parks and Recreation. It covers 45 acres. Guided and self-guiding tours are available. The center is open all year; closed on Mondays, Tuesdays and major holidays.

Stone Valley Recreation Area, R.D. #1, Petersburg 16669; (814) 238-5872. The area is operated by Pennsylvania State University. It covers 600 acres and is open all year.

Tinicum National Environmental Center, 744 Darby Avenue, Prospect Park 19076. Contact: Kenneth Chitwood, Suite 104, Scott Plaza 2, Philadelphia 19113; (215) 521-0662 for information. The center is operated by the federal government; it is located just outside Philadelphia. To reach the center from the airport area, take Island Avenue northwest to Lindbergh Boulevard, turn left and continue to the entrance on 86 Street. Tinicum was established to preserve freshwater tidal marsh. It presently covers 255 acres (acquisition is not yet complete) of woods, fields, and marshes. There is an observation platform; a naturalist is on staff. Look for: Greater Scaup, Ruddy Duck, Blue-winged Teal, Rough-legged Hawk, Ruddy Turnstone, Virginia Rail, Common Gallinule, and Yellow Warbler.

Todd Sanctuary. The sanctuary is operated by the Audubon Society of Western Pennsylvania. To reach the sanctuary (which is located north of Pittsburgh), take SR 28 to Freeport, turn left (northwest) on SR 356, continue for about 2 miles, and watch for signs. The sanctuary totals 160 acres and is open to the public in the summer only. For further information, contact the Audubon Society of Western Pennsylvania, 24 Woodland Road, Sewickley 15143. Among the nesting species are Ruffed Grouse, Acadian Flycatcher, Chestnut-sided Warbler, Canada Warbler, and Louisiana Waterthrush.

Wildflower Reserve, Box 723, Clinton 15126; (412) 899-2767. The preserve is operated by the Western Pennsylvania Conservancy. It totals 300 acres. Guided tours are offered. The center is open all year, closed on Mondays.

NATURE CONSERVANCY PRESERVES

The following preserves are protected and/or managed by the Northeastern Pennsylvania Chapter of The Nature Conservancy, c/o Lacawac Sanctuary, R.D. 1, Lake Ariel 18436.

Lacawac Sanctuary, R.D. 1, Lake Ariel 18436; (717) 689-2814. The sanctuary is located 3 miles south of Lakeville. The most interesting feature of this 400-acre sanctuary is its lake — the southernmost glacial lake in the United States. Floating bog mats and a hardwood swamp adjoin the lake. Lacawac has a laboratory and is staffed by a resident naturalist. It is open to the public by appointment. Interpretive walks are schedules for Saturday mornings at 10 during July and August.

Salt Springs State Park, at Franklin Forks. To reach the park, take SR 29 north from Montrose for about 8 miles. This 408-acre park has an unusual salt spring, a 10-acre stand of hemlock, and a narrow gorge with small waterfalls. Salt Springs is maintained by the state.

Tannersville-Cranberry Bog. The preserve is located near Tannersville. It covers 120 acres and has been closed for an indefinite period due to abuse and over use.

Woodbourne Forest and Wildlife Sanctuary. The sanctuary is located 2 miles south of Montrose. This 555-acre preserve has a remarkable stand of virgin hemlock. There are also 2 ponds and a northern hardwood forest. The sanctuary is open to the public and guided tours are given by the resident naturalist. Among the 54 species of breeding birds found here are: Cooper's Hawk, Red-tailed Hawk, Red-shouldered Hawk, Great Horned Owl, and Barred Owl. Also look for migrating warblers in spring and fall.

STATE PARKS AND FORESTS

Pennsylvania's state park and forest system is unusually extensive and covers most of the state. Most parks offer camping in addition to a variety of recreational activities. Some parks have nature and/or environmental education centers. Nearly all have nature/hiking trails. Those parks that are also well-known spots for birdwatching are marked with an asterisk (*). Following the listing of state parks is a listing of state forests, many of which incorporate natural areas. These areas have been set aside and are of special scenic, historic, geologic, or ecological value. No development will be permitted on those lands. Primitive camping (only) is permitted in the natural areas.

STATE PARKS

Allegheny River, R.D. 1, Oil City 16301; (814) 676-5915; under development.
Archbald Pothole, c/o Lackawanna, see below; day use only.
Bald Eagle, R.D. Hoawar 16841; (814) 625-2775.
*Beltzville, Box 252, R.D. 3, Lehighton 18235; (215) 377-3170; day use only.
Bendigo, Box A, Johnsonburg 15845; (814) 965-2666; day use only.
Big Pocono, c/o Hickory Run, see below; day use only.
Big Spring, c/o Col. Denning, see below; day use only.
Black Moshannon, Box 104, R.D. 1, Phillipsburg 16866; (814) 342-1101.
Blue Knob, R.D. 1, Imler 16655; (814) 276-3576.
*Bucktail, Box 1A, R.D. 1, Emporium 15834; (814) 483-3365; state natural area.
*Caledonia, R.D. 2, Fayetteville 17222; (717) 352-2161.
*Chapman, in Allegheny National Forest.
Clear Creek, Route 1, Sigel 15860; (814) 752-2368.
*Codorus, R.D. 3, Hanover 17331; (717) 637-2816; day use only.
Colonel Denning, R.D. 3, Newville 17241; (717) 776-5272.
Colton Point, c/o Leonard Harrison, see below.
*Cook Forest, Cooksburg 16217 (814) 744-8407.
Cowans Gap, Fort Loudon 17224; (717) 485-3948.
Crooked Creek, R.D. 3, Ford City 16226; (412) 763-3161.
Curwensville, Box 106A, R.D. 1, Curwensville 16833; (814) 236-1184; day use only.
Denton Hill, Box 407, Coudersport 16915; (814) 435-6372; day use only.
Elk, c/o Bendigo, see above; day use only.
Frances Slocum, R.D. 3, Wyoming 18644; (717) 696-3607; day use only.
French Creek, R.D. 1, Elverson 19520; (215) 582-8125.

George W. Childs, Dingmans Ferry 18328; (717) 828-3913; day use only.

Gifford Pinchot, R.D. 1, Lewisberry 17339; (717) 432-5011.

Gouldsboro, c/o Tobyhanna, see below; day use only.

*Greenwood Furnace, R.D. 2, Huntington 16652; (814) 667-3808.

Hickory Run, R.D. 1, White Haven 18661; (717) 443-9991.

Hillman, c/o Raccoon Creek, see below.

Hills Creek, R.D. 1, Crooked Creek 16919; (717) 724-4246.

Hyner Run, R.D. 1, Renovo 17764; (717) 923-0257; day use only.

Jacobsburg, 734 Jacobsburg Road, Nazareth 18064; (215) 759-7616; under development.

Kettle Creek, Star Route, Renovo 17764; (717) 923-9925.

Keystone, Box 101, R.D. 2, Derry 15627; (412) 668-2939.

Kinzua Bridge, c/o Bendigo, see above; day use only.

Kooser, R.D. 6, Somerset 15501; (814) 445-8673.

Lackawanna, R.D. 1, Dalton 18419; (717) 945-3239; day use only.

*Laurel Hill, R.D. 4, Somerset 15501; (814) 445-7725.

*Laurel Mountain, Box 527, Ligonier 15658; (412) 238-4317; day use only.

Laurel Ridge, R.D. 3, Rockwood 15557; (412) 455-3744.

Leonard Harrison, R.D. 6, Wellsboro 16901; (717) 724-3061.

*Linn Run, Box 87, Rector 16901; (412) 238-6895; day use only.

Little Buffalo, Box 256, R.D. 2, Newport 17074; (717) 567-9255; day use only.

Little Pine, Waterville 17776; (717) 847-3200.

Locust Lake, c/o Tuscarora, see below.

Lyman Run, c/o Denton Hill, see above.

*Marsh Creek, Lyndell Raod, Downington 19335; (215) 458-8515.

Maurice K. Goddard, R.D. 3, Sandy Lake 16145; (412) 253-4833; day use only.

*McConnells Mill, R.D. 1, Portersville 16057; (412) 368-8091; day use only.

Memorial Lake, Annville 17003; (717) 271-2601, ext. 2806; day use only.

Milton, c/o Shikellamy Marina, see below; day use only.

Mont Alto, c/o Caledonia, see above; day use only.

*Moraine, R.D. 1, Portersville 16057; (412) 368-8811; day use only.

Neshaminy, 201 Dunks Ferry Road, Cornwells Heights 19020; (215) 639-6822; day use only.

Nockamixon, R.D. 3, Quakertown 18951; (215) 257-3646; day use only.

*Nolde Forest, Box 392, R.D. 1, Shillington, Reading 19067; (215) 775-1411; day use only; environmental education center.

*Ohiopyle, R.D. 1, Ohiopyle 15470; (412) 329-4707.

Oil Creek, c/o Allegheny River, see above; under development.

Ole Bull, R.D. 1, Cross Fork 17729; (814) 435-2169.

Parker Dam, Penfield 15849; (814) 765-5082.

Pine Grove Furnace, R.D. 2, Gardners 17324; (717) 486-7174.

Poe Valley, c/o Reeds Gap, see below.

*Presque Isle, Box 1115, Erie 16512; (814) 833-0741; day use only.

Prince Gallitzin, Patton 16668; (814) 674-3691.

Promised Land, R.D. 1, Greentown 18426; (717) 676-3428.

Prompton, c/o Lackawanna, see above; day use only.

*Pymatunig, Box 425, Jamestown 16134; (412) 932-3141.

*Raccoon Creek, R.D. 1, Hookstown 15050; (412) 763-3161.

Ralph Stover, Point Pleasant 18950; (215) 297-5090; day use only.

Ravensburg, c/o R. B. Winter, see below; day use only.

Raymond B. Winter, R.D. 2, Mifflinburg 17844; (717) 966-1455.

Reeds Gap, R.D. 1, Milroy 17063; (717) 667-3622; day use only.

Ricketts Glen, R.D. 2, Benton 17814; (717) 477-5675.

*Ridley Creek, Route 36, Sycamore Mills Road, Media 19063; (215) 566-4800; day use only.

Roosevelt, Upper Black Eddy 18972; (215) 982-5560; day use only.

*Ryerston Station, R.D. 1, Wind Ridge 15380; (412) 428-4254.

Samuel S. Lewis, R.D. 2, Hellam Branch, York 17406; (717) 252-1134; day use only.

S. B. Elliott, c/o Parker Dam, see above.

Shawnee, Schellsburg 15559; (814) 733-4218.

Shikellamy, c/o Shikellamy Marina, Island Blvd., Sunbury 17801; (717) 286-7880; day use only.

Sinnemahonig, R.D. 1, Austin 16721; (814) 647-8945.

Sizerville, Box 238A, R.D. 1, Emporium 15834; (814) 486-5605.

Snyder-Middleswarth, c/o Reeds Gap, see above; day use only.

Susquehanna, c/o Shikellamy Marina, see above; day use only.

*Susquehannock, c/o French Creek, see above; day use only.

Tobyhanna, Tobyhanna 18466; (717) 894-8671.

Trough Creek, Box 565, R.D. 1, James Creek 16657; (814) 658-3847.

Tuscarora, R.D. 1, Barnesville 18214; (717) 467-2404; day use only.

Tyler, Newtown 18940; (215) 968-2021; day use only.

Warrior's Path, Saxton 16678; (814) 635-2680; day use only.

*Whipple Dam, c/o Greenwood Furnace, see above; day use only.

Worlds End, Forksville 18616; (717) 924-3287.

*Yellow Creek, R.D. 1, Penn Run 15765; (412) 479-2161; day use only.

STATE FORESTS AND NATURAL AREAS

Bald Eagle State Forest, near Lock Haven: *Joyce Kilmer* (77 acres); *The Hook* (5119 acres); *Mt. Logan* (600 acres); *Rosecrans Bog* (140 acres); *Snyder-Middleswarth* (500 acres); and *Tall Timbers* (1000 acres).

Buchanan State Forest, near Bedford: *Sweet Rood* (1403 acres) and *Pine Ridge* (568 acres).

Delaware State Forest, near Blooming Grove: *Pine Lake* (67 acres); *Bruce Lake* (2845 acres); *Buckhorn* (471 acres); *Stillwater* (1931 acres); and *Pennel Run* (936 acres).

Elk State Forest, near Driftwood: *Lower Jerry Run* (32 acres); *Wycoff Run* (1245 acres); *Pine Tree Trail* (200 acres); *Bucktail* (15,682 acres); and *Johnson Run* (200 acres).

Forbes State Forest, near Myersdale: *Mt. Davis* (581 acres) and *Roaring Run* (3070 acres).

Gallitzin State Forest, near Johnstown: *Dr. Charles F. Lewis* (384 acres).

Michaux State Forest, near Waynesboro: *Carbaugh Run* (848 acres) and *Meeting of the Pines* (603 acres).

Moshannon State Forest, near Medix Run: *Marion Brooks* (917 acres).

Rothrock State Forest, near State College: *Bear Meadows* (833 acres); *Alan Seeger* (118 acres); *Big Flat Laurel* (142 acres); *Detweiler Run* (185 acres); and *Little Juanita* (624 acres).

Sproul State Forest, near Renovo: *East Branch Swamp* (186 acres); *Tamarack Swamp* (86 acres); and *Cranberry Swamp* (144 acres).

Susquehannock State Forest, near Beech Creek: *Beech Bottom Hemlocks* (1500 acres).

Tiadaghton State Forest, near Jersey Mills: *Bark Cabin* (73 acres); *Miller Run* (4000 acres); and *Algerine Swamp* (84 acres).

Tioga State Forest, near Ansonia: *Black Ash Swamp* (308 acres); *Pine Creek Gorge* (5720 acres); and *Reynolds Spring* (1302 acres).

Tuscarora State Forest, near Waterloo: *Laurel Run* (1270 acres); *Box Huckleberry* (10 acres); and *The Hemlocks* (131 acres).

Wyoming State Forest, near Hillsgrove: *Kettle Creek Gorge* (774 acres) and *High Knob* (32 acres).

In addition, there are several thousand acres of "wild areas" that have also been set aside. These, too, are located in state forests. For a complete list of them, write: Pennsylvania Department of Environmental Resources, Box 1467, Harrisburg 17120.

RHODE ISLAND

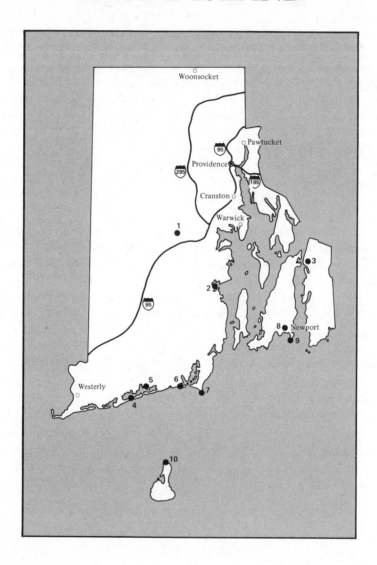

1. George Parker Woodland
2. Davis Memorial Wildlife Refuge
3. Emilie Ruecker Wildlife Refuge
4. Ninigret NWR
5. Kimball Wildlife Refuge
6. Moonstone Waterfowl Refuge
   Trustom Pond NWR

7. Galilee Bird Sanctuary
8. Norman Bird Sanctuary
9. Sachuest Point NWR
10. Block Island NWR

Although Rhode island is the smallest state in the union, it is a big state for birdwatching. The Audubon Society's checklist of Rhode Island birds (1900-1965) lists 295 species plus accidentals. Probably the single most rewarding time and place to go birdwatching in Rhode Island is early October at Block Island. The Audubon Society of Rhode Island sponsors an annual trip there, usually the first weekend in October. Recent bird counts during this trip have recorded 150 species or more.

Shearwaters, alcids, petrels, phalaropes, and jaegers can be seen off the southern coast of Rhode Island. Much of the interior of the state remains wooded. There are swamps, ponds, streams, and old fields. These all combine to provide habitat for a wide variety of landbirds.

There are 13 state management areas totaling 21,400 acres. While these are designed primarily for hunting, birdwatching at these areas can also be productive. There are upland fields and woods, salt marshes, and freshwater wetlands. Two of the best of these areas are *Great Swamp*, just west of Kingston, and *Sapowet Marsh*, which is south of Tiverton. Another fine state-owned birdwatching spot is the *Galilee Bird Sanctuary*, located in the southeastern corner of the state. The sanctuary is off Galilee Road, in Galilee, about 8 miles south of Wakefield via Point Judith Road.

The Audubon Society of Rhode Island is extremely active. They own and/or maintain several sanctuaries throughout the state as well as areas that they call open space areas. These latter areas are mostly woodlands and salt marshes. For further information about birdwatching in Rhode Island, contact the Audubon Society of Rhode Island, 40 Bowen Street, Providence 02903; (401) 521-1670.

Block Island National Wildlife Refuge. Administered by Ninigret NWR. The refuge is located on Block Island in Block Island Sound; access is by boat only. Ferries run from New London (Connecticut) and Newport in the summer. The Point Judith and Providence ferries run all year. Camping is not permitted on the refuge. Each October the Audubon Society of Rhode Island sponsors a 3-day trip to Block Island.

This 30-acre refuge was established in 1973 and is administered under a cooperative agreement with the town of New Shoreham. The refuge is on the northern tip of Block Island, about 10 miles from the coast of Rhode Island. Situated along the Atlantic Flyway, the refuge provides protection and resting places for waterfowl, songbirds, and other migrating birds. Nesting species include Spotted Sandpipers, Piping Plovers, gulls, and terns. The refuge is accessible by boat or on foot from the main part of the island.

Among the many species of birds sighted here are: Red-throated Loon, Gannet, Great and Double-crested Cormorants, Gadwall, Surf Scoter, Black Scoter, Sharp-shinned Hawk, Peregrine Falcon, Clapper Rail, Golden Plover, Black-bellied Plover, Pectoral Sandpiper, White-rumped Sandpiper, Black-billed Cuckoo, Eastern and Western Kingbirds, Willow Flycatcher, White- and

Red-breasted Nuthatches, Hermit Thrush, Long-billed Marsh Wren, Water Pipit, Cedar Waxwing, Red-eyed Vireo, Black-throated Blue Warbler, Bay-breasted Warbler, Mourning Warbler, Wilson's Warbler, Bobolink, Yellow-headed Blackbird, Scarlet Tanager, Rose-breasted Grosbeak, Indigo Bunting, Dickcissel, Evening Grosbeak, Sharp-tailed Sparrow, and Lapland Longspur.

Davis Memorial Wildlife Refuge, Davisville Road, North Kingston. The refuge is owned by the Audubon Society of Rhode Island. To reach Davis Refuge from Wickford, take US 1 north to Quonset Point, then turn northwest (left) on Devils Foot Road (SR 403), which becomes Davisville Road, proceed to refuge entrance (about 2 miles).

Davis borders the Hunt River. It totals 96 acres of mixed woodlands and freshwater wetlands. Canoeing is good on the Hunt River — only boats without motors are permitted. A network of trails throughout the refuge is maintained. Look for herons, ducks, woodpeckers, thrushes, and warblers.

Emilie Ruecker Wildlife Refuge, Seapowet Avenue, Tiverton 02878. The refuge is owned by the Audubon Society of Rhode Island. To reach the refuge from Tiverton, take SR 77 South to Seapowet Avenue, turn west (right), and proceed to the entrance.

This 30-acre refuge is located on the Sakonnet River. There are old fields, mixed woodlands, and both freshwater and saltwater marshes. A network of trails is maintained — through the woods, along the marshes, over the fields. Among the many birds to be seen here are: Osprey, Bobwhite, Ring-necked Pheasant, Great Blue Heron, Little Blue Heron, Black-crowned Night Heron, Snowy Egret, Glossy Ibis, Virginia Rail, American Woodcock, White-eyed Vireo, Yellow-rumped (Myrtle) Warbler, Common Yellowthroat, Yellow Warbler, American Redstart, American Goldfinch, Sharp-tailed Sparrow, and Field Sparrow.

Nearby *Brigg's Marsh* is a very good spot for wintering ducks. Look for American Wigeon, Pintail, Blue-winged Teal, Oldsquaw, Common Goldeneye, Black Scoter, and other waterfowl including loons, grebes, Gannets, and Razorbills.

George B. Parker Woodland, Town Farm and Biscuit Hill Roads, Coventry 02816. The sanctuary is owned by the Audubon Society of Rhode Island. It is located west of Providence, near the Connecticut border. To reach the sanctuary from Coventry Center, take SR 117 (Flat River Road) east for about a mile to the entrance (about 4 miles). There are no parking facilities and no trails are maintained.

The refuge totals 450 acres of mixed hardwoods and conifers. There is a stand of mature chestnut oak — one of the last in Rhode Island. The 2 streams that traverse the area and the rock bluffs make the Woodland a valuable natural habitat. A diversified community of plant and animal life is supported here. Look for landbirds.

Kimball Wildlife Refuge, Charlestown 02813. The refuge is owned by the Audubon Society of Rhode Island. Kimball is located off Prosser Trail on the south side of Watchaug Pond. From Charlestown, take US 1 west/south to Kings Factory Road, turn north (right) and go to Prosser Trail, turn left and continue to the refuge entrance. Trails are maintained and interpretive programs are offered. A naturalist is on duty during the summer months and is available to conduct guided tours. The refuge lies between Ninigret NWR and Burlingame State Park (where camping facilities are available).

Kimball is made up of 30 acres that are mostly mixed woodlands bordering Watchaug Pond. Among the birds to be found at the refuge are: Ring-necked Duck, Lesser Scaup, Great Horned Owl, Downy Woodpecker, Yellow-bellied Sapsucker, Wood Thrush, White-breasted Nuthatch, Carolina Wren, Golden-crowned Kinglet, Black-and-white Warbler, Northern Parula, Pine Warbler, Evening Grosbeak, and Pine Siskin.

Moonstone Waterfowl Refuge. Moonstone Beach Road, South Kingston. The refuge is owned by the Audubon Society of Rhode Island. Visitors are required to have *written* permission to use the refuge. Contact: Audubon Society of Rhode Island, 40 Bowen Street, Providence 02903. A parking fee is charged. The refuge is located southeast of Wakefield; from US 1, turn south on Moonstone Beach Road.

The refuge consists of a 115-acre barrier beach with brackish ponds. There are also fresh and saltwater marshes and farmlands. Bird banding and other research projects are carried out at Moonstone Refuge. Among the many species of birds to be found here are: Canada Goose, Common Goldeneye, Bufflehead, Red-breasted Merganser, Great Blue Heron, Great (Common) Egret, American Bittern, and many more shorebirds, marshbirds, and waterfowl.

Ninigret National Wildlife Refuge, Box 307, Charlestown 02813; (401) 364-3106. Ninigret is located 2 miles south of Charlestown along the south shoreline of Ninigret Pond. Vehicles are not permitted on the refuge; the nearest access (for a car) is to turn south from US 1 onto East Beach Road. Foot travel along the East Beach is permitted. Camping is not allowed on the refuge; however camping facilities are available at nearby state parks.

The refuge was established in 1970 and totals over 27 acres. Ninigret serves as a resting area for gulls, terns, waterfowl, and migrating shorebirds.

Norman Bird Sanctuary, Third Beach Road, Middletown 02840; (401) 846-2477. The sanctuary is owned by a private trust and managed by the Audubon Society of Rhode Island. An admission fee is charged. The sanctuary is open all year. To reach the sanctuary from Middletown, take Valley Road south to Green End Avenue; turn east (left) and continue to Third Beach Road, then turn south (right) and proceed to the entrance.

This 350-acre sanctuary, located on Rhode Island Sound, is comprised of salt marsh, mixed woodlands, freshwater wetlands, and farmlands. Trails are maintained and interpretive programs are offered. There is a trailside museum; guided tours are available. The marshes, woods, and bluffs all combine to support a diverse community of plant and animal life. Among the many species of birds seen here are: Common Loon, Pied-billed Grebe, Canada Goose, Marsh Hawk, Green Heron, Snowy Egret, and a variety of ducks, gulls, and warblers.

Sachuest Point National Wildlife Refuge. Administered by Ninigret NWR. The refuge is located near the Norman Bird Sanctuary. To reach Sachuest Point from Providence, take I-95 south to SR 138 going east through Middletown. The refuge is near Newport, off SR 138. Camping is not permitted on the refuge.

Sachuest Point NWR covers 75 acres, mostly wetlands. A wide spectrum of coastal birdlife is present on the refuge. Use of the area by migrating shorebirds, ducks, and Canada Geese is significant — with peak numbers of 1000 or more birds.

Trustom Pond National Wildlife Refuge. Administered by Ninigret NWR. Trustom Pond, established in 1973, covers 350 acres. The property adjoins the Audubon Society's Moonstone Beach Refuge and is between Ninigret NWR (to the west) and Galilee Bird Sanctuary (to the east). To reach the refuge from Charlestown, take Matunuck School Road toward Green Hill. The refuge is on Matunuck School Road near its intersection with Green Hill Road. Camping is not permitted at the refuge, however facilities are available at nearby state parks.

Trustom Pond NWR consists of barrier beach, salt marsh, and upland — including a shallow, brackish pond. Large numbers of migrating shorebirds and waterfowl use Trustom Pond as a resting and feeding ground. The marsh and upland portions of the refuge are frequented by deer and foxes. Among the many birds to be seen in the upland areas are American Kestrel (Sparrow Hawk), Great Horned Owl, Hermit Thrush, and Evening Grosbeak.

AUDUBON SANCTUARIES

The Audubon society of Rhode Island maintains 25 open space areas in addition to their sanctuaries. Arrangements to visit them should be made in advance. Some of these areas require *written* permission to visit. These areas are all undeveloped and are, in most cases, unsuitable for casual hiking. No trails are maintained and there are no parking facilities. Some of these areas adjoin state lands and act as buffers; others provide unique wildlife habitat. These open space areas are listed below. For additional information about these open space areas, contact: Audubon Society of Rhode Island, 40 Bowen Street, Providence 02903; (401) 521-1670.

Beech Grove, South Kingston; in Point Judith Pond; 14 acres of salt marsh on a wooded island; permission to visit is required.

Cocumscussoc Brook Reserve, North Kingston; near Cocumscussoc State Park; 16 acres of mixed woodlands.

The Dumpling, Jamestown; offshore nerar Fort Wetherill State Park; a ½-acre rocky island.

Eldred Wildlife Refuge, South Kingstown; near Hundred Acre Pond; 48 acres of mixed woodlands and freshwater marsh.

Fayette E. Bartlett Woodland, Burrilville; on Massachusetts border, off Fayette Bartlett Woodland Road, about 4 miles north of Harrisville; 70 acres of mixed woodlands.

Fox Hill Pond Salt Marsh, Jamestown; off Beaver Tail Road; 45 acres of salt marsh; permission to visit is required.

Gould Island Rookery, Portsmouth; south of Tiverton, in the Sakonnet River; 5-acre wooded island; heronry; northernmost nesting area for Cattle Egrets; permission to visit is required.

Grey Craig Overlook, Middletown; northwest of Norman Bird Sanctuary; 29 acres of mixed woodlands with rocky ledges.

Hundred Acre Cove, Barrington; north of Barrington, on Barrington River, off New Meadow Road; 43 acres of salt marsh.

Indian Run Woods, South Kingstown; off Saugatucket Road, north of Wakefield; 50 acres of mixed woodlands.

John Francis Brown Ravine, Warwick; off Narragansett Parkway, south of Pawtuxet; 6 acres of woodlands.

Lonesome Swamp, Cumberland; off Pound Road, east of Manville; ½ acre of freshwater wetland and mixed woodland.

Margaret Robinson Knight Wildlife Refuge, Cranston; near Fiskeville, east of J. L. Curran State Park, off Laten Knight Road; 52 acres of mixed woodlands.

Marsh Meadows Wildlife Preserve, Jamestown; between North Road and East Shore Road, north of Jamestown; 21 acres of saltwater marsh.

Matunuck Hills Woods, South Kingstown; near Tucker Pond; 35 acres of mixed woodlands.

Occupessatuxet Cove Salt Marsh, Warwick; between West Shore Road and Narragansett Parkway, south of Pawtuxet, near Hoxie; 3-acre salt marsh; permission to visit is required.

Ocean Drive Marsh, Newport; south of Newport, near Prices Neck Public Fishing Area; 9 acres of salt marsh; good for gulls, ducks, alcids, and other waterfowl and shorebirds.

Pettaquamscutt River Wildlife Habitat, Narragansett; just north of Narragansett Pier; 10 acres of saltwater marsh; good for shorebirds and alcids.

Racquet Road Thicket, Jamestown; near Fort Wetherhill State Park; 19 acres of mixed woodlands.

Ram Island, South Kingstown; in Point Judith Pond; 14 acres of salt marsh on a wooded island; permission to visit is required.

Sheffield Cove Salt Marsh, Jamestown; off Narragansett Avenue; 5 acres of salt marsh.

Spectable Island, Briggs Marsh, Little Compton; at Sakonnet off the Sakonnet Point Road; 4 acres of salt marsh on a wooded island; good for ducks, gulls, alcids, and other waterbirds; permission to visit is required.

Third Beach Road Lots, Middletown; northwest of Norman Bird Sanctuary; a buffer area; 18 acres of farmland.

Usher Cove Salt Marsh, Bristol; near Colt State Park; 3-acre salt marsh; permission to visit is required.

Wesquage Pond, Narragansett; off Boston Neck Road (US 1A), north of Narragansett Pier; 30 acres of fresh- and saltwater marshes.

STATE PARKS AND FORESTS

There are many state parks in Rhode Island. Most of them offer a variety of recreational activities including camping, swimming, boating, hiking, and picnicking. Although not designed for nature study, several of these parks are also good birdwatching places; they are marked with an asterisk (*). For additional information about state parks, contact: Rhode Island Department of Economic Development, Tourist Promotion Division, 1 Weybosset Hill, Providence 02903.

Arcadia State Park, Arcadia; (401) 539-7643.
*Beach Pond State Park, Escoheag 02821.
*Block Island State Beach, Block Island; day use only.
*Brenton Point State Park, Newport 02840; day use only.
*Charlestown Breachway, Charlestown Beach 02813; (401) 364-7000.
Burlingame State Park, US 1, Charlestown 02813; (401) 277-2632.
*Colt State Park, Bristol 02809; day use only.
Dawley Memorial State Park/Dawley Memorial State Forest, Arcadia; day use only.
Diamond Hill State Park, Diamond Hill 02895; day use only.
*East Matunick State Beach, Jerusalem; day use only.
*Fisherman's Memorial State Park, Point Judith Road, Narragansett 02882; (401) 789-8374.
Fort Adams State Park, Newport 02840; day use only.

*Galilee State Park/Galilee Bird Sanctuary, Point Judith Road, Narragansett 02882.

George Washington Management Area, Pulaski Memorial Forest, Pascoag 02859; (401) 568-6700.

*Goddard State Park, East Greenwich 02818; day use only.

Haines Memorial Park, West Barrington 02890; day use only.

Lincoln Woods State Park, Saylesville; day use only.

*Misquamicut State Beach, Misquamicut 02891; day use only.

*Ninigret Conservation Area, East Beach Road, Charlestown 02813; (401) 277-2632.

Pulaski Memorial State Park, Pascoag 02859; (401) 568-6700.

*Quonochontaug Breachway, Quonochontaug; day use only.

*Roger Wheeler Memorial State Beach, Sand Hill Cove Road, Galilee 02882; day use only.

Scarborough Beach, Ocean Road, Point Judith; day use only.

World War II Memorial State Park, Woonsocket 02895; day use only.

Killdeer

VERMONT

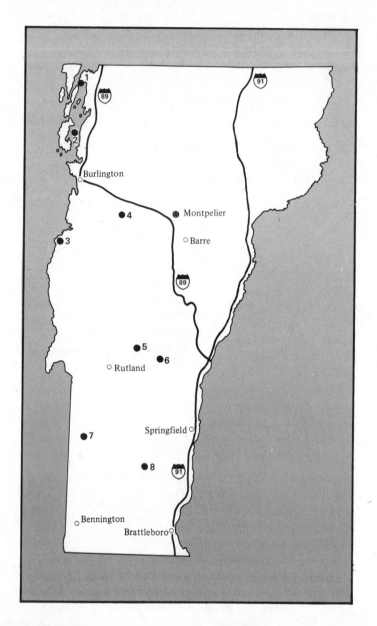

1. Missiquoi NWR
2. Sand Bar Refuge
3. Dead Creek Waterfowl Area
4. Green Mountain Audubon NC

5. Green Mountain National Forest
6. Vermont Institute of Natural Science
7. Merck Forest
8. West River Valley Greenway

Vermont is relatively small (9609 square miles) and largely mountainous. Its entire central section, from north to south, is dominated by the Green Mountains. The Connecticut River is its eastern boundary; Lake Champlain forms much of its western boundary. Famous for farming, marble, skiing, cheese, and maple sugar, Vermont is characterized by forests, lakes, rivers, and open fields. The Appalachian Trail traverses the southern part of the state — from the Massachusetts border to Sherburne Center, where it veers off into New Hampshire. At Sherburne, the Long Trail continues northward to Canada. The Long Trail, over 260 miles in length, is maintained by the Green Mountain Club.

The Agency of Environmental Conservation/Vermont Fish and Game Department maintains 68 wildlife management areas (13 waterfowl, 55 upland) which are located throughout the state. These areas, totaling nearly 83,000 acres, are open to the public. Some waterfowl refuges, however, are closed during the nesting season.

Along Lake Champlain, the Connecticut River, and the Long Trail; throughout the Green Mountains; and in and around the marshes near Rutland and Newport — birdwatching is always rewarding. There are 258 species of birds that occur in Vermont. Of these, 143 are regular nesting species. For additional information about birdwatching in Vermont, contact the Green Mountain Audubon Society, P. O. Box 33, Burlington 05401. They publish a very good booklet — *Birds of Vermont,* which has a section on birding places in Vermont. Additional information about Vermont can be obtained from the Vermont Fish and Game Department and the Agency of Environmental Conservation, Montpelier 05602.

Green Mountain National Forest, 22 Evelyn Street, Rutland 05702. There are district ranger offices in Manchester Center, Middlebury, and Rochester. Green Mountain Forest is divided into 2 basic units: northern and southern. They total 240,000 acres of woodlands, mountains, brooks, and open fields. Of special interest are: the Texas Falls area; the Robert Frost farm (located near Ripton); and the Long Trail, which is maintained by the Green Mountain Club (in Rutland) and extends through the Forest (it totals 260 miles). In addition there are many scenic areas, drives, and trails. Camping facilities are available, too, as are a variety of other recreational activities, including skiing.

Among the many birds that can be seen throughout Green Mountain National Forest are: Common Loon, Wood Duck, Blue-winged Teal, Hooded Merganser, Red-tailed Hawk, American Kestrel (Sparrow Hawk), Ruffed Grouse, Green Heron, Black-crowned Night Heron, Common Gallinule, Killdeer, Greater Yellowlegs, Ring-billed Gull, Black Tern, Great Horned Owl, Barred Owl, Whip-poor-will, Ruby-throated Hummingbird, Yellow-bellied Sapsucker, Hairy Woodpecker, Black-backed Three-toed Woodpecker (rare), Eastern Kingbird, Cliff Swallow, Common Raven, Boreal Chickadee (rare), Long-billed Marsh Wren, Gray-cheeked Thrush, Veery, Cedar Waxwing, Red-eyed Vireo,

Magnolia Warbler, Black-throated Green Warbler, Chestnut-sided Warbler, Common Yellowthroat, Bobolink, Scarlet Tanager, Evening Grosbeak, Red Crossbill, and Snow Bunting.

Missiquoi National Wildlife Refuge, R.D. #2, Swanton 05488; (802) 868-4781. Missiquoi is located about 40 miles north of Burlington, near the Canadian border; refuge headquarters are on SR 78, 2 miles northwest of the village of Swanton. Interested visitors should apply to refuge headquarters for permits and further information. Camping is not permitted at the refuge; however, facilities are available at nearby state parks and private campgrounds.

The refuge was established in 1943. It now totals nearly 4800 acres of brushland, ponds, river delta, and lowland hardwood swamp. Refuge objectives are to provide food and protection for migratory waterfowl, and to provide ideal habitat for summer breeders and resident wildlife. The refuge supports a population of about 100 white-tailed deer; the marshes are home for muskrat, beaver, otter, mink, and weasel. There are about 300 nesting boxes and baskets that are used to supplement natural nesting areas — nearly 65 percent of the 1000 waterfowl born each year are hatched in these structures.

Missiquoi (an Indian word meaning "much waterfowl" and "much grass") is on the Atlantic Flyway, and during fall migration there may be as many as 10,000 ducks present on the refuge at one time. There have been 185 species of birds (35 nesting) sighted at Missiquoi. Among these are: Mallard, Wood Duck, Ring-necked Duck, Marsh Hawk, Great Blue Heron, Virginia Rail, White-rumped Sand-piper, Common Tern, Saw-whet Owls, Pileated Woodpecker, Downy Woodpecker, Bank Swallow, Brown Creeper, Yellow-throated Vireo, Blackburnian Warbler, White-winged Crossbill, Song Sparrow, and Snow Bunting. Checklist available.

NATURE CENTERS

In addition to the federal properties discussed above, there are several nature centers and preserves that are also good birdwatching places. They are described below.

Green Mountain Audubon Nature Center, P. O. Box 68, Huntington 05462; (802) 434-3068. The center is operated by the Green Mountain Audubon Society. This 235-acre sanctuary consists of open fields, mixed woodlands, and freshwater marshes. Its elevations range from 550 feet at the Huntington River to about 1200 feet. The varied wildlife community reflects the diverse habitat. A wide range of educational and interpretive programs is offered at the center. Five miles of trails take visitors through the area. There have been 126 species of birds recorded here; among the nesting species are American Woodcock and Hermit Thrush. A checklist and booklet on birding are available at the center.

Merck Forest, Rupert 05768. The forest covers 2600 acres. A variety of educational and interpretive programs is offered. Guided tours are available for groups. The center is open all year.

Black-capped Chickadee

Vermont Institute of Natural Science, Woodstock 05091; (802) 457-2779. Bird banding and environmental research programs are offered. The 57-acre center is open all year.

West River Valley Greenway, Conservation Society of Southern Vermont, Townshend 05353; (802) 365-7754. The 2500-acre area is located near Jamaica, on the West River. A variety of educational and interpretive programs is available. Guided tours are offered; self-guiding trails are maintained. The center is open all year.

There are also several state wildlife management areas that are well known as good birdwatching places. These include the Sand Bar State Wildlife Refuge, a 1668-acre area, and the Dead Creek Waterfowl Area, an area of 2223 acres. The *Sand Bar Refuge* is located on the coast of Lake Champlain, north of Burlington, outside of Milton. The refuge includes the marsh area on either side of US 2 as one approaches the Sand Bar causeway from Milton. The marsh is an important nesting and feeding area for waterfowl. It is known for its large Wood Duck population. Common Goldeneyes and Black Ducks nest here too. Rails and herons also use the area. A portion of the refuge is wooded, and the large trees along the Lamoille River provide habitat for Pileated Woodpeckers. The refuge is open only with permission. Contact: Refuge Manager, Sand Bar State Wildlife Refuge, Milton 05468; (802) 893-7859. Camping facilities are available at nearby Grand Isle State Park.

Dead Creek Waterfowl Area, called one of Vermont's most valuable wildlife areas, is a nesting site for Canada Geese. Black Terns also nest in the area. In the many marshes, Osprey, herons, rails, and a variety of shorebirds can be seen. Several access points have been made available to the public; there is also a public observation area. Dead Creek is located on the coast of Lake Champlain, east of Vergennes. Camping facilities are available at nearby Button Bay State Park.

STATE PARKS AND FORESTS

There are many state parks and forests in Vermont. Most of these offer camping in addition to a full range of recreational facilities such as swimming, boating, and hiking. Some parks also have nature interpretation programs, nature centers, and resident naturalists. Those parks that are well known for birdwatching are marked with an asterisk (*). For additional information about state parks and forests in Vermont, write the Vermont Agency of Environmental Conservation, Department of Forests and Parks, Montpelier 05602.

Allis, Randolph 05060; (802) 276-2975; 487 acres.
*Ascutney, Windsor 05089; (802) 674-2060; 1984 acres.
Bomoseen, Fair Haven 05743; (802) 265-4242; 2795 acres.
Branbury, Brandon 05733; (802) 247-5925; 96 acres.
Brighton, Island Pond 05846; (802) 723-4360; 152 acres.
Burton Island, St. Albans Bay 05481; (802) 524-6353; 253 acres.
*Button Bay, Vergennes 05491; (802) 475-2377; 236 acres.
*Camel's Hump, Waterbury (no mail address); 16,995 acres; day use only.
*Calvin Coolidge State Forest, Plymouth 05056; (802) 672-3612; 16,118 acres.
Crystal Lake, Barton 05822; (802) 525-6205; 16 acres; day use only.
D. A. R., Vergennes 05491; (802) 759-2354; 100 acres.
*Darling, East Burke 05832; 2029 acres.
Dutton Pines, Brattleboro 05301; (802) 254-2277; 13 acres; day use only.

Elmore, Lake Elmore 05657; (802) 888-2982; 709 acres.

Emerald Lake, East Dorset 05253; (802) 362-1655; 430 acres.

Fort Dummer, Brattleboro 05301; (802) 254-2610; 217 acres.

*Gifford Woods, Killington 05751; (802) 775-5354; 114 acres; Appalachian Trail crosses park.

Grand Isle, Grand Isle 05458; (802) 372-4300; 226 acres.

Granville Gulf Reservation; 1171 acres; south of Waterbury; day use only.

*Groton Falls State Forest, Marshfield 05658; (802) 584-3820; 23,057 acres.

Knight Point, North Hero 05474; 60 acres; day use only.

Lake Carmi, Enosburg Falls 05450; (802) 933-8383; 482 acres.

Lake St. Catherine, Poultney 05764; (802) 287-9158; 117 acres.

Maidstone State Forest, North Stratford, New Hampshire 03590; (802) 676-3930; 469 acres.

Molly Stark, Wilmington 05363; (802) 464-5460; 158 acres.

*Mount Mansfield State Forest, Waterbury 05676; (802) 244-7103; 27,377 acres. There are two additional areas: Smugglers Notch and Underhill.

Mt. Philo, North Ferrisburg 05473; (802) 425-2390; 163 acres.

North Hero, North Hero 05474; (802) 372-8727; 399 acres.

Quechee Gorge Recreation Area; (802) 295-2990; 76 acres.

*St. Albans Bay, St. Albans Bay 05481; (802) 524-6324; 45 acres; day use only.

*Sand Bar, Milton 05468; (802) 372-8240; 20 acres; day use only.

Shaftsbury, Shaftsbury 05262; (802) 375-9978; 85 acres; day use only.

Silver Lake, Barnard 05031; (802) 234-9451; 34 acres.

Thetford Hill State Forest, Thetford 05074; (802) 785-2441; 262 acres.

Townshend State Forest, Newfane 05345; (802) 365-7500; 856 acres.

Wilgus, Ascutney 05030; (802) 674-5422; 100 acres.

Woodford, Bennington 05201; (802) 447-7169; 400 acres.

VIRGINIA

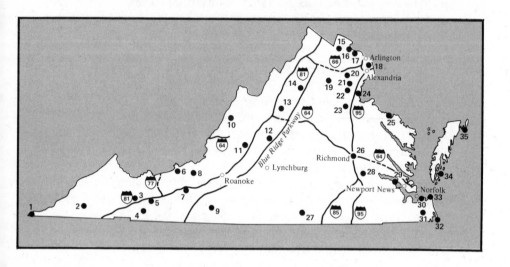

1. Cumberland Gap National Historic Park
2. Natural Tunnel State Park NC
3. Hungry Mother State Park NC
4. Mount Rogers National Recreation Area
5. Mountain Meadow Preserve
6. Jefferson National Forest
7. Clayton Lake State Park NC
8. Falls Ridge Nature Preserve
9. Fairy Stone State Park NC
10. George Washington National Forest
11. Douthat State Park NC
12. Blue Ridge Parkway/Skyline Drive
13. Fernbrook Natural Area
14. Shenandoah National Park
15. Furnace Mountain
16. Fraser Preserve
17. Great Falls National Park
18. { Gulf Branch NC
     Hidden Oaks NC
     Laurel Ridge NC
     Potomac Overlook Regional Park
19. Wildcat Mountain Natural Area

20. Signal Hill Preserve
21. Bull Run
22. Prince William Forest Park
23. Alexander Berger Memorial Sanctuary
24. Marumsco NWR
    Mason Neck NWR
    Mason Neck Wildlife Refuge and Park
25. Westmoreland State Park NC
26. Maymont NC
    The Nature Center
    Pocahontas State Park NC
27. Staunton River State Park NC
28. Presquile NWR
29. Chippokes Plantation State Park NC
30. Fisherman Island NWR
31. Dismal Swamp NWR
    Nansemond NWR
32. Back Bay NWR
    Mackay Island NWR
33. Seashore State Park NC
34. Virginia Coastal Reserve
35. Chincoteague NWR

Virginia's sharply contrasting environments — from the Blue Ridge Mountains to the Atlantic barrier islands — make possible a great diversity of wildlife. The tidewater, Virginia's coastal plain, consists mostly of 4 peninsulas formed by the Chesapeake Bay and the James, York, Rappahannock, and Potomac rivers. Much of Virginia's coastline, along both the Chesapeake and the Atlantic, has been preserved as refuges for wildlife. Since this area lies along the Atlantic Flyway, it is particularly attractive to vast numbers of migrating birds. The western part of the state is largely mountainous. The Alleghenys are paralled by the Blue Ridge. The latter are more accessible to the birdwatcher owing primarily to the parkway.

The state of Virginia also maintains several thousand acres as wildlife management areas. Although these areas are designed primarily for hunting and fishing, birdwatching is also usually good. Among the areas well known as good birding places are: *Back Bay, Mockhorn Island, Saxis Marsh, Hog Island, Elm Hill, Fairy Stone Farms, Amelia,* and *Lands End.* Camping is not permitted at any wildlife management area. Other restrictions, depending upon the time of year, may be in force. It is advisable to arrange visits in advance. Contact: Commission of Game and Inland Fisheries, P. O. Box 11104, Richmond 23230.

Other good birdwatching places in Virginia include the James River Plantations: Berkeley and Shirley, in the Charles City area and Carter's Grove, near Williamsburg. These are all open daily 9-5; an admission fee is charged.

Birdwatching at any season of the year is rewarding. Spring and fall, of course, are best in the mountains and on the shore. Wintering populations of waterfowl are most spectacular at Chincoteague and Back Bay NWRs. In the summer, many woodland breeding birds can be seen in Shenandoah National Park. Additional information about wildlife in Virginia can be obtained from the Commission of Game and Inland Fisheries, at the above address.

Alexander Berger Memorial Sanctuary. Owned by The Nature Conservancy. Contact: Ray M. Culter, preserve manager, The Nature Conservancy, 1800 North Kent Street, Arlington 22209; (703) 524-3151. The sanctuary is open to the public. It is located south of Fredericksburg. To reach the sanctuary, take SR 17 to New Post, turn right (west) on SR 2 and continue 200 yards to parking area (on the left).

Alexander Berger Sanctuary covers 846 acres of mixed woodlands and rhododendron. There is a pond, and streams traverse the sanctuary. Among the many birds to be seen here are: Wood Duck, Greater Scaup, Red-tailed Hawk, Osprey, Little Blue Heron, Belted Kingfisher, Red-headed Woodpecker, Pileated Woodpecker, Rough-winged Swallow, White-breasted Nuthatch, Long- and Short-billed Marsh Wrens, Wood Thrush, Eastern Bluebird (nesting), Ruby- and Golden-crowned Kinglets, Cedar Waxwing, Yellow-throated Vireo, Prothonotary Warbler, Common Yellowthroat, Rufous-sided Towhee, Chipping Sparrow, and Swamp Sparrow.

Back Bay National Wildlife Refuge, Suite 218, 287 Pembroke Office Park, Virginia Beach 23462; (804) 490-0505. To reach the refuge from Norfolk, take SR 165 southeast to SR 149, then south on SR 149 to SR 615. Take SR 615 south to Back Bay. Camping is not permitted at the refuge; however, facilities are available at nearby Seashore State Park.

Back Bay Refuge was established in 1938. It comprises 4600 acres of dunes, beach, marsh, woodland, and cultivated fields. Winter visitors are greeted by large flocks of Whistling Swans, Snow Geese, Canada Geese, and many species of ducks. Among the 257 species of birds (60 nesting) that have been sighted here are: Red-throated Loon, Gannet, Gadwall, Black Scoter, Marsh Hawk, Merlin (Pigeon Hawk), Great (Common) Egret, Glossy Ibis, Sora, Whimbrel, Marbled Godwit, Laughing Gull, Chuck-will's-widow, Red-bellied Woodpecker, Horned Lark, Short-billed Marsh Wren, Swainson's Thrush, Water Pipit, Yellow-breasted Chat, Eastern Meadowlark, Summer Tanager, Rose-breasted Grosbeak, and Savannah Sparrow. Checklist available.

Blue Ridge Parkway, P. O. Box 7606, Asheville, North Carolina 28807. The Blue Ridge Parkway, a unit of the National Park System, is 469 miles long. It goes from Afton (near Waynesboro, Virginia) south — through George Washington, Jefferson, and Pisgah National Forests — to Cherokee (near Bryson City, North Carolina). The Appalachian Trail roughly parallels the parkway for a distance of 100 miles. There are many self-guiding trails beginning at overlooks along the parkway. Gully Creek at Cumberland Knob is a favorite during the fall. In summer, there are conducted nature walks. Among the many species of birds sighed in the Roanoke area are: American Kestrel (Sparrow Hawk), Screech Owl, Whip-poor-will, Chimney Swift, Red-bellied Woodpecker, Eastern Wood Pewee, Common Raven, Carolina Wren, Eastern Bluebird, Black-and-white Warbler, Ovenbird, American Redstart, Eastern Meadowlark, and Song Sparrow. Checklist available.

Chincoteague National Wildlife Refuge, Box 62, Chincoteague 23336; (804) 336-6122. The refuge is located in the far northeast corner of Virginia, 3 miles east of the town of Chincoteague on SR 175. Camping is not permitted at the refuge; however, facilities are available at adjoining Assateague Island National Seashore (Maryland).

Chincoteague Refuge was established in 1943 to preserve a significant portion of coastal wetlands. Chincoteague occupies part of Assateague Island (see entry in Maryland chapter, page 29). It is 13 miles long. A wildlife haven, Chincoteague comprises over 9000 acres of marshes, dunes, and beaches — one of the finest ocean beaches on the eastern seaboard. The well-known Chincoteague ponies roam the refuge. Fox, shrews, and the rare Delmarva Peninsula Fox Squirrel are among the mammals to be found at Chincoteague. The refuge is located along the Atlantic Flyway. The variety of habitat at Chincoteague supports a variety of birdlife. There have been more than 275 species of birds sighted here. Among the common summer birds are:

Double-crested Cormorant, Blue-winged Teal, Black Duck, Willet, Clapper Rail, Gull-billed Tern, and American Oystercatcher. Common winter birds include: Red-throated Loon, Common Snipe, American Woodcock, Hermit Thrush, Horned Lark, and Evening Grosbeak. Rare occurrences have been: Sooty Shearwater, Parasitic Jaeger, Northern Phalarope, Snowy Owl, Philadelphia Vireo, and Worm-eating Warbler. Checklists available.

Cumberland Gap National Historic Park, For information, see entry in Kentucky chapter, page 198.

Dismal Swamp National Wildlife Refuge, P. O. Box 349, Suffolk 23434; (804) 539-7479. The refuge is located near Norfolk. To reach it, take I-64 southwest to Deep Creek, turn south on US 13 and go to Suffolk. The Canal can be approached from US 17. Camping is not permitted at the refuge; however, facilities are available at nearby Seashore State Park.

Dismal Swamp Refuge was established in 1973. The land (49,097 acres) was acquired through The Nature Conservancy. In March 1976, an additional 11,000 acres (in North Carolina) were added to the refuge. Features of the refuge include the Dismal Swamp Canal and Lake Drummond. The circular lake is in the heart of the swamp. Although very shallow (average depth is 6 feet), its waters are unusually pure. Stands of cypress border the lake. The refuge is being managed to retain the essential natural character of the swamp. Travel by bicycle or on foot is permitted on established roads that border the numerous ditches. Boat access is permitted by way of the Feeder Ditch that connects the Canal to Lake Drummond. Access by motor vehicles is permitted only by special permission, given at the discretion of the refuge manager. Public tours are given three days during each month; for information about the scheduling of these tours, contact the refuge manager. Among the 177 species of birds (95 nesting) seen at the refuge are: Double-crested Cormorant, Black Duck, Red-tailed Hawk, Marsh Hawk, Merlin (Pigeon Hawk), Black-crowned Night Heron, Killdeer, King Rail, Whimbrel, Northern Phalarope, Barred Owl, Red-cockaded Woodpecker, Great Crested Flycatcher, Tree Swallow, Carolina Chickadee, Brown-headed Nuthatch, Red-eyed Vireo, Worm-eating Warbler, Swainson's Warbler, Bachman's Warbler (rare), Blue-winged Warbler, Golden-winged Warbler, Prothonotary Warbler, Hooded Warbler, Wilson's Warbler, Orchard Oriole, and Blue Grosbeak. Checklist available.

Fisherman Island National Wildlife Refuge. Administered by Back Bay NWR. This 1000-acre island became a refuge in 1969. It is located near the north end of the Chesapeake Bay Bridge-Tunnel. The refuge is unmanned and special permission to visit it must be secured from the refuge manager at Back Bay.

Fisherman Island is one of the truly outstanding shorebird areas on the east coast. It provides habitat for migratory waterfowl and a wide variety of other birds including: Peregrine Falcons, Bald Eagles, Ospreys, and Savannah (Ipswich) Sparrows.

George Washington National Forest. Contact: Forest Supervisor, 210 Federal Building, P. O. Box 233, Harrisonburg 22801. George Washington is adjacent to Jefferson National Forest, near Monongahela National Forest (Kentucky), and encompasses part of the Blue Ridge Parkway. George Washington Forest is also near many limestone caverns famous for their beautiful formations and coloring — such as: Shenandoah Caverns, Skyline Caverns, and Luray Caverns. The Forest is located in the southwestern corner of Virginia, along the Kentucky and West Virginia borders, north of Roanoke. Camping facilities are available in addition to a wide range of recreational activities.

The Forest covers an area of about 1.8 million acres. It was established in 1911, making it one of the first national forests in the East. There are networks of canoeing, horseback riding, and hiking trails — including a 70-mile portion of the Appalachian Trail (which goes through the Pedlar Ranger District). The diversified habitat of George Washington Forest provides for food and shelter for many species of birds. Annual hawk counts are made here during fall migration. Among the 150 species of birds seen here are: Great Horned Owl, Common Nighthawk, Common (Yellow-shafted) Flicker, Acadian Flycatcher, Brown Thrasher, Wood Thrush, Red-eyed Vireo, Cerulean Warbler, Northern Parula, and Scarlet Tanager.

Great Falls National Park, 9200 Old Dominion Drive, Great Falls 22066; (202) 426-6931. Great Falls Park is located just outside of Washington, D.C. To reach the park take the Capital Beltway (I-495) to Exit 13 (Old Georgetown Pike/SR 193); continue west on SR 193 to Old Dominion Drive; turn north and continue to the park entrance. Great Falls Park is the beginning of the Chesapeake and Ohio Canal National Historical Park. Although there are no camping facilities at Great Falls, C & O Park has them (see entry in Maryland chapter, page 31). Park service employees conduct interpretive tours of the falls. In addition, there are more than 4 miles of trails and roads available for exploration. There are many natural overlooks that give striking views of the Potomac River and gorge.

A wide variety of plants and animals live along the banks of the river and in the swamps and upland forests of the park. Here grow the pawpaw tree and the delicate trailing arbutus. Among the birds likely to be seen here are: Wood Duck, Red-shouldered Hawk, Bobwhite, Killdeer, Ruffed Grouse, Turkey, Screech Owl, Whip-poor-will, Hairy Woodpecker, Barn Swallow, Tree Swallow, Carolina Chickadee, Winter Wren, Wood Thrush, Blue-gray Gnatcatcher, Prothonotary Warbler, Northern Parula, Pine Warbler, Scarlet Tanager, Northern (Baltimore) Oriole, Indigo Bunting, and Fox Sparrow.

Jefferson National Forest. Contact: Forest Supervisor, 3517 Brandon Avenue, SW, P. O. Box 4009, Roanoke 24015. Jefferson National Forest is located in the southwestern corner of Virginia, along the Kentucky border, near

Roanoke, adjacent to George Washington National Forest. It is also near the Blue Ridge Parkway and Monongahela National Forest (Kentucky).

Jefferson Forest covers 575,000 acres in the Allegheny and Blue Ridge Mountains. There are camping facilities in addition to a range of recreational activities. Many hiking trails — including a portion of the Appalachian Trail — traverse the area; there are also some self-guiding nature walks. Several district ranger stations are located throughout the Forest. Among the 110 species of birds (41 nesting) sighted at Jefferson National Forest are: Red-tailed Hawk, Ruffed Grouse, Turkey, Barred Owl, Pileated Woodpecker, Tufted Titmouse, Brown Thrasher, Cedar Waxwing, Yellow Warbler, Indigo Bunting, and Rufous-sided Towhee.

Mackay Island National Wildlife Refuge. Administered by Back Bay NWR. Mackay Island is located just south of Back Bay NWR. Most of Mackay lies in North Carolina. Refuge headquarters are reached by driving south on SR 615 to the town of Knotts Island. Contact the refuge manager at: Box 6128, Virginia Beach 23456 for additional information. Camping is not permitted at the refuge; however, facilities are available at nearby state parks.

The 6995-acre refuge was established in 1960 primarily as a wintering ground for migratory waterfowl — especially for Snow Geese. As many as 20,000 of these geese rest and feed on the beach and marshlands of the refuge throughout the winter. Among the 150 species of birds (32 nesting) to be seen at the refuge are: American Wigeon, Hooded Merganser, Cooper's Hawk, Great Blue Heron, American Bittern, American Woodcock, Common Snipe, Barn Owl, Tree Swallow, Mockingbird, Prothonotary Warbler, and Cardinal. Checklist available.

Marumsco National Wildlife Refuge. Administered by Mason Neck NWR. Marumsco is located ½ mile east of US 1, adjacent to Woodbridge, about 17 miles south of Washington, D.C. It was established as a refuge in 1973 and totals 63 acres of freshwater tidal marsh. Primary species include Black Ducks, Mallards, and other migratory birds. Since Marumsco is so close to Mason Neck, much of the birdlife is similar.

Mason Neck National Wildlife Refuge, 14015 Jefferson Davis Highway, Woodbridge 22191; (703) 494-6479. Mason Neck is located 18 miles south of Washington, D.C. To reach the refuge, take US 1 south for about 17 miles, than take SR 242 southeast to Gunston Hall; watch for signs to Mason Neck. Camping is not permitted at the refuge; however facilities are available at Prince William Forest Park.

Mason Neck was established in 1969 as a sanctuary for the Bald Eagle. The 918-acre refuge is a unique blend of low boggy areas, upland forest, and river front marsh. Woodland ponds; the Great Marsh (285 acres); and stands of hemlock, oak, and beech all combine to provide habitat for a great variety of wildlife — especially birds. One of the refuge's primary objectives is to provide nesting areas for the Bald Eagle. Several techniques are being used to encourage nesting, including the planting, pruning, and replacing of pine trees. Future plans include development of a wildlife interpretive complex with foot trails. A major portion of the refuge, about 600 acres, will be closed to all visitors. This will help to provide the maximum protection that the Bald Eagle requires. There have been 210 species of birds (85 nesting) sighted at Mason Neck. Among them are: Black Duck, Red-breasted Merganser, Bald Eagle, Bobwhite, Great Blue Heron, Spotted Sandpiper, Bonaparte's Gull, Screech Owl, Chimney Swift, Pileated Woodpecker, Bank Swallow, House Wren, Wood Thrush, Blue-gray Gnatcatcher, Black-and-white Warbler, Kentucky Warbler, Ovenbird, Orchard Oriole, Summer Tanager, Indigo Bunting, and Fox Sparrow. Checklist available.

Mount Rogers National Recreation Area, 1102 North Main Street, Marion 24354; (703) 783-5196. Mount Rogers Area lies between Jefferson National Forest and Cherokee National Forest (Tennessee) in southwestern Virginia. To reach Mount Rogers Area from Marion, go south on SR 16 for about 10 miles. Recreational facilities available include camping and fishing. Several roads traverse the area and a network of trails is maintained. Mount Rogers itself rises over 5700 feet; nearby is White Top Mountain, 5200 feet high. A paved road leads to the summit of White Top. The Appalachian Trail crosses the Mount Rogers Area near these two peaks.

Among the many birds seen here are: Ruffed Grouse, Whip-poor-will, Saw-whet Owl, Brown Creeper, Red-breasted Nuthatch, Wood Thrush, Swainson's Thrush, Swainson's Warbler, Magnolia Warbler, Hooded Warbler, Scarlet Tanager, and Rose-breasted Grosbeak.

Nearby, about 20 miles north, are the *Saltville ponds*. These ponds are just outside of Saltville, off SR 91, to the southwest. This is a good place for waterfowl and shorebirds, including: Gadwall, Green-winged Teal, Bufflehead, Hooded Merganser, Common Snipe, Greater Yellowlegs, and Pectoral Sandpiper.

Nansemond National Wildlife Refuge. Administered by Dismal Swamp NWR. This 208-acre refuge is mostly marshland. It was established in 1973 and is located in Nansemond County. Public access is by permit only; contact the refuge manager at Dismal Swamp NWR. Owing to their proximity to each other, the birdlife of Nansemond is basically the same as that of Dismal Swamp NWR.

Presquile National Wildlife Refuge, P. O. Box 620, Hopewell 23860; (804) 458-7541. Refuge headquarters are located in Room 202, Tarton Building, Hopewell. The refuge is accessible by private boat or by refuge-operated ferry (which runs at irregular intervals). Information as to good birding areas and ferry schedules may be secured by telephoning the refuge.

Presquile Refuge was established in 1952. It is located on a 1329-acre man-made island in the James River and is surrounded by 1000 acres of protected waters. Three distinct types of habitat are found on the refuge: tidal marsh, tidal swamp, and uplands. The refuge is managed primarily for waterfowl; birdlife is of most interest in winter when there are large concentrations of ducks and geese. Among the 199 species of birds normally expected to be present on the refuge at some time during the year are: Horned Grebe, Snow (Blue) Goose, Wood Duck, Hooded Merganser, Broad-winged Hawk, Bald Eagle, Peregrine Falcon (rare), Greater Yellowlegs, Lesser Yellowlegs, Semipalmated Sandpiper, Forster's Tern, Caspian Tern, Black Skimmer, Short-eared Owl, Red-headed Wood-pecker, Pileated Woodpecker, Acadian Flycatcher, Bank Swallow (nesting), Bewick's Wren (rare), Carolina Wren, Prothonotary Warbler, Blue-winged Warbler (rare), Summer Tanager, Blue Grosbeak, Indigo Bunting, American Goldfinch, Bachman's Sparrow, and Henslow's Sparrow (rare). Checklist available.

Prince William Forest Park, Box 208, Triangle 22172; (7703) 221-7181. Prince William is administered by the National Park Service. It is located 35 miles south of Washington, D.C., just west of US 1 between Dumfries and Triangle. Camping, hiking, and picnicking are among the activities available at the park.

Prince William Park totals 11,000 acres of hardwood forest, pine groves, old fields, and ponds and streams. There are trails (some self-guiding) and a nature center. A variety of interpretive programs is offered at the center. In addition, a park naturalist is on duty. Among the 75 species of birds seen here in the summer are: Black Vulture, Red-tailed Hawk, Osprey, Bobwhite, Turkey, Green Heron, Mourning Dove, Black-billed Cuckoo, Barred Owl, Whip-poor-will, Pileated Woodpecker, Hairy Woodpecker, Acadian Flycatcher, Blue Jay, Tufted Titmouse, Gray Catbird, Cedar Waxwing, Prairie Warbler, Common Yellow-throat, Summer Tanager, Scarlet Tanager, Rufous-sided Towhee, and Chipping Sparrow. Checklist available.

Shenandoah National Park, Luray 22835. The park adjoins the Blue Ridge Parkway. The 105-mile Skyline Drive, a continuation of the Blue Ridge Parkway, goes through the center of the park. There are 66 overlooks along the Skyline Drive. As in most national parks, there are camping and picnicking facilities available. There is also a park concessioner that operates a lodge and cottages, camp stores, and shower and laundry buildings. The park service conducts various interpretive programs such as hikes and campfire talks. There are also several self-guiding trails throughout the park. The Appalachian Trail runs the length of the park. Shenandoah is located near the Luray Caverns and George Washington National Forest.

The park covers over 300 square miles of waterfalls, forests, and mountains. Streams, lakes, and woodlands all combine to support a varied wildlife community. There are over 17 varieties of orchids to be found at Shenandoah. Bear, raccoon, opossum, and skunk are among the mammals commonly found here. There have been 188 species of birds identified at Shenandoah National Park. Among them are: Wood Duck, Sharp-shinned Hawk, Golden Eagle (rare), Osprey, Peregrine Falcon (rare), Ruffed Grouse, Bobwhite, Turkey, Green Heron, American Woodcock, Black- and Yellow-billed Cuckoos, Barred Owl, Common Nighthawk, Belted Kingfisher, Pileated Woodpecker, Red-headed Woodpecker, Eastern Phoebe, Barn Swallow, Common Raven, White- and Red-breasted Nuthatches, Winter Wren, Eastern Bluebird, Golden- and Ruby-crowned Kinglets, Cerulean Warbler, Blackpoll Warbler, Blue-winged Warbler, Golden-winged Warbler, Blackburnian Warbler, Scarlet Tanager, Rose-breasted Grosbeak, Blue Grosbeak, Indigo Bunting, Red Crossbill, and Bachman's sparrow (rare). Checklist available.

Least Tern

Virginia Coastal Reserve. Owned and managed by The Nature Conservancy. Contact: The Nature Conservancy, 1800 North Kent Street, Arlington 22209; (703) 524-3151. The Virginia Coastal Reserve is made up of a 45-mile chain of barrier beach islands fronting on the Atlantic Ocean. Access is by boat only. The preserve is open only with special permission; contact The Nature Conservancy at the above address.

The islands that make up the preserve are (from north to south): Metomkin (2000 acres); Cedar; Parramore (5870 acres); Revel's; Sandy; Hog (3651 acres); Rogue (390 acres); Cobb; Mink (28 acres); Godwin (850 acres); and Smith, Myrtle, and Ship Shoal (8760 acres combined). The islands consist of cordgrass marshes, dunes, brackish ponds, salt marsh, and pine groves. Hog Island has a large heronry, with 2000 birds including Glossy Ibis, Snowy Egret, Great (Common) Egret, and Great Blue Heron. Rogue Island, which lies just to the west of Hog Island, provides habitat for American Oystercatcher, Forster's Tern, Black Skimmer, Laughing Gull, and Wilson's Plover. There have been over 100 species of birds recorded on the islands. Among them are: Common Scoter, Peregrine Falcon, Merlin, Marsh Hawk, Osprey, Yellow-crowned Night Heron, Clapper Rail, Piping Plover, Ruddy Turnstone, Whimbrel, Willet, Red Knot, Semipalmated Sandpiper, Western Sandpiper, Marbled Godwit, Skua, Iceland Gull, Royal Tern, Sandwich Tern, Barn Owl, House Wren, Prairie Warbler, and Sharp-tailed Sparrow.

Wildcat Mountain Natural Area. Owned by The Nature Conservancy. This 633-acre woodland is located about 7 miles north of Warrenton. It lies on the western slope of Wildcat Mountain, a high point of the Rappahannock Ridge, in the foothills of the Blue Ridge Mountains. There are oak-hickory forests, pine groves, and abandoned farmlands. Of special interest are the wildcats that live on the slopes. There have been 94 species of birds identified at Wildcat Mountain. Among them are: Red-tailed Hawk, Bobwhite, Green Heron, Solitary Sandpiper, Yellow-billed Cuckoo, Chimney Swift, Pileated Woodpecker, Great Crested Flycatcher, Purple Martin, White-breasted Nuthatch, Carolina Wren, Mockingbird, Brown Thrasher, Wood Thrush, Eastern Bluebird, Blue-gray Gnatcatcher, Cedar Waxwing, Loggerhead Shrike, Red-eyed Vireo, Cape May Warbler, Black-throated Green Warbler, Prairie Warbler, Louisiana Waterthrush, Hooded Warbler, Summer Tanager, Indigo Bunting, and Grasshopper Sparrow. Checklist available.

NATURE CENTERS

Throughout Virginia there are various nature centers, many of which are located in state or city parks. A variety of recreational, educational, and interpretive programs is offered at these centers. In addition, camping facilities are available at the state parks. The centers are described briefly below.

Chippokes Plantation State Park, Nature Center, Surry 23883; (804) 294-3625. The center is operated by the Virginia State Park Commission. The park totals 1683 acres. Guided and self-guiding tours are offered. Of special interest is the living historical farm. The center is open April through October, closed on Mondays.

Clayton Lake State Park, Nature Center, Dublin 24084; (703) 674-5492. The center is operated by the Virginia State Park Commission. The park covers 472 acres; guided tours are given. Trails are maintained. The center is open every day, June through August.

Douthat State Park, Nature Center, Box 212, Millboro 24460 (703) 862-0612. The center is operated by the Virginia State Park Commission. The park covers 4493 acres. Guided tours are offered; trails are maintained. The center is open every day, June through August.

Fairy Stone State Park, Nature Center, Route 2, Box 134, Stuart 24171; (703) 930-2424. The center is operated by the Virginia State Park Commission. The park covers 4570 acres. Guided tours are available. Trails are maintained. The center is open every day, June through August.

Gulf Branch Nature Center, 3608 North Military Road, Arlington 22207; (703) 558-2340. The center is operated by the Arlington County Department of Environmental Affairs. It totals 30 acres. Teacher training programs are offered. Guided and self-guiding tours are available. The center is open all year, closed on Mondays.

Hidden Oaks Nature Center, Box 236, Annandale 22003; (703) 941-5009. The 38-acre center is operated by the Fairfax County Park Authority. A variety of educational programs is offered. Guided and self-guiding tours are available. The center is open all year, closed on Mondays and holidays.

Hungry Mother State Park, Nature Center, Marion 24354; (703) 783-3422. The center is operated by the Virginia State Park Commission. The park covers 2180 acres. Guided tours are offered; trails, some self-guiding, are maintained. The center is open every day, June through August.

Laurel Ridge Nature Center, 8925 Leesburg Pike (Route 7), Vienna 22180; (703) 790-4000. The center is operated by the National Wildlife Federation. The center covers 20 acres. A variety of educational and interpretive programs is offered. Guided tours are available Monday through Friday; the trails are open all year.

Maymont Nature Center, Maymont Park, Richmond 23220; (804) 649-5175. The center is operated by the Richmond Department of Recreation and Parks. The park covers 95 acres. A variety of programs is available to the general public. Guided and self-guiding tours are offered. The center is open all year, closed on holidays.

Natural Tunnel State Park, Nature Center, Route 1, Box 271, Clinchport 24227; (703) 940-2674. the center is operated by the Virginia State Park Commission. The park totals 567 acres. Guided tours are offered; trails, some self-guiding, are maintained. The center is open every day, June through October.

The Nature Center, 1606 Washington Plaza, Reston 22070; (703) 471-7472. This is an environmental education center which offers management programs in and for a "planned city."

Pocahontas State Park, Nature Center, Chesterfield 23832; (804) 748-5929. The center is operated by the Virginia State Park Commission. The park covers 2005 acres. Guided and self-guiding tours are available. The center is open every day, June through August.

Potomac Overlook Regional Park, Arlington. For further information, contact: Chief Naturalist, Northern Virginia Regional Park Authority, 11001 Popes Head Road, Fairfax 22030.

Seashore State Park, Nature Center, 2500 Shore Drive, Virginia Beach 23451; (804) 481-2131. The center is operated by the Virginia State Park Commission. The park totals 2770 acres. Guided and self-guiding tours are offered. The center is open all year.

Staunton River State Park, Nature Center, Route 2, Box 295, Scottsburg 24589. The center is operated by the Virginia State Park Commission. The park totals 1287 acres. Guided and self-guiding tours are available. The center is open every day, June through August.

Westmoreland State Park, Nature Center, Box 465, Montross 22520; (804) 493-6167. The center is operated by the Virginia State Park Commission. The park covers 1302 acres. Guided and self-guiding tours are available. The center is open every day, June through August.

NATURE CONSERVANCY PRESERVES

In addition to the properties described in the previous pages, The Nature Conservancy owns and manages several preserves that are located throughout the state of Virginia. Following are brief descriptions of these preserves.

Bull Run-Occoquan. Contact: Northern Virginia Regional Park Authority, 10680 Main Street, Fairfax 22030; (703) 591-3990. The 468-acre preserve is open to the public. The land will be transferred to the Northern Virginia Regional Park Authority which currently owns 3337 acres in the area. To reach the preserve, take I-95 south from Washington, D.C., to the Woodbridge exit; then take SR 123 northwest to CR 640 (Old Shirley Highway), turn left (south) on CR

640; and continue to the preserve. The preserve is a woodland covered with mixed hardwoods.

Falls Ridge Nature Preserve. Contact: Mr. William P. Bradley, RFD #2, Box 1382, Christiansburg 24073; (703) 382-2220. The preserve is open with permission only. To reach the preserve from Roanoke, take I-81 south to Ironto exit, turn right on SR 603, go for nearly 8 miles to a small private bridge, which is painted red. The property is on the left side of the road; access is by the bridge. This 457-acre preserve is characterized by deciduous woodlands, wild azaleas, mountain laurel, trailing arbutus, redbud, rhododendron, hepatica, and dogwood. Large sinkholes on the property indicate the existence of unexplored caverns. Among the birds to be found here are: Ruffed Grouse, Turkey, Red-tailed Hawk, Red-shouldered Hawk, Great Horned Owl, Common Raven, and Pileated Woodpecker.

Fernbrook Natural Area. Contact: Mr. George R. Paschall, Fernbrook Farm, Route 4, Box 235, Charlottesville 22901; (804) 973-6602. The preserve is open with permission only. This 62-acre natural area consists of a woodland bordering the Rivanna River. A variety of ferns and wildflowers border the many small springs. To reach the preserve from Charlottesville, take SR 20 north to Stony Point and turn west (left) on SR 600, go for about ½ mile to SR 784, turn left again, and enter the preserve.

Fraser Preserve. Contact: Dr. Robert Watson, 2636 Marcey Road, Arlington 22207; (702) 528-5547. The preserve is open with permission only. To reach the preserve from Washington, D.C., take SR 123 west to SR 193 (Georgetown Pike), take SR 193 to Great Falls; about 3 miles beyond Great Falls, turn right on CR 633, go to CR 755 which dead ends at the Fraser Preserve. This 220-acre preserve consists of mixed hardwoods, pine plantations, abandoned farmland, and a pond. A trail traverses the property. Fraser Preserve is jointly managed by The Nature Conservancy and the Calvary Baptist Church of Washington, D.C. A variety of educational programs is offered at the preserve.

Furnace Mountain. Contact: Wayne C. Bevan, Route 2, Box 40, Lovettsville 22080; (703) 822-5035. The preserve is open to the public. To reach it from Leesburg, take SR 15 north to the Virginia side of Rocks Bridge, turn west on SR 672 and go for 50 yards to SR 662, turn south and follow SR 662 for 1½ miles to preserve entrance, which is on the right (west). This 29-acre area is well forested with mixed hardwoods. There are gently rolling hills and steep slopes which descend to Chatoctin Creek. Breeding birds include Turkey, Bobwhite, and Ruffed Grouse.

Mason Neck Wildlife Refuge and Park. Contact: Mr. Richard N. Antonette, Mason Neck Wildlife Refuge, 14015 Jefferson Davis Highway,

Woodbridge 22191; (703) 494-6479. This 2883-acre preserve adjoins Mason Neck NWR. For further information, see page 133.

Mountain Meadow Preserve. Contact: Mr. Sebert Sisson, P. O. Box 606, Hillsville 24343; (703) 728-9505. The preserve is open with permission only. To reach Mountain Meadow, from Roanoke, take I-81 south to SR 100, turn south (left); continue on SR 100 to US 221 and turn west toward Hillsville; proceed 1½ miles on US 221; the preserve is on the right. Mountain Meadow Preserve totals over 40 acres of white pine plantation and mowed grasslands. Among the birds seen here are: Common (Yellow-shafted) Flicker, Gray Catbird, Carolina Wren, Indigo Bunting, and Rufous-sided Towhee.

Signal Hill Preserve. Contact: Town of Manassas Park, Town Hall, Manassas 22110. The 13-acre preserve is open to the public. It is currently leased to the Town of Manassas Park and will eventually be transferred to the Town of Manassas. To reach the preserve from downtown Manassas, take SR 28 north to SR 616, turn right (east) on SR 616, and continue for about 1½ miles to the preserve. Signal Hill lies on the east side of the road.

STATE PARKS AND FORESTS

Virginia has many state parks, forests, and natural areas. Most of these areas offer camping, hiking, and picnicking in addition to a variety of public recreational activities. Although not designed as bird sanctuaries, state parks can be rewarding bird finding areas. Those that are well known as such are marked with an asterisk (*). For additional information regarding state parks in Virginia, contact: Division of Parks, 1201 State Office Building, Capitol Square, Richmond 23219.

STATE PARKS

Bear Creek Lake, Cumberland 23040; (804) 492-3351.
Breaks Interstate Park, Breaks 24607; (703) 865-4413.
*Chippokes Plantation, Surry 23883; (804) 294-3625; 1683 acres; day use only.
*Clayton Lake, Dublin 24084; (703) 674-5492; 470 acres.
*Douthat, Clifton Forge 24422; (703) 862-0612; 4500 acres.
*Fairy Stone, Route 2, Box 134, Stuart 24171; (703) 930-2424; 4570 acres.
Goodwin Lake-Prince Edward, Green Bay 23942; (804) 392-3435.
Grayson Highlands, Independence 24348; under development.
Holliday Lake, Appomattox 24522; (804) 983-4571.
*Hungry Mother, Marion 24354; (703) 783-3422; 2180 acres.
*Natural Tunnel, Route 1, Box 271, Clinchport 24227; (703) 940-2674; 567
    acres.
*Occoneechee, Clarksville 23927.

*Pocahontas, Chesterfield 23832; (804) 748-5929; 2005 acres.
*Seashore, 2500 Shore Drive, Virginia Beach 23451; (804) 481-2131; 2770
    acres.
*Staunton River, Scottsburgh 24589; (804) 572-4623; 1290 acres.
*Westmoreland, Montross 22520; (804) 493-6167; 1302 acres.

STATE FORESTS

There are 4 state forests in Virginia: Buckingham-Appomattox, Cumberland,
Pocahontas, and Prince Edward-Gallion. All these have wildlife management
areas and state parks within their boundaries. For camping information, see
entries under state parks.

Carolina Wren

NATURAL AREAS

There are 6 natural areas in Virginia. These offer no recreational facilities and camping is not permitted. Some trails are maintained. Although they are all probably good birdwatching places, the 4 located in eastern Virginia are well known as such. They are marked with an asterisk (*).

*Charles C. Steirly Heron Rookery. The heronry is about five miles northeast of Waverly. From Waverly, take SR 603 over Blackwater Bridge and go east from there along a logging road for 1½ miles. This will lead directly into the swamp. This is a dense swamp surrounded by timber. Visitors are advised to wear hip boots.

Goshen Pass Natural Area. This area is off SR 39 near Lexington, on the edge of George Washington National Forest.

Lick Creek Natural Area. Lick Creek totals 870 acres and is located about 20 miles northeast of Marion in Jefferson National Forest. From Marion, take SR 42 north for 3 miles, then go north on SR 621.

*Parkers Marsh Natural Area. The area is located near Onanock. It is bordered on the south by Onanock Creek, on the north by Back Creek, and on the west by the Chesapeake Bay. It is accessible by boat or by wading.

*Seashore Natural Area. The area encompasses a large portion of Seashore State Park at Cape Henry. It totals 2700 acres.

*Wreck Island Natural Area. The area is accessible by boat only; boats leave from Oyster, off US 13. The island is about 7 miles from Oyster. It consists mostly of salt marsh and dunes; only one-fifth of it can be considered high ground. Wreck Island is about 3 miles long and ½ mile wide. It is a haven for wildlife.

WEST VIRGINIA

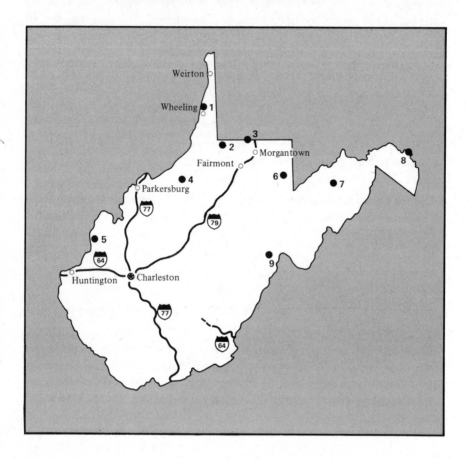

1. Brooks NC
   Oglebay Park
   Parkinson Estate Preserve
2. West Virginia University Arboretum
   West Virginia University Forest
3. Mason-Dixon Historical Park
4. Murphy Preserve
5. McClintic Wildlife Area
6. Cranesville Swamp
7. Greenland Gap
8. Yankauer Preserve
9. Monongahela National Forest

West Virginia — the mountain state — occupies a remarkable geographic position due to its peculiar shape. The tip of its northern panhandle is nearly as far north as New York City; its eastern extremity extends nearly to Washington, D.C.; its southernmost point is further south than Richmond (Virginia); and its western boundary, near Huntington where the Ohio River leaves West Virginia, is at almost the same longitude as Port Huron (Michigan). This diversity, including the state's many mountains, makes possible a wide variety of plant and animal life.

West Virginia lies between the Atlantic and Mississippi Flyways, on a westward arm of the former. It therefore lacks spectacular waterfowl migrations. Even so, there is plenty of good birdwatching. In Monongahela National Forest, 35 species of warblers have been sighted. There are 164 breeding species in West Virginia.

The state maintains hundreds of acres of public hunting and fishing areas. Many of them have campgrounds, mostly either rustic or primitive. Although good for birdwatching, the primary objective of these areas is hunting and fishing. Therefore, there may be certain restrictions to visiting them, especially during some seasons of the year. It is best to arrange in advance, by contacting: West Virginia Department of Natural Resources, State Capitol, Charleston 25305. The best known of these areas, for birding, is *McClintic Wildlife Area,* Route 1, Box 125, Point Pleasant 25550. It is located 2 miles off SR 62, 7 miles north of Point Pleasant.

For further information about birdwatching in West Virginia, contact: Brooks Bird Club, 707 Warwood Avenue, Wheeling 26003. The club sponsers many activities, including bird counts and various trips.

Monongahela National Forest, Elkins 26241. The Forest is located along the eastern border of West Virginia. To reach the area from Elkins, take US 33 east and/or US 219/250 south/southeast. Monongahela Forest borders on George Washington National Forest (Virginia). Camping, hiking, and picnicking are among the wide range of public recreational facilities offered at the Forest.

Monongahela National Forest covers 824,000 acres. The Allegheny Mountains cut through its center. Of special interest is the Cranberry Glades Botanical Area, which supports subalpine tundra. There are also unexplored limestone caves; Spruce Knob (4860 feet high); Blackwater Canyon and 60-foot waterfalls; the Seneca Rocks on the historic Seneca Indian Trail; Smoke Hole; the Gaudineer Scenic Area (a vast virgin spruce forest); and the Dolly Sods Scenic Area, which is noted for fall migratory birds. Other locations in the Forest that are good for birdwatching include: Gaudineer Knob and Great Mountain Wilderness. There are miles of streams and trails, scenic drives, and man-made lakes. In this vast, mountainous region can be seen over 180 species of birds. Among these are: Common Loon, Horned Grebe, Canada Goose, Wood Duck, Turkey Vulture, Goshawk, Marsh Hawk, Merlin (Pigeon Hawk), Bobwhite,

Little Blue Heron, Killdeer, Screech Owl, Common Nighthawk, Pileated Woodpecker, Red-headed Woodpecker, Least Flycatcher, Eastern Wood Pewee, Cliff Swallow, Black-billed Magpie, Common Raven, Bewick's Wren, Hermit Thrush, Water Pipit, Philadelphia Vireo, Blue-winged Warbler, Cerulean Warbler, Mourning Warbler, Summer Tanager, Scarlet Tanager, Dickcissel, White-winged Crossbill, Henslow's Sparrow, and Lapland Longspur.

NATURE CENTERS

There are several nature centers, arboretums, and parks located in northern West Virginia. These are generally good birdwatching places. They are described briefly below.

Brooks Nature Center, Oglebay Institute, Wheeling 26003; (304) 242-6855. The center is maintained by the Brooks Bird Club. It covers 1500 acres. A variety of educational and interpretive programs is offered at the center. Guided and self-guiding tours are available. The center is open all year.

Oglebay Park, Wheeling. This 1400-acre park is located 6 miles outside of Wheeling. There is a trailside museum and a naturalist is on duty. Among the birds found here are: Black Duck, Blue-winged Teal, Cooper's Hawk, Ruffed Grouse, Green Heron, Yellow-billed Cuckoo, Belted Kingfisher, Pileated Woodpecker, Eastern Kingbird, Purple Martin, Tufted Titmouse, Brown Creeper, Blue-gray Gnatcatcher, Philadelphia Vireo, Blue-winged Warbler, Worm-eating Warbler, Hooded Warbler, Bobolink, Rose-breasted Grosbeak, and Indigo Bunting.

Parkinson Estate Preserve. The preserve is maintained by the George M. Sutton Audubon Society. This 100-acre sanctuary is located at Bethany College and is open to the public. To reach the preserve from Wheeling, take SR 88 north to the college.

West Virginia University Arboretum, Department of Biology, West Virginia University, Morgantown 26506; (304) 293-4794. The arboretum covers 75 acres. A variety of educational and interpretive programs is offered. Guided and self-guiding tours are available. The arboretum is open all year.

West Virginia University Forest, New Forestry Building, Morgantown 26506; (304) 293-2301. The Forest covers 7500 acres. A variety of educational and interpretive programs is offered. Guided and self-guiding tours are available. The area is open all year.

For additional information about birdwatching in the northern panhandle region of West Virginia, the reader is referred to an unpublished paper, "Birds of the West Virginia Northern Panhandle," by Albert Bucklew, Jr.

NATURE CONSERVANCY PRESERVES

The Nature Conservancy maintains several preserves in West Virginia. They are described briefly below. For additional information, contact: The Nature Conservancy, West Virginia Chapter, Mr. Maxwell Smith, Chairperson, Route 3, Box 55, Grafton 26354.

Cranesville Swamp. The preserve totals 293 acres and is located in Preston County, near Terra Alta. Due to the altitude, a colony of northern plants has been preserved since the ice age.

Greenland Gap Nature Preserve. The preserve totals 255 acres and is located in Grant County, near Scherr. It consists mostly of a pine forest. Quartz and sandstone cliffs tower above a creek lined with vegetation.

Murphy Preserve. The preserve totals 276 acres and is located in Ritchie County, near Harrisville. It consists of an oak-hickory forest with two small ponds.

Yankauer Preserve. The preserve comprises 107 acres of mostly open fields in Berkeley County, near Hedgesville.

Other preserves, previously owned by The Nature Conservancy, have been transferred to either the United States Forest Service, for inclusion in a national forest, or to West Virginia State Parks, for inclusion in a state park. *Mason-Dixon Historical Park,* a 285-acre preserve, is being held for an historical and recreational park. This park is located on the Pennsylvania border, just north of Morgantown.

STATE PARKS AND FORESTS

West Virginia has a well-developed system of state parks and forests. Most of them offer camping in addition to a wide range of other public recreational facilities. Some are also good birdwatching places; those are marked with an asterisk (*). Further information about state parks can be obtained from: West Virginia Department of Natural Resources, Division of Parks and Recreation, State Capitol, Charleston 25305. Information regarding Sutton Lake, Summersville Lake, and other large impoundments can be obtained from the U.S. Army Corps of Engineers, Huntington District, Federal Building, Huntington 25701. There is usually free camping available at lakes maintained by the Corps.

STATE PARKS

Audra, Route 4, Box 564, Buckhannon 26201; (304) 457-1162; 355 acres.
Babcock, Clifftop 25822; (304) 438-6205; 3640 acres.
Beartown, Droop 24933; (304) 653-4254; 100 acres; day use only.
*Blackwater Falls, Davis 26260; (304) 259-5216; 1690 acres.

Bluestone, Hinton 25951; (304) 466-1922; 4980 acres.

Cacapon, Berkeley Springs 25411; (304) 258-1022; 6155 acres.

*Canaan Valley, Davis 26260; (304) 866-4121; 6015 acres.

Carnifex Ferry, Kelsers Cross Lanes 26675; (304) 872-3773; 155 acres; day use only.

Cathedral, Aurora 26705; (304) 735-3771; 135 acres; day use only.

Cedar Creek, Route 1, Box 9, Glenville 26351; (304) 462-7158; 2030 acres.

Chief Logan, Logan 25601; (304) 752-8558; 3305 acres; day use only.

Droop Mountain, Droop 24933; (304) 653-4254; 290 acres; day use only.

Grandview, Route 9, Beaver 25813; (304) 763-3145; 880 acres; day use only.

Hawk's Nest, Ansted 25812; (304) 658-5212; 240 acres.

*Holly River, Hacker Valley 26222; (304) 493-6353; 7800 acres.

Little Beaver, Route 9, Beaver 25813; (304) 763-2494; 385 acres; day use only.

Lost River, Mathias 26812; (304) 897-5372; 3680 acres.

North Bend, Cairo 26337; (304) 643-2931; 1400 acres.

Pinnacle Rock, Box 121, Bramwell 24715; (304) 945-4137; 245 acres; day use only.

Pipestem Resort, Pipestem 25979; (304) 466-1800; 4030 acres.

Prickett's Fort, Route 3, Box 403, Fairmont 26554; (304) 363-3731; 190 acres; day use only.

*Tomlinson Run, P. O. Box 97, New Manchester 26056; (304) 564-3651; 1400 acres; day use only.

Twin Falls, P. O. Box 236, Mullens 25882; (304) 249-4000; 3780 acres.

Tygart Lake, Route 1, Grafton 26354; (304) 265-2320; 1380 acres.

Valley Falls, Route 6, Box 244, Fairmont 26554; (304) 363-3319; 1035 acres; day use only.

*Watoga, Burr Route, Box 57, Marlinton 24954; (304) 799-4087; 10,060 acres.

Watters Smith, Lost Creek 26385; (304) 745-3081; 280 acres; day use only.

STATE FORESTS

Cabwaylingo, Route 1, Dunlow 25511; (304) 272-5415; 8150 acres.

*Cal Price, Dunmore 24934; day use only.

Camp Creek, Camp Creek 25820; (304) 425-1283; 4900 acres

*Cooper's Rock, Route 1, Box 80, Bruceton Mills 26525; (304) 296-6065; 12,750 acres.

*Greenbrier, Caldwell 24925; (304) 536-1944; 5060 acres.

*Kanawha, Route 2, Box 185, Charleston 25314; (304) 346-5654; 6600 acres.

Kumbrabow, P. O. Box 10, Huttonsville 26273; (304) 335-3319; 9430 acres.

Panther, Panther 24872; (304) 938-2252; 7810 acres.

*Seneca, Dunmore 24934; (304) 799-6213; 11,690 acres.

Barred Owl

The Southeast

Alabama   Mississippi
Florida   North Carolina
Georgia   South Carolina
Kentucky   Tennessee

Anhinga

ALABAMA

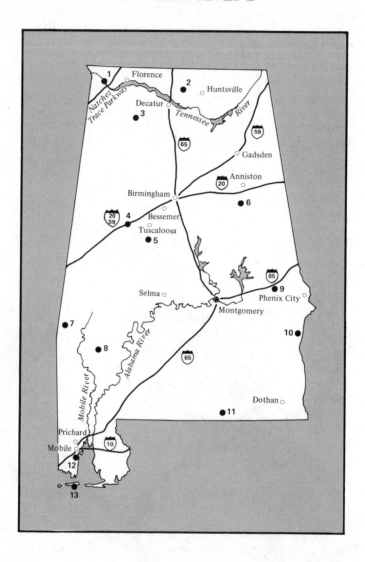

1. Natchez Trace Parkway
2. Wheeler NWR
3. William Bankhead National Forest
4. Moody Swamp
   University of Alabama Arboretum
5. Talladega National Forest
6. Talladega National Forest
7. Choctaw NWR

8. Fred T. Stimpson Game Sanctuary
   Salt Springs Game Sanctuary
9. Tuskegee National Forest
10. Eufala NWR
11. Conecuh National Forest
12. Bellingrath Gardens
13. Dauphin Island Sanctuary

Alabama — the heartland of the South — has not been explored in depth by birdwatchers although the swamps, deltas, beaches, and pineland forests are rich in avian life. In the swamps, cypress trees are draped with moss; the coastal pinelands are characterized by longleaf and slash pine, the mountains are covered with hickory and oak forests.

During the winter months, birdwatching in Alabama can be very productive; large congregations of waterfowl winter over in Mobile and Bon Secour bays and on the outlying waters of the Gulf. The large impoundments of the NWRs are also particularly attractive to waterfowl.

Alabama has many state-owned sanctuaries and wildlife management areas. These are administered by the Department of Conservation, 64 North Union Street, Montgomery 36104.

Choctaw National Wildlife Refuge, Box 325, Jackson 36545; (205) 246-3583. Choctaw is located in western Alabama, about 100 miles north of Mobile. From Butler, take SR 17 south to the fire tower; then turn east on the county road; turn east again at Womack Hill. Camping is not allowed on the refuge; however, there are camping facilities at nearby Coffeeville Dam and at De Soto National Forest just across the state line in Mississippi.

The 4200-acre refuge was established in 1964 and lies on the Tombigbee River. The terrain is flat. Its rich river bottomland, with numerous lakes and sloughs, is ideal for waterfowl. Management programs on the refuge include developing impoundments and farmlands. Construction of Wood Duck nesting boxes is another important refuge program. Although designed primarily as a refuge for waterfowl, Choctaw provides food and shelter for a great number of birds. There have been 139 species of birds (67 nesting) reported on the refuge. Among these are: Anhinga, Gadwall, Blue- and Green-winged Teals, Ring-necked Duck, Bufflehead, Ruddy Duck, Swallow-tailed Kite, Cooper's Hawk, Red-tailed Hawk, Golden Eagle (rare), Bald Eagle, Turkey, Great Blue Heron, Yellow-crowned Night Heron, American Bittern, Wood Stork (Ibis), White Ibis, Virginia Rail, Purple Gallinule, Common Snipe, Yellow-billed Cuckoo, Barred Owl, Whip-poor-will, Pileated Woodpecker, Red-headed Woodpecker, Purple Martin, Tufted Titmouse, Carolina Wren, Blue-gray Gnatcatcher, Loggerhead Shrike, Prothonotary Warbler, Hooded Warbler, Orchard Oriole, Blue Grosbeak, Lark Sparrow, and Fox Sparrow. Checklist available.

Conecuh National Forest, Box 310, Andalusia 36420. Conecuh is located about 100 miles south of Montgomery. To reach the Forest, take US 65 south from Montgomery to Evergreen; then turn east on US 84 to Andalusia; then south on US 29. Camping, in addition to other recreational activities, is available at Conecuh.

The 85,000-acre Forest, on the Florida border, is known for its large, clear ponds and lush pine forests. Conecuh is in the flat, sandy coastal plain. Here the streams wander through semitropical vegetation. A large portion of the Forest is devoted to a wildlife management area. Among the birds likely to be seen here are: Cooper's Hawk, Turkey, Yellow-billed Cuckoo, Barred Owl, Chuck-will's-widow, Pileated Woodpecker, Hairy Woodpecker, Great Crested Flycatcher, Carolina Chickadee, Wood Thrush, Blue-gray Gnatcatcher, Kentucky Warbler, and Hooded Warbler.

Dauphin Island Sanctuary. Owned by the National Audubon Society. To reach the sanctuary from Mobile, take SR 163 south to Dauphin Island. Historic Fort Gaines is also on the island. Dauphin lies between the Florida and Mississippi sections of Gulf Islands National Seashore (see entry in Florida chapter, page 164). Camping is not permitted at the sanctuary; private campgrounds are located nearby. The sanctuary is open during the day all year round; there is a naturalist/warden on duty.

The 164-acre sanctuary covers about ⅓ of Dauphin Island, west of the mouth of Mobile Bay. Dauphin Island is a 14-mile barrier beach island with salt marshes, beaches, dunes, tidal flats, freshwater ponds, mixed deciduous and pine woods, thickets, and open meadows. This is an important concentration area for migratory songbirds which migrate across the Gulf of Mexico. Although rewarding throughout the year, Dauphin Island is the best in spring, fall, and winter. Among the many birds that can be seen here are: Eared Grebe, Magnificent Frigatebird, Brown Pelican, Gannet, Mottled Duck (nesting), Fulvous Tree Duck (nesting), Great Blue Heron, Cattle Egret, American Oystercatcher, Snowy Plover, Wilson's Plover, Least Tern (nesting), Royal Tern, Gull-billed Tern, Gray Kingbird, Red-cockaded Woodpecker, Scissor-tailed Flycatcher (rare), Bell's Vireo, Cerulean Warbler, Hooded Warbler, Blue Grosbeak, and Painted Bunting.

Eufaula National Wildlife Refuge, Box 258, Eufaula 36027; (205) 687-4065. To reach the refuge from Eufaula, take US 431 north for about 5 miles, turn north on SR 165, and continue for 2 additional miles. Eufaula was established in 1964 and now consists of over 11,000 acres; it is located on the Chattahoochee River, and ⅓ of the refuge lies in Georgia. Facilities include 2 self-guiding automobile trails, numerous foot trails, and an observation tower. Camping facilities are available nearby.

Eufaula was originally created to provide feeding and resting habitat for migrating waterfowl. Management programs on the refuge include water control (by means of dikes and impoundments), greentree reservoirs, and the planting of supplemental waterfowl foods (such as grain, sorghum, corn, and Japanese millet). These management programs also benefit other wildlife on the refuge — such as beaver, raccoon, opossum, bobcat, skunk, shrew, vole, and rabbit. There have been 204 species of birds identified at Eufaula. Among these are: Pied-billed Grebe, White Ibis, Snow Goose, Northern Shoveler, Wood Duck, Ruddy Duck, Bald Eagle, Golden Eagle, Osprey, Marsh Hawk, Great Blue

Heron, Louisiana Heron, American Bittern, Virginia Rail, Purple Gallinule, American Coot, Piping Plover, Ruddy Turnstone, Willet, Ring-billed Gull, Ground Dove, Barred Owl, Common. Nighthawk, Pileated Woodpecker, Red-cockaded Woodpecker (rare), Eastern Kingbird, Rough-winged Swallow, Carolina Chickadee, Tufted Titmouse, Long- and Short-billed Marsh Wrens, Blue-gray Gnatcatcher, Loggerhead Shrike, Northern Parula, Kentucky Warbler, Yellow-breasted Chat, Bobolink, Brewer's Blackbird (rare), Summer Tanager, Indigo Bunting, and Vesper Sparrow. Checklist available.

Natchez Trace Parkway. For information, see entry in Mississippi chapter, page 207.

Talladega National Forest, Box 35, Talledega 35160. Talladega Forest is divided into 2 sections: Oakmulgee and Talladega; these total 360,000 acres. The latter is the larger area. The Oakmulgee Division is located between Montgomery and Tuscaloosa, off US 82. The Talladega Division is near Sylacauga, Talladega, and Anniston; use US 431 and/or SR 49 and SR 77. There are camping facilities in both divisions. Near the Oakmulgee Division is a national fish hatchery — 5 miles north of Marion on SR 5. Talladega has an observation tower and a scenic drive in addition to trails and other paved roads. Both areas are mountainous and have streams running through vast forests.

Talladega Forest captures the southernmost section of the Appalachian Mountain chain, affording the visitor spectacular views of wooded valleys and waterfalls. Wildlife is abundant here. Among the birds likely to be seen at Talladega are: Red-tailed Hawk, Marsh Hawk, Ground Dove, Red-headed Woodpecker, Pileated Woodpecker, Eastern Kingbird, Dickcissel, Horned Lark, Tufted Titmouse, Carolina Chickadee, Barn Swallow, Mockingbird, Gray Catbird, Brown Thrasher, Loggerhead Shrike, White-eyed Vireo, Northern Parula, Blue-winged Warbler, Kentucky Warbler, Hooded Warbler, Blue Grosbeak, Rufous-sided Towhee, Vesper Sparrow, Fox Sparrow, and Henslow Sparrow. Near the fish hatchery can be seen: Pied-billed Grebe, Pectoral and Solitary Sandpipers, American Coot, and many ducks.

Tuskegee National Forest, Box 390, Tuskegee 36084. Tuskegee Forest is located between Montgomery and Columbus (Georgia). From Montgomery, take US 80 east for about 30 miles to the ranger station. As in most national forests, there are camping facilities in addition to other recreational activities. Tuskegee is the smallest national forest in Alabama, totaling 11,000 acres.

Attractions include a pine plantation, fishing streams, and nature trails. Tuskegee is in the rolling hills of the piedmont. This land, midway between the mountains and the coast, takes on some of the flavor of both types of terrain. There is a network of all-weather paved roads through the Forest. These, combined with the foot trails, make vast areas of Tuskegee accessible to birdwatchers. Among the 145 species of birds likely to be seen here are:

Sharp-shinned Hawk (rare), Marsh Hawk, Osprey, Great Blue Heron, Killdeer, Common Snipe, Least Sandpiper, Ring-billed Gull (rare), Ground Dove, Screech Owl, Ruby-throated Hummingbird, Pileated Woodpecker, Red-headed Woodpecker, Acadian Flycatcher, Rough-winged Swallow, Carolina Chickadee, Tufted Titmouse, Brown-headed Nuthatch, Winter Wren, Water Pipit, Prothonotary Warbler, Golden-winged Warbler, Kentucky Warbler, Orchard Oriole, Summer Tanager, Indigo Bunting, and Bachman's Sparrow.

Wheeler National Wildlife Refuge, Box 1643, Decatur 35601; (205) 353-7243. Wheeler is located in northern Alabama, just outside of Decatur. To reach the refuge from Decatur, take SR 67 for 1½ miles east of its junction with US 31. Camping is not permitted on the refuge; facilities are available at Bankhead National Forest. Of special interest is nearby Shelta Cave

Brown Thrasher

(owned by The Nature Conservancy) — a cave with a rare degree of preservation of aquatic life. For information, contact the National Speleological Society, Cave Avenue, Huntsville 35810.

Wheeler was established in 1938 and now covers over 34,000 acres. It is located on a TVA reservoir (on the Tennessee River), and is a good example of multiple land use. Situated east of the Mississippi Flyway, Wheeler supports a large winter population of geese and ducks. Other primary species include Bald Eagle and Bobwhite. There is a network of graveled roads (mostly open year-round) that permits easy access to nearly all parts of the refuge. There have been 277 species of birds (85 nesting) sighted at Wheeler. Among these are: White Pelican, American Wigeon, Oldsquaw (rare), Mississippi Kite, Swainson's Hawk, Rough-legged Hawk, Green Heron, Wood Stork (Ibis), White Ibis, Sora, Upland Sandpiper (Plover), Baird's Sandpiper (rare), Buff-breasted Sandpiper, Black Tern, Yellow- and Black-billed Cuckoos, Short-eared Owl (rare), Pileated Woodpecker, Horned Lark, Cliff Swallow, Mockingbird, Eastern Bluebird, Blue-gray Gnatcatcher, Cedar Waxwing, Yellow-throated Vireo, Prothonotary Warbler, Tennessee Warbler, Ovenbird, Louisiana Waterthrush, Scarlet Tanager, Blue Grosbeak, Evening Grosbeak, Dickcissel, and Bachman's Sparrow (rare). Checklist available.

William B. Bankhead National Forest, Box 278, Double Springs 35553. Bankhead Forest is located about 30 miles south of Decatur; take SR 24 southwest to Moulton; then SR 33 south into the Forest. A variety of recreational activities, including camping, is offered.

Of special interest at Bankhead are the limestone gorges, the natural bridges, the Lewis Smith Reservoir, the Sipsey Wilderness Area, and the Black Warrior Wildlife Management Area. Bankhead comprises 181,000 of streams, lakes, rock bluffs, and waterfalls. Wheeler NWR is located nearby. Geese, ducks, Bobwhite, Mourning Dove, and Bald Eagle are among the more easily seen birds. Others include: Red-headed Woodpecker, Eastern Wood Pewee, Veery, Eastern Bluebird, Mourning Warbler, American Redstart, Indigo Bunting, Rufous-sided Towhee, and Le Conte's Sparrow.

NATURE CENTERS

In addition to the properties described in the previous pages, the following gardens and nature centers can also be rewarding birdfinding areas.

Bellingrath Gardens, Theodore 36582; (205) 973-2217. Bellingrath is located a few miles south of Mobile. There are 755 acres of landscaped gardens; Bellingrath is open daily 8-6; an admission fee is charged.

Fred T. Stimpson Game Sanctuary. The sanctuary is located near Jackson and is state owned. For information about visiting it, contact the Department of Conservation. Stimpson is a good place to look for Mississippi Kites.

Moody Swamp. The swamp is southwest of Tuscaloosa. Drive west on US 11/43 as far as 32nd Avenue; turn south (left) on 32nd Avenue and proceed for about 2 miles. Look for Pileated Woodpecker, Cerulean Warbler, and American Redstart.

Salt Springs Game Sanctuary. Salt Springs is 13 miles south of Jackson. This state-owned sanctuary comprises 5500 acres of mixed woodlands and thicketed areas. It is open to the public with permission only—contact the Department of Conservation, Montgomery 36101.

University of Alabama Arboretum, P. O. Box 1927, University 35486; (215) 348-5960. The arboretum is located near Tuscaloosa. Guided tours of the 65-acre area are available by appointment. The arboretum is open all year. Among the birds seen here are: Carolina Wren, Carolina Chickadee, and Blue Grosbeak.

STATE PARKS AND FORESTS

State parks in Alabama are administered by the Alabama Department of Conservation and Natural Resources, Division of State Parks, 64 North Union Street, Montgomery 36104. Most of the parks offer camping, swimming, picnicking, and hiking. The parks are designed primarily for recreational use; however, birdwatching there can also be productive. Those parks that are especially good for birdwatching are marked with an asterisk (*).

Bladon Springs, Bladon Springs 36092; day use only; 357 acres.
Blue Springs, Route 1, Clio 36017; (205) 397-8703; 103 acres.
Buck's Pocket, Route 1, Box 24, Groveoak 35975; (205) 659-2000; 2000 acres.
Camden, P. O. Box 128, Camden 36726; (205) 682-4838; 200 acres.
Chattahoochee, Gordon 36343; (205) 552-3607; 596 acres.
*Cheaha, Lineville 36266; (205) 488-5111; 2719 acres.
Chewacla, Route 2, Box 350, Auburn 36830; (205) 887-5621; 696 acres.
Chicksaw, Route 1, Gallion 36742; (205) 295-8230; 580 acres.
*DeSoto, Route 1, Box 210, Fort Payne 35967; (205) 845-0051; 4869 acres.
Florala, Florala 36441; (205) 858-7622; day use only; 40 acres.
*Gulf, Star Route, Box 9, Gulf Shores 36452; (205) 968-7544; 6000 acres.
*Joe Wheeler, Route 2, Town Creek 35672; (205) 685-3306; 2550 acres.
Lake Guntersville, Star Route 2, Guntersville 35976; (205) 582-2061; 5559 acres.
Lake Lurleen, Route 1, Coker 35452; (205) 339-1558; 1625 acres.
*Lakepoint Resort, Route 2, Box 94, Eufaula 36027; (205) 687-9591; 1220 acres.
*Little River, Route 2, Box 77, Atmore 36502; (205) 862-2511; 960 acres.

*Monte Sano, Huntsville 35801; (205) 534-3575; 2140 acres.
Oak Mountain, P. O. Box 278, Pelham 35124; (205) 663-6771; 9940 acres.
Paul M. Grist, Route 2, Selma 36701; (205) 872-5846; 1080 acres.
Rickwood Caverns, Route 2, Warrior 35180; (205) 647-9692; 380 acres.
Wind Creek, Route 2, Alexander City 35010; (205) 234-2101; 1400 acres.

Red-shouldered Hawk

FLORIDA

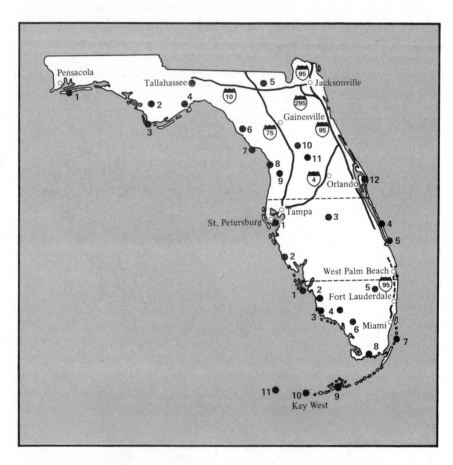

Florida is one of the most rewarding places to go birdwatching in the entire country: it has species and subspecies of birds not found elsewhere, it attracts large wintering bird populations, and it lies along principal migration routes. Florida's great, wet freshwater prairies, thousands of miles of shoreline, immense swamps, and large forests all combine to provide habitat for a wide diversity of plant and animal life — especially birdlife. This chapter deals with defined areas, such as NWRs, that are set aside for birdwatching and other naturalist pursuits. Birdwatching from a roadside or in a city park, however, can be equally rewarding. For specific, local information the reader is advised to consult a booklet published by the Florida Audubon Society: *Where to Find Birds and Enjoy Natural History in Florida*. Copies may be obtained by writing to Florida Audubon, P.O. Drawer 7, Maitland 32751; (305) 647-2615.

Of special interest to birdwatchers is the Audubon House in Key West. The house was built in 1830 and has been completely restored and furnished. On permanent display is the 4-volume Elephant Folio edition of Audubon's *Birds of America*. The house is open every day from 9-5; an admission fee is charged.

Because there are so many birdwatching sites in Florida, the state has been divided into 3 sections: northern, central, and southern Florida. Within each section, the entries are arranged alphabetically.

Northern Florida

Apalachicola National Forest, Tallahassee 32301. Apalachicola NF is located in northwestern Florida near Tallahassee; to reach the Forest, use US 10, US 98, US 319 and/or SR 20, SR 60, SR 267, SR 375. The 557,000-acre forest is characterized by pine-hardwood swamps along large rivers. There are numerous ponds and streams. Public facilities include fishing, swimming, camping, canoeing, boating, and picnicking. There is a network of forest service roads that traverse the area. The Bradwell Bay Wilderness Area (see below) is located within forest boundaries. Nearby are St. Marks NWR, St. Vincent NWR, and the Audubon Society's Wakulla Springs Sanctuary.

Among the endangered species that are sheltered at Apalachicola are the Florida panther, American alligator, Red-cockaded Woodpecker, Sandhill Crane, (Southern) Bald Eagle, and Osprey. Other birds that can be seen here include: Wood Duck, Red-breasted Merganser, Swallow-tailed Kite, Marsh Hawk, Limpkin, Bobwhite, Purple Gallinule, Yellow-billed Cuckoo, Barred Owl, Common Nighthawk, Pileated Woodpecker, Tree Swallow, Carolina Wren, Eastern Bluebird, Cedar Waxwing, Prothonotary Warbler, Prairie Warbler, American Redstart, Orchard Oriole, Indigo Bunting, and Bachman's Sparrow.

Bradwell Bay Wilderness Area, P.O. Box 68, Crawfordville 32327; (904) 926-3561. Bradwell Bay is located in the Apalachicola National Forest;

access to this 22,000-acre wilderness area is via forest service roads. The climate of the general area reflects the subtropical conditions that are common in Florida. The drier periods are spring and early summer; heavy rainfalls occur during the late summer and fall. The terrain is flat; shallow water usually stands in low areas. The slightest change in elevation is shown by differing vegetation. The main swamp (''Bay'') consists of a dense titi swamp with some areas sparsely intermingled with scrubby pond pine. This area is normally covered with a few inches of water throughout.

Many rare and endangered species of wildlife find refuge in Bradwell Bay. Among them are the Florida black bear, white-tailed deer, and American alligator; also the Red-cockaded Woodpecker.

There are few existing access points and identifiable landmarks in the Bradwell Bay Wilderness Area. Persons who plan to hike into the core area should be experienced and properly equipped; there are no trails or old roadbeds. For further information, see entry for Apalachicola National Forest.

Canaveral National Seashore, P.O. Box 2583, Titusville 32780; (305) 867-4675. Headquarters for Canaveral Seashore are located on SR 402 (across the street from those of Merritt Island NWR), 7 miles east of Titusville. The Seashore totals 67,500 acres, 41,000 of which have been previously administered as Merritt Island NWR. No camping is permitted at Canaveral; there are several private campgrounds in the vicinity.

Canaveral Seashore, established in 1975, has 25 miles of beaches, vegetated barrier dunes, mangrove stands, hammocks, and Mosquito Lagoon — a subtropical estuary. The shallow, island-dotted lagoon is subject to ocean tides through Ponce de Leon Inlet at New Smyrna Beach. Visitors are advised to beware of poisonous snakes; to use insect repellent when at Mosquito Lagoon; and to swim only in protected areas — the ocean currents are strong and dangerous.

Canaveral Seashore is home to a wide variety of plant and animal life including a number of endangered species: the beaches serve as nesting sites for giant loggerhead and green turtles; manatees are frequently spotted in the lagoon; and American alligators feed and nest here. Nearly 300 species of birds have been observed at Canaveral and at adjacent Merritt Island NWR. A large nesting population of Brown Pelicans occupies a mangrove rookery in the heart of the Seashore. For information about the birds likely to be seen here, consult the entry for Merritt Island (page 165).

Cedar Keys National Wildlife Refuge. Under management of Chassahowitzka NWR. Access is by boat only. Arrangements to visit the refuge must be made in advance by contacting the refuge manager at Chassahowitzka; the refuge is open to the public from mid-July through October. Camping is not permitted. There are no plans at the present time to further develop the refuge, as improved facilities would be incompatable with refuge and wilderness objectives.

Cedar Keys is made up of 4 islands totaling 378 acres; it was established as a refuge in 1929. Narrow sandy beaches, salt marshes, and mangrove swamps characterize the shores while a hammock forest of live oak, cabbage palm, and bay dominates the uplands. The lack of permanent fresh water has been a major factor in limiting the wildlife population. However the islands are of tremendous value as a nesting area of colonial birds — especially Double-crested Cormorant, Great (Common) Egret, Snowy Egret, Louisiana Heron, Great Blue Heron, and White Ibis; there are also 32 Osprey nests and a Bald Eagle nest on the refuge. In addition, many species of terns, gulls, and shorebirds use the beaches and mud flats. Passerine birds are most abundant during migration periods.

Chassahowitzka National Wildlife Refuge, Route 1, Box 153, Homosassa 32646. The refuge is about 50 miles north of St. Petersburg, headquarters are approximately 4 miles south of Homosassa Springs on US 19. Camping is not permitted on the refuge; facilities are available at nearby state forests.

Established in 1943, Chassahowitzka is managed principally for waterfowl. The refuge totals nearly 30,000 acres of brackish marshes, estuaries, and coastal salt bays on the Gulf of Mexico. Primary species include Bald Eagle, Sandhill Crane, Limpkin, White Ibis, American alligator, and Florida manatee. There have been 234 species of birds observed on the refuge (plus 14 accidentals). Among these are: Sooty Shearwater (rare), White and Brown Pelicans, Brown Booby, Anhinga, Magnificent Frigatebird, Mottled Duck (rare), Swallow-tailed Kite, Great Blue Heron, Wood Stork (Ibis), Yellow Rail, Black Rail, Wilson's Plover, Whimbrel, Greater Yellowlegs, Ruddy Turnstone, Red Knot, Marbled Godwit, Sandwich Tern, Pileated Woodpecker, Scrub Jay, Long-billed Marsh Wren, Gray-cheeked Thrush, Loggerhead Shrike, Yellow-throated Vireo, Orange-Crowned Warbler, Worm-eating Warbler, Yellow-throated Warbler, Northern Parula, Connecticut Warbler, Hooded Warbler, Northern (Baltimore) Oriole, Summer Tanager, Rose-breasted Grosbeak (rare), Painted Bunting (rare), and Bachman's Sparrow. Checklist available.

Chinsegut Nature Center, 404 Highland Street, Brooksville 33512; (904) 796-2198. Operated by Florida Fish Commission in cooperation with the Hernando Audubon Society. This 408-acre center is located north of Brooksville, near the Robins Memorial Forest. To reach the center, take US 41 north from Brooksville for about 5 miles to SR 581, continue for ½ mile to entrance; permission to tour the center must be obtained in advance from the director in Brooksville. Guided tours can be arranged; a variety of educational and interpretive programs is offered.

The varied habitat — mixed woodlands, open fields, and ponds — provides food and shelter for a large number of birds. There have been 155 species reported here since 1966. Among these are: Double-crested Cormorant, Anhinga, American Wigeon, Ring-necked Duck, Sharp-shinned Hawk, Marsh Hawk, Louisiana Heron, American Bittern, Wood Stork (Ibis), Roseate

Spoonbill, Sandhill Crane, Purple Gallinule, Black Tern, Barred Owl, Chimney Swift, Rough-winged Swallow, Carolina Chickadee, Short-billed Marsh Wren, Wood Thrush, White-eyed Vireo, Cape May Warbler, Cerulean Warbler, Hooded Warbler, Boat-tailed Grackle, Summer Tanager, Rose-breasted Grosbeak, and Bachman's Sparrow. Checklist available.

Cummer Sanctuary, Route 1, Chiefland 32626. Owned by The Nature Conservancy; preserve director: Mr. Alton Marsh. The sanctuary is open with permission only. Cummer Sanctuary is located about 15 miles from Chiefland, southwest of Flowler's Bluff, on SR 347, southeast of the Suwannee River.

The 985-acre sanctuary includes about 4 miles of river bank and 2 small islands. It is essentially a river preserve. The land along the Suwannee is low and is often submerged. Behind the river swamp, with its characteristic vegetation, are sections of pine flatwoods and hardwood hammock; beyond the flatwoods are small islands of white sand hills with typical scrub flora. These 3 main different plant communities and the river itself combine to provide habitat for a variety of birds. Among the birds seen regularly at the Cummer Sanctuary are: Wood Duck, Cooper's Hawk, Bald Eagle, Osprey, Bobwhite, Black-crowned Night Heron, American Bittern, American Coot, Common Snipe, American Woodcock, Screech Owl, Whip-poor-will, Belted Kingfisher, Red-headed Woodpecker, Eastern Kingbird, Eastern Wood Pewee, Carolina Chickadee, House Wren, Gray Catbird, Blue-gray Gnatcatcher, Black-and-white Warbler, Common Yellowthroat, Cardinal, Rufous-sided Towhee, and Swamp Sparrow.

Gulf Islands National Seashore, P.O. Box 100, Gulf Breeze 32561. Gulf Islands Seashore is located on the Gulf of Mexico, and extends into Mississippi. To reach the park from Pensacola, take US 98 south to SR 399. There are camping facilities at the Fort Pickens area of the Seashore. Gulf Islands became part of the National Park System in 1971. Acquisition is not yet complete — the park will total 125,000 acres. Visitors are asked to respect the rights of private property owners.

There are forts of historic interest at the park. There are also self-guiding nature trails; and various interpretive programs are offered. The park embraces a variety of habitats from beaches to freshwater marshes. Each area provides homes for wildlife. There have been 159 species of birds (20 nesting) sighted here. Among these are: Red-throated Loon, Horned Grebe, White and Brown Pelicans, Brown Booby, Gannet, Magnificent Frigatebird, Green- and Blue-winged Teals, Wood Duck, Bufflehead, Sharp-shinned Hawk, Peregrine Falcon, Osprey, Reddish Egret, Louisiana Heron, White Ibis, Black Rail, American Oystercatcher, Snowy Plover, Wilson's Plover, Ruddy Turnstone, Willet, Red Knot, Marbled Godwit, Laughing Gull, Sooty Tern, Yellow-billed Cuckoo, Burrowing Owl, Yellow-bellied Sapsucker, Gray Kingbird, Bank Swallow, Winter Wren, Ruby-crowned Kinglet, Cedar Waxwing, Loggerhead Shrike,

Black-whiskered Vireo, Prothonotary Warbler, Worm-eating Warbler, Blue-winged Warbler, Louisiana Waterthrush, Bobolink, Orchard Oriole, Scarlet Tanager, Painted Bunting, and Song Sparrow.

Lake Woodruff National Wildlife Refuge, P.O. Box 488, DeLeon Springs 32028; (904) 985-4673. To reach the refuge, take SR 40A ½ mile southwest from DeLeon Springs. Much of the refuge is accessible only by boat. There is a wildlife management demonstration area located a mile west of refuge headquarters; this area can be reached by car. In addition, the refuge maintains a self-guiding nature trail and an interpretive exhibit at refuge headquarters; guided tours of the management area are also offered. The best time for these tours is from November to February. Lake Woodruff Refuge is located near Canaveral National Seashore and Merritt Island NWR; it is adjacent to Ocala National Forest. Although there is no camping allowed on the refuge, facilities are available at Ocala as well as at several smaller state and private campgrounds in the vicinity.

Lake Woodruff NWR was established in 1963 and consists of 18,417 acres of marsh and hardwood swamp areas as well as some pinelands. Situated on the Atlantic Flyway, the primary concern of the refuge is to provide wintering grounds for migratory waterfowl. The diverse habitat of the refuge provides food and shelter for a variety of wildlife. Deer, black bear, river otter, armadillo, and the endangered Florida panther are among the animals that live here. There have been 192 species of birds (72 nesting) reported at Lake Woodruff. Among them are: Double-crested Cormorant, Fulvous Tree Duck, American Wigeon, Wood Duck, Ring-necked Duck, Swallow-tailed Kite, Everglade Kite (rare), Broad-Winged Hawk, Little Blue Heron, Least Bittern, Wood Stork (Ibis), White Ibis, Sandhill Crane (rare), Limpkin, Sora, Black-necked Stilt, Bonaparte's Gull, Ground Dove, Barn Owl, Whip-poor-will, Pileated Woodpecker, Red-headed Woodpecker, Eastern Wood Pewee, Purple Martin, Carolina Chickadee, Long- and Short-billed Marsh Wrens, Hermit Thrush, Orange-crowned Warbler, Swainson's Warbler, Black-throated Blue Warbler, Louisiana Waterthrush, Boat-tailed Grackle, Blue Grosbeak, and Bachman's Sparrow. Checklist available.

Merritt Island National Wildlife Refuge, P.O. Box 6504, Titusville 32780. Merritt Island shares a common boundary with the John F. Kennedy Space Center. The refuge is about 35 miles east of Orlando; take SR 50 east to Titusville; then SR 402 for 7 miles east (from Titusville) to the refuge. Merritt Island is part of Cape Canaveral National Seashore. Camping is not permitted on the refuge; however private campgrounds are located nearby. *St. Johns NWR,* also administered by Merritt Island NWR, is located 5 miles west of Titusville. *Ulumay Wildlife Refuge,* a 460-acre county preserve, is nearby — on Sykes Creek Parkway. The refuge consists of salt marsh and thickets. Herons, ibises, rails, and passerines frequent the area.

Merritt Island NWR was established in 1963 and now totals over 140,000 acres. The habitat of the refuge includes freshwater impoundments, brackish impoundments and marshlands, ocean beach, oak hammocks, mangrove islands, citrus groves, and palmetto-pine uplands. A primary management objective of the refuge is to continue to maintain favorable conditions for the breeding populations of the (Southern) Bald Eagle, Brown Pelican, and (Dusky) Seaside Sparrow.

Spring and fall are particularly rewarding times for birdwatching at Merritt Island. Winter peak concentrations of waterfowl reach 70,000 or more. There have been 251 species of birds (80 nesting) observed on the refuge (plus 31 accidentals). Among the birds likely to be seen here are: Double-crested Cormorant, Magnificent Frigatebird, Fulvous Tree Duck, Mottled Duck, Cinnamon Teal, Wood Duck, Marsh Hawk, Great Blue Heron, Reddish Egret, Wood Stork (Ibis), American Flamingo, Roseate Spoonbill, Black Rail, American Oystercatcher, Wilson's Plover, Purple Sandpiper (rare), American Avocet, Pomarine Jaeger, Long-tailed Jaeger, Gull-billed Tern, Black Tern, Smooth-billed Ani, Barn Owl, Downy Woodpecker, Scrub Jay, Brown-headed Nuthatch, Swainson's Thrush, Black-whiskered Vireo, Swainson's Warbler, Orange-crowned Warbler, Worm-eating Warbler, Painted Bunting, Henslow's Sparrow (rare), and Bachman's Sparrow (rare). Checklist available.

Ocala National Forest, Lake George Ranger District, Ocala 32670; (904) 622-6577; or Seminole Ranger District, Eustis 32726; (904) 357-3721. Ocala Forest is located in northeastern Florida about 50 miles south of Jacksonville and 40 miles north of Orlando. To reach the Forest, use SR 19, SR 40, SR 42, SR 314. Ocala is quite near Lake Woodruff NWR. Public facilities available at Ocala include camping, picnicking, swimming, fishing, canoeing, and hiking. During the summer, guided nature walks are scheduled. Self-guiding interpretive trails are also maintained.

Ocala Forest covers 366,000 acres; it is characterized by vast stands of sand pine. This tree is the only one capable of growing to usable size in the dry sand. Along the streams, palms tower above the subtropical vegetation. Ocala provides habitat for a wide variety of plant and animal life. Among the birds seen here are: Pied-billed Grebe, Anhinga, Wood Duck, Turkey Vulture, Osprey, Bobwhite, Green Heron, Least Bittern, White Ibis, King Rail, Mourning Dove, Screech Owl, Whip-poor-will, Common (Yellow-shafted) Flicker, Scrub Jay, Carolina Chickadee, Mockingbird, Brown Thrasher, Prothonotary Warbler, Common Yellowthroat, Orchard Oriole, Indigo Bunting, and Bachman's Sparrow (occasionally).

Osceola National Forest, U.S. Forest Service, P.O. Box 1649, Lake City 32055. Osceola Forest is located in northern Florida. To reach Osceola, take US 10 west from Jacksonville for about 40 miles. The 157,000-acre Forest has a network of hiking and canoeing trails. Other public recreational activities available include camping, swimming, and picnicking. Of special interest is the Olustee Experimental Forest, which is a center for research in forest genetics. This 3315-acre area is located on the south side of Osceola.

Although Osceola Forest is composed primarily of slash and longleaf pine, it also has numerous hardwood swamps of cypress, maple, and black gum. The terrain is mostly flat, dotted with ponds, sinks, and cypress swamps. Osceola shelters a variety of snakes (including some that are poisonous), turtles, lizards, frogs, skunks, mice, bears, weasels, squirrels. Among the 66 most common birds of Osceola Forest are: Wood Duck, Turkey Vulture, Red-tailed Hawk, Bobwhite, Little Blue Heron, Barred Owl, Common Nighthawk, Red-cockaded Woodpecker, Northern Parula, Common Yellowthroat, and Summer Tanager. Partial checklist available.

Robins Memorial Forest. Owned by The Nature Conservancy. The preserve is located 6 miles north of Brooksville, on US 41 (about 50 miles north of Tampa). The 31-acre area is open with permission only; contact the wildlife biologist at nearby Chinsegut Nature Center (see page 163).

Robins Memorial Forest, also known as McCarty Woods, is a virgin longleaf pineland. Over 150 species of birds have been recorded in the area. Among them are: Mottled Duck, Swallow-tailed Kite, Red-shouldered Hawk, Bobwhite, Little Blue Heron, Least Bittern, Wood Stork (Ibis), Chuck-will's-widow, Red-bellied Woodpecker, Pileated Woodpecker, Tufted Titmouse, Carolina Wren, Yellow-billed Cuckoo, Gray Kingbird, Great Crested Flycatcher, Tree Swallow, Brown Thrasher, Red-eyed Vireo, Cedar Waxwing, Loggerhead Shrike, Black-throated Green Warbler, Pine Warbler, Bay-breasted Warbler, Scarlet and Summer Tanagers, Indigo Bunting, and Bachman's Sparrow.

St. Marks National Wildlife Refuge, Box 68, St. Marks 32355. St. Marks Refuge is located approximately 20 miles south of Tallahassee. To reach refuge headquarters, take SR 363 south from Tallahasee to its junction with US 98; turn east on US 98, and proceed to the entrance. St. Marks Refuge is situated near Wakulla Springs Audubon Sanctuary, Apalachicola National Forest, St. Vincent NWR, and Aucilla Wildlife Management Area. Although no camping is permitted at the refuge, facilities are available at Apalachicola.

St. Marks was established in 1931. The refuge totals about 65,000 acres along the Gulf of Mexico; an additional 32,000 acres of water in Apalachee Bay are also protected. There are salt and brackish marshes, hardwood swamps, pine-oak uplands, and pine flatwoods. Myrtle, gallberry, slash and longleaf pine, saw palmetto, and other vegetation characterize the flatwoods. The refuge supports and protects several endangered species: American alligator, Red-cockaded Woodpecker, Bald Eagle, and Osprey. The best birdwatching opportunities are during fall, winter, and spring. Shorebirds are most common during late spring and early fall. There have been 263 species of birds (98 nesting) identified on the refuge (plus 41 accidentals). Among the birds likely to be seen here are:

Magnificent Frigatebird, White-fronted Goose, Fulvous Tree Duck (rare), Gadwall, Pintail, Bufflehead, Ruddy Duck, Swallow-tailed Kite, Mississippi Kite, Little Blue Heron, Snowy Egret, Wood Stork (Ibis), White Ibis, Roseate Spoonbill (rare), Limpkin, Black Rail, American Oystercatcher, Piping Plover, American Golden Plover, Ruddy Turnstone, Red Knot, Dunlin, American Avocet (rare), Royal Tern, White-winged Dove, Great Horned Owl, Pileated Woodpecker, Western Kingbird, Vermilion Flycatcher, Cliff Swallow, Brown Creeper, Blue-gray Gnatcatcher, Swainson's Warbler, Worm-eating Warbler, Golden-winged Warbler, Cerulean Warbler (rare), Kentucky Warbler, Orchard Oriole, Scarlet Tanager, Indigo Bunting, Henslow's Sparrow (rare), and Bachman's Sparrow. Checklist available.

St. Vincent National Wildlife Refuge, P.O. Box 447, Apalachicola 32320. Access is by boat only; there are no public transportation facilities; visitors must provide their own boats. The refuge manager should be contacted before the refuge is visited. The island is located in Apalachicola Bay; the east end of the island is about 9 miles offshore from the town of Apalachicola. The refuge is located near St. Marks NWR, Wakulla Springs Audubon Sanctuary, and Apalachicola National Forest.

St. Vincent Refuge was established in 1968 and totals 12,350 acres. Beaches, tidal marsh, freshwater ponds, pine flatwoods, scrub oak ridges, and magnolia hammocks cover the island. In some sections large live oaks are laced together with hanging spanish moss. The 14 miles of beach are open to daytime public use; a permit (from the refuge manager) is needed to explore the interior of the island. Camping is not permitted at St. Vincent; facilities are available at Apalachicola National Forest.

American alligators and loggerhead turtles are among the endangered species that use the refuge. In addition, many species of shorebirds, waterbirds, ducks, gulls, and terns, are either visitors or residents. Among the birds likely to be seen here are: Anhinga, Canada Goose, Mallard, Northern Shoveler, Ring-necked Duck, Sharp-shinned Hawk, Bald Eagle, Osprey, Green Heron, Snowy Egret, American Bittern, Clapper Rail, Limpkin, American Oystercatcher, Wilson's Plover, Willet, Least Sandpiper, Laughing Gull, Black Skimmer, Great Horned Owl, Chuck-will's-widow, Red-bellied Woodpecker, Tree Swallow, Long- and Short-billed Marsh Wrens, Brown Thrasher, Magnolia Warbler, Yellow Warbler, Common Yellowthroat, Brown-headed Cowbird, Summer Tanager, and Sharp-tailed Sparrow.

Wakulla Springs Wildlife Sanctuary. Owned and maintained by the Florida Audubon Society. The sanctuary is located 15 miles south of Tallahassee, off SR 363. It is comprised of 4500 acres of mixed woodlands divided by the Wakulla River. There are guided and self-guiding tours; cruises in glass-bottom boats can be taken. The sanctuary is located near several state parks and recreation areas, gardens, and the Apalachicola National Forest (where camping facilities are available). An admission fee is charged. Among the many birds to be seen here are: Anhinga, Wood Duck, Osprey, Purple Gallinule, Limpkin, Prothonotary Warbler, and Northern Parula.

Central Florida

Blowing Rocks Preserve. For information, contact: Southeast Regional Office, The Nature Conservancy, 148 International Blvd. NE, Atlanta, Georgia 30303; (404) 659-0240. Blowing Rocks is located on the eastern coast of Florida, about 20 miles north of West Palm Beach. The 58-acre preserve is bisected by SR 707 near the southern end of Jupiter Island. Blowing Rocks is quite near Hobe Sound NWR; other nearby NWRs include Loxahatchee and Pelican Island. Camping facilities are available at nearby Jonathan Dickinson State Park.

The preserve is an Atlantic barrier island with 4400 feet of ocean frontage. It consists mainly of coral outcroppings and sand beach. The beach is a sea turtle spawning area; and Brown Pelicans, Double-crested Cormorants, and Osprey frequent the preserve. Birdlife is somewhat limited, owing to the accessibility of the area to people and prey. For additional information about birds of the area, see the entry for Hobe Sound NWR (page 170).

Buttonwood Rookery. Owned by Lemon Bay Conservancy, P.O. Box 508, Englewood 33533. Preserve director: Ms. Joan Eckert, 185 Sabal Lane, Englewood 33533; (813) 474-8438; Ms. Eckert lives across from the preserve. Visits to the preserve must be arranged with the director. Buttonwood Rookery is across Lemon Bay from Grove City. From Englewood, take SR 776 across the Bay, then go south on Gulf Boulevard. Buttonwood is located near Sanibel Island and several NWRs.

The 47-acre preserve is made up of 2 mangrove islands which are in Lemon Bay, a wholly unpolluted estuarial system. Both islands are completely wild — there are no buildings of any kind on either island; neither are there any roads, trails, or paths. The land is characterized by sand and mud flats and beds of eel and turtle grass. The vegetation is typically subtropical, including sabal palm, silver buttonwood, mangroves (mostly white and black) and a variety of low shrubs, succulents, grasses, and other plants.

Rookery Island (the smaller of the 2) has had a nesting colony of egrets (Great and Snowy). Both islands are resting, feeding, and breeding grounds for a wide variety of birds. Among the birds likely to be seen here are: Magnificent Frigatebird, Double-crested Cormorant, Brown and White Pelicans, Osprey, Great Blue Heron, Louisiana Heron, Black-crowned Night Heron, Wood Stork (Ibis), White Ibis, Roseate Spoonbill, Black Skimmer, Laughing Gull, Arctic Tern, Barred Owl, Whip-poor-will, Downy and Hairy Woodpeckers, Yellow-bellied Sapsucker, Loggerhead Shrike, and numerous warblers.

Egmont Key National Wildlife Refuge. Under management of J. N. "Ding" Darling NWR. Egmont Key is one of the more recent additions to the refuge system — it was established in 1974. The refuge now totals 240 acres. Egmont Key is located in Tampa Bay, a mile north of Passage Key NWR.

Loggerhead turtles nest on the island as do Black Skimmers, Least Terns, and Mourning Doves. For information about visiting the refuge, contact the refuge manager at J. N. "Ding" Darling NWR. Access to Egmont Key is by boat only; public use is not encouraged. All visiting is prohibited during nesting season.

Hobe Sound National Wildlife Refuge, P.O. Box 645, Hobe Sound 33455; (305) 546-6141. The refuge is managed by South Florida National Wildlife Refuges, Route 1, Box 278, Delray Beach 33444. Hobe Sound NWR is located about 20 miles north of West Palm Beach; headquarters are on US 1, just south of the town of Hobe Beach. Nearby wildlife refuges include Loxahatchee and Pelican Island. Hobe Sound NWR borders Jonathan Dickinson State Park where camping facilities are available.

Hobe Sound Refuge was established in 1968 and presently covers about 400 acres. The landscape is characterized by mangroves and Australian pines. The habitat of Hobe Sound Refuge may be its most interesting feature. It is typical of a rapidly diminishing type in Florida — very high dunes, reaching 50 feet or more, dropping sharply to the shoreline.

Although wildlife populations are not large, they are varied including such mammals as raccoon, river otter, armadillo, bobcat, and white-tailed deer. Birdlife is also varied. Among the birds seen here are: Pied-billed Grebe, Anhinga, Brown Pelican, Red-breasted Merganser, Red-shouldered Hawk, Bald Eagle, Osprey, Louisiana Heron, Black- and Yellow-crowned Night Herons, White Ibis, Roseate Spoonbill, American Coot, Willet, Least Tern, Screech Owl, Scrub Jay, Yellow-bellied Sapsucker, House Wren, Cape May Warbler, American Redstart, Common Yellowthroat, and Cardinal.

Island Bay National Wildlife Refuge. Under management of J. N. "Ding" Darling NWR. Island Bay was established in 1908 and totals over 20 acres. The refuge is located 23 miles northwest of Fort Myers and 75 miles south of Tampa in the Cape Haze area. The 6 separate tracts that make up the refuge are not entire islands, but rather higher areas of several mangrove islands. The refuge includes 2 Indian midden mounds. These historic sites are on Turtle Bay.

The vegetation of the refuge is characterized by red and black mangroves, buttonwood, cabbage palms, rubber trees, gumbo limbo, palmettos, sea grape, and low shrubs and vines. The islands serve as a feeding and resting area for shorebirds, gulls, and terns. Primary species on the refuge include herons, Brown Pelicans, and White Ibises. For information about visiting the refuge, contact the refuge manager at J. N. "Ding" Darling NWR. Access to Island Bay is by boat only; public use is not encouraged. During the nesting season, all visiting is prohibited.

Jack Island State Preserve. For information contact the Florida Department of Natural Resources, Crown Building, 202 Blount Street, Tallahassee 32304. Jack Island is adjacent to Pepper Park State Recreation Area; it was known formerly as the Indian River Inlet Area. An access road leads from SR A1A to the visitors' parking lot. There is a footbridge that goes across to the island. Only foot traffic is permitted on the 958-acre sanctuary. Camping facilities are available at Pepper Park.

Jack Island is composed of salt marsh, mangrove, and hardwood hammock. Buttonwoods, sabal palms, and gumbo limbos are characteristic of the island. The mud flats and marshy areas are nesting and feeding grounds for a wide variety of birds (141 species). Among the birds likely to be seen here are: Horned Grebe, White and Brown Pelicans, Anhinga, Pintail, Redhead, Osprey, Peregrine Falcon (rare), Snowy Egret, Reddish Egret (rare), Green Heron, Wood Stork (Ibis), Roseate Spoonbill, Virginia Rail, Piping Plover, Ruddy Turnstone, Willet, Sanderling, Black-necked Stilt, Laughing Gull, Forster's Tern, Caspian Tern, Yellow-billed Cuckoo, Barn Owl, Yellow-bellied Sapsucker, Pileated Woodpecker, Barn Swallow, Carolina Wren, Hermit Thrush, Loggerhead Shrike, Black-whiskered Vireo, Black-and-white Warbler, Black-throated Blue Warbler, American Redstart, and Rufous-sided Towhee. Checklist available.

Mountain Lake Sanctuary, P.O. Box 268, Lake Wales 33853; (813) 638-1355. The sanctuary and the Singing Tower are located 3 miles north of Lake Wales, off US 27. The grounds are open all year from 8-5:30; there is a parking fee. Mountain Lake and the Singing Tower are owned and maintained by The American Foundation (a private organization). The Singing Tower houses a 53-bell carillon; it is not an observation tower.

The sanctuary comprises 128 acres of mixed woodlands, pools, and lawns. With the exception of the pine trees, all trees and shrubbery on the grounds have been planted. There are various self-guiding trails, observation blinds, and interpretive facilities. A naturalist is on duty. Among the 103 species of birds seen here regularly are: Pied-billed Grebe, Wood Duck, Bald Eagle, Osprey, Green Heron, White Ibis, Killdeer, Screech Owl, Common Nighthawk, Red-headed Woodpecker, Purple Martin, Tufted Titmouse, Mockingbird, Veery, Ruby-crowned Kinglet, Loggerhead Shrike, Solitary Vireo, Orange-crowned Warbler, Palm Warbler, Hooded Warbler, Summer Tanager, Rose-breasted Grosbeak, and Bachman's Sparrow. Checklist available.

Passage Key National Wildlife Refuge. Under management of J. N. "Ding" Darling NWR. Passage Key was established in 1905 as a refuge for migratory birds. It now totals over 36 acres. Passage Key is located at the entrance to Tampa Bay, about 25 miles from Tampa. The key is a sand spit whose size changes drastically with the tide. At high tide, the refuge is about 20 acres; at low tide it may be 3 times that size.

Passage Key is a wave-formed island that has been greatly influenced by hurricane storm tides that have stripped the key of vegetation. Until 1956, the island was covered with Australian pine, beach grass, sea oats, and morning glories. Wildlife on the refuge includes Loggerhead turtles, Laughing Gulls, Black Skimmers, terns, gulls, shorebirds, pelicans, cormorants, and other waterbirds which use the refuge for loafing, feeding, and nesting.

Passage Key is now classified as a Wilderness Area. Access is by boat only and public use is discouraged. During nesting season, all visiting is prohibited. For further information, contact the refuge manager at J. N. "Ding" Darling NWR.

Pelican Island National Wildlife Refuge. Under management of Merritt Island NWR. The refuge is located between the towns of Sebastian and Wabasso, about 25 miles south of Melbourne (45 miles south of Merritt Island NWR). The island is near Sebastian Inlet State Recreation Area where camping facilities are available.

The refuge was established in 1903 and now consists of nearly 4400 acres of bottomlands and mangrove islands. Although best known for its nesting colonies of pelicans, the refuge provides habitat for many other species. Abundant nesting birds include Double-crested Cormorant, Anhinga, Brown Pelican, Wood Stork (Ibis), Roseate Spoonbill, Louisiana Heron, and egrets.

While public use of the refuge must be limited to avoid disturbing the birds, there are opportunities for birdwatching (and photography) from a reasonable distance offshore. An interpretive center is planned for the refuge, to be located on a nearby shore where it will not affect the wilderness character of the islands.

Pinellas National Wildlife Refuge. Under management of J. N. "Ding" Darling NWR. The 377-acre refuge was established in 1921. It consists of 2 mangrove islands — Bush Key and Indian Key — and is located in Tampa Bay. The islands are flat with small depressions and potholes — ideal mosquito-breeding habitat. Bush Key, in addition, has interior tidal flats connected to the bay waters by a natural canal. Vegetation on the islands consists mostly of red and black mangroves, cordgrass, and *batis*. Nesting birds include Brown Pelicans, Double-crested Cormorants, Great Blue Herons, and Great (Common) Egrets. Roseate Spoonbills and Magnificent Frigatebirds also use the islands. The heavy oil damage in 1970 has had an adverse effect on the vegetation and wildlife of the refuge.

Access to Pinellas is by boat only; public use is discouraged. During nesting season, all visiting is prohibited. For further information, contact the refuge manager at J. N. "Ding" Darling NWR.

Walk-in-the-Water Creek, Lake Wales 33853. Owned by The Nature Conservancy; preserve director: Dr. Bruce Newell, 1128 Carlton Avenue, Lake Wales 33853; (813) 676-4722. The preserve is open with permission only. To reach the preserve, take US 60 north from Indian Estate for about 5 miles; the preserve is reached from US 60 just east of Walk-in-the-Water Creek through Dr. Newell's property. This 13-acre preserve is characterized by mixed pine and hardwood forests, palms with bromeliads, spanish moss, and orchids; there are marshy areas; a swampy, open area; and ponds. Fall, winter, and spring are the most confortable times to visit; the bromeliads and orchids are in bloom in February. The many birds seen at the preserve include: Turkey, Bobwhite, Great (Common) Egret, Great Blue Heron, Wood Stork (Ibis), Killdeer, Barred Owl, Red-bellied Woodpecker, Common (Yellow-shafted) Flicker, Scrub Jay, Mockingbird, Brown Thrasher, Cardinal, and migrating passerines.

Southern Florida

Big Cypress National Fresh Water Reserve. Contact: Mr. Pank Defendorf, National Park Service, P.O. Box 1515, Naples 33904; (813) 261-4477. The preserve is between Naples and Miami and abuts the Everglades. Boundaries are along US 41, SR 94, and SR 838. Most of the area cannot be reached by car. For information about visiting the reserve, contact the National Park Service. Big Cypress adjoins the northwest section of the Everglades National Park; it provides the freshwater which is crucial to the survival of the Everglades. Acquisition is not yet complete; Big Cypress Reserve will total 585,000 acres. Nearby is the Audubon Society's Corkscrew Swamp Sanctuary.

The wet sawgrass prairie and cypress hammocks provide habitat for 17 endangered species. Among these are: Florida panther, West Indian (Florida) manatee, American alligator, (Southern) Bald Eagle, Brown Pelican, Everglade Kite, Red-cockaded Woodpecker, Mangrove Cuckoo, Reddish Egret, Wood Stork (Ibis), Roseate Spoonbill, and Great Blue (White) Heron. Other birds (210 species) that can be seen here include: White Pelican, Peregrine Falcon, Sharp-shinned Hawk, Caracara, American Flamingo, Limpkin, Black-necked Stilt, Piping Plover, Whimbrel, Long-billed Curlew, Marbled Godwit, Willet, Pectoral Sandpiper, Red Knot, Burrowing Owl, Pileated Woodpecker, Carolina Wren, Black-whiskered Vireo, Swainson's Warbler, Worm-eating Warbler, Kentucky Warbler, Ovenbird, Painted Bunting, and Seaside (Cape Sable) Sparrow.

Biscayne National Monument, P.O. Box 1369, Homestead 33030. Biscayne is located south of Miami and east of Homestead. The temporary park headquarters are at Homestead Bayfront Park. There are public and private campgrounds in the area. On Elliott Key itself there is a primitive campground; fresh water is not available. Access is by boat only. Other facilities at Elliott Key include a small boat marina, saltwater showers, and a picnic area. Most of Biscayne's 96,000 acres are water and reef. The park borders the temperate and tropic zones and because of this it has wildlife of both zones on the land and in the surrounding waters. Nearby is the famed John Pennekamp Coral Reef State Park.

Biscayne has about 25 islands (keys) forming an almost continuous chain. Woody vegetation covers the keys almost completely. Mangroves line the shoreline and a startling variety of tropical hardwoods dominates the higher interior. Bobcat, raccoon, and opossum are found here. There are 93 species of birds (12 nesting) known to occur at Biscayne; an additional 100 species are likely to occur. Among the birds generally seen here are: Brown Pelican, Brown Booby (rare), Blue-footed Booby (rare), Double-crested Cormorant, Magnificent Frigatebird, Red-breasted Merganser, Sharp-shinned Hawk, Bald Eagle, Osprey, Great Blue (White) Heron, Reddish Egret (nesting), White Ibis, Wilson's Plover, Willet, Caspian Tern, Black Skimmer, White-crowned Pigeon, Mangrove Cuckoo (rare, may nest), Screech Owl, Red-bellied Woodpecker, Blue-gray Gnatcatcher, Black-whiskered Vireo, Prairie Warbler, American Redstart, Bobolink, and Boat-tailed Grackle. Checklist available.

Caloosahatchee National Wildlife Refuge. Under management of J. N. "Ding" Darling NWR. This 40-acre refuge was established in 1908. It is located 12 miles east of Fort Myers in the Caloosahatchee River. The primary species of the refuge are Louisiana Heron, Brown Pelican, egrets, and other waders and shorebirds. Caloosahatchee consists of 4 low, marshy islands which are covered by small bay trees, shrubs, and mixed freshwater growth. For information about visiting Caloosahatchee, contact the refuge manager at J. N. "Ding" Darling. Access is by boat only; public use is not encouraged. During nesting season, all visiting is prohibited.

Corkscrew Swamp Sanctuary, Box 1875, Route 2, Sanctuary Road, Naples 33940; (813) 657-3771. Corkscrew is owned and maintained by the National Audubon Society. The sanctuary is located near Bonita Springs, 16 miles southwest of Immokalee, off SR 846; follow signs. An entrance fee is charged; a guidebook is available. A staff of naturalists is on duty and there are various interpretive displays and programs. Picnicking is allowed in an area adjacent to the parking lot. Camping is not permitted, although facilities are available at nearby private campgrounds.

Corkscrew covers 11,000 acres — including the last remaining large stand of virgin bald cypress in the state. A mile-long boardwalk through the heart of the swamp leads to the Wood Stork (Ibis) rookery. Among the 168 species of birds (65 nesting) reported here are: Anhinga, Red-shouldered Hawk, Louisiana Heron, White Ibis, Sandhill Crane, Limpkin, Pileated Woodpecker, Carolina Wren, Loggerhead Shrike, Northern Parula, Painted Bunting, Rufous-sided Towhee, and Bachman's Sparrow. Checklist available.

Dry Tortugas. The Dry Tortugas are a group of small islands located about 70 miles west of Key West in the Gulf of Mexico. Chapters of the Florida

Audubon Society generally sponsor trips to the Tortugas in May. It is not recommended to make the trip alone. Trips are either by boat or by chartered seaplane from Key West or Marathon. Fort Jefferson National Monument is located on Garden Key. If a visit to the islands is planned, remember to bring everything — including all water (there is no fresh water on the islands). The best time to visit the Tortugas is during spring and fall. Among the many birds to be seen there are Double-crested Cormorant, Sooty Tern, Black Noddy Tern, Roseate Tern, Magnificent Frigatebird, Brown Booby, Blue-faced Booby, Smooth-billed Ani (on Loggerhead Key), and various warblers.

Everglades National Park, Box 279, Homestead 33030. The park is located about 50 miles south of Miami, 12 miles from Homestead on SR 27. A visitors' center is at the park entrance; there is an entrance fee to the park. The road through the park is 38 miles long, ending at Flamingo on Florida Bay. Camping facilities are available at the Long Pine Key and Flamingo areas. There are many elevated boardwalk trails along the way; birding opportunities are myriad in the Everglades.

In addition to the Flamingo area, which is the largest — it has a museum, ranger-sponsored activities, boat trips, hikes and hiking trails, canoeing opportunities, and much more — there is the Shark Valley area. Shark Valley can be reached from US 41 about 30 miles west of Miami. At Shark Valley there is a ranger-escorted tram tour that leaves every hour. Be prepared to wait for trams during the winter (tourist) season. (Insects, especially mosquitoes, make summer visits to the Everglades unpleasant.) The tram travels through freshwater sloughs, sawgrass, and marshes to an observation tower. There is a third area of the park which is the least developed. This is also reached from US 41, about 40 miles west of Shark Valley, turn south on SR 29 to Everglades City. The Sandfly Island National Environmental Study Area is nearby, and accessible by boat only. There are boat tours operating out of Everglades City. For information regarding recreational facilities and opportunities, contact the park ranger (at the above address) and/or the Everglades Park Company, 18494 South Federal Highway, Miami 33157; (305) 695-3101. The Everglades Park Company operates boat tours, boat rentals, restaurants, and housing in the park.

There are 240 species of birds (81 nesting) that occur regularly in the park (plus 86 accidentals). Among these are: Anhinga, Magnificent Frigatebird, White and Brown Pelicans, Northern Shoveler, Ruddy Duck, Everglade Kite, Bald Eagle, Great Blue (White) Heron, Wood Stork (Ibis), White Ibis, Roseate Spoonbill, Limpkin, Purple Gallinule, Willet, Laughing Gull, Royal Tern, Sandwich Tern, Barred Owl, Red-bellied Woodpecker, Scissor-tailed Flycatcher, Blue-gray Gnatcatcher, Northern Parula, Yellow-breasted Chat, Orchard Oriole, Painted Bunting, and Lark Sparrow. Checklist available.

J. N. "Ding" Darling National Wildlife Refuge, P.O. Drawer B, Sanibel 33957. The refuge is located on Sanibel Island, in the Gulf of Mexico, 5 miles from the Florida coast. To reach Sanibel from Fort Myers, take SR 867 southwest for 17 miles to the causeway (a toll road). The refuge was established in 1945 and comprises 4300 acres. Sanibel Island is famous for the many varieties of shells on its beaches. Nearby are Corkscrew Swamp Sanctuary, Rookery Bay, Buttonwood Rookery, and several small NWRs that are administered by "Ding" Darling Refuge. Facilities at the refuge include a wildlife interpretive center, hiking and canoeing trails, an observation tower, a boardwalk, and a nature drive. Camping is not permitted at the refuge; facilities are available at nearby private campgrounds.

The island is composed of shell, sand, and silt. On the north side mangroves, interspersed with shallow bays, provide ideal habitat for wading birds. The refuge is mainly on the north side of the island with small areas elsewhere, including Point Ybel, at the eastern end, where refuge headquarters are located. There have been 226 species of birds identified on the refuge (68 nesting) plus 41 accidentals. Among the birds likely to be seen here are: Common Loon, White and Brown Pelicans, Gannet, Magnificent Frigatebird, Mottled Duck, American Wigeon, Swallow-tailed Kite, Sharp-shinned Hawk, Green Heron, Great Blue (White) Heron, Least Bittern, Wood Stork (Ibis), White Ibis, Roseate Spoonbill, Black Rail, Purple Gallinule, American Oystercatcher, American Avocet, Black-necked Stilt, Piping Plover, Snowy Plover, Wilson's Plover, Laughing Gull, Caspian Tern, White-winged Dove, Mangrove Cuckoo, Smooth-billed Ani, Burrowing Owl, Common Nighthawk, Red-headed Woodpecker (rare), Scissor-tailed Flycatcher (rare), Purple Martin, Brown Thrasher, Loggerhead Shrike, Black-whiskered Vireo, Prothonotary Warbler, Orange-crowned Warbler, Cape May Warbler, Black-throated Blue Warbler, Orchard Oriole, Painted Bunting, and Seaside Sparrow (rare). Checklist available.

Key West National Wildlife Refuge; Key Deer NWR; Great White Heron NWR, P. O. Box 385, Big Pine Key 33043. These 3 refuges are at the southern tip of Florida and are composed of scattered islands stretching for about 60 miles. All of the refuge islands are accessible only by boat, except for parts of Key Deer on Big Pine Key. Camping is not permitted on the islands; there are state campgrounds near Big Pine Key.

Key West NWR was established in 1908 and totals over 2000 acres; Great White Heron NWR (part of which overlaps part of Key West NWR) was established in 1938 and totals nearly 2000 acres; Key Deer NWR was established in 1954 and covers over 7400 acres. Both Key West and Great White Heron NWRs are managed primarily as migratory bird refuges. The latter gives permanent protection to the Great Blue (White) Heron, the largest North American wading bird. Key Deer NWR is managed primarily as a refuge for the Key Deer — the smallest North American deer. Near extinction in the 1950s, the Key Deer population exceeded 600 animals by 1970. Other endangered species which receive protection on the refuges include American alligator, White-crowned Pigeon, and Mangrove Cuckoo.

There have been 185 species of birds (44 nesting) and one hybrid (Wurdemann's Heron) observed on the refuges of the Florida Keys. Among these are: Brown Pelican, Gannet, Magnificent Frigatebird, Red-shouldered Hawk, Bald Eagle, Reddish Egret, Roseate Spoonbill, Limpkin, Clapper Rail, Black-necked Stilt, Wilson's Plover, Killdeer, Gull-billed Tern (rare), Sooty Tern, Noddy Tern (rare), White-winged Dove, Smooth-billed Ani, Ruby-throated Hummingbird, Scissor-tailed Flycatcher, Black-whiskered Vireo, Worm-eating Warbler, Palm Warbler, Louisiana Waterthrush, Bobolink, and Blue Grosbeak. Checklist available.

Loxahatchee National Wildlife Refuge, Route 1, Box 278, Delray Beach 33444. Loxahatchee is located about 50 miles north of Miami; the refuge headquarters are just off US 441, 12 miles west of Delray Beach. Camping is not permitted on the refuge.

Loxahatchee was established in 1951; it contains 145,635 acres of the Everglades. Sawgrass marshes, sloughs, hammocks, and wet prairies combine to form a habitat suitable to an unusual community of plant and animal life — including rare and endangered species such as the Florida panther, American alligator, and Everglade Kite. Because the vast marshes of the refuge support the sole food of this bird, Loxahatchee is one of the few places where the Everglade Kite can be seen.

The refuge is a southern terminus for waterfowl migrating down the Atlantic and Mississippi Flyways. A primary management objective of the refuge is providing winter habitat for these birds. There have been 245 species of birds (62 nesting) identified on the refuge. Among these are: Double-crested Cormorant, Fulvous Tree Duck, Mottled Duck, Masked Duck (rare), Swallow-tailed Kite, Short-tailed Hawk, Bald Eagle, Louisiana Heron, Glossy Ibis, White Ibis, Roseate Spoonbill, Sandhill Crane, Limpkin, Black-necked Stilt, Pectoral Sandpiper, Long- and Short-billed Dowitchers, Black Tern, Black Skimmer, Smooth-billed Ani, Short-eared Owl, Red-bellied Woodpecker, Scissor-tailed Flycatcher, Carolina Wren, Water Pipit, Yellow-throated Vireo, Swainson's Warbler, Golden-winged Warbler, Magnolia Warbler, Painted Bunting, and Bachman's Sparrow (rare). Checklist available.

Matlacha Pass National Wildlife Refuge. Under management of J. N. "Ding" Darling NWR. This 10-acre refuge was established in 1908. It is located 13 miles southwest of Fort Myers in Matlacha Pass. The 3 islands of the Matlacha Pass Refuge are important nesting and roosting sites for Black-crowned Night Herons, White Ibises, and Brown Pelicans. In addition, the islands provide resting and feeding areas for gulls, terns, and shorebirds. For information about visiting Matlacha Pass Refuge, contact the refuge manager at J. N. "Ding" Darling NWR. Access is by boat only; public use of the refuge is not encouraged. During nesting season, all visiting is prohibited.

Pine Island National Wildlife Refuge. Under management of J. N. "Ding" Darling NWR. This 31-acre refuge is located near Fort Myers, north of Sanibel Island in Pine Island Sound. The refuge was established in 1908.

Mammals on the refuge include manatees, raccoons, and marsh rabbits. Among the birds commonly seen here are: Magnificent Frigatebird, Great Blue (White) Heron, Reddish Egret, Wood Stork (Ibis), and Roseate Spoonbill. Nesting species include Little Blue Heron, Louisiana Heron, Great Blue (White) Heron, Great (Common) Egret, Snowy Egret, and the endangered Brown Pelican. Gulls and terns also use the refuge. For information about visiting Pine Island, contact the refuge manager at J. N. "Ding" Darling NWR. Access is by boat only; public use of the refuge is not encouraged. All visiting is prohibited during nesting season.

Rookery Bay Wildlife Sanctuary. Owned by the National Audubon Society, P.O. Box 997, Naples 33940; contact Mr. John Allen, Biologist, 1880 Kingfish Road, Naples 33940; (813) 774-0737. Rookery Bay is located 3 miles south of Naples and is accessible only by boat at high tide. To reach the sanctuary, take US 41 south from Naples to SR 951 (Isles of Capri Road); take SR 951 south to Shell Island Road. Rookery Bay is located near Sanibel Island, Corkscrew Swamp Sanctuary, and the western part of the Everglades. Although camping is not permitted on the island, there are camping facilities at nearby state parks.

Rookery Bay is an unspoiled estuary, an ideal place for waterfowl, wading birds, and shorebirds. Bobcat, black bear, deer, and diamondback rattlesnakes also find refuge at the sanctuary. Porpoises play in the bay. Brown Pelicans, Bald Eagles, and Osprey breed here. Among the other birds that can be seen at Rookery Bay are: White Pelican, Magnificent Frigatebird, Anhinga, Mottled Duck, Swallow-tailed Kite, Great Blue (White) Heron, Louisiana Heron, Reddish Egret, Roseate Spoonbill, Wood Stork (Ibis), White Ibis, and many species of gulls and terns.

NATURE CENTERS

Florida is well known to birdwatchers as having some of the best birdwatching areas on the eastern seaboard. In addition to those federal, local, and private preserves described above, there are the following nature centers. Most of these centers offer a variety of educational and interpretive programs. These centers are discussed briefly below. Owing to a lack of space, none of them are shown on the map.

Babson Park Audubon Center, Route 1, Box 149 E, Babson Park 33827; (813) 638-1355. The center is operated by the Florida and the Ridge Audubon Societies. It is located on US Alt. 27, just north of Webber College. Guided and self-guiding tours are available. The center is open all year.

Big Cypress Nature Center, Route #3, Box 140, Naples 33940; (813) 642-2812. The center consists of 5 acres plus the use of additional areas. Guided and self-guiding tours are available. The center is open all year; closed on Thanksgiving, Christmas, Easter, and weekends.

Boyd Hill Nature Park, 1101 Country Club Way South, St. Petersburg 33710; (813) 894-2111. The park covers 627 acres including open fields and swampy areas. Guided tours are available by appointment. There have been 161 species of birds seen here including: Magnificent Frigatebird, Screech Owl, Orange-crowned Warbler, and American Redstart.

Fairchild Tropical Gardens, 10901 Old Cutler Road, Miami 33156; (305) 667-1651. The gardens cover 83 acres. Guided tours are available by appointment. Paths and trails are maintained. The gardens are open 10-5, every day; an admission fee is charged.

The Koreshan Unity, Inc., P.O. Box 57, Estero 33928; (813) 922-2184. The center consists of 305 acres in a state park. Guided tours are available by appointment. Trails wind through extensive tropical gardens. The gardens are open every day from October through May.

Morningside Park Nature Center, 3540 East University Avenue, Gainesville 32601; (904) 378-3289. The center is operated by the Gainesville Department of Buildings and Grounds. It covers 278 acres. Guided and self-guiding tours are available. The park is open all year; closed on Thanksgiving, Christmas, and New Year's Day.

Pine Jog Environmental Sciences Center, 6301 Summit Boulevard, West Palm Beach, 33406; (305) 686-6600. The center is operated by Florida Atlantic University. It totals 40 acres; guided tours only are available. The center is open all year.

Street Nature Center, Lameraux Road (east of Cypress Gardens), Winter Haven 33880; (813) 299-2984. The center is operated by the Florida and the Lake Region Audubon Societies. It covers 40 acres. Guided tours are available; trails, some self-guiding, are maintained. The center is open all year.

Tallahassee Junior Museum, 3945 Museum Drive, Tallahassee 32304; (904) 576-1636. The center totals 50 acres. A special aspect of the museum is the pioneer farm with native animals. Guided tours are available; trails are maintained. The museum is open all year; closed on Mondays and holidays.

AUDUBON SANCTUARIES

There is a good deal of Audubon activity in Florida — 44 local chapters in addition to the Florida Audubon Society. Many of these local chapters maintain sanctuaries and/or nature centers. For additional information about these properties, contact the local chapter responsible. These are not shown on the map.

Crowley Museum and Nature Center, Inc., Sarasota; (813) 322-1414; naturalist on staff. Maintained by Miakka Audubon Society.

Doc Thomas Audubon House; 3 acres; visits by arrangement. Maintained by Tropical Audubon Society, Ms. Alice Wainwright, 3301 SW 27 Avenue, Miami 33133.

Hallman Island; 2 acres; naturalist on staff; visits by arrangements. Maintained by Bay County Audubon Society, Ms. M. F. Parker, 1546 Cincinnati Avenue, Panama City 32401.

Indian River Audubon Society Nature Education Center and Sanctuary; 19 acres; open to the public. Maintained by Indian River Audubon Society, Mr. Harold Wyle, 207 Broadview Drive, Cocoa Beach 32922.

Sawpit Creek Sanctuary; 60 acres; open to the public. Maintained by Duval and Florida Audubon Societies.

The following sanctuaries are maintained by the Florida Audubon Society. For specific information, including arrangements to visit their sanctuaries, contact them at: P. O. Drawer 76, Maitland 32751; (305) 647-2615.

Audubon House, Maitland; 3 acres; headquarters of Florida Audubon Society; open to the public.

Babson Park Audubon Center. Route 1, Box 149 E. Babson Park 33827; (813) 638-1355; open to the public.

Becky Price Sanctuary (Lake County); 6 acres; visits by arrangement.

Coclough Pond Wildlife Sanctuary; 24 acres; naturalist on staff; administered by Alachua Audubon Society; visits by arrangement.

Cuyler Lanier Sanctuary (Lake County); 36 acres; visits by arrangement.

Daughtrey's Creeek (Lee County); several islands in a tidal zone; visits by arrangement.

Egret Island Sanctuary (Orange County); 10 acres; visits by arrangement.

Fred Schultz Memorial (Hillsborough County); 1¼-acre island; visits by arrangement.

Froitzheim Wilderness Sanctuary (Nassau County); 10 acres; visits by arrangement.

Grove and Cypress Wildlife Sanctuary (Lake County); 5 acres; visits by arrangement.

Hatton Wildlife Sanctuary (Brevard County); 10 acres; visits by arrangement.

J. Russell Errett Wildlife Sanctuary; 21 acres; naturalist on staff; administered by St. Lucie Audubon Society; visits by arrangement.

Mary Krune Bird Refuge (Dade County); 2 acres; visits by arrangement.

May Male Wildlife Sanctuary (Polk County); 20 acres; look for Limpkins, Pileated Woodpeckers, and warblers; visits by arrangement.

Orange Lake Sanctuary — Bird Island (Alachua County); 36 acres; visits by arrangement.

Perry Boswell, Jr. Wildlife Sanctuary (Martin County); 3 acres; visits by arrangement.

Saddle Creek Sanctuary (Polk County); visits by arrangement.

Scarborough Sanctuary (Orange County); 10 acres; visits by arrangement.

Sebastian Sanctuaries (Indian River County); 70 acres; visits by arrangement.

Smith Island Sanctuary (Monroe County); 2½ acres; visits by arrangement.

The following sanctuaries are owned by the National Audubon Society. Visits to them are restricted and must be arranged in advance by contacting the warden in charge.

Cowpens Key; 10 acres in Florida Bay, west of Tavernier. This is a low, mangrove-covered island with the largest nesting colony of Roseate Spoonbills in Florida. Other nesting species include Great Blue (White) Herons and Magnificent Frigatebirds. For information, contact NAS, Research Department, 115 Indian Mount Trail, Tavernier 33070.

Kissimmee Prairie Region; 60,000 acres north and west of Okeechobee (includes some private property). Among the nesting species are Sandhill Cranes, Burrowing Owls, Caracaras, and wading birds. For information, contact the Lake Okeechobee warden (see below).

Kitchen Creek Wildlife Sanctuary; 42 acres along the Loxahatchee River in Martin County; characterized by bald cypress and pinelands. Maintained by the Audubon Society of the Everglades, c/o Tom Tomlinson, 4906 N. Dixie Highway, West Palm Beach 33407.

Lake Okeechobee; 2 parcels on the west side of the lake totaling over 28,000 acres. This is a principal nesting ground for Everglade Kites and wading birds. For information, contact the warden at: 505 SW 10 Street, Okeechobee 33472; (813) 763-3946.

Lake Worth Islands; about 100 acres of islands in the town of Palm Beach. The islands are a nesting site for egrets, herons, and ibises. For information, contact the Audubon Society of the Everglades (see above).

Tampa Bay; about 200 acres made up of small islands south of Tampa in Tampa and Hillsboro Bays. Nesting species on the islands include Brown Pelicans, herons, egrets, ibises, and terns. For information, contact the warden at: Route 1, Box 205-U, Ruskin 33570; (813) 645-9484.

NATURE CONSERVANCY PRESERVES

The Nature Conservancy is also very active in Florida — acquiring property themselves and helping other organizations to preserve what is left of natural areas in the state. General information about The Nature Conservancy's activities in Florida can be obtained by writing to their Southeast Regional Office (see page 337 for address) or to the Florida Chapter of The Nature Conservancy, Box 224, Homestead 33030. In addition to those preserves already described, The Nature Conservancy also maintains (or is in the process of acquiring) the following areas:

Akers Reservation. Preserve director: Mr. Dick Workman, Sanibel-Captiva Conservation Foundation, Inc., P.O. Box 25, Sanibel 33957; (813) 472-2329. This 12½-acre preserve is located 25 miles west of Fort Myers; take SR 867 to Sanibel Island and Chateaux Sur Mer; take a private road to the bayou and then to the preserve by boat. The preserve is made up of hammocks and marshlands and is located at the mouth of the Sanibel Slough.

Fuch's Hammock. Preserve director: Ms. Sally Black, Castellow Hammock Education Center, 22301 SW 162 Avenue, Gould; (305) 245-4321. The 25-acre preserve is located a mile west of Krome Avenue (SR 27), near Homestead, on the corner of 312 Street SW (King's Highway) and 198 Avenue SW. This is an ancient hammock in which is found a rare bromeliad growing nowhere else in the United States. The property serves as a watering place for shorebirds and the surrounding thickets attract many smaller birds, especially during migration. The preserve is open with permission only; contact the preserve director.

Janet Butterfield Brooks Preserve, in Hernando County. Managed by the Florida Chapter. The 80-acre preserve is part of a proposed 290-acre area. It contains a mixture of high hammock, longleaf pine, and turkey oak uplands which are inhabited by opossum, bobcat, armadillo, fox, and fox squirrel.

New River Natural Area, in Broward County; 2 acres of mixed bottomland climax forest with upland mature swamp; cypress trees and knees; river frontage with sand beach. For information, contact the Florida Chapter.

Saint John's River Bluff; leased by The Nature Conservancy; 176 acres adjacent to the Theodore Roosevelt Preserve (see below).

Theodore Roosevelt Preserve. Preserve director: Dr. Ted Allen, Department of Biology, Jacksonville University, Jacksonville 32211. To reach the preserve from Jacksonville, take US 115 east to Monument Road (SR 113), then go north to Mount Pleasant Road. The property is located just south of Fort Carolina National Park. The 603-acre preserve is characterized by a hardwood forest blending into a magnolia-hickory forest with a rich understory of shrubs; there are two large swamps with ponds. Marshlands border the St. John's River and provide habitat for alligators. A heronry is located on the preserve.

Tiger Creek. Preserve director: Mr. Ken Morrison, P.O. Box 268, Lake Wales 33853; (813) 676-1355. To reach Tiger Creek, from Lake Wales, go east on SR 60 for 7 miles to Walk-in-the-Water Road, turn right, proceed to the end of the road. The area known as Tiger Creek is on the right. This preserve totals 2040 acres. Tiger Creek is a beautiful, crystal-clear stream. Since the creek is largely inaccessible, it would be wise to check with the preserve director before visiting it. Wildlife common to the area includes deer, squirrel, fox, raccoon, opossum, rabbit, bobcat, armadillo, skunk, and numerous birds.

STATE PARKS AND FORESTS

There are numerous parks located throughout Florida. They are administered by the Florida Department of Natural Resources, Division of Recreation and Parks, Crown Building, Tallahassee 32304; (904) 488-7326. No pets are permitted in campgrounds or on the beaches; pets are allowed in picnic areas if they are leashed and well behaved. Admission fees are charged. Facilities at Florida state parks include camping, boating, swimming, skin and scuba diving, and picnicking. In addition, there are museum exhibits, historic features, guided tours, and nature trails. Those parks that are well known as good birdwatching places are indicated as such by an asterisk (*). For additional information, contact the Department of Natural Resources at the above address.

STATE PARKS

Anastasia, St. Augustine 32084.
Bahia Honda, Bahia Honda Key.
Basin Bayou, Freeport 32439.
Bill Baggs (Cape Florida), Key Biscayne; day use only.
Blackwater River, Milton 32570.
Blue Springs, Orange City 32763.
Caladesi Island, Dunedin 33528; day use only.
Chekika, Homestead 33030.
Collier-Seminole, Marco 33937.
Dead Lakes, Wewahitchka 32465.
Falling Waters, Chipley 32428.
Faver-Dykes, Marineland.

Flagler Beach, Flagler Beach 32036.
Florida Caverns, Marianna 32446.
Fort Clinch, Fernandina Beach 32034.
Fred Gannon Rocky Bayou, Niceville 32578.
Grayton Beach, Grayton Beach.
*Highlands Hammock, Sebring 33870.
Hillsborough River, Zephyrhills 33599.
Hontoon Island, DeLand 32720.
Hugh Taylor Birch, Fort Lauderdale 33300.
Ichetucknee Springs, Fort White 32038; day use only.
John C. Beasley, Fort Walton Beach 32548; day use only.
John Pennekamp Coral Reef, Key Largo 33037.
*Jonathan Dickinson, Jupiter 33458.
Lake Griffin, Fruitland Park 32731.
*Little Talbot Island, Jacksonville 32200.
Long Key, Long Key.
Manatee Springs, Chiefland 32626.
Mike Roess (Gold Head Branch), Keystone Heights 32656.
*Myakka River, Myakka.
Ochlockonee River, Sopchoppy 32358.
O'Leno, High Springs 32643.
Oscar Scherer, Osprey 33559.
Pahokee, Pahokee 33476.
*Pepper Park (St. Lucie Museum), Fort Pierce 33450.
Ponce de Leon, Ponce de Leon 32455; day use only.
St. Andrews, Panama City 32401.
Sebastian Inlet (McLarty Museum), Sebastian 32958.
Suwanee River, Falmouth.
Three Rivers, Sneads 32460.
T.H. Stone Memorial (St. Joseph Peninsula), Port St. Joe 32456.
Tomoka, Ormond Beach 32074.
Torreya, Bristol 32321.
Wekiwa Springs, Apopka 32703.
Withlacoochee State Forest, Lacoochee 33537.

   DAY USE AREAS *(including ornamental gardens and special feature sites)*

Alfred B. Maclay Gardens, Tallahassee 32301.
Bulow Plantation Ruins, Bunnell 32010.
Cedar Key Museum, Cedar Key 32625.
Constitution Convention, Port St. Joe 32456.
Crystal River, Crystal River 32629.
Dade Battlefield, Bushnell 33513.
DeBary Hall, DeBary 32713.
Eden Gardens, Point Washington 32454.

Fort Gadsden, Sumatra.
Gamble Mansion, Ellenton 33532.
Huguenot Memorial, Fort George 32037.
John Gorrie, Apalachicola 32320.
Kingsley Plantation, Fort George 32037.
*Koreshan, Estero 33928.
Lake Jackson Mounds, Tallahassee 32301.
Madira Bickel Mounds, Terra Ceia Island 33591.
Marjorie K. Rawlings (Cross Creek), Island Grove 32654.
Natural Bridge Battlefield, Woodville 32362.
New Smyrna Sugar Mill Ruins, New Smyrna Beach 32069.
Olustee Battlefield, Olustee 32072.
*Ravine Gardens, Palatka 32077.
San Marcos de Apalache, St. Marks 32355.
Turtle Mound, New Smyrna Beach 32069.
*Washington Oaks Gardens, Marineland; 340 acres.
Yulee Sugar Mill Ruins, Homosassa 32646.

Limpkin

GEORGIA

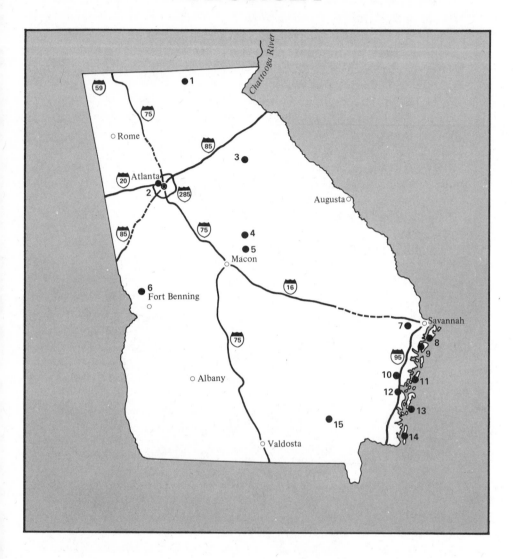

1. Chattahoochee National Forest
2. Lullwater Conservation Garden
   Fernbank Science Center
3. Sandy Creek NC
4. Oconee National Forest
5. Piedmont National Wildlife Refuge
6. Callaway Gardens
7. Savannah National Wildlife Refuge

8. Tybee NWR
9. Wassaw NWR
10. Harris Neck NWR
11. Blackbeard Island NWR
12. Wolf Island NWR
13. St. Simon's Island
14. Cumberland Island National Seashore
15. Okefenokee NWR

Georgia, the largest state east of the Mississippi, offers many opportunities to birdwatchers. About 75 percent of the 440 birds indigenous to the eastern United States can be seen in Georgia — including such endangered and local birds as Fulvous Tree Duck, Mississippi Kite, Limpkin, Purple Sandpiper, Red-cockaded Woodpecker, Common Raven, Gray Kingbird, Swainson's Warbler, Painted Bunting, and Bachman's Sparrow. The 96-mile coastline is primarily a succession of national wildlife refuges that lie along the Atlantic Flyway.

Most of the areas described in this chapter are owned by the federal government. Other areas that are worth checking for birds are Georgia's state wildlife management areas. Although established for hunting, such areas as *Allatoona, Berry College, Cedar Creek, Ocmulgee, Arabia Bay, Brunswick,* and *Altamaha* are particularly good for birding. For information regarding these areas, contact: Georgia Department of Natural Resources, Game and Fish Division, 270 Washington Street, SW, Atlanta 30334; (404) 656-3500; and request their brochure: Georgia Hunting Regulations and Management Area Guide. This brochure gives complete addresses of and traveling directions to these areas. In some areas, camping is permitted.

The state of Georgia has a comprehensive preservation program called the Georgia Heritage Trust Program, whereby lands of historical and/or ecological importance are acquired. For information about these preserves, contact the State of Georgia, Department of Natural Resources, 270 Washington Street, SW, Atlanta 30334.

For particular and local information regarding birdwatching in Georgia, the reader is advised to consult *A Birder's Guide to Georgia,* published by the Georgia Ornithological Society. It is an excellent book and gives specific information and detailed traveling directions. It is available from the GOS, P. O. Box 362, Atlanta 30301. For up-to-date birding information, contact the *Atlanta Audubon Society Rare Bird Alert:* (404) 634-5497.

Blackbeard Island National Wildlife Refuge. Administered by Savannah NWR. A refuge employee resides on the island. Blackbeard is located 18 miles off the coast of Georgia, not far from Wolf Island and Harris Neck NWRs. There is no regular boat service available, therefore visitors should make advance arrangements for transportation.

Blackbeard Refuge was established in 1924; it covers an area of about 5600 acres. The main body of the island is made up of a series of narrow ridges with valleys known as savannas. The ridges are mostly covered with live oak. Other prominent vegetation on the refuge includes slash pine, cabbage palmetto, holly, and magnolia. Some of the savannas have been diked to form pools. The island has 9 miles of beach on the ocean side which receive tremendous use by shorebirds. Thousands of skimmers, pelicans, and terns also make regular use of the island. The tidal marsh is a favorite nesting place for the Clapper Rail. Blackbeard Island is also a nesting ground for loggerhead turtles — over 100 nest on the island each year. There is an outstanding American alligator population, too. The varied habitat of the refuge enables many small land birds, especially in winter, to find food and cover. Yet several common mainland birds, such as the Blue Jay and Tufted Titmouse, are absent here. There have been 198 species of birds (74 nesting) recorded on the island. Among these are: Brown Pelican, Gannet, Fulvous Tree Duck (rare), Blue- and Green-winged Teals, Oldsquaw, Osprey, Chachalaca, Little Blue Heron, Black- and Yellow-crowned Night Herons, White Ibis, American Oystercatcher, Piping Plover, Dunlin, Marbled Godwit, Sandwich Tern, Chimney Swift, Pileated Woodpecker, Carolina Chickadee, Carolina Wren, Ruby- and Golden-crowned Kinglets, Northern Parula, Magnolia Warbler, Blackpoll Warbler, Cape May Warbler, Orchard Oriole, Summer Tanager, Painted Bunting, and Ipswich Sparrow (rare). Checklist available.

Chattahoochee National Forest, Forest Supervisor, U.S. Forest Service, Box 1437, Gainesville 30501; (404) 532-6366. Chattahoochee is located north of Atlanta, about 20 miles north of Gainesville; use US 23/441 and/or SR 60. There are 5 ranger districts. The Forest borders several other national forests: Nantahala (North Carolina), Cherokee (Tennessee) and Sumter (South Carolina). Camping facilities are available. Attractions in the 720,000-acre Forest include Brasstown Bald (highest point in Georgia — 4784 feet); a section of the Blue Ridge Mountains; Tallulah Gorge; lakes and waterfalls; and the southern end (an 83-mile portion) of the Appalachian Trial. In addition, there are scenic overlooks and drives and miles of hiking trails. The Cohutta Wilderness Area — mostly mixed hardwoods interspersed with hemlock and pine with an understory of mountain laurel and rhododendron — is located in the northwest section of the Forest. This 34,500-acre area is truly wild — no motorized vehicles are allowed; there are no roads, although roads do skirt the area. Six trails totaling 38 miles traverse the area.

The Chattahoochee National Forest offers endless opportunities for hiking, photography, and the study and enjoyment of nature. The hardwood forest areas and the many lakes and streams provide habitat for a wide variety of birds. Among the birds seen here are: Wood Duck, Broad-winged Hawk, American Kestrel (Sparrow Hawk), Turkey, Green Heron, Screech Owl, Great Horned Owl, Common Raven, Blue Jay, Hairy Woodpecker, Eastern Phoebe, Tufted Titmouse, American Robin, Veery, Eastern Meadowlark, Brown-headed Cowbird, Black-throated Blue Warbler, Chestnut-sided Warbler, Blackburnian Warbler, Le Conte's Sparrow, and Field Sparrow.

Cumberland Island National Seashore, P.O. Box 806, St. Marys 31558; (912) 882-4335. Cumberland has been open to the public since June 1975. The island can be reached only by ferry; half-day and all-day trips are available. Reservations are recommended; contact the park service at the above address. Cumberland Island is located off the coast of Georgia, south of Brunswick. From

Brunswick take US 95 south to SR 40, then take SR 40 east to St. Marys. Camping is permitted on the island with prior permission; there are no facilities on the island other than drinking water and toilets.

The island is made up of dunes, beaches, and freshwater lakes; the Seashore totals over 36,800 acres. Opportunities for birdwatching are numerous. Among the many species of birds likely to be seen here are: Ruddy Duck, White-winged Scoter, Red-shouldered Hawk, Green Heron, Least Bittern, Snowy Egret, Virginia Rail, Willet, Wood Stork (Ibis), Whimbrel, Piping Plover, Lesser Yellowlegs, Red-headed Woodpecker, Tree Swallow; Long- and Short-billed Marsh Wrens, Painted Bunting, and various warblers and sparrows.

Harris Neck National Wildlife Refuge. Administered by Savannah NWR. Harris Neck is located 43 miles south of Savannah and 20 miles north of Darien, near Blackbeard Island NWR. To reach the refuge from Darien, take US 17 north to SR 131, turn east on SR 131 and proceed for about 7 miles to the entrance.

Harris Neck was established in 1962 primarily for wintering Canada Geese and other migratory waterfowl. Despite its relatively small size (2687 acres), this refuge maintains a variety of habitat attractive to many birds — there are wooded tracts, several small ponds, salt marshes, and tidal streams. There have been 204 species of birds (58 nesting) recorded at Harris Neck. Among these are: Horned Grebe, Anhinga, Brown Pelican, Gadwall, Ring-necked Duck, Cooper's Hawk, Merlin (Pigeon Hawk), Green Heron, Least Bittern, Glossy Ibis, White Ibis, Virginia Rail, Purple Gallinule, American Oystercatcher, Ruddy Turnstone, Black-bellied Plover, American Woodcock, Bonaparte's Gull, Black Tern, Chuck-will's-widow, Pileated Woodpecker, Vermilion Flycatcher (rare), Winter Wren, Hermit Thrush, Sprague's Pipit (rare), Orange-crowned Warbler, Pine Warbler, Cape May Warbler, Hooded Warbler, Brown-headed Cowbird, Cardinal, Painted Bunting, Bachman's Sparrow, and Lapland Longspur (rare). Checklist available.

Oconee National Forest. There are 2 districts, each with a ranger: Redlands District, Greensboro 30642; and Uncle Remus District, Monticello 31064. Redlands is located just north of Greensboro off SR 15; Uncle Remus is north of Macon (south of Monticello) on SR 11. Oconee is in the piedmont section of the state; it totals 104,000 acres and was established in 1959. Points of interest in or near Oconee include: the Scull Shoals Indian Mounds; the Hitchiti Experimental Forest (4700 acres of pine-hardwood type); Rock Eagle Lake (and the rock eagle, built of rock by unknown tribes centuries ago); and various archeological remains. There is a network of gravel roads, paved roads, and hiking trails throughout the Forest. Camping, picnicking, and swimming are among the public facilities available at Oconee. Piedmont NWR is located nearby.

Forests, streams, and lakes all provide habitat for birds as well as other wild animals. Among the many birds likely to be seen here are: Mallard, Wood Duck,

Black Vulture, Cooper's Hawk, Bobwhite, American Coot, Least Sandpiper, Barred Owl, Ruby-throated Hummingbird, Hairy Woodpecker, Eastern Kingbird, Purple Martin, Tufted Titmouse, Brown-headed Nuthatch, House Wren, Carolina Wren, Wood Thrush, Red-eyed Vireo, Louisiana Waterthrush, Kentucky Warbler, American Goldfinch, and Fox Sparrow.

Okefenokee National Wildlife Refuge, Box 117, Waycross 31501; (912) 283-2580. Headquarters are in Room 228-230, Bunn Building, Waycross. The refuge itself is located south of Waycross. There are 3 public entrances: Stephen C. Foster State Park (west entrance), off SR 177; Okefenokee Swamp Park (north entrance), off SR 177; and Suwannee Canal Recreation Area (east entrance), off SR 23. The visitors' center and interpretive facilities are located at the east entrance. Certain designated parts of the Okefenokee are open to the public; these areas are conspicuously posted and easily reached. Other areas may be seen only with a guide. For detailed information, contact the refuge manager at the above address. The wildlife-oriented facilities at the east entrance (Suwannee Canal) include a wildlife drive, walking trails, a 4000-foot boardwalk over the swamp, and observation towers. Concessioners at all entrances offer a wide variety of boat trips, guided tours, and so forth. There are camping facilities at the state park at the west entrance.

The refuge was established in 1937. It extends 38 miles from north to south, about 25 miles across at its widest, and contains approximately 412,000 acres. It is one of the oldest and most primitive swamps in America. Okefenokee is actually a vast peat bog covered with many unusual forms of plant life. Streams move slowly through the cypress forests of the swamp; their principal outlet is the Suwannee River.

Raccoons, opossums, and bobcats live in the forest; otters and alligators haunt the streams; Sandhill Cranes inhabit the prairies. Most of the swamp is covered with black gum, cypress, and bay forests. About 15 percent is flooded or semiflooded prairie; and islands make up another 6 percent. This diversified habitat is attractive to a wide variety of birds. There have been 210 species (76 nesting) seen on the refuge. Among these are: Pintail, Swallow-tailed Kite, Peregrine Falcon (rare), Great Blue Heron, Louisiana Heron, Wood Stork (Ibis), Sandhill Crane, Sora (rare), Killdeer, Ground Dove, Common Nighthawk, Red-cockaded Woodpecker, Barn Swallow, Tufted Titmouse, Brown-headed Nuthatch, Winter Wren, Eastern Bluebird, Swainson's Warbler (rare), Blue-winged Warbler, Cape May Warbler, Black-throated Green Warbler (rare), Yellow-throated Warbler, Yellow-breasted Chat (rare), Eastern Meadowlark, Scarlet Tanager (rare), Indigo Bunting, Painted Bunting, and Bachman's Sparrow (nesting). Checklist available.

Piedmont National Wildlife Refuge, Round Oak 31080; (912) 986-3651. The refuge is located 15 miles north of Macon. To reach the refuge from Macon, take US 129 north to Gray; turn northwest on SR 11 and continue to Round Oak;

just north of Round Oak, take the paved road west for 3 miles to Piedmont NWR. Camping is not permitted on the refuge; facilities are available at nearby Oconee National Forest.

The refuge was established in 1939 and now totals 34,600 acres. The land is quite hilly and is interspersed with small streams that drain into the Ocmulgee River. Most of the land, formerly used for cotton farming, has now reverted to loblolly-shortleaf pine timber mixed with hardwoods. Timber harvesting is an important program in the management of the refuge. The cutting keeps the pine canopy from becoming too dense, thus shading out the ground vegetation which provides a considerable amount of wildlife food. Impoundments are under construction; they will help to increase the waterfowl population on the refuge.

Piedmont Refuge is divided into compartments; compartments 14 and 25 are the only ones open to birdwatchers. Compartment 14 is closed during deer hunts; compartment 25 is open all year. There are county and state roads that traverse the refuge. These are always open for driving and walking. There is a parking area and wildlife trail at Allison Lake; walking the trail provides opportunities to observe marsh- and waterbirds, shorebirds, and raptorial birds. In compartment 14 there is a colony of Red-cockaded Woodpeckers. There have been 182 species of birds (70 nesting) observed on the refuge. Among these are: Wood Duck, Canvasback (rare), Ruddy Duck, Hooded Merganser, Cooper's Hawk, Bald Eagle (rare), Golden Eagle (rare), Bobwhite, Great Blue Heron, American Woodcock, Upland Sandpiper (Plover), Screech Owl, Common Nighthawk, Red-headed Woodpecker, Horned Lark (rare), Brown-headed Nuthatch, Winter Wren, Swainson's Thrush, Golden-winged Warbler, Northern Parula, Bay-breasted Warbler, (rare), Yellow-breasted Chat, Bobolink, Evening Grosbeak, Indigo Bunting, and Bachman's Sparrow (nesting). Checklist available.

Savannah National Wildlife Refuge, Route 1, Hardeeville, South Carolina 29927; (912) 964-0231. Savannah is located a few miles north of the city of Savannah off US 17, near the South Carolina border. The refuge is divided between the 2 states, with the larger portion lying in Georgia. The 13,000-acre refuge was established in 1927 and is primarily a waterfowl area, although many other kinds of wildlife are also protected.

Savannah is one of the outstanding refuges along the Atlantic Flyway — about 15 species of ducks winter here. Waders frequent the many pools and marshes of the refuge. Birdwatching is encouraged: there is a nature drive (along the dikes) which encircles several pools and a network of trails is maintained. The impoundments are managed diversely — some are kept at maximum depth for growing aquatic plants, others are drained and farmed. Savannah is extremely flat — most of it varies less than 2 inches in elevation. The timberlands, therefore, consist mainly of scattered islands surrounded by cutgrass marsh. Dominant on these islands (hammocks) is black gum; bald cypress, red maple, spruce pine, and swamp chestnut oak occur in mixed stands. These woodlands support many kinds of plants — more than 900 species have been recorded. The former rice fields, impoundments, marshes, and timberlands all contribute to provide an environment for a wide variety of birds. Among the 213 species of birds (84 nesting locally) sighted here are: Horned Grebe, Brown Pelican, Fulvous Tree Duck, Wood Duck, Red-breasted Merganser, Marsh Hawk, Cooper's Hawk, Great Blue Heron, Louisiana Heron, Yellow Rail, Black Rail, Wilson's Plover, Pectoral Sandpiper, Caspian Tern, Black Tern, Ground Dove, Short-eared Owl (rare), Whip-poor-will, Red-cockaded Woodpecker (rare), Carolina Wren, Brown Thrasher, Blue-gray Gnatcatcher, Swainson's Warbler (rare), Black-throated Blue Warbler, Kentucky Warbler, American Redstart, Blue Grosbeak, Painted Bunting, and Bachman's Sparrow. Checklist available.

Tybee National Wildlife Refuge. Administered by Savannah NWR. Tybee Refuge is a 100-acre island off the coast of Georgia; it is next to Wassaw Island NWR and quite near Savannah NWR. Tybee is another in a chain of NWRs that are situated along the Atlantic Flyway. It was established in 1938 and is an important refuge for shorebirds.

To reach the island, take SR 80 from Thunderbolt (which is just south of Savannah) to its termination at Savannah Beach. Among the many species of birds that can be seen at Tybee are: Red-throated Loon, Brown Pelican, Gannet, Common Merganser, Purple Sandpiper, Pectoral Sandpiper, Ruddy Turnstone, Red Knot, American Oystercatcher, Dunlin, Wilson's Plover, Piping Plover, Black-bellied Plover, Caspian Tern, Sandwich Tern, Yellow-billed Cuckoo, Orange-crowned Warbler, and Painted Bunting.

Wassaw Island National Wildlife Refuge, P. O. Box 4008, Port Wentworth 31407. Wassaw is located 15 miles south of Savannah, just south of Tybee Island NWR. The refuge is accessible only by boat. Wassaw was established in 1969; it comprises 10,240 acres of tidal marsh and timbered dunes, and is administered by Savannah NWR.

The beaches and limited interior trails are open to the public on a day-use basis for wildlife observation, shelling, picnicking, and so forth. The large areas of salt marsh and mud flats provide habitat for many birds. Hundreds of migrating shorebirds visit the beaches in spring and fall. There have been 205 species of birds (73 nesting) sighted on the refuge. Among these are: Red-throated Loon, Anhinga, Gannet, Northern Shoveler, Ruddy Duck, Bufflehead, Sharp-shinned Hawk, Peregrine Falcon, Green Heron, Wood Stork (Ibis), Sandhill Crane, Piping Plover, Ruddy Turnstone, Willet, Whimbrel, Red Knot, Parasitic Jaeger, Least Tern, Ground Dove, Barred Owl, Red-headed Woodpecker, Tree Swallow, Brown Creeper, Long- and Short-billed Marsh Wrens, Eastern Bluebird, Nashville Warbler, Prothonotary Warbler, Worm-eating Warbler, Cape May Warbler, Orchard Oriole, Boat-tailed Grackle, Scarlet Tanager, Rufous-sided Towhee, Painted Bunting, and Savannah Sparrow. Checklist available.

Wolf Island National Wildlife Refuge. Administered by Savannah NWR. Wolf Island is located off the coast of Georgia near Darien. The refuge was originally established in 1930; it was significantly enlarged in 1971 by means of a cooperative acquisition program with The Nature Conservancy. The refuge now totals about 4200 acres of tidal marsh and beach. There are low dunes and small ridges of scrub cedar and pine. It is particularly suited for water- and shorebirds which are numerous throughout the year. There have been 113 species of birds (39 nesting) reported on Wolf Island. Among these are: Red-throated Loon, Gannet, Anhinga, Northern Shoveler, Wood Duck, Bufflehead, Marsh Hawk, Great Blue Heron, Snowy Egret, Wood Stork (Ibis), Clapper Rail, Purple Gallinule, Piping Plover, Wilson's Plover, Ruddy Turnstone, Pectoral Sandpiper, Whimbrel, Dunlin, Great Black-backed Gull, Royal Tern, Sandwich Tern, Black Tern, Caspian Tern, Long-billed Marsh Wren, Yellow-rumped (Myrtle) Warbler, Magnolia Warbler, Belted Kingfisher, Tree Swallow, Indigo Bunting, and Savannah Sparrow. Checklist available.

NATURE CENTERS

In addition to the places described above, the following nature centers and gardens are also rewarding places for birdwatchers.

Callaway Gardens. The gardens are located 30 miles north of Columbus, off US 27. The visitors' center has maps of the gardens. The Laurel Springs area is often the best spot for birding, especially during spring and fall migration periods. In summer this area is good for Kentucky Warblers, Hooded Warblers, Black-and-white Warblers, and Louisiana Waterthrushes. In winter, ducks can be seen on the lakes along the drive through the gardens. The greenhouse area is a good place for Ruby-throated Hummingbirds. In addition, there are birding trails near the log cabin. The preserve totals 2500 acres and includes 12 lakes, a beach, and several picnic areas. An admission fee is charged. The gardens are open daily, 9-6.

Fernbank Science Center, 156 Heaton Park Drive, NE, Atlanta 30307; (404) 378-4311. This is a 70-acre preserve, primarily composed of a mature hardwood forest. There are paved nature trails and an experimental garden. The center is open Sunday through Friday, 2-5; on Saturdays, 10-5. Look for woodpeckers.

Lullwater Conservation Garden, Atlanta 30300. To reach the garden from the corner of Ponce de Leon Avenue and Peachtree Street, take Ponce de Leon Avenue east for nearly 3 miles; turn left on Lullwater Road and proceed for nearly ½ mile.

Okefonokee Outdoor Education Program, Route 5, P. O. Box 406, Waycross 31501; (912) 283-8494. The center covers 1235 acres; various educational and interpretive programs are offered. There are four miles of boat trails through the swamp, a boardwalk, and guided tours (by appointment). The program operates throughout the year.

Sandy Creek Nature Center, Athens 30601. The entrance to the center is north of the junction of US 441 and US 29. After turning north on US 441, take a dirt road to the left which will lead to the center.

There are also two national monuments of note: *Fort Pulaski,* which is located 17 miles east of Savannah via US 80; and *Fort Frederica,* which is on St. Simons Island, 12 miles from Brunswick via US 17. There have been 260 species of birds recorded on St. Simons Island, including: Gannet, Whimbrel, Limpkin, Avocet, Red-cockaded Woodpecker, Swainson's Warbler, and Sharp-tailed Sparrow.

STATE PARKS AND FORESTS

Georgia has many state parks, most of which offer a variety of recreational facilities including camping, picnicking, and hiking. State parks and historic sites in Georgia are managed by the Georgia Department of Natural Resources, Parks and Historic Sites Division, 270 Washington Street, SW, Atlanta 30334. Although not designed primarily as bird sanctuaries, several of the following parks are well known as good birdwatching spots. Those are indicated as such by an asterisk (*).

PARKS WITH CAMPING FACILITIES

Amicola Falls, Juno 30551; (404) 265-2885; 296 acres.
Bainbridge, Donalsonville 31745; (912) 861-3137.
Blackburn, Dahlonega 30533; (404) 864-3789.
Black Rock Mountain, Mountain City 30562; (404) 746-2141; 1182 acres.
Bobby Brown, Elberton 30635; (404) 283-3313; 664 acres.
Chattooga Lakes, Summerville 30747 (404) 857-5211.
*Cloudland Canyon, Rising Fawn 30738; (404) 657-4050; 1699 acres.
*Crooked River, Kingsland 31548; (912) 882-5256; 500 acres.
Elijah Clark, Lincolnton 30817; (404) 359-3458; 447 acres.
Fairchild, Donalsonville 31745; (912) 861-3137.
*Fort Mountain, Chatsworth 30705; (404) 695-2621; 1897 acres.
Fort Yargo, Winder 30680; (404) 867-3489; 1680 acres.
*Franklin D. Roosevelt, Pine Mountain 31822; (404) 663-4858; 4980 acres.
General Coffee, Nicholls 31554; (912) 384-7082; 1495 acres.
George Carver, Cartersville 30120; (404) 974-5182.
George T. Bagby, Georgetown 31754; (912) 768-2660; 289 acres.
Georgia Veterans Memorial, Cordele 31015; (912) 273-2190; 1307 acres.
Gordonia Alatamaha, Reidsville 30453; (912) 557-4763; 1204 acres.

Hamburg, Mitchell 30820; (912) 552-2393; 1495 acres.
Hard Labor Creek, Rutledge 30663; (404) 557-2863; 5804 acres.
Hart, Hartwell 30643; (404) 376-8756.
High Falls, Jackson 30233; (404) 994-5080; 981 acres.
Indian Springs, Indian Springs 30231; (404) 775-7241; 510 acres.
James H. Floyd, Summerville 30747; (404) 832-7545; 169 acres.
*Jekyll Island, Brunswick 31520; (912) 635-2236.
John Tanner, Carrollton 30117; (404) 832-7545; 139 acres.
Keg Creek, Appling 30802.
Kolomoki Mounds, Blakely 31723; (912) 723-5296, 1293 acres.
Lake Chatuge; in Chattahochee National Forest.
Laura S. Walker, Waycross 31501; (912) 283-4424; 306 acres.
Lincoln, Millen 30442; (912) 982-2499.
Little Ocmulgee, McRae 31055; (912) 868-2832; 1397 acres.
*Magnolia Springs, Millen 30442; (912) 982-1660; 948 acres.
Mistletoe, Appling 30802; (404) 541-0321; 1920 acres.
Moccasin Creek, Clarkesville 30523; (404) 947-3194; 31 acres.
Red Top Mountain, Cartersville 30120; (404) 974-5182; 1246 acres.
Reed Bingham, Adel 31620; (912) 896-7788; 1605 acres.
Reynoldsville, Donalsonville 31745; 100 acres.
Richmond Hill, Richmond Hill 31324; (912) 861-3137; 190 acres.
Seminole, Donalsonville 31745; (912) 861-3137; 343 acres.
Skidaway Island, Savannah 31406; (912) 352-8599; 480 acres.
*Stephen C. Foster, Fargo 31631; (912) 496-7509; 80 acres.
Stone Mountain, Stone Mountain 30083; (404) 469-9831.
Tugaloo, Lavonia 30553; (404) 356-3377; 393 acres.
Unicoi, Helen 30545; (404) 878-2201; 1000 acres.
Victoria Bryant, Royston 30662; (404) 245-6270; 407 acres.
*Vogel, Blairsville 30512; (404) 745-2628; 221 acres.
Watson Mill, Comer 30629; (404) 783-5349.
Whitewater Creek, Montezuma 31063; (912) 472-8061.

DAY USE PARKS

Chattahoochee River, off US 41, north of Atlanta.
Panola Mountain, off SR 155, 18 miles southeast of Atlanta.
Providence Canyon, on SR 39, 8 miles west of Lumpkin.
Santa Maria, on SR 40, near Cumberland Island National Seashore.
*Sweetwater Creek, off SR 5, about 20 miles west of Atlanta.

In addition there are 14 historic sites (not listed here), including museums, archaeological areas, forts, and plantations. These are day use areas as well.

KENTUCKY

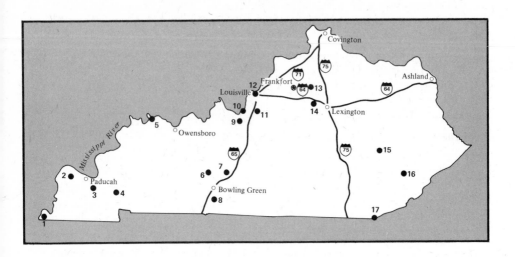

1. Reelfoot NWR
2. Ballard County Wildlife Management Area
3. Murphey's Pond
4. Land Beween the Lakes
5. John James Audubon State Park
6. Shanty Hollow Lake
7. Mammoth Cave National Park
8. Transient Lakes of Woodburn
9. Vernon-Douglas Wildlife Sanctuary
10. Otter Creek Park
11. Bernheim Forest
12. Jefferson County Forest Audubon Sanctuary
13. Kleber Wildlife Area
14. Clyde E. Buckley Wildlife Sanctuary
15. Daniel Boone National Forest
16. Lilly Cornett Woods
17. Cumberland Gap National Historic Park

Kentucky's rivers and mountains and streams and forests provide multiple birdwatching opportunities — for resident and visitor alike. The most historic spot for birdwatching in Kentucky is the famous falls of the Ohio River, just outside of Louisville. John James Audubon lived here (and in Henderson) in the early nineteenth century. There is a museum at John James Audubon State Park (in Henderson) honoring the famous ornithologist. Audubon's description of this area is fascinating — especially his accounts of the enormous flights of Passenger Pigeons. The rock shelf just below the McAlpine Dam is a fossil coral reef — more than 900 kinds of coral have been found. Among the birds seen at the falls but rarely seen anywhere else in the state are: White Pelican, Wood Stork (Ibis), Sandhill Crane, Red Knot, Red and Northern Phalaropes, Black-legged Kittiwake, Glaucous Gull, and Snowy Owl.

Other unusual birding places in Kentucky are the *"transient lakes of Woodburn."* These lakes — Chaney and McElroy — are located in the southern part of Warren County, south of Bowling Green. Chaney is reached by taking US 31W south from Bowling Green for 8 miles, turning right on a gravel road, and driving ½ mile. To reach McElroy from this point, continue south on US 31W for 2 more miles to Woodburn, turn left on SR 240 and go for ⅓ mile, turn left again on SR 884 and continue for 2½ miles to arrive at the lake (and owner's home). The most rewarding time for birdwatching at the lakes is in the spring — March and April. Almost any species of inland waterfowl can be found here sometime during the late winter and early spring. Among the unusual species seen here have been: Whistling Swan, Oldsquaw, Osprey, Glossy Ibis, Ruddy Turnstone, Common Gallinule, and Forster's Tern. It is essential to obtain permission to visit the lake from the owner (or manager) of the farm on which the lake is located.

Other good birding places in Kentucky include the *Lloyd Wildlife Area* and other wildlife management areas operated by the Kentucky Department of Fish and Wildlife Resources, Capitol Plaza Tower, Frankfort 40601; (502) 564-4336. For detailed information about birdwatching in Kentucky, the reader is advised to consult: *Kentucky Birds; A Finding Guide,* an excellent book published by the University Press of Kentucky, Lexington 40506.

Ballard County Wildlife Management Area, Route 1, La Center 42056; (502) 224-2244. The area is managed by the Kentucky Department of Fish and Wildlife Resources. To reach the area, take US 60 from Paducah west to Barlow, then go north on SR 1105 to SR 473; look for directional signs. The area is managed chiefly for waterfowl hunting, and is closed to the public from 15 October to 15 March. When open, no pets or firearms are allowed. There are a limited number of primitive campsites in the area; permission to use them must be obtained at headquarters. Among the many birds likely to be seen here are: Turkey, Least Tern, Red-headed Woodpecker, Common Yellowthroat, Yellow-breasted Chat, Cerulean Warbler, and herons, egrets, and waterfowl in considerable variety.

Bernheim Forest. Bernheim Forest Nature Center, State Highway 245, Clermont 40110; (502) 543-2355. The center is owned and operated by the Isaac W. Bernheim Foundation. The forest is located 25 miles south of Louisville. To reach it, take I-65 (Kentucky Turnpike) south from Louisville to the Bernheim Forest Ramp; from Shepherdsville, take SR 61 south for 4 miles to SR 245, turn east and continue for 2 miles. Bernheim Forest is open every day; it is closed from 15 November to 15 March, although hikes may be taken with permission of the ranger. There are no camping facilities; swimming and boating are prohibited.

This 10,000-acre wildlife sanctuary is situated in the Knobs — a region so-named for its flat-topped hills. At the sanctuary, there are several marked hiking trails, a nature center, and a 47-foot-tall fire tower. Interpretive programs, guided tours, and exhibits are sponsored by the center. In addition, there is an arboretum, and live animals (native to the region) are on display in outdoor pens. Birding is excellent — nearly 200 species have been recorded. A checklist is available at the nature center. Among the birds likely to be seen here are: Canada Goose, Wood Duck, Red-breasted Nuthatch, Yellow-bellied Sapsucker, and warblers. Waterbirds and shorebirds stop over during migration.

Clyde E. Buckley Wildlife Sanctuary, Route 3, Frankfort 40601; (606) 873-5711. The sanctuary is owned and operated jointly by the National Audubon Society and the Buckley Hills Audubon Society. It is located 2½ miles west of Millville. From Frankfort, take US 60 south for about 3 miles to SR 1681 (Jett Road); then turn west toward Millville. Camping is not permitted at the sanctuary; however, facilities are available at nearby private and state campgrounds. The sanctuary is open Wednesday through Sunday, closed in January and February.

The woods are characterized by black locust, ash, and American elm. There are 3 hiking trails, a bird watch house, and a barn containing natural history displays. Interpretive programs are given by the resident naturalist. The 285-acre sanctuary has open fields and steep hillsides and bluffs. The Elk Lick Branch bisects the preserve; and along its bluffs and ravines are found many spring flowers and deciduous trees not found elsewhere in the sanctuary. Nearly 150 species of birds have been sighted here since 1967. Among them are: Black Duck, Red-bellied Woodpecker, Red-headed Woodpecker, and 26 species of warblers. Occasional waterbirds are seen, but the sanctuary's 2 ponds are too small to attract large numbers of them.

Cumberland Gap National Historic Park, Box 840, Middlesboro 40965. The visitors' center is near Middlesboro, and can be reached by taking US 58 west from Ewing for about 15 miles. Camping facilities are available, and there are several hiking trails.

The park covers 20,000 acres in three states — Virginia, Tennessee, and Kentucky. Of special interest are the overlooks and caves, the White Rocks, the

Iron Furnace, and the Hensley Settlement. This region is of geologic interest as it has been subjected to great earth stresses which produce folded and faulted rocks. A wide range of visitor activites is available, including campfire programs, talks, guided hikes, and various interpretive programs. Among the many birds that are likely to be seen here are: Red-tailed Hawk, Common (Yellow-shafted) Flicker, Barn Swallow, Eastern Phoebe, Eastern Meadowlark, White-eyed Vireo, Pine Warbler, Ovenbird, Hooded Warbler, Northern Waterthrush, American Redstart, Dark-eyed Junco, Scarlet Tanager, and Chipping Sparrow.

Daniel Boone National Forest, 100 Vaught Road, Winchester 40391. Daniel Boone Forest is located east and south of Lexington; use the Daniel Boone Parkway (toll), Mountain Parkway (toll), or US 60, US 64, US 75, and/or SR 15. In addition, there are many smaller roads that traverse the Forest. Camping facilities are available.

Daniel Boone Forest covers 487,000 acres. Sandstone cliffs 100 feet high, natural rock arches, limestone caves, mineral springs, waterfalls, and wooded valleys — all are to be seen here. There are hundreds of miles of streams and numerous lakes and ponds. A wide variety of hiking trails offers excellent opportunities to observe native plants and wildlife. Over 46 types of mammals are to be found here including red and gray foxes, deer, muskrat, and raccoon. In addition, over 150 species of birds frequent the wooded habitats, the fields, and the marshy areas which lie within the Forest boundaries. Among these are: Mallard, Wood Duck, Red-tailed Hawk, Turkey, Ruffed Grouse, Common Nighthawk, Common (Yellow-shafted) Flicker, Great Crested Flycatcher, Barn Swallow, Winter Wren, Brown Thrasher, Tennessee Warbler, Yellow Warbler, Mourning Warbler, Eastern Meadowlark, Brown-headed Cowbird, Summer Tanager, Dickcissel, and Chipping Sparrow. Checklist available.

Kleber Wildlife Area. The area is located northwest of Lexington in Owen County. The 685-acre tract is about 7 miles southeast of Monterey on SR 368. Take US 127 south from Monterey to its intersection with SR 368, turn east and continue for about 2 miles. Camping is not allowed at Kleber.

The area is covered mostly with immature second-growth hardwood; there are some brushfields of redbud and honey locust. Grasslands are maintained by mowing and food crops (such as wheat, sorghum, and millet) are produced. Two rock-bottomed creeks run most of the year. The birds found here are those usually found in upland woods and meadows. Finches and sparrows are abundant. Other birds likely to be seen here are: Red-tailed Hawk, Bobwhite, Great Horned Owl, Belted Kingfisher, Red-headed Woodpecker, Carolina Chickadee, Tufted Titmouse, House Wren, Mockingbird, American Robin, Cedar Waxwing, Common Yellowthroat, Eastern Meadowlark, and Rufous-sided Towhee. About 40 species of birds nest at Kleber.

Land Between the Lakes, Golden Pond 42231; (502) 924-5602. This 170,000-acre recreation area is located south of Paducah, between Lake Barkley and Kentucky Lake. The area is owned by the TVA (Tennessee Valley Authority). Camping facilities are available. Although there are many wildlife management programs at LBL, they are all administered from a multiple-use perspective. There are pine and hardwood forests and some small impound-ments, including a number of artificial ponds. There is a considerable variety of habitats, and although there are no great numbers of birds, LBL does support a flock of Turkeys. In addition, Canada Geese, Yellow-crowned Night Herons, Green Herons and Cliff Swallows nest at LBL. Among the other birds that can be seen here are: herons, egrets, sandpipers and other marshbirds (during migration), Wood Duck, Common Merganser, Hooded Merganser, Ring-necked Duck, Bald Eagle, Golden Eagle (rare), Red-tailed Hawk, Great (Common) Egret, Caspian Tern, Least Tern, Pileated Woodpecker, Carolina Wren, Tufted Titmouse, Eastern Bluebird, Horned Lark, Red-eyed Vireo, Common Yellow-throat, and Rufous-sided Towhee.

Lilly Cornett Woods, P. O. Box 78, Skyline 40851; (606) 663-5828. This 554-acre preserve is owned by the state and operated by the Division of Forestry. Visiting the preserve is by prior arrangement only; call or write the superintendent in advance. No one is permitted in the undisturbed part of the woods without a guide. To reach the Woods, take US 7 south from Hazard to Ulvah; at Ulvah, take SR 1103 south to the preserve. Camping is not permitted on the property; facilities are available at nearby Daniel Boone National Forest.

Line Fork Creek runs through the property, and the cleared land (about 60 acres) is mostly along the creek. The major portion of the preserve is a remnant of one of the greatest forests of all time — the mixed mesophytic forest. There are over 150 species of trees, grasses, and shrubs. There is one good trail through the forest. To hike it takes about 4 hours and it is not easy. There are easier walks: along Line Fork Creek and through the meadow; or on the east side of the road around a pond. Among the many birds that can be seen here are: Barred Owl, Common Yellowthroat, Hooded Warbler, Indigo Bunting, Chipping Sparrow, Field Sparrow, and Song Sparrow.

Mammoth Cave National Park, Mammoth Cave 42259. The park is located about 25 miles north of Bowling Green; take US 31W north to Park City, then SR 70 into the park; follow directional signs to the visitors' center. There are camping facilities in the park; in addition, National Park Concessions, Inc., operates a lodge and cabins. Other recreational activities include: cave tours, river cruising, interpretive programs, and self-guiding trails (both foot and auto). Be advised: all cave tours are strenuous and require stooping and walking over unlevel terrain. Poisonous snakes and poison ivy are common, even around the most heavily visited areas.

Mammoth Cave has been a national park since 1941. The limestone cave, formed over 200 million years ago, is the prime attraction of the park. Nonetheless, the miles of hiking trails throughout the park's 52,000 acres afford the naturalist many opportunities for observing wildlife. There have been over 190 species of birds observed at Mammoth Cave National Park. Among these are: Snow Goose, Wood Duck, Sharp-shinned Hawk, Bobwhite, Green Heron, Sandhill Crane, American Woodcock, Least Tern (rare), Snowy Owl (rare), Whip-poor-will, Ruby-throated Hummingbird, Pileated Woodpecker, Red-cockaded Woodpecker (rare), Eastern Wood Pewee, Rough-winged Swallow, Carolina Chickadee, Winter Wren, Brown Thrasher, Blue-gray Gnatcatcher, Water Pipit, Loggerhead Shrike, Philadelphia Vireo (rare), Prothonotary Warbler, Swainson's Warbler (rare), Worm-eating Warbler, Golden-winged Warbler, Cerulean Warbler, Mourning Warbler, Rose-breasted Grosbeak, Indigo Bunting, and Bachman's Sparrow. Checklist available.

Murphey's Pond. Owned by the state; for information, contact: Dr. Constantine Curris, President, Murray State University, Murray 42071. Murphey's Pond is located about 30 miles southwest of Paducah. Take SR 1748 from Beulah to Henderson Road, south on Henderson Road until the first house on the right, turn at the first road before the house. Murphey's Pond is relatively inaccessible, and despite its being well known, it is not particularly rich in birdlife. Waterfowl use the pond during migration but do not winter in large numbers. Wading, marsh-, and shorebirds are attracted to the edges of the swamp. Almost every species of turtle, frog, fish, and salamander can be found; copperheads, timber rattlesnakes, cottonmouth moccasins, and various non-poisonous water snakes are also at the pond. There is a virgin cypress stand which contains a heronry. Wood Duck, Hooded Merganser, Black Vulture, Yellow-crowned Night Heron, and Blue Grosbeak are among the birds seen here.

Otter Creek Park. Otter Creek Park Visitors' Center, Route 1, Vine Grove 40175; (502) 583-3577. The park is operated by the city of Louisville and is located 25 miles southwest of Louisville. To reach the park, take US 31W/60 south to Muldraugh, then go west on SR 1638 for 4 miles. The 2400-acre park has camping and picnicking facilities, swimming areas, and hiking trails. A nature center is maintained, and the staff includes a naturalist. The park is closed from November to March. Special features include guided and self-guiding tours, farm animals, native wildlife, and a pioneer area.

The Ohio River is the park's northern boundary. Most of the land adjoining the park is part of a military reservation, and, as such, is uninhabited. The variety and abundance of plant and animal life in this region has been known for many years. Audubon Christmas Bird Counts are taken here — as many as 63 species recorded in a single day. Hawks, thrushes, vireos, and warblers can be seen here. The high bluffs overlooking the Ohio River are ideal spots for observing migrating waterfowl.

Reelfoot National Wildlife Refuge. For information, see entry in Tennessee chapter (page 234).

Shanty Hollow Lake. Owned by the Kentucky Department of Fish and Wildlife Resources. Shanty Hollow Lake is located near Mammoth Cave National Park, 17 miles north of Bowling Green. From Bowling Green, take SR 67 north for 15 miles to SR 185, continue for less than a mile to the Shanty Hollow Lake Road. Primitive camping is permitted; the state operates a dock and a small concession stand; boats are for rent and there is a ramp for launching boats. The lake itself is maintained for public fishing. Swimming and high-speed boating are prohibited.

At either end of the lake there are marshes; the surrounding countryside is made up of uncultivated, hilly fields and woods. Oak, hickory, beech, maple, tulip, sweet gum, and dogweed characterize the wooded areas. Among the birds likely to be seen here are: Pied-billed Grebe, Red-tailed Hawk, Osprey, Least Bittern, Clapper Rail, American Coot, Belted Kingfisher, Barn Swallow, White-eyed Vireo, Scarlet Tanager, and warblers.

AUDUBON SANCTUARIES

In addition to the preserves discussed in the foregoing pages, there are 2 National Audubon sanctuaries in Kentucky.

Jefferson County Forest Audubon Sanctuary, P.O. Box 5248, Louisville 40205; (502) 451-0331. This 1800-acre sanctuary is owned by Louisville's Metropolitan Park and Recreation Board and protected by the Louisville Audubon Society. The sanctuary is a mixed woodland and is located just outside the city.

Vernon-Douglas Wildlife Sanctuary, Route 1, Box 19, Mauckport, Indiana 47142; (812) 732-2349. This 682-acre sanctuary is located 10 miles east of Elizabethtown (south of Louisville); its habitat is typical of the Knobs region. The sanctuary is operated in cooperation with the Lincoln Trail Audubon Society. Visits to the sanctuary are limited and must be arranged in advance.

STATE PARKS AND FORESTS

Kentucky has numerous state parks, many of which are good places to go birdwatching. Some are near large, undeveloped forests or on the shores of lakes. All the parks listed below offer camping in addition to a variety of recreational facilities. Those that are particularly noteworthy for birding are marked with an asterisk (*). For additional information, contact the Kentucky Department of Public Information, Frankfort 40601. They publish a booklet called ''Kentucky Camping,'' which also lists private campgrounds.

*Barren River Lake, Lucas 42156; (502) 646-2151.

Big Bone Lick, Union 41091; (606) 384-3522.

Blue Licks Battlefield, Mt. Olivet 41064; (606) 289-5507.

Breaks Interstate Park, Breaks, Virginia 24607; (703) 865-4413.

*Buckhorn Lake, Buckhorn 41721; (606) 398-7510.

*Carter Caves, Olive Hill 41164; (606) 286-4411.

*Columbus-Belmont Battlefield, Columbus 42032; (502) 677-2327.

*Cumberland Falls, Corbin 40701; (606) 528-4121.

*Fort Boonesboro, Route 5, Richmond 40475; (606) 527-3328.

*General Burnside, Burnside 42519; (606) 561-4104.

*General Butler, Carrollton 41008; (502) 732-4384.

Grayson Lake, Grayson 41143; (606) 474-9727.

Greenbo Lake, Greenup 41144; (606) 473-7324.

*Green River Lake, Campbellsville 42718; (502) 465-8255.

*Jenny Wiley, Prestonburg 41653; (606) 886-2711.

*John James Audubon, Henderson 42420; (502) 826-2247; includes Audubon museum.

Kenlake, Hardin 42048; (502) 474-2211.

*Kentucky Dam Village, Gilbertsville 42044; (502) 362-4271.

Kincaid Lake, Falmouth 41040; (606) 654-3531.

Kingdom Come, near Cumberland, off SR 463.

Lake Barkley, Cadiz 42211; (502) 924-1171.

*Lake Cumberland, Jamestown 42629; (502) 343-3111.

*Lake Malone, Dunmor 42339; (502) 657-2111.

*Levi Jackson Wilderness Road, London 40741; (606) 864-5108.

My Old Kentucky Home, Bardstown 40004; (502) 348-3502.

*Natural Bridge, Slade 40376; (606) 663-2214.

*Pennyrile Forest, Dawson Springs 42408; (502) 797-3421.

*Pine Mountain, Pineville 40977; (606) 337-3066.

*Rough River Dam, Falls of Rough 40119; (502) 257-2311.

In addition, there are many county- and city-owned parks; recreation areas managed by the US Army Corps of Engineers; Land Between the Lakes, managed by the TVA; and state wildlife areas managed by the Department of Fish and Wildlife Resources — all offer camping. For information, contact these agencies.

MISSISSIPPI

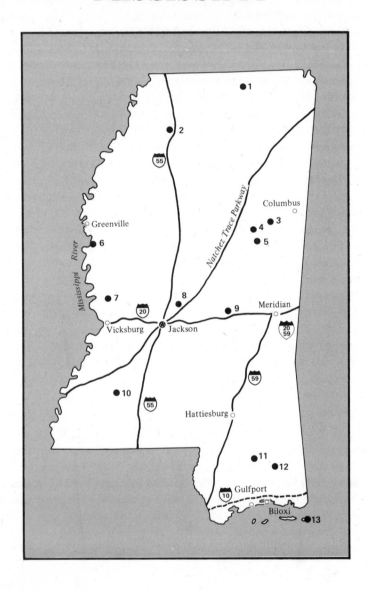

1. Holly Springs National Forest
2. Sardis Waterfowl Area
3. Plymouth Bluff
4. Noxubee NWR
   Tombigbee National Forest
5. Clytenville Heronry
6. Yazoo NWR

7. Delta National Forest
8. Natchez Trace Parkway
9. Bienville National Forest
10. Homochitto National Forest
11. DeSoto National Forest
12. Mississippi Sandhill Crane Sanctuary
13. Gulf Islands National Seashore

Most of Mississippi lies in the coastal plain. There are some hills in the northeast corner; the state's highest point, Woodall Mountain, is 806 feet above sea level. More than half the land in Mississippi is classified as forest. The state's most distinctive feature is the Yazoo-Mississippi Delta — a vast alluvial flood plain. Although most of the Delta area is under cultivation, it has many meandering streams, bayous, and sloughs. Several of these meanders have been cut off to form oxbow lakes, and these lakes lie along the Mississippi Flyway. With the exception of the coast of the Gulf of Mexico (around Biloxi and Gulfport), the most rewarding birdwatching to be done in the state is along these waterways. There have been 325 species of birds identified in Mississippi.

The Mississippi Game and Fish Commission owns over a million acres which are incorporated into 21 state wildlife management areas. These are scattered all over the state, and range from pine and hardwood forests to marshy areas to open fields. Many of these areas are within US Forest Service boundaries. Although designed for hunting and fishing, these areas are often good for birdwatching. Camping is usually permitted on or near the area. One of the best is the *Sardis Waterfowl Area* near the town of Sardis in northern Mississippi. For further information, contact the Mississippi Game and Fish Commission, Box 451, Jackson 39205.

For further and more detailed information about birdwatching in Mississippi, the reader is referred to the Mississippi Ornithological Society, 111 North Jefferson Street, Jackson 39202.

Bienville National Forest, Forest 39074. Bienville is located between Jackson and Meridian; US 20 bisects it. To reach the Forest, use US 80 and/or SR 35. Bienville totals 177,000 acres and is characterized by coastal plain second-growth pine and hardwood forest. There are numerous forest management demonstration areas. Camping, fishing, swimming, and hiking are among the recreational activities offered. Of special interest are the 70-acre Marathon Lake and the Bienville Pines Scenic Area. The northern part of Bienville is near the Natchez Trace Parkway.

The lakes, streams, rivers, forests, freshwater marshes, and open fields provide diverse habitat for a variety of birdlife. Among the species of birds common to the area are: Canada Goose, Pintail, American Wigeon, Wood Duck, Red-tailed Hawk, Bobwhite, Turkey, Great Blue Heron, Green Heron, Yellow-crowned Night Heron, Least Bittern, Upland Sandpiper (Plover), Ground Dove, Black-billed Cuckoo, Pileated Woodpecker, Yellow-bellied Sapsucker, Eastern Kingbird, Blue Jay, Tree Swallow, Red-breasted Nuthatch, Winter Wren, Hermit Thrush, White-eyed Vireo, Prothonotary Warbler, Tennessee Warbler, Cerulean Warbler, Bobolink, Rose-breasted Grosbeak, Indigo Bunting, Pine Siskin, and Vesper Sparrow.

Delta National Forest, Rolling Fork 39159. Delta is located just north of Vicksburg; to reach the Forest, take US 61 north. This 59,000-acre area is characterized by hardwood forests and greentree reservoirs. It is in the west central part of the Mississippi Delta. Of special interest is the Red Gum Natural Area which is a fine example of a natural bottomland hardwood stand. Recreational activities available at Delta include camping, boating, fishing, and hiking. Delta is near Yazoo NWR and just east of the Mississippi River; it is located along the Mississippi Flyway and spring and fall migration periods are the best times for birdwatching.

The streams, forests, and open fields provide food and shelter for many birds. Among the species of birds likely to be seen here are: Black Duck, Pintail, Northern Shoveler, Wood Duck, Marsh Hawk, Sharp-shinned Hawk, Bobwhite, Black-crowned Night Heron, Green Heron, Barn Owl, Whip-poor-will, Red-bellied Woodpecker, Eastern Phoebe, Bank Swallow, House Wren, Gray Catbird, Wood Thrush, Cedar Waxwing, Orange-crowned Warbler, Yellow Warbler, Blackpoll Warbler, Northern Waterthrush, Painted Bunting, Rufous-sided Towhee, and Field Sparrow.

DeSoto National Forest. Forest supervisor's office at Jackson 39200; district ranger offices at: Laurel 39440; Gulfport 39501; Wiggins 39577; and Hattiesburg 39401. DeSoto Forest totals 500,000 acres and is located south of Hattiesburg. To reach the Forest, use US 11, US 49, and US 90 and/or SR 26, SR 29, and SR 15.The southernmost section of the Forest is near Gulf Islands National Seashore (see entry in Florida chapter, page 164). Public facilities at DeSoto include camping, fishing, swimming, boating, and hiking. Of special interest is the Ashe Forest Service Nursery where about 40 million seedlings are produced annually. The majority of the seedlings are pine, but small quantities of several hardwood species are also produced. Many miles of horseback riding and hiking trails are maintained. Float trips down creeks are also offered.

The moist soils of DeSoto are ideal for the pitcher plants (insectivores). Other insect-eating plants found in the same areas are the butterworts and sundews. Certain marshy areas called "pitcher plant flats" have been designated for special protection. Abundant rainfall and a long, hot growing season combine to make the pine forests of DeSoto especially productive. The southern pine forests that are there now are predominately planted — much of the area of DeSoto Forest was acquired after the original forests had been cut. Desoto is rich in plant and animal life. Among the birds that can be seen here are: Wood Duck, Black Vulture, Red-shouldered Hawk, Killdeer, Yellow-billed Cuckoo, Barred Owl, Chimney Swift, Pileated Woodpecker, Common (Yellow-shafted) Flicker, Acadian Flycatcher, Blue-gray Gnatcatcher, Carolina Chickadee, Brown Creeper, Carolina Wren, Eastern Bluebird, Prothonotary Warbler, Hooded Warbler, Kentucky Warbler, Louisiana Waterthrush, Blue Grosbeak, and Summer Tanager.

Gulf Islands National Seashore. The islands are about 10 miles off the coast of Mississippi. For further information about the Seashore, see entry in Florida chapter (page 164).

Holly Springs National Forest, Holly Springs 38635. Holly Springs is located north of Oxford. To reach the Forest, use US 78 and/or SR 5, SR 7, and SR 30. Public facilities at this 145,000-acre Forest include camping, swimming, fishing, boating, and hiking. Of special interest is the restored Indian mound at the Chewalla Lake area.

Holly Springs National Forest sponsors intensive erosion control programs, and is operated under multiple-use management practices. Deer, cottontail rabbit, raccoon, and opossum find shelter in the mixed woodlands. There is also a wide variety of birdlife to be found. Among the species of birds likely to be seen at Holly Springs are: Wood Duck, Northern Shoveler, Broad-winged Hawk, Killdeer, Greater Yellowlegs, Ground Dove, Yellow-billed Cuckoo, Barn Owl, Chuck-will's-widow, Red-bellied Woodpecker, Red-headed Woodpecker, Acadian Flycatcher, Rough-winged Swallow, Tufted Titmouse, Carolina Wren, Brown Thrasher, Ruby-crowned Kinglet, Carolina Chickadee, Blue-gray Gnatcatcher, Red-eyed Vireo, Prothonotary Warbler, Kentucky Warbler, Prairie Warbler, Hooded Warbler, Pine Warbler, Orchard Oriole, Indigo Bunting, Purple Finch, Grasshopper Sparrow, and Bachman's Sparrow.

Homochitto National Forest, Gloster 39638. Homochitto is located near Natchez in the southwestern corner of the state. From Jackson, take US 55 south to US 84 (at Brookhaven); then take US 84 west to Homochitto. Public facilities at this 192,000-acre Forest include camping, fishing, swimming, picnicking, and hiking. Of special interest are the numerous forest management demonstration areas and the picturesque eroded loess country near Natchez. Homochitto is near the southern end of the Natchez Trace Parkway. A 13-acre lake forms the central attraction of the Clear Springs area.

The streams, forests, and fields typical of the coastal plain combine to provide a diversified habitat for a wide variety of plant and animal life. Among the many species of birds that can be seen here are: Cooper's Hawk, Killdeer, Yellow-billed Cuckoo, Barred Owl, Red-bellied Woodpecker, Hairy Woodpecker, Brown-headed Nuthatch, Wood Thrush, Brown Thrasher, Red-eyed Vireo, Prothonotary Warbler, American Redstart, Indigo Bunting, and Bachman's Sparrow.

Natchez Trace Parkway. National Park Service, Rural Route 1, NT-143, Tupelo 38801. The Natchez Trace Parkway cuts across Mississippi — from Natchez to Tupelo; then it crosses the northwestern corner of Alabama and continues into Tennessee, terminating at Nashville. It was once an Indian path, then a wilderness trail, and during the early 1880s it served as a highway binding the old southwest to the Union. Along the 306-mile parkway are many archeological sites, historic landmarks, and natural areas. There are camping and picnicking facilities along the Trace. Of special interest to naturalists are the Loess Bluff, Bullen Creek, and Cypress Swamp — the latter has an elevated walkway. In addition there are Indian mounds, old battlefields, and areas where the old Trace is open for hiking — paralleling the main road. Other recreational activities include campfire programs, swimming, conducted walks, sorghum-making demonstrations, and crafts festivals. The Tupelo visitors' center sponsors an artists-in-parks program. At various points on the parkway there are self-guiding nature trails and information centers.

Among the birds likely to be seen along the Trace (depending, of course, on the habitat) are: Red-tailed Hawk, Turkey, Bobwhite, Killdeer, Yellow-billed Cuckoo, Great Horned Owl, Red-cockaded Woodpecker, Eastern Phoebe, Rough-winged Swallow, Carolina Chickadee, Carolina Wren, Wood Thrush, Red-eyed Vireo, Black-and-white Warbler, Yellow-throated Warbler, Pine Warbler, American Redstart, Eastern Meadowlark, Indigo Bunting, Blue Grosbeak, and Grasshopper Sparrow.

Wood Duck

Noxubee National Wildlife Refuge, Route 1, Box 84, Brooksville 39739; (601) 323-5548. To reach the refuge from the junction of US 82 and SR 12, in Starkville, drive to the stadium at Mississippi State University and then follow directional signs for 17 miles (south). Camping is not allowed on the refuge; facilities are available at nearby Tombigbee National Forest.

When Noxubee was established in 1940, it was an eroded, depleted area. Now the 47,000-acre refuge, owing to careful management, is a land of forests, streams, ponds, and fields. Public facilities include nature trails and scenic auto routes. Several endangered species — American alligator, Red-cockaded Woodpecker, and (Southern) Bald Eagle — are found at Noxubee; special efforts are devoted to their protection. The pine, cypress, and hardwood forests; greentree reservoirs; and shallow lakes provide ideal habitat for a wide variety of wildlife. There have been 216 species of birds recorded on the refuge. Among these are: Anhinga, Gadwall, Ruddy Duck, Bald Eagle, Yellow-crowned Night Heron, American Bittern, American Woodcock, Pectoral Sandpiper, Short-eared Owl, Pileated Woodpecker, Eastern Wood Pewee, Rough-winged Swallow, Brown-headed Nuthatch, Bewick's Wren, Swainson's Warbler, Golden-winged Warbler, Black-throated Green Warbler, Cerulean Warbler, Mourning Warbler, Scarlet Tanager, and Bachman's Sparrow. Checklist available.

Tombigbee National Forest, Ackerman 39735. Tombigbee is located between Bienville and Holly Springs national forests and adjoins Noxubee NWR. To reach Tombigbee, which is near Louisville and Ackerman, use US 82 and/or SR 9 and SR 25. Camping facilities are available.

Tombigbee totals 65,000 acres and is characterized by upper coastal plain pine and hardwood forests. Of special interest are the Indian mounds, Davis and Choctaw Lakes, and nearby Natchez Trace Parkway. Public recreational activities include boating, swimming, fishing, picnicking, and hiking. Owing to its proximity to Noxubee NWR and the Mississippi Flyway, birdwatching at Tombigbee is especially rewarding. Among the species common to the area are: Red-shouldered Hawk, Bobwhite, Yellow-bellied Cuckoo, Screech Owl, Hairy Woodpecker, Brown-headed Nuthatch, Acadian Flycatcher, Carolina Chickadee, Western Wood Pewee, Brown Thrasher, Red-eyed Vireo, Prothonotary Warbler, Pine Warbler, Hooded Warbler, Common Yellowthroat, Orchard Oriole, Indigo Bunting, and Bachman's Sparrow.

Yazoo National Wildlife Refuge, Route 1, Box 286, Hollandale 38748; (601) 839-2638. Yazoo is located about 30 miles south of Greenville and a few miles east of the Mississippi River. From Greenville, take SR 1 south to Hampton, then go northeast on SR 436 for about 4 miles; watch for directional signs. Roads may become impassible during the wet winter months. Camping is not permitted on the refuge; facilities are available at nearby Delta National Forest.

Yazoo was established in 1956 starting with an area of 2500 acres; it now totals 12,470 acres. Impoundments, greentree reservoirs, and croplands are managed by refuge personnel to provide additional habitat and food for waterfowl. The flooded forest lands, open water, and fields provide habitat for a wide variety of birds. Birdlife on the refuge is probably most interesting during the fall and winter. Hiking and driving trails wind through the refuge making sightseeing easy for the visitor. Among the 140 species normally found on the refuge during the year are: Ring-necked Duck, Gadwall, Canvasback, Mississippi Kite, Marsh Hawk, Bobwhite, Green Heron, Black-crowned Night Heron, Upland Sandpiper (Plover), Barn Owl, Red-headed Woodpecker, Long- and Short-billed Marsh Wrens, Lawrence's Warbler (rare), Kentucky Warbler, Painted Bunting, and Summer Tanager. Checklist available.

NATURE CENTERS

In addition to those federal properties described in the previous pages, there are several private and state-owned areas that can prove to be rewarding to the birdwatcher.

The Nature Conservancy has been associated with 2 projects in Mississippi: first, they have conveyed to the Mississippi State College for Women (in Columbus) a 30-acre tract called *Plymouth Bluff*. This preserve, in Lowndes County, consists of a pine forest overlooking the Tombigbee River. Their second project has been the addition to the *Mississippi Sandhill Crane Sanctuary* (in Jackson County). A present total of nearly 500 acres — providing habitat for the rare and endangered Sandhill Crane — is being held for transfer to the US Fish and Wildlife Service for inclusion in a proposed NWR. The sanctuary is located in the southeastern corner of the state.

One of Mississippi's 3 local Audubon chapters — the Oktibbeha Audubon Society — maintains a sanctuary. It is the 7½-acre *Clytenville Heronry,* established in 1967. It is leased from the Mississippi Ornithological Society and is open to the public. Primary species are Little Blue Heron and various egrets. The sanctuary is near Noxubee NWR. For specific information, contact MOS, 111 North Jefferson Street, Jackson 39202.

STATE PARKS AND FORESTS

Mississippi has 15 state parks, all of which offer a variety of recreational activities including camping, swimming, picnicking, fishing, and hiking. Those which are known for birdwatching as well are so indicated by an asterisk (*). For additional information regarding Mississippi state parks and/or historic sites, contact Mississippi Park Commission, 717 Robert E. Lee Building, Jackson 39201; (601) 354-6321.

Carver Point, State 7, Route 2, Coffeeville 38922; (601) 628-5199; 750 acres.
Clarkco, US 45, Quitman 39355; (601) 776-6651; 792 acres.
Holmes County, US 51, Durant 39063; (601) 653-3351; 463 acres.
Hugh White, State 8, Grenada 38901; (601) 226-4934; 745 acres
*John W. Kyle, US 51, Sardis 38666; (601) 487-1345; 740 acres.
*J. P. Coleman, State 25, Iuka 38852; (601) 423-6629; 1468 acres.
Leroy Percy, US 61, Hollandale 38748; (601) 827-5320; 2442 acres.
Magnolia, US 90, Ocean Springs 39564; (601) 875-2424; 200 acres.
Paul B. Johnson, US 49, Hattiesburg 39401; (601) 582-7721; 805 acres.
Percy Quin, State 48, McComb 39648; (601) 684-3931; 1620 acres.
Roosevelt, US 80, Morton 39117; (601) 732-6075; 562 acres.
*Tishomingo, State 25, Tishomingo 38873; (601) 438-3303; 1400 acres.
Tombigbee, US 78, Tupelo 38801; (601) 842-7669; 822 acres.
Wall Doxey, State 7, Holly Springs 38635; (601) 252-4231; 855 acres.
Yocona Ridge, State 32, Route 1, Oakland 38948; (601) 623-7356; 825 acres.

In addition there are 4 historic sites that are day use areas.

Red-cockaded Woodpecker

NORTH CAROLINA

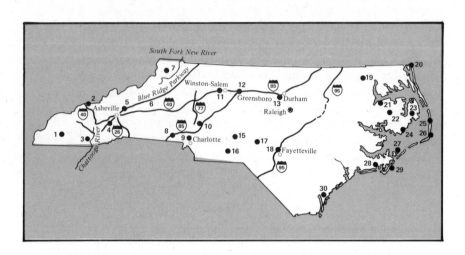

1. Nantahala National Forest
2. Great Smoky Mountain National Park
3. Highlands
4. Pisgah National Forest
   Connemara
5. Pisgah National Forest
6. Blue Ridge Parkway
7. New River
8. Schiele Museum
9. Charlotte Nature Museum
   Independence Outdoor Laboratory
10. Supplementary Educational Center
11. Nature Science Center
12. Natural Science Center
    T. Gilbert Pearson Wildlife Sanctuary
    Trailing Cedar Farm
13. Sara P. Duke Gardens
14. Hymettus Woods Preserve

15. Uwharrie National Forest
16. Pee Dee NWR
17. Clarendon Gardens
18. Boyd Forest Preserve
19. Chowan Swamp
20. Mackay Island NWR
21. Pungo NWR
22. Mattamuskeet NWR
23. Jockey's Ridge
24. Swan Quarter NWR
25. Pea Island NWR
26. Cape Hatteras National Seashore
27. Cedar Island NWR
28. Croatan National Forest
29. Cape Lookout National Seashore
30. Greenfield Gardens
    Airlie Gardens
    Orton Plantation

North Carolina's diverse habitats — ranging from the Great Smoky Mountains to the coastal plain — provide many rewarding birdwatching opportunities. Most visitors concentrate on the coastal regions, the long chain of sand islands which front on the Atlantic; but the birds of the forests and mountains are equally deserving of attention. The Red Crossbill and Saw-whet Owl both breed in the mountains. Common birds of the piedmont plateau include hawks, cuckoos, woodpeckers, flycatchers, and warblers. Much of the coast — notably Cape Lookout and Cape Hatteras — is preserved, either as a national seashore or wildlife refuge. Among the regularly nesting birds on the beaches and marshes are terns, Black Skimmer, Willet, and Seaside Sparrow.

There are 6 local Audubon chapters, one of which maintains 2 sanctuaries. Unfortunately the famed Gaddy's (Wild Goose) Refuge near Ansonville has had to be closed — due, in part, to lack of funds. However, the New River, in western North Carolina, has been saved — no dams to be built for a 26½-mile stretch of the river. This area, lying between Jefferson and Stratford, has been declared a scenic river area. Additional information regarding wildlife in North Carolina can be obtained from the State of North Carolina, Department of Natural and Economic Resources, Raleigh 27611.

Blue Ridge National Parkway. For complete information, see entry in Virginia chapter (page 130). A section of the parkway runs through Pisgah National Forest. Of special interest in North Carolina are: the Craggy Gardens at milepost #370 — over 1500 species of wildflowers bloom here from late spring through fall; the Linville Gorge Wilderness Area, located a short distance from the parkway; and the Linville Caverns, which are on US 221 near Linville Gorge.

Cape Hatteras National Seashore, Box 457, Manteo 27954. Cape Hatteras is located off the eastern coast of North Carolina and is a continuation of the chain of barrier islands that make up Cape Lookout National Seashore. Cape Hatteras can be reached by road from Manteo by going east on US 64 and then south on SR 12. It can also be reached by ferry from Cedar Island (near Beaufort). Camping is permitted at the Seashore.

Cape Hatteras National Seashore was established in 1937 and covers 45 square miles of beach land. It includes Pea Island NWR. For information about birds, see entry for Pea Island, page 216. A checklist for Cape Hatteras is available.

Cape Lookout National Seashore, P.O. Box 690, Beaufort 28516. Access is by boat only. There are no facilities on the islands. Visitors are cautioned to bring adequate supplies of food and water. As there is little shade or shelter, it is advisable to bring a shirt and a hat as well. Camping is permitted at Cape Lookout — be sure that tents are strong enough to withstand wind. Mosquito netting and insect repellent are also needed. The islands are relatively undeveloped; ferry service is available to some of the areas. For information, contact the superintendent at the above address. A visitors' center is planned for Harkers Island and this center will be accessible by car.

Cape Lookout National Seashore is composed of 58 miles of barrier island — low, narrow ribbons of sand. The islands consist mostly of wide, bare beaches, flat grasslands, and large expanses of salt marshes. (Note: The sea oats are protected by law; do not pick them.) Snakes and turtles live on the islands — mammals are rare. On Shackleford there are some domestic animals now gone wild — sheep, goats, cows, and horses. Cape Lookout is a wintering area for such northern birds as loons, mergansers, cormorants, and bay and sea ducks. Among the birds sighted at the Seashore are: Marsh Hawk, Peregrine Falcon (during migration), Glossy Ibis, Green Heron, Snowy Egret, American Coot, American Oystercatcher, Virginia Rail, Wilson's Plover, Piping Plover, Red Knot, Ruddy Turnstone, Least Tern, Forster's Tern, Black Skimmer, Common Nighthawk, Barn Swallow, Mockingbird, Common Yellowthroat, Eastern Meadowlark, and Seaside Sparrow. Occasionally, pelagic birds will also visit the area.

Cedar Island National Wildlife Refuge. Administered by Mattamuskeet NWR. Cedar Island is located in Pamlico Sound near Mattamuskeet, Swan Quarter, and Pea Island NWRs. To reach the refuge from Beaufort, take US 70 north for about 30 miles, continue north on SR 12 to Cedar Island. Camping is not permitted on the refuge; however, facilities are available at nearby Croatan National Forest.

The refuge was established in 1964, and now totals over 12,500 acres; acquisition is not yet complete. Over 80 percent of the refuge is salt marsh, but there are also pine-hardwood ridges and 2 small islands. Primary species at Cedar Island include Snow Geese, Black Ducks, and rails; however, over 200 species of birds visit or reside here.

Croatan National Forest. Forest Supervisor, 50 South French Broad Avenue, Asheville 28802; (704) 258-2850. Croatan Forest is located in eastern North Carolina; it lies between New Bern and Morehead City. To reach the Forest, use US 70. Public facilities at Croatan include camping, fishing, swimming, boating, and hiking.

Croatan Forest comprises 152,000 acres of pine and swamp hardwoods, rivers and lakes. There is a swamp that borders Great Lake in the center of Croatan. The area is characterized by cypress and gum. On the south side of the lake is a small rookery of Double-crested Cormorants. Herons also nest here, as do Prothonotary and Swainson's Warblers. Other birds which can be seen at Croatan include Turkey, Bobwhite, Red-bellied Woodpecker, Carolina Chickadee, Tufted Titmouse, Blue-gray Gnatcatcher, Whip-poor-will, Wood Thrush, Northern Parula, American Redstart, and Blue Grosbeak.

Great Smoky Mountain National Park. For information, see entry in Tennessee chapter (page 232).

Mackay Island National Wildlife Refuge. For information, see entry in Virginia chapter (page 133).

Mattamuskeet National Wildlife Refuge, New Holland 27885; (919) 926-4021. The refuge is located in New Holland on US 264, approximately 10 miles between Swan Quarter and Englehard. Mattamuskeet is near Swan Quarter, Pungo, and Cedar Island NWRs and across Pamlico Sound from Cape Hatteras National Seashore. Upon arrival, visitors can obtain instructions from the staff regarding travel on the refuge. This is necessary because some roads are impassable during wet periods. Camping is not permitted on the refuge; however, facilities are available at nearby Pettigrew State Park.

Mattamuskeet was established in 1934 and consists of 50,000 acres of marsh, water, timber, and croplands. Lake Mattamuskeet, a shallow lake averaging only 2 feet in depth, is 18 miles long and 5 to 6 miles wide. Mattamuskeet's climate is characterized by hot, humid summers and moderate winters; snowfall is rare. The refuge lies in the middle of the Atlantic Flyway. Although noted primarily for waterfowl, Mattamuskeet provides habitat for 214 species of birds. Among these are: Canada Goose, Snow (Blue) Goose, Red-cockaded Woodpecker, Prothonotary Warbler, Common Yellowthroat, Summer Tanager, Henslow's Sparrow, and over 22 species of ducks. Checklist available.

Nantahala National Forest. Forest Supervisor, 50 South French Broad Avenue, Asheville 28802; (704) 258-2850. Nantahala is bordered by Pisgah, Cherokee, and Chattahoochee national forests and by Great Smoky Mountain National Park. A wide range of public recreational activities are available, including camping. To reach the Forest from Asheville, use US 19.

The 420,000-acre Forest is a land of waterfalls, rushing streams, wildflowers, and virgin timber. An 80-mile portion of the Appalachian Trail passes through Nantahala. Nantahala also includes the 3800-acre Joyce Kilmer Memorial Forest — a living monument to the poet.

Of special interest is the Highlands Biological Station also located within Forest boundaries. The station is located on 16 acres bordering Lake Ravenel, less than ½ mile east of the center of Highlands. The station maintains several other natural areas as well: the Margaret Cannon Howell Wildlife Refuge, a primeval forest; and the Frank Dulany tract, a bog supporting a unique assemblage of plants and animals, are just 2 examples. Highlands also maintains a museum that is open to the general public. The heavy rainfall and high elevation of the Highlands area make it an interesting and important one for study.

Within the borders of Nantahala National Forest are several Nature Conservancy preserves. The following 3 are located in the area of the Highlands Biological Center.

Timber Ridge Preserve — 20 acres, hardwood forest; and *Henry M. Wright Preserve* — 22 acres, mixed conifer and hardwood forest. Both preserves are open with permission only. For further information, contact The Nature Conservancy or Dr. Lindsay Olive, Department of Botany, University of North Carolina, Chapel Hill 27514. Also in this area is the *Olive Tract Preserve,* a 4-acre hardwood forest with an understory of laurel and rhododendron. Wildflowers include wild orchids and trilliums. For further information, contact the Botanical Garden Foundation, P.O. Box 2241, Chapel Hill 27514. There have been 183 species of birds sighted in the area. Among these are: Pied-billed Grebe, Wood Duck, Sharp-shinned Hawk, Peregrine Falcon, Green Heron, Killdeer, Screech Owl, Chimney Swift, Pileated Woodpecker, Least Flycatcher, Olive-sided Flycatcher (rare), Brown Creeper, Brown Thrasher, Hermit Thrush, Solitary Vireo, Swainson's Warbler, Palm Warbler, Connecticut Warbler (rare), Field Sparrow, and Song Sparrow.

Pea Island National Wildlife Refuge, P.O. Box 1026, Manteo 27954; (919) 987-2394. The refuge is located on Cape Hatteras National Seashore, on SR 12, about 10 miles south of Nags Head. Although camping is not permitted on the refuge, there are campgrounds on Cape Hatteras.

Pea Island Refuge was established in 1938. The refuge contains 5915 acres of tidal marsh, ocean dunes, and beach. In addition there are 25,700 acres of protected waters in Pamlico Sound. Pea Island is a midpoint in the Atlantic Flyway, and is a much-used and valuable feeding and resting area for numerous species of wintering waterfowl. The area also provides habitat for the endangered Brown Pelican and Peregrine Falcon. Among the 265 species of birds (plus 50 accidentals) that visit the refuge regularly are: Red-throated Loon, Gannet, Sooty Shearwater, Leach's Storm-Petrel, Wilson's Storm-Petrel, Gadwall, Cooper's Hawk, Osprey, Great Blue Heron, Yellow-crowned Night Heron, Glossy Ibis, Black Rail, Purple Gallinule, American Oystercatcher, American Avocet, Black-necked Stilt, Western Sandpiper, Buff-breasted Sandpiper (rare), Red Knot, Baird's Sandpiper, Hudsonian Godwit, Wilson's Phalarope, American Woodcock, Pomarine Jaeger, Glaucous Gull (rare), Black-legged Kittiwake, Dovekie, Gull-billed Tern, Black Skimmer, Short-eared Owl, Swainson's Thrush, Magnolia Warbler, Orange-crowned Warbler, Connecticut Warbler (rare), Summer Tanager, Ipswich Sparrow (rare), and Lark Sparrow. Checklist available.

Pee Dee National Wildlife Refuge, Box 780, Wadesboro 28170; (704) 694-4424. Refuge headquarters are in the Wadesboro Post Office building, approximately 6 miles from the refuge. From Charlotte, take US 74 east to Wadesboro. The refuge is located between US 52 and SR 109 near Ansonville. Camping is not permitted at the refuge; however, facilities are available at nearby Uwharrie National Forest. Pee Dee is also near Carolina Sandhills NWR (South Carolina).

Established in 1964, Pee Dee is still in the acquisition stage. When complete, the refuge will contain 11,000 acres; its present size is 4500 acres. The Pee Dee

River bisects the refuge which is located in the piedmont area of the state. The primary management objective of the refuge is to restore the dwindling populations of geese and ducks. Among the 159 species of birds sighted here are: White-fronted Goose (rare), Wood Duck, Golden Eagle (rare), (Southern) Bald Eagle (rare), Little Blue Heron, Belted Kingfisher, Red-cockaded Woodpecker, Prothonotary Warbler, Louisiana Waterthrush, Bobolink, Scarlet Tanager, and Blue Grosbeak. Checklist available.

Pisgah National Forest. Forest Supervisor, 50 South French Broad Avenue, Asheville 28802; (704) 258-2850. Pisgah is located near Asheville; it borders Nantahala and Cherokee national forests and Great Smoky Mountain National Park. Part of the Blue Ridge Parkway traverses Pisgah (see entry in Virginia chapter, page 130). To reach Pisgah from Asheville, use the Blue Ridge Parkway or US 276 and/or SR 115. Camping facilities are available at Pisgah in addition to a wide range of recreational activities.

Pisgah was among the first of our national forests; established in 1914, it now encompasses 157,000 acres. There are more than 250 miles of hiking trails; a fish hatchery; and an experimental forest. A portion of the Appalachian Trail crosses Pisgah where it borders on Cherokee. Attractions include Shining Rock Wilderness — 14,000 acres of mountains and waterfalls, the name comes from the white quartz atop Shining Rock Ridge; Mount Mitchell — 6684 feet, highest point east of the Mississippi; and Linville Falls and Gorge (including the Linville Caverns). Craggy Gardens and Roan Mountain are famous for their purple rhododendron which covers the mountainside in the spring. The Cradle of American Forestry visitors' center is also found at Pisgah. Pisgah National Forest is home for many fish, birds, and wild animals. Among the 50 most frequently seen birds at the Mount Mitchell area are: Red-tailed Hawk, Hairy Woodpecker, Downy Woodpecker, Winter Wren, Eastern Bluebird, Ruby-throated Hummingbird, Cliff Swallow, Golden- and Ruby-crowned Kinglets, Cedar Waxwing, Swainson's Thrush, Solitary Vireo, Chestnut-sided Warbler, Ovenbird, Rose-breasted Grosbeak, and Indigo Bunting.

Pungo National Wildlife Refuge, P.O. Box 267, Plymouth 27962; (919) 793-2143. Pungo is located in eastern North Carolina. From Plymouth, take SR 32 south for 5 miles, then turn south on SR 99, and continue for 12 more miles to the entrance. Pungo is near Mattamuskeet, Swan Quarter, and Dismal Swamp NWRs. Camping is not permitted on the refuge; however, facilities are available at nearby Pettigrew State Park.

Pungo was established in 1963, primarily as a wintering area for Canada Geese. Its 12,300 acres are composed of freshwater marshes, farmland, hardwood forests, and Pungo Lake. Nature trails, observation points, photography blinds, and other facilities are planned. Birdwatching for species other than waterfowl is best during spring and fall migration. Among the 174 species of birds recorded here are: Fulvous Tree Duck (rare), Wood Duck,

Bufflehead, Bald Eagle, Osprey, American Kestrel (Sparrow Hawk), Snowy Egret, Louisiana Heron, American Bittern, Glossy Ibis, Ruddy Turnstone (rare), Pectoral Sandpiper (rare), Pileated Woodpecker, Golden-crowned Kinglet, Yellow-rumped (Myrtle) Warbler, and Indigo Bunting. Checklist available.

Swan Quarter National Wildlife Refuge. Administered by Mattamuskeet NWR. The refuge is located in Swan Quarter, off US 264. Nearby NWRs include Pungo, Cedar Island, and Mattamuskeet. Camping is not permitted on the refuge; however, facilities are available at nearby Pettigrew State Park.

Swan Quarter was established in 1932 and consists of 15,500 acres of marshland bordering on Pamlico Sound. An additional 24,450 acres of water (in the Sound) have been closed to migratory waterfowl hunting. Among the 227 species of birds recorded here are: Pied-billed Grebe, Brown Pelican, Pintail, Bald Eagle, Great Blue Heron, Great (Common) Egret, Clapper Rail, Killdeer, Pectoral Sandpiper, Screech Owl, Red-bellied Woodpecker, Brown-headed Nuthatch, Long-billed Marsh Wren, Cedar Waxwing, Worm-eating Warbler, Eastern Meadowlark, and Fox Sparrow. Checklist available.

Uwharrie National Forest. Forest Supervisor, 50 South French Broad Avenue, P.O. Box 2750, Asheville 28802; (704) 258-2850. Uwharrie is located in the center of the state, south of Greensboro. From Greensboro, take US 220 south to Ulah, then take SR 134 south to Troy. A network of state and county roads traverse Uwharrie. Facilities for camping and picnicking are available; other recreational facilities include horseback riding, fishing, and hiking.

The forest totals 44,000 acres. Attractions include the Uwharrie wildlife management area. Among the birds likely to be seen here are: Red-shouldered Hawk, Bobwhite, Yellow-billed Cuckoo, Barred Owl, Pileated Woodpecker, Great Crested Flycatcher, House Wren, Wood Thrush, Brown Thrasher, Mockingbird, Red-eyed Vireo, Black-and-white Warbler, and Song Sparrow.

NATURE CENTERS

Located throughout North Carolina are various nature centers, gardens, and preserves. These are often good birding places. They are described briefly below.

Boyd Forest Preserve. Maintained by State of North Carolina, Department of Natural and Economic Resources, Raleigh 27611. This 403-acre preserve is located near Fayetteville. It is characterized by rolling sandhills; broad, shallow ravines; an open forest of longleaf pines; and a swamp.

Charlotte Nature Museum, 1658 Sterling Road, Charlotte 28209; (704) 333-0506. The center covers 29 acres and features a planetarium; guided and self-guiding tours are offered. A range of educational and interpretive programs are available. It is open all year, closed on holidays.

Chowan Swamp. Located in Gates County, this 6059-acre preserve is characterized by bald cypress, gum, and white cedar. The swamp is habitat for bobcat, opossum, Osprey, woodpeckers, and waterfowl. For further information, contact the Department of Natural and Economic Resources at the above address.

Clarendon Gardens. Located in Southern Pines, Clarendon has one of the nation's top collections of holly. The gardens are open during daylight hours; an admission fee is charged.

Connemara. The 240-acre Carl Sandburg Farm located near Flat Rock is now a National Historic Site. It is open to the public daily 9-5. Flat Rock is south of Asheville, near Hendersonville.

Greenfield Gardens, Airlie Gardens; and Orton Plantation. All 3 gardens are located near Wilmington and all are open during daylight hours; admission fees are charged. They are all very good for birdwatching. Marsh birds, wading birds, ducks, woodpeckers, and passerines (especially warblers) are to be found. Painted Buntings can be seen at Airlie Gardens.

Hymettus Woods Preserve. The preserve is located in the city of Raleigh. The 5-acre woodlands are mixed southern hardwoods with a dogwood understory; the preserve is traversed by a stream.

Independence Outdoor Laboratory, 1967 Patriot Drive, Charlotte 28212; (704) 545-4536. The laboratory is operated by the Charlotte-Mecklenburg Schools; it totals 27 acres. Guided and self-guiding tours are offered. It is open Monday through Friday from 1 September to 31 May.

Jockey's Ridge. Located in Dare County, this 6-acre preserve acts as feeder land for nearby Jockey's Ridge — the tallest sand dune in the eastern United States. The preserve is to be included in a proposed state park. For further information, contact the Department of Natural and Economic Resources at the above address.

Natural Science Center, 4301 Lawndale Drive, Greensboro 27408; (919) 288-3769. The center is operated by the city of Greensboro; it totals 83 acres. Various educational and interpretative programs are offered; guided and self-guiding tours are available. The center is open all year, closed on Mondays.

Nature Science Center, Museum Drive, Winston-Salem 27105; (919) 767-6642. The center totals 31 acres and is open all year, closed on Mondays and holidays.

Sara P. Duke Gardens. Located north of Pinehurst in Durham, the gardens are near the main entrance to the west campus of Duke University. The gardens are open during daylight hours; an admission fee is charged.

Schiele Museum of Natural History and Planetarium, 1500 East Garrison Boulevard, Gastonia 28052; (704) 864-3962. The museum is operated by the city of Gastonia. It covers 15 acres; educational and interpretive programs are offered; guided and self-guiding tours are available. The museum is open all year, closed on Mondays.

Supplementary Educational Center, 1636 Parkview Circle, Salisbury 28144; (704) 636-3462. The center is operated by the city of Salisbury and Rowan and Davie counties. It totals 34 acres; educational and interpretive programs are offered; guided and self-guiding tours are available. The center is open all year, closed on weekends.

Trailing Cedar Farm — Audubon Wildlife Sanctuary. This 200-acre sanctuary is maintained by the T. G. Pearson Audubon Society, and is located near Greensboro. Visiting is by prior arrangement only.

T. Gilbert Pearson Wildlife Sanctuary. The sanctuary is leased permanently from Guilford College; the college is located on US 421 just west of Greensboro. This 125-acre sanctuary is maintained by the T. G. Pearson Audubon Society.

STATE PARKS

In addition to the federally and privately owned properties described in the foregoing pages, there are the following state-owned parks and recreation areas. The first 9 listed offer camping facilities; the others do not but do offer many other activities. The parks that are likely to be best for birdwatching are marked with an asterisk (*). Information about camping in North Carolina can be obtained from the State of North Carolina, Travel Development Section, Division of Economic Development, Department of Natural and Economic Resources, Raleigh 27611. Firearms and pets (except for dogs on leashes) are prohibited at all times. No pets are allowed at any time in the swimming areas or cabins.

PARKS WITH CAMPING FACILITIES

*Carolina Beach, P.O. Box 475, Carolina Beach 28428; (919) 458-8206; 340 acres.

Cliffs of the Neuse, Route 2, Seven Springs 28578; (919) 734-2617; 570 acres.

Duke Power, Route 1, Troutman 28166; (704) 528-6350; 1130 acres.

*Hanging Rock, P.O. Box 96, Danbury 27016; (919) 593-8480; 4040 acres.

Jones Lake, Route 2, Box 215, Elizabethtown 28337; (919) 588-4550; 1890 acres, in Bladen Lakes State Forest.

Morrow Mountain, Route 2, Albemarle 28801; (704) 982-4402; 4425 acres.

*Mount Mitchell, Route 5, Box 400, Burnsville 28714; (704) 675-4611; 1470 acres.

*Pettigrew, Route 1, Creswell 27928; (919) 787-4475; 17,370 acres.

*William B. Ulmstead, Route 8, Box 130, Raleigh 27607; (919) 787-3033; 5210 acres.

DAY USE PARKS

Crowder's Mountain; (704) 867-1181; 1100 acres (near Gastonia).

*Dismal Swamp Land; 14,400 acres north of Elizabeth City located east of US 17.

*Eno River, Route 2, Box 436-C, Durham 27705; (919) 383-1686; 1200 acres.

*Fort Macon, P.O. Box 127, Atlantic Beach 28572; (919) 726-3775; 385 acres.

*Goose Creek, Route 2, Box 382, Washington 27889; (919) 946-2050; 1300 acres.

*Hammocks Beach, P.O. Box 38, Swansboro 28584; (919) 326-4881; 890 acres; access by boat only.

*Jockey's Ridge; 300 acres near Nags Head; supervised by superintendent of Pettigrew State Park (see above).

Medoc Mountain, P.O. Box 58, Hollister 27844; (919) 445-2280; 2300 acres.

*Merchants Millpond; 1800 acres near Murfreesboro and Ahoskie bordering Great Dismal Swamp.

Mount Jefferson, P.O. Box 174, Jefferson 28640; (919) 246-9653; 540 acres.

Pilot Mountain, Route 1, Box 13, Pinnacle 27403; (919) 325-2355; 3540 acres.

*Raven Rock, Route 3, Box 447, Lillington 27546; (919) 893-4888; 2700 acres.

*Stone Mountain, Roaring Gap 28668; (919) 957-8185; 2110 acres.

*Theodore Roosevelt Natural Area; 250 acres; 4 miles south of Morehead City on US 24.

*Weymouth Woods (Sandhills Nature Preserve), P.O. Box 1368, Southern Pines 28387; (919) 692-2167; 410 acres.

In addition to those parks listed above, there are 7 recreation areas associated with Kerr Reservoir (Buggs Island Lake). These are all located in the north central part of the state near Henderson. For additional information about this area, contact the Kerr Reservoir Development Commission, Route 3, Box KRDC, Henderson 27536; (919) 438-7791.

SOUTH CAROLINA

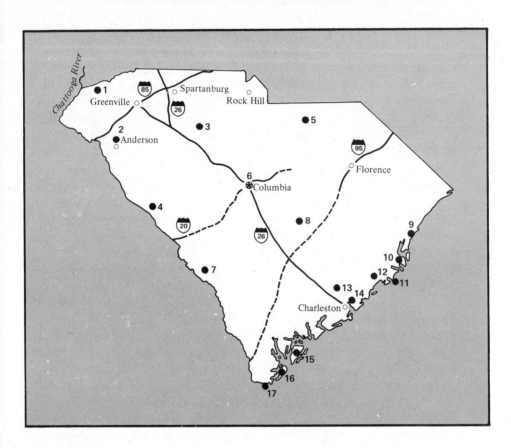

1. Sumter National Forest
2. Woodfern Environmental Center
3. Sumter National Forest
4. Sumter National Forest
5. Carolina Sandhills NWR
6. Columbia Science Museum
7. Silver Bluff Plantation
8. Santee NWR
9. Brookgreen Gardens
10. Santee Coastal Reserve

11. Cape Romain NWR
12. Francis Marion National Forest
13. Francis Beidler Forst (Four Hole
    Swamp)
14. Cypress Gardens
    Magnolia Gardens
    Middleton Place Gardens
15. Island Wildlife Preserve
16. Turtle Island
17. Savannah NWR

South Carolina has long been recognized by birders as one of the best birding areas in the East — there have been 443 species of birds recorded in South Carolina. The state's 281-mile coastline lies along the Atlantic Flyway. This coastal plain is always productive for the birdwatcher; it is not unusual at Bulls Island (Cape Romain NWR), for example, to sight well over 100 species. The center of the state is known as the piedmont region. This area includes several major lakes and many streams and rivers. Black gum, sweet gum, maple, and willow grow in the river valleys. In the northern corner of South Carolina lie the mountains — part of the Blue Ridge. Here at least 3 peaks exceed 3000 feet. Hemlock, white pine, and mountain laurel characterize the landscape.

There are 3 local Audubon chapters, one of which maintains a sanctuary (Hilton Head). National Audubon maintains 3 sanctuaries in South Carolina (one of which is closed to the public).

Cape Romain National Wildlife Refuge, Route 1, Box 191, Awendaw 29429; (803) 928-3368. The refuge lies about 20 miles northeast of Charleston, east of US 17, south of the Santee River. Cape Romain is between Francis Marion National Forest and Bulls Bay (on the Atlantic). To reach refuge headquarters (and Bulls Island), turn off US 17 onto See Wee Road for 5 miles to Moore's Landing. Boat access is generally available at this point. Camping is not permitted on the refuge; however, facilities are available at nearby Francis Marion National Forest.

Cape Romain Refuge was established in 1932 and comprises 34,000 acres of woodland, marsh, and water; an additional 30,000 acres of open water has been closed to migratory waterfowl hunting. The refuge is located on the Atlantic Flyway, and occupies a 20-mile section of the coast. Cape Romain's sea islands, intricate coastal waterways, salt marshes, and sandy beaches combine to form one of the outstanding wildlife refuges in the East. Bulls Island, an ancient barrier reef, is the most popular part of the refuge. It is the refuge's only wooded island; it has a forest of live oaks, magnolias, pines, and palmettos. In addition, the island has several shallow brackish and freshwater ponds. For birdwatching, too, Bulls Island presents perhaps the best opportunities.

But while the most attractive and accessible, Bulls Island is not the only important biological area of the refuge. Many of the small, treeless islands in Bulls Bay are nesting areas for gulls, terns, and pelicans. Other small islands on the refuge are nesting sites for herons, egrets, oystercatchers, skimmers, willets, plovers, and other shorebirds.

The best opportunities for observing a large variety and quantity of birds are during the fall, winter, and spring months. The diversity of birdlife is shown when the 1-day Christmas Bird Counts are reviewed. Among the 251 species of birds (108 nesting) that have been sighted here are: Wilson's Storm-Petrel (rare), Gannet, Brown Pelican, Surf Scoter, Swallow-tailed Kite, Mississippi Kite, Wood Stork (Ibis), Purple Gallinule, American Oystercatcher, American Avocet (rare), Piping Plover, Wilson's Plover, Long-billed Curlew, Marbled Godwit, Stilt Sandpiper, White-rumped Sandpiper, Red Knot, Northern Phalarope (rare), Parasitic Jaeger (rare), Gull-billed Tern, Red-cockaded Woodpecker, Long- and Short-billed Marsh Wrens, Black-throated Blue Warbler, Chestnut-sided Warbler, Hooded Warbler, Painted Bunting, and Bachman's Sparrow. Checklist available.

Carolina Sandhills National Wildlife Refuge, P. O. Box 477, McBee 29101; (803) 335-8401. Sandhills NWR is located about 55 miles northeast of Columbia, 3 miles north of McBee on US 1. Camping is not permitted at the refuge; however, facilities are available at nearby state parks and private campgrounds.

Established in 1939 as an upland game refuge, emphasis in recent years has been directed toward management for geese and ducks. The 46,000-acre refuge is part of a wide band of sandhills along the coastal plain. In prehistoric times, these sandhills were part of the shores of an ancient ocean. Now hardwood forests, freshwater ponds and lakes, and croplands combine to support a varied and abundant wildlife community.

Carolina Sandhills has one of the largest remaining colonies of Red-cockaded Woodpeckers, an endangered species which builds its nesting cavity in a living pine tree suffering from red heart disease. The refuge is home to an additional 184 species of birds (72 nesting). Among these are: Wood Duck, Bald Eagle (rare), Osprey, Little Blue Heron, Least Sandpiper (rare), Great Horned Owl, Ruby-throated Hummingbird, Pileated Woodpecker, Tree Swallow, Brown-headed Nuthatch, Carolina Wren, Northern Parula, Yellow-throated Warbler, Prairie Warbler, Hooded Warbler, Summer Tanager, Bachman's Sparrow (rare), and Chipping Sparrow. Checklist available.

Francis Beidler Forest (Four Hole Swamp). Owned by the National Audubon Society; preserve director: Norman Brunswig, P.O. Box 47, Dorchester 29437; (803) 563-4313. The preserve is located in Berkeley and Dorchester Counties, about 40 miles from Charleston. Contact the preserve director for specific traveling directions. The preserve is open with permission only. A full-time biologist-warden is on staff. Camping facilities are available at nearby state parks.

This 3415-acre preserve is perhaps the last significant remaining virgin tupelo-bald-cypress stand in the world. The trees range from 3 to 4 feet in diameter, some exceed 5 feet. Spanish moss drapes the limbs of the large trees, and the cypress knees are covered with ferns, mosses, and orchids. The swamp is truly wild. There are about 40 miles of waterways, via the mainstream and its many branches and meanders. Canoes take visitors through the area. Throughout much of the year, water levels permit extensive walking throughout the forest, which is remarkably free of undergrowth. At least 2 roads, probably dating back to colonial times, allow hikers access for considerable distances into the swamp. These trails traverse highly scenic and typical cross-sections of the original forest. American alligator, mink, raccoon, weasel, otter, and various species of snakes breed in the swamp. Among the many species of birds seen here are: Anhinga, Red-tailed Hawk, Great (Common) Egret, Great Horned Owl, Pileated Woodpecker, Red-bellied Woodpecker, White-eyed Vireo, Red-eyed Vireo, Blue-gray Gnatcatcher, Carolina Wren, Prothonontary Warbler, and Summer Tanager..

Francis Marion National Forest. National Forests in South Carolina, 1612 Marion Street, Columbia 29201. Francis Marion is located just north of Charleston. To reach it, take US 17/701 north and/or SR 41 north. Camping, in addition to other recreational facilities, is offered. Francis Marion is adjacent to Cape Romain NWR and borders the southern edge of Santee NWR.

Established in 1936, the Forest now covers over 180,000 acres. Francis Marion is famous for its pure strain of Turkey. Resident mammals include deer, rabbit, raccoon, and opossum. The American alligator, an endangered species, is also found here. Francis Marion is located along the Atlantic Flyway; and in winter as many as 250 different species of birds have been counted. The creeks, swamps, bays, and marshes are favorite spots for birdwatchers. Among the bird species sighted are: Anhinga, Fulvous Tree Duck, Pintail, American Wigeon, Canvasback, Northern Shoveler, Redhead, Oldsquaw, Swallow-tailed Kite, Mississippi Kite, Bald Eagle, Peregrine Falcon, Louisiana Heron, Least Bittern, Wood Stork (Ibis), Purple Gallinule, Clapper Rail, American Oystercatcher, American Avocet, Ruddy Turnstone, Whimbrel, Dowitcher, Marbled Godwit, Caspian Tern, Short-eared Owl, Common Nighthawk, Barn Swallow, Brown-headed Nuthatch, Short-billed Marsh Wren, Swainson's Thrush, Water Pipit, Blue-winged Warbler, Cape May Warbler, Brewer's Blackbird, Western Tanager, Henslow's Sparrow, and Sharp-tailed Sparrow. Checklist available.

The Island Wildlife Preserve, Hilton Head Audubon Society, P.O. Box 6185, Hilton Head Island 29928. The preserve is located between Beaufort and Savannah (Georgia). To reach the preserve from Beaufort, take US 21 west to SR170; then go southwest to SR 462, take that south to US 278; take US 278 east to Hilton Head Island. Camping is not permitted on the preserve, facilities are available at nearby private campgrounds or at Hunting Island State Park.

The 49-acre preserve is maintained by the Hilton Head Audubon Society; the preserve is open to the public. There are wooded areas, ponds fringed with rushes, and marshes. Wildflowers thrive. The wide variety of plant life provides habitat for many birds. Over 50 species of birds have been reported here. Among them are: Pied-billed Grebe, Wood Duck, Osprey, White Ibis, Killdeer, Common (Yellow-shafted) Flicker, Hairy Woodpecker, Tree Swallow, Blue-gray Gnatcatcher, Cedar Waxwing, Yellow-throated Warbler, and Summer Tanager. Checklist and booklet available.

Santee National Wildlife Refuge, Box 158, Summerton 29148; (803) 478-2217. Santee is located southeast of Columbia, near Sumter. Take US 15 south to Summerton, then take US 301 south for about 7 miles to the refuge.

Camping is not permitted at the refuge; however, facilities are available at nearby Santee State Park. Caution should be exercised in walking around this area as there are numerous poisonous snakes.

Santee Refuge was established in 1941 and contains about 73,300 acres; it comprises Lakes Marion and Moultrie. In late fall and early spring, waterfowl populations are at their peak; in summer, the Wood Duck is chief denizen, and considerable management is devoted to the production of this species. Many birds are present throughout the year, but it is during spring and fall migration that the species and numbers reach their spectacular peaks. Among the 234 species of birds (78 nesting locally) are: Pied-billed Grebe, Anhinga, Snow (Blue) Goose, Green-winged Teal, Mississippi Kite, Sharp-shinned Hawk, Broad-winged Hawk, Little Blue Heron, Wood Stork (Ibis), Limpkin (rare), Piping Plover, Sanderling, Western Sandpiper, Screech Owl, Red-cockaded Woodpecker, Eastern Kingbird, Brown Creeper, Short-billed Marsh Wren, Wood Thrush, Veery, Solitary Vireo, Orange-crowned Warbler, Northern Waterthrush, Boat-tailed Grackle, Blue Grosbeak, and Vesper Sparrow. Checklist available.

Savannah National Wildlife Refuge, Route 1, Hardeeville 29927; (912) 964-0231. For information, see entry in Georgia chapter (page 191).

Sumter National Forest. Forest Supervisor, 1801 Assembly Street, Columbia 29201. There are 3 sections (5 districts): Andrew Pickens, in the northwest corner of the state, near Walhalla; Enoree and Tyger Districts, near Union; and Edgefield and Long Cane Districts, near Greenwood. Sumter totals 346,000 acres of mountains, forests, and streams. Camping facilities are available at all 5 districts.

In the Andrew Pickens District is the Walhalla Trout Hatchery. Other attractions of this district include the Ellicott Rock Scenic Area and the Chattooga River, one of our National Wild and Scenic Rivers. Since this district borders the Nantahala National Forest (in North Carolina), the birdlife in both areas is nearly the same.

The Enoree and Tyger districts are less mountainous than Andrew Pickens. There are auto routes as well as hiking and horseback riding trails throughout the area. The Edgefield and Long Cane districts have more recreational opportunities than the other districts. They, too, offer hiking and horseback riding trails; in addition, there are 2 lakes and 2 reservoirs.

There are about 230 species of birds to be seen at Sumter. Among them are: Common Loon, Wood Duck, Canvasback, Sharp-shinned Hawk, Cooper's Hawk, American Kestrel (Sparrow Hawk), American Bittern, King Rail, Common Snipe, Upland Sandpiper (Plover), Pectoral Sandpiper, Wilson's Phalarope (rare), Barred Owl, Chimney Swift, Belted Kingfisher, Red-cockaded Woodpecker, Eastern Phoebe, Brown-headed Nuthatch, House Wren, Wood Thrush, Swainson's (Olive-backed) Thrush, Loggerhead Shrike, Solitary

Vireo, Golden-winged Warbler, Nashville Warbler, Ovenbird, Yellow-breasted Chat, Orchard Oriole, and Grasshopper Sparrow.

NATURE CENTERS

In addition to the federally and privately owned properties discussed in this chapter, the following gardens and preserves may also prove profitable for the birdwatcher.

Brookgreen Gardens. Brookgreen is located about 20 miles south of Myrtle Beach along US 17. This is a 4000-acre outdoor museum and garden. Brookgreen is open all year; an admission fee is charged. Among the birds likely to be seen here are: Bobwhite, Green Heron, Red-cockaded Woodpecker, Brown-headed Nuthatch, Swainson's Warbler, Black-throated Green Warbler (the South Carolina race, known as Wayne's Warbler), and — during the winter — many species of ducks. Spring and fall reveal migratory warblers and other birds of passage.

Columbia Science Museum, 1519 Senate Street, Columbia 29201; (803) 252-6974. The museum is operated by the Columbia Art Commission; it consists of 4 acres plus use of private, city, and state lands. There is a wildflower garden; various interpretive and educational programs are offered. The center is open all year, closed on Mondays.

Cypress Gardens. The gardens are located about 20 miles north of Charleston; use US 52 to get there. Cypress Gardens is open 9-5, every day; an admission fee is charged. Francis Marion National Forest and Cape Romain NWR are located nearby. Among the landbirds to be found at Cypress Gardens are the Pileated Woodpecker, Yellow-throated Warbler, and Painted Bunting.

Magnolia Gardens, Highway 61, Charleston 29400; (803) 571-1266. The gardens are located just outside Charleston. An admission fee is charged. To get there from Charleston, take US 17 south to SR 61, turn north (right), and continue for 12 miles. The gardens cover 350 acres, including a large freshwater pond. The gardens are at their peak of bloom in late March and early April. Look for Anhinga, Yellow-crowned Night Heron, White Ibis, Least Bittern, Fulvous Tree Duck, Pileated Woodpecker, Mockingbird, Yellow-throated Vireo, Wood Thrush, Prothonotary Warbler, and Painted Bunting.

Middleton Place Gardens, Highway 61, Charleston 29400; (803) 556-6020. The gardens are located off SR 61 a few miles north of Magnolia Gardens. An admission fee is charged. The mixed woodlands and open fields are good for a variety of landbirds — orioles, thrushes, and warblers.

Santee Coastal Reserve. The preserve is owned by The Nature Conservancy. This 23,000-acre preserve (including Blake's Reserve) is located about 50 miles north of Charleston; it provides habitat for 2 endangered species:

the American alligator and the (Southern) Bald Eagle. A vast cypress swamp; Atlantic beaches; and salt, brackish, and freshwater marshes combine to support a diversified wildlife community. A very large egret rookery is located on the preserve. Among the other birds that inhabit the reserve are: Anhinga, Osprey, Louisiana Heron, and White Ibis. Loggerhead turtles nest on the beaches. The preserve adjoins Cape Romain NWR and Francis Marion National Forest.

Silver Bluff Plantation. The preserve is owned by the National Audubon Society. For information, contact the warden, Route 1, Box 391, Jackson 29831; (803) 471-2367. The sanctuary is open with permission only; arrangements must be made in advance. This 3000-acre tract is located in Jackson, not far from Augusta (Georgia).

Turtle Island. The island is located near Savannah (Georgia). Under the direction of The Nature Conservancy, this 1700-acre island is being transferred to the South Carolina Wildlife and Marine Resources Department. Its beaches, brackish water marsh, and pine uplands provide habitat for an abundance of birds, including; Blue-winged Teal, Marsh Hawk, Louisiana Heron, Great Blue Heron, Clapper Rail, Black Skimmer, and flocks of gulls, terns, egrets, and shorebirds.

Woodfern Environmental Center, P.O. Box 439, Anderson 29621; (803) 224-3244. The center is operated by the Anderson School District. It totals 45 acres; guided and self-guiding tours are available and a variety of interpretive programs is offered. The center is open all year and closed on weekends, Thanksgiving, and Christmas.

STATE PARKS AND FORESTS

State parks in South Carolina are administered by South Carolina Department of Parks, Recreation, and Tourism, Edgar A. Brown Building, 1205 Pendleton Street, Columbia 29201; (803) 758-3622. Most state parks offer a variety of facilities among which are camping, picnicking, boating, swimming, and hiking. In addition, there are organized activities and interpretive programs during the summer. Pets are permitted but must be leashed. Although not designed for birdwatching, several of the following parks do offer rewarding birding opportunities. Those that do are preceded by an asterisk (*).

Aiken, Windsor 29856; (803) 649-2857; 1070 acres.
Andrew Jackson, Route 1, Lancaster 29720; (803) 285-3344; 360 acres.
Baker Creek, Route 1, Box 219, McCormick 29835; (803) 443-5866; 1300 acres.
Barnwell, Blackville 29817; (803) 284-2212; 300 acres.
Charles Towne Landing, 1500 Old Towne Road, Charleston 29407; (803) 556-4450; 670 acres; day use only.
Cheraw, Cheraw 29520; (803) 537-2215; 7360 acres.

*Chester, Chester 29706; (803) 385-2680; 520 acres.

Colleton, Canadys 29433; (803) 538-8206; 35 acres.

Croft, Route 4, Box 28-A, Spartanburg 29302; (803) 585-1283; 7100 acres.

Dreher Island, Route 1, Box 66-A, Chapin 29036; (803) 364-3933; 340 acres.

*Edisto Beach, Route 1, Box 40, Edisto Island 29438; (803) 869-2156; 75 acres.

Givhans Ferry, Route 3, P.O. Box 49, Ridgeville 29472; (803) 873-0692; 1240 acres.

Greenwood, Ninety Six 29666; (803) 543-3535; 900 acres.

Hamilton Branch, Route 1, Box 88, Plum Branch 29845; (803) 443-2115; 200 acres.

Hickory Knob, McCormick 29835; (803) 443-2151; 960 acres.

*Hunting Island, Frogmore 29920; (803) 838-2011; 5000 acres.

*Huntington Beach, Murrells Inlet 29576; (803) 237-4440; 2500 acres.

Kings Mountain, Box 230, Blacksburg 29702; (803) 222-3209; 6150 acres.

Lee, Bishopville 29010; (803) 428-3833; 2840 acres.

Little Pee Dee, Dillon 29536; (803) 774-8872; 835 acres.

*Myrtle Beach, US 17 — south, Myrtle Beach 29577; (803) 238-5325; 300 acres.

N. R. Goodale, Camden 29020; (803) 432-2772; 700 acres; day use only.

*Oconee, Walhalla 29691; (803) 638-5353; 1165 acres.

Old Dorchester, Summerville 29483; (803) 873-1740; 9740 acres.

Paris Mountain, Route 5, Box 221, Greenville 29609; (803) 244-5565; 1275 acres.

Pleasant Ridge, P.O. Box 2, Cleveland 29635; (803) 836-6589; 300 acres.

Poinsett, Wedgefield 29168; (803) 494-8177; 1000 acres.

Rivers Bridge, Ehrhardt 29801; (803) 267-3675; 390 acres.

Rose Hill, Route 2, Union 29379; (803) 427-5966; 45 acres; day use only.

Sadlers Creek, Route 4, Anderson 29621; (803) 226-8950; 400 acres.

*Santee, Route 1, Box 255-A, Santee 29142; (803) 854-2167; 2365 acres.

Sesquicentennial, Route 3, Box 254, Columbia 29206; (803) 788-2706; 1445 acres.

*Table Rock, Route 3, Pickens 29671; (803) 878-9813; 2860 acres.

Wildcat Wayside, 4 miles north of Cleveland on US 276; 63 acres; day use only.

In addition to the state parks listed above, there are several federal campgrounds in South Carolina. Besides the ones in the national forests discussed in this chapter, there are campgrounds at the Anderson Reservoir, the Hartwell Reservoir, and the Clark Hill Reservoir. For information regarding these areas, contact the South Carolina Department of Parks, Recreation, and Tourism at the address given above.

TENNESSEE

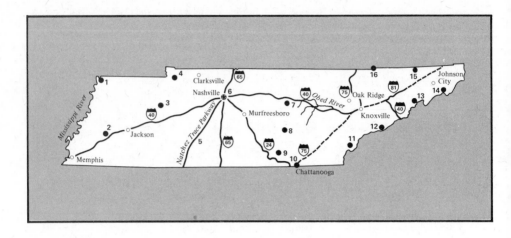

1. Lake Isom NWR
   Reelfoot NWR
2. Hatchie NWR
3. Tennessee NWR
4. Cross Creeks NWR
5. Natchez Trace Parkway
6. Tennessee Botanical Gardens
7. Catoosa Wildlife Management Area
8. Cane Creek NC
9. Savage Gulf

10. Chickamauga and Chattanooga National
    Military Park
11. Cherokee National Forest
12. Great Smoky Mountain National Park
13. Cherokee National Forest
14. Roan Mountain
15. Allanadale
    Bays Mountain Nature Education Center
16. Cumberland Gap National Historic Park

Tennessee — from the Great Smoky Mountains to the Mississippi River — encompasses hundreds of lakes, forests, and rivers. The state has 3 natural divisions: the low plateau in the west, the central bluegrass plain, and the mountainous east. Birds are everywhere — in the forests of the mountains, on the myriad lakes that cover the state, and along the Mississippi Flyway to the west.

Among the most remarkable natural features of Tennessee are Roan Mountain and Reelfoot Lake. Roan Mountain, in Cherokee National Forest, is over 6280 feet high — its sides covered with rhododendrons. Violets, wild geraniums, forget-me-nots, and flame azaleas — all combine to make Roan Mountain unique. Its massive floral displays are unequaled. In the extreme northwestern corner of the state is Reelfoot Lake — as different from Roan Mountain as a place can be. Reelfoot, Tennessee's largest natural lake, was formed by a remarkable series of earthquakes in 1811 and 1812. The lands along Reelfoot Creek sank and filled with water. Now cypress and dense swamp forest provide habitat for many varieties and large numbers of birds.

Of special interest are the lakes connected to the TVA. Loons, grebes, geese, ducks, herons, and shorebirds frequent these lakes; the woodlands bordering the lakes provide shelter for small landbirds. For information about these lakes, contact the Information Office, Tennessee Valley Authority, Knoxville 37902.

Cherokee National Forest. US Forest Service, P.O. Box 400, Cleveland 37311. Cherokee is divided into 2 major districts, with Great Smoky Mountain National Park separating them. The southern section is near Cleveland (via US 64); the northern is near Johnson City (via US 321 and/or US 23). Camping facilities are available at Cherokee in addition to a variety of other public recreational facilities.

The 615,000-acre Forest is managed by 6 district rangers. Most of the areas of Cherokee are accessible by road. The terrain is rugged; mountainsides are covered with rhododendron and laurel blooming in season. Of special interest are: Roan Mountain, which is well known for its spectacular rhododendron blooms in mid-June; and Andrew Johnson Deer Refuge, an 8000-acre wilderness area. Over a thousand miles of streams and rivers wind their way through Cherokee. A large portion, about 65 miles, of the Appalachian Trail runs through the center of the northern section of the Forest. Cherokee Forest provides the vital food, water, and shelter for many species of birds and animals. The Cherokee Management Area is known for hawk and warbler migrations. Among the many (over 200) species of birds that are to be seen here are: Turkey Vulture, Broad-winged Hawk, Ruffed Grouse, Turkey, Yellow-billed Cuckoo, Great Horned Owl, Common Nighthawk, Common (Yellow-shafted) Flicker, Downy and Hairy Woodpeckers, Great Crested Flycatcher, Purple Martin, Common Raven, Carolina Wren, Acadian Flycatcher, Gray Catbird, Wood Thrush, Black-throated Blue Warbler, Magnolia Warbler, Prairie Warbler, Canada

Warbler, Louisiana Waterthrush, Indigo Bunting, Scarlet Tanager, Rose-breasted Grosbeak, Purple Finch, and White-throated Sparrow.

Cross Creeks National Wildlife Refuge, Route 1, Box 229, Dover 37058; (615) 232-7477. Refuge headquarters may be reached by driving east from Dover on SR 49 for about 2 miles, then turning north for about one mile on a county road. Camping is not permitted on the refuge; however, facilities are available at nearby state parks.

Cross Creeks was established in 1962; and comprises 9700 acres of pond, marsh, and hardwood forest. Barkley Lake, the heart of the refuge, is a major impoundment on the Cumberland River. One of the refuge's major management programs is the raising of Wood Ducks; numerous broods can be seen throughout spring and summer. Bird banding is another important management activity. Throughout the year, various species of birds visit the refuge offering year-round birdwatching opportunities. There have been 204 species recorded here. Among them are: Horned Grebe, Snow (Blue) Goose, Oldsquaw (rare), Bald Eagle, Golden Eagle, Least Bittern, Virginia Rail (rare), Upland Sandpiper (Plover), Pectoral Sandpiper, Caspian Tern, Yellow-billed Cuckoo, Barred Owl, Chimney Swift, Common (Yellow-shafted) Flicker, Cliff Swallow, Winter Wren, Eastern Bluebird, Blue-winged Warbler, Cerulean Warbler, American Redstart, and Lark Sparrow. Checklist available.

Cumberland Gap National Historic Park. See entry in Kentucky chapter (page 198).

Great Smoky Mountains National Park, Gatlinburg 37738. Park headquarters are 2 miles south of Gatlinburg on US 441. The park, one of the few national parks in the East, totals nearly 515,000 acres. Although there are roads throughout the park, much of it remains virtually unspoiled. Great Smoky Mountains National Park lies between Cherokee National Forest and Nantahala National Forest. A 68-mile portion of the Appalachian Trail cuts through the center of the park. There are scenic drives, observation towers, 600 miles of hiking and horseback riding trails, and several short self-guiding nature trails. The park service schedules interpretive programs during the summer; during spring and fall these programs are limited. Camping facilities are located at various points throughout the park. Visitors are advised not to approach the bears closely; even though they appear tame, they can turn suddenly and inflict serious injury.

The varied landscape — high conifer forests, deciduous woodlands, freshwater ponds and streams — provides habitat for many birds. Among the 205 species of birds (102 nesting) that have been sighted here are: Broad-winged Hawk, Ruffed Grouse, Turkey, Sandhill Crane (rare), Mourning Dove, Yellow- and Black-billed Cuckoos, Screech Owl, Saw-whet Owl, Chuck-will's-widow, Ruby-throated Hummingbird, Pileated Woodpecker, Acadian Flycatcher, Rough-winged Swallow, Carolina Chickadee, Red- and White-breasted

Nuthatches, Winter Wren, Mockingbird, Eastern Bluebird, White-eyed Vireo, Worm-eating Warbler, Tennessee Warbler, Hooded Warbler, Black-throated Blue Warbler, Bay-breasted Warbler, Indigo Bunting, Red Crossbill, Bachman's Sparrow, and Song Sparrow. Checklist available.

Hatchie National Wildlife Refuge, Box 187, Brownsville 38102; (901) 772-0501. The refuge is located about 10 miles south of Brownsville on the Hatchie River; refuge headquarters are at 34 North Lafayette Street, Brownsville. Camping is not permitted on the refuge; however, facilities are available at nearby private and state campgrounds.

Hatchie Refuge was established in 1964; when acquisition is complete it will contain 11,000 acres (it now covers 9400 acres) of forest, grasslands, and open water. Located on the Mississippi Flyway, Hatchie is important as a refuge for migrating waterfowl that total up to 100,000 in peak numbers. The refuge is also managed for Wood Duck production. Hatchie is mainly a timbered bottomland with oxbow lakes and winding streams throughout. With its trails and roads, the refuge offers excellent opportunities for birdwatching. Flood waters occur annually from mid-January to mid-May. However, visitors may observe birds from public roads that cross or adjoin the refuge. Among the 200 species of birds (87 nesting) sighted here are: Anhinga, Snow Goose, Gadwall, Wood Duck, Mississippi Kite, Marsh Hawk, Little Blue Heron, Wood Stork (Ibis), Upland Sandpiper (Plover), Pectoral Sandpiper, Western Sandpiper (rare), Short-eared Owl, Chuck-will's-widow, Hairy Woodpecker, Yellow-bellied Flycatcher, Horned Lark, Carolina Chickadee, Carolina Wren, Gray Catbird, Ruby-crowned Kinglet, Philadelphia Vireo, Prothonotary Warbler, Swainson's Warbler, Golden-winged Warbler, Cerulean Warbler, Yellow-throated Warbler, Louisiana Waterthrush, Rusty Blackbird, and Lark Sparrow. Checklist available.

Lake Isom National Wildlife Refuge. Administered by Reelfoot NWR. Lake Isom Refuge is located about 5 miles south of Samburg in western Tennessee — just south of Reelfoot. Camping is not permitted on the refuge; however, facilities are available at nearby Reelfoot Lake State Park.

The refuge was established in 1938; and it totals 1850 acres. Its management objectives are much the same as those of Reelfoot NWR. Birdlife, too, is similar. For further information, see entry for Reelfoot NWR, page 000.

Natchez Trace Parkway. See entry in Mississippi chapter (page 207). Of special interest along the Parkway in Tennessee is Natural Bridge, located near Waynesboro.

Radnor Lake Natural Area, Otter Creek Road, Nashvile 37200; (615) 834-6186. Radnor Lake Area is located south of the center of Nashville; take US 31 (Franklin Pike) south to Otter Creek Road and continue to the park. This state-owned natural area covers nearly 800 acres of mixed woodlands, old fields, marshlands, and a 60-acre reservoir. Trails are maintained; the area is open during daylight hours.

Among the many species of birds seen here are: Black Duck, Ring-necked Duck, Canvasback, Pintail, Wood Duck, Red-tailed Hawk, Little Blue Heron, Yellow-billed Cuckoo, Screech Owl, Pileated Woodpecker, Acadian Flycatcher, Carolina Chickadee, Carolina Wren, Blue-gray Gnatcatcher, Prothonotary Warbler, Blue-winged Warbler, Cerulean Warbler, and Summer Tanager.

Reelfoot National Wildlife Refuge, Box 295, Samburg 38254; (901) 538-2481. Refuge headquarters can be reached from Union City by driving south on US 51; then turning west on SR 21; then north to Samburg on SR 22. Part of the refuge lies in Kentucky. Camping is not allowed on the refuge; however, facilities are located at nearby Reelfoot Lake State Park.

The 9600-acre refuge was established in 1941. It includes a portion of Reelfoot Lake, which was formed in 1811 and 1812 by a series of earthquakes. The entire district is in the flood plain of the Mississippi River, which once flowed through what is now the refuge. On the Mississippi Flyway, Reelfoot Lake has always been known for its great concentrations of waterfowl. The lake is bordered by a dense swamp forest. Scattered giant cypress trees grow in the water against a background of flowering aquatic plants. Farmland on the refuge is used to raise supplemental food for waterfowl. Although the primary objective of Reelfoot NWR is to provide habitat for waterfowl, large numbers of wading, marsh, and shorebirds are usually present. Great (Common) Egrets and Great Blue Herons occupy a rookery on the Kentucky part of the refuge. Also found at Reelfoot are mink, gray squirrel, swamp rabbit, and red fox. Not the least important is the attraction the varied habitat holds for passerine birds. The warbler migrations are of special interest. Among the 242 species of birds (102) nesting) sighted here are: Horned Grebe, Snow (Blue) Goose, Pintail, Cinnamon Teal, Ring-necked Duck, Mississippi Kite, Osprey, Green Heron, Black Rail, American Golden Plover, Upland Sandpiper (Plover), Stilt Sandpiper, Sabine's Gull (rare), Barn Owl, Red-headed Woodpecker, Least Flycatcher, Purple Martin, Winter Wren, Blue-gray Gnatcatcher, Swainson's Warbler, Orange-crowned Warbler (rare), Cerulean Warbler, Connecticut Warbler (rare), Orchard Oriole, Indigo Bunting, Lark Sparrow, and Harris' Sparrow (rare). Checklist available.

Tennessee National Wildlife Refuge, Box 849, Paris 38242; (901) 642-2091. Refuge headquarters are located in the Masonic Building, Blythe Street, Paris. The refuge consists of 3 units: the Big Sandy Unit, which is located east of Paris near the town of Big Sandy; the Duck River Unit, which is located between the towns of Camden and Waverly; and the Busseltown Unit, which is located near the town of Parsons. For specific traveling directions, contact the refuge manager at the above address. Camping is not permitted on the refuge; however, facilities are available at nearby Natchez Trace State Park.

The lands and waters included in the 51,350-acre refuge are currently owned by the TVA. The refuge was established in 1945 to provide sanctuary for waterfowl and other wildlife. A large farming program is conducted on the refuge to provide supplemental waterfowl foods for the thousands of ducks and geese that winter here. The Tennessee River is a spur route of the Mississippi Flyway, and funnels about 200,000 ducks and 35,000 geese into the area each fall and spring. The refuge also conducts a bird banding program. Band returns provide much of the information needed to establish efficient management programs along the Flyway. Birds banded here have been recorded as far south as Venezuela and as far north as Manitoba. Management practices are designed to improve populations of turkeys, eagles, ducks, herons, and deer. Among the 211 species of birds (92 nesting) identified on the refuge are: White Pelican, White-fronted Goose (rare), Northern Shoveler, Ruddy Duck, Goshawk, Golden Eagle, Bald Eagle, Peregrine Falcon (rare), Green Heron, Upland Sandpiper (Plover), Pectoral Sandpiper, Franklin's Gull (rare), Forster's Tern, Screech Owl, Pileated Woodpecker, Gray-cheeked Thrush, Water Pipit, Blue-winged Warbler, Black-throated Green Warbler, Chestnut-sided Warbler, Dickcissel, and Lark Sparrow. Checklist available.

NATURE CENTERS

In addition to the federally owned refuges and forests described in the foregoing pages, there are several nature centers, private preserves, wildlife management areas, and botanical gardens that can be rewarding to the birdwatcher.

Allandale. This mansion and gardens area is located in Kingsport. It is open all year, closed on Mondays; an admission fee is charged.

Bays Mountain Nature Education Center, Route 4, Bays Mountain Park Road, Kingsport 37660; (615) 245-4192. This 1300-acre area is operated by the city of Kingsport. A variety of educational programs is offered. There are a display gallery and a planetarium. Guided and self-guiding tours are available. The center is open all year.

Cane Creek Nature Center, Fall Creek Falls State Park, Pikeville 37367; (615) 881-3708. The center is operated by Tennessee State Parks and is open all year. Guided and self-guiding tours are offered.

Catoosa Wildlife Management Area. The area is located near Crossville; it is well known for Red-cockaded Woodpeckers. For further information about this and other wildlife management areas, contact the Tennessee Wildlife Resources Agency in Nashville.

Chickamauga and Chattanooga National Military Park. This 8000-acre park is located in the city of Chattanooga; part of the park extends into Georgia. Maple, oak, hickory, and tulip trees are characteristic of the wooded areas; bushy fields and grassy meadows adjoin. Spring warbler migrations are particularly rewarding. Among the birds to be seen here are: Bobwhite, Pileated Woodpecker, Bewick's Wren, Mockingbird, Wood Thrush, Rufous-sided

Towhee, Eastern Meadowlark, and Field Sparrow. For further information, contact the park supervisor, P.O. Box 2126, Fort Oglethorpe, Georgia 30742. The park is open all year.

Savage Gulf. Located in Grundy County (southeastern Tennessee), this 192-acre area is a breeding area for the Red-cockaded Woodpecker. For further information, contact the southeast regional office of The Nature Conservancy.

Tennessee Botanical Gardens and Fine Arts Center, Cheekwood, Cheek Road, Nashville 37205; (615) 356-3306. This 5310-acre center has greenhouses, wildflower gardens, and an art gallery. Various educational programs and guided and self-guiding tours are offered. The center is open all year.

STATE PARKS AND FORESTS

Tennessee has 26 state parks. Although these parks are designed primarily for recreation, some are well-known birdwatching places as well; those that are likely to be good for birding are preceded by an asterisk (*). All the following parks have camping facilities. For further information about state parks in Tennessee, contact the Division of State Parks, Tennessee Department of Conservation, 2611 West End Avenue, Nashville 37203.

*Big Ridge, Maynardville 37807; (615) 992-5523; 3600 acres.
*Booker T. Washington, Route 2, Box 369, Chattanooga 37416; (615) 894-4955.
 Cedars of Lebanon, Lebanon 37087; (615) 444-9394.
 Chickasaw, Henderson 38340; (901) 989-5141; 11,215 acres.
*Cove Lake, Carryville 37714; (615) 562-8355.
*Cumberland Mountain, Route 8, Box 164, Crossville 38555; (615) 484-6138; 1400 acres.
 Davy Crockett, Lawrenceburg 38464; (615) 762-9408.
*Fall Creek Falls, Pikeville 37367; (615) 881-3241; 16,000 acres.
 Harrison Bay, Harrison 37341; (615) 344-6214.
 Henry Horton, Chapel Hill 37034; (615) 364-2222.
*Meeman-Shelby, Millington 38053; (901) 876-5111.
 Montgomery Bell, Burns 37029; (615) 797-3101.
*Natchez Trace, Wildersville 38388; (901) 968-3742; 48,000 acres.
*Nathan Bedford, Eva 38333; (901) 584-6356.
*Norris Dam, Norris 37828; (615) 494-7197; 4000 acres.
 Old Stone Fort, Manchester 37355; (615) 728-0751.
 Panther Creek, Morristown 37814; (615) 581-2623.
*Paris Landing, Buchanan 38222; (901) 642-4311.
*Pickett, Jamestown 38556; (615) 879-7017.
 Pickwick Landing, Pickwick Dam 38365; (901) 689-3135.
*Reelfoot Lake, Tiptonville 38079; (901) 253-7756.

*Roan Mountain, Roan Mountain 37687; (615) 772-3303; Appalachian Trail crosses park.

Rock Island, Rock Island 37581; (615) 686-2471.

*Standing Stone, Livingston 38570; (615) 823-1158.

T. O. Fuller, 3269 Boxtown Road, Memphis 38109; (901) 785-3950.

*Warrior's Path, Box 5026, Kingsport 37663; (615) 239-8531.

Black-throated Blue Warbler

The North Central

Illinois   Ohio

Indiana   Wisconsin

Michigan

Sandhill Crane

ILLINOIS

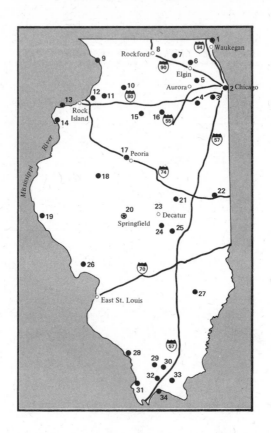

1. Illinois Beach State Park
   - Chicago Commons
   - Gensburg-Markham Prairie
2. The Landing
   - Lincoln Park
   - Lombard Park District
   - Sand Ridge NC
3. Little Red Schoolhouse NC/McGinnis Sough
4. Pilcher Park Nature Museum
5. Morton Arboretum
6. Crabtree NC
   - Crystal Lake Outdoor Education Center
7. Pleasant Valley Farm
8. Aldeen Nature Trail Environmental Education Department Rock Cut State Park NC

9. Mississippi Palisades State Park NC
10. Green River Conservation Area
11. Sinnissippi Park
12. Illiniwek
13. Credit Island
14. Loud Thunder Forest Preserve
15. Starved Rock State Park NC
16. Goose Lake Prairie
17. Forest Park NC
18. Chautauqua NWR
19. Mark Twain NWR
20. Abraham Lincoln Memorial Garden
    - Carpenter Park
    - Washington Park
21. Lodge Park
    - Robert Allerton Park

22. Willow Shores NC
23. Lincoln Park
24. Shelbyville Wildlife Management Area
25. Lake Paradise
26. Pere Marquette State Park NC
27. Prairie Chicken Sanctuaries
28. Union County Conservation Area
29. Southern Illinois University Outdoor Laboratory
30. Crab Orchard NWR
31. Horseshoe Lake Wildlife Refuge
32. Shawnee National Forest
33. Giant City State Park NC
34. Fort Massic State Park NC

Although remarkably flat, Illinois is more than prairie and grasslands. The southern section of the state is richly forested. The Ohio and Mississippi rivers provide southern and western boundaries, while the Illinois and Rock rivers cross the state. There are also many smaller rivers, a network of canals, and some lakes. Illinois is basically an agricultural state, led only by California in farm crops; however there are also large pockets of industry and manufacturing.

Special birds of Illinois are Bell's Vireo and the Greater Prairie Chicken. Thanks to preservation efforts by The Nature Conservancy and the Illinois Department of Conservation, much of the Greater Prairie Chicken's habitat is being restored and preserved.

There are many local reservoirs, lakes, small parks, preserves, and roadside areas that are well known as good birdwatching places. For a complete description of them, the reader is advised to consult *Bird Finding in Illinois,* published by the Illinois Audubon Society, 1017 Burlington Avenue, Downers Grove 60515. The Chicago Audubon Society maintains a *rare bird alert.* For up-to-date telephone information, call (312) 283-2144. For additional information about natural areas in Illinois, contact the Illinois Department of Conservation, State Office Building, Springfield 62705 and the Illinois Nature Preserves Commission, 819 North Main Street, Rockford 61103.

Abraham Lincoln Memorial Garden, Springfield. The garden is located near Lake Springfield, about 7 miles south of City Square. From the north end of Lake Springfield, take East Lake Drive for 3½ miles; the garden is on the left.

This 60-acre garden is not a formal, landscaped area, but rather a grouping of a wide variety of trees, shrubs, and ground covers. The lakefront and all the foot paths are good birding places. Look for Double-crested Cormorant, Snow Goose, American Woodcock, Bell's Vireo, Golden-winged Warbler, Connecticut Warbler, Orchard Oriole, and other woodland birds and waterfowl.

Carpenter Park, Springfield. The park entrance is just west of the intersection of US 66 and SR 124. It is about 4 miles north of the center of Springfield. The park is on the Sangamon River and totals 438 acres of woodland; a cliff borders the river. Paths interlace the park. The best birding spots are: along the path that follows the river; on both sides of the railroad tracks; and in a weedy area in the park's northwest corner. No cars are allowed in the park. Be on the alert for people who are target practicing in the woods. Mosquitoes are abundant after the third week in May.

Among the many birds seen here are: Great Horned Owl, Barred Owl, Whip-poor-will, Great Crested Flycatcher, Tufted Titmouse, Brown Creeper, Carolina Wren, Wood Thrush, Blue-gray Gnatcatcher, Warbling Vireo, Prothonotary Warbler, Kentucky Warbler, Scarlet Tanager, and Rose-breasted Grosbeak.

Other good birding places in the Springfield area include *Lake Springfield* (waterfowl, marshbirds, and shorebirds), *Oak Ridge Cemetery*, and *Calvary Cemetery* (woodpeckers, thrushes, and warblers).

Chautauqua National Wildlife Refuge, Rural Route 2, Havana 62644; (305) 595-2290. The refuge is administered by Mark Twain NWR. To reach Chautauqua Refuge from Pekin, drive 30 miles south and west on the Manito Blacktop Road; when approaching the refuge, directional signs will point the way. Opportunities for observing wildlife at the refuge are increased by use of trails, roads, and an observation tower. Camping is not permitted at the refuge; however facilities are available at nearby Spring Lake State Conservation Area.

Chautauqua Refuge was established in 1936. It is a resting and wintering area for waterfowl and has supported populations of over 1½ million ducks. It provides an important link in the chain of waterfowl refuges along the Mississippi Flyway. The refuge is located near several state conservation areas and parks. Chautauqua totals nearly 5200 acres of land and water and is located within the flood plain of the Illinois River. The forests are mostly oak and hickory in the upland areas and red maple, cottonwood, and black willow in the flood plain area.

An interesting feature of the east shoreline of Lake Chautauqua is that the seepage springs keep the shoreline open even in the coldest winter weather. The varied environment provides habitat for a wide assortment of animals including badger, deer, fox, and coyote. Although managed primarily for waterfowl, Chautauqua is also home to many passerines. There have been 246 species of birds (70 nesting) sighted on the refuge. Among these are: Red-necked Grebe (rare), Western Grebe (rare), Whistling Swan (rare), Snow (Blue) Goose, Pintail, Wood Duck, Lesser Scaup, Bufflehead, Ruddy Duck, Cooper's Hawk, Bald Eagle, American Kestrel (Sparrow Hawk), Bobwhite, Great Blue Heron, Sora, Black-bellied Plover, Baird's Sandpiper, Hudsonian Godwit, Wilson's Phalarope (rare), Forster's Tern, Yellow- and Black-billed Cuckoos, Short-eared Owl, Pileated Woodpecker, Alder (Traill's) Flycatcher, Barn Swallow, Black-capped Chickadee, Winter Wren, Gray-cheeked Thrush, Loggerhead Shrike, Northern Shrike (rare), Bell's Vireo, Tennessee Warbler, Orange-crowned Warbler, Mourning Warbler (rare), European Tree Sparrow (rare), Eastern and Western Meadowlarks, Bobolink, Indigo Bunting, Lark Sparrow, and Tree Sparrow. Checklist available.

Crab Orchard National Wildlife Refuge, P.O. Box J, Carterville 62918; (618) 997-3344. Crab Orchard is located just north of Shawnee National Forest. To reach the refuge from Marion, take SR 13 west for about 4 miles to the intersection with SR 148; turn south and continue into the refuge. Camping is not permitted at the refuge, however facilities are available at Shawnee.

Crab Orchard Refuge was established in 1947 and totals over 43,000 acres. The refuge is a unique blend of wildlife conservation, recreation, agriculture, and industry. The large lakes, abundant forests, greentree reservoirs, and croplands are all managed for wildlife. There are over 50 species of trees, mostly oak and hickory, to be found in Crab Orchard's forests. Located along the Mississippi Flyway, the primary purpose of the refuge is to provide a winter home for thousands of geese and ducks. The refuge also draws many other birds. There have been 238 species of birds (97 nesting) recorded at Crab Orchard. Among the birds likely to be seen here are: Horned Grebe, White Pelican, Snow Goose, Gadwall, Wood Duck, Common Goldeneye, Ruddy Duck, Goshawk (rare), Bald Eagle, Great (Common) Egret, American Bittern, Sora, American Avocet, American Golden Plover, Upland Sandpiper (Plover), Pectoral Sandpiper, White-rumped Sandpiper, Baird's Sandpiper, Wilson's Phalarope, Franklin's Gull, Black Tern, Screech Owl, Chimney Swift, Red-headed Woodpecker, Yellow-bellied Flycatcher, Cliff Swallow, Tufted Titmouse, Winter Wren, Eastern Bluebird, Cedar Waxwing, Bell's Vireo, Swainson's Warbler, Cerulean Warbler, Golden-winged Warbler, Blue-winged Warbler, Kentucky Warbler, Canada Warbler, Orchard Oriole, Scarlet Tanager, Rose-breasted Grosbeak, Purple Finch, Henslow's Sparrow, and Bachman's Sparrow. Checklist available.

Crabtree Nature Center, Palatine Road, Barrington Hills; (312) 381-6592. The center is operated by the Cook County Forest Preserve District. Crabtree is northwest of Chicago, 3 miles southwest of Barrington; from I-90, take Barrington Road Exit and drive 2½ miles north, turn left on Palatine Road and proceed to the center.

Crabtree Center covers 1100 acres of mixed woodlands, open fields and pastures, a restored prairie, marshy areas, and lakes (Crabtree and LaBuy's). Management programs include providing supplemental waterfowl food. There is a 100-acre wildfowl sanctuary. Various interpretive and educational programs are offered at the center. Trails are maintained. There have been 228 species of birds (40 nesting) observed at Crabtree. Among them are: Common Loon, Horned Grebe (rare), Canada Goose, ducks (17 species), Marsh Hawks, Gray Partridge (rare), herons, egrets, rails, shorebirds (15 species), gulls, terns, owls, woodpeckers (6 species), Hermit Thrush, Water Pipit, warblers (31 species), finches (10 species), and Snow Bunting.

Credit Island, Davenport. The island is a city park. From the center of town, go west on US 61; 3 miles past the Centennial Toll Bridge, turn left on a road marked "Credit Island."

The harbor area is good for ducks and shorebirds. Also look for Barred Owls and Pileated Woodpeckers. Among the 225 species of birds recorded here are: Double-crested Cormorant, Bald Eagle, Osprey, Great (Common) Egret, Carolina Wren, and various species of gulls, terns, shorebirds, vireos, warblers, and sparrows.

Duck Creek Park and *Fejervary Park,* both also in Davenport, are other good birdwatching places.

Gensburg-Markham Prairie, Markham. This 94-acre preserve is located just south of downtown Chicago in the suburb of Markham. It is owned by The Nature Conservancy and maintained by Northeastern Illinois University.

The preserve consists of grasslands and a sandy beach. Among the many birds to be seen here are Red-tailed Hawk, American Woodcock, Bobwhite, and Common Snipe.

Goose Lake Prairie Nature Preserve. The preserve is located in Goose Lake Prairie State Park, just outside of Morris. From Joliet, take I-55 to Lorenzo Road, exit right and go west for about 3 miles to Jugtown Road; turn right and go north for almost a mile to park entrance. The park is undeveloped and there are no roads or facilities. Some areas, which are wet in the spring, may become impassible; check with the ranger. Located nearby are William G. Stratton and Gebhard Woods state parks, the Des Plains Conservation Area (273 acres), and the Grundy County Wildlife Management Area (100 acres).

The preserve (in the 2380-acre park) consists of dry and wet prairies, marshes, and potholes. Trails are maintained. Those that skirt the ponds are often the best for birdwatching. Look for Short-eared Owls, hawks, flycatchers, vireos, warblers, and sparrows. Nesting birds include 3 species of rails, Bell's Vireo, and Henslow's Sparrow.

Green River Conservation Area, Dixon; (815) 379-2324. The preserve is located south of Dixon; go 5 miles north from Ohio on SR 26; turn left and continue for 3 miles, following the state signs. The 2330-acre preserve is open to hunting and is also a wildlife conservation area. Request permission from the refuge manager to go birdwatching. There are various paved and gravel roads throughout the area.

The preserve is mostly flat with sandy prairies, rose thickets, and some pine plantings. Look for rails, Ring-necked Pheasant, American Woodcock, Upland Sandpiper (Plover), Bell's Vireo, Dickcissel, Le Conte's Sparrow, and various warblers.

Horseshoe Lake Wildlife Refuge, Olive Branch. The refuge is located just south of the Union County Conservation Area, between Shawnee National Forest and the Mississippi River. To reach the refuge from Olive Branch, take SR 3 south for 2 miles, turn west (right) onto the lake road.

Horseshoe is an oxbow lake formed from an old Mississippi River meander. The area around the lake is a typical river bottomland. There are numerous roads throughout the 7000-acre refuge. Look for waterfowl, waders, and passerines. Bald Eagles are permanent residents; Swainson's Warblers are found here in the summer. In other respects, the birdlife here is much the same as for Crab Orchard NWR (see page 242).

Illiniwek, East Moline. Illiniwek is a forest preserve of Rock Island County. To reach the preserve from East Moline, drive up-river on SR 84; 2 miles east, turn onto a gravel road; look for U.S. Lock and Dam No. 14 where parking is available.

The bluff provides views of the Mississippi River and allows the birdwatcher to see birds at treetop level. Ducks and waterfowl can best be seen with a scope.

Illiniwek is known for woodland birds. On windy, winter days Bald Eagles can be seen.

Adjacent to the preserve is the beginning (105 acres) of what will be a 225-acre sanctuary for Bald Eagles. Owned by the National Wildlife Federation, *Oak Valley Eagle Refuge* protects a critical feeding and winter roosting area for Bald Eagles.

Lake Paradise, Mattoon. Lake Paradise is a wildlife sanctuary located west of Mattoon on SR 16. From Mattoon, take US 45 south for nearly 2½ miles to a small sign that reads "Lake Paradise." Turn right (west) and continue to the lake. Beware of poison ivy in the area.

Waterfowl and herons are seen near the lake. Mockingbirds and Blue Grosbeaks have been found nesting in the surrounding shrubbery.

In Mattoon there are 2 city parks that are also good birdwatching places: *Lytel* and *Peterson*.

Lincoln Park, Chicago. The park lies along Lake Michigan and is accessible from Lake Shore Drive — numbers 3200 north and 4400 north. It extends from Oak Street Beach to Foster Avenue. The best birding areas are Belmont and Montrose harbors, the lagoons on either side of Fullerton Avenue, and Diversey Harbor. In the winter, look for Oldsquaw, Common Merganser, Common Goldeneye, Black Duck, Lesser Scaup, and an occasional Common Eider (rare). During migration periods, look for flycatchers, vireos, warblers, and sparrows. Around Montrose Harbor, one can see Glaucous, Iceland, and Little Gulls during the winter. In September, huge flocks of Purple Martins visit the harbor.

Other good parks in Chicago include *Navy Pier Park* (waterfowl); *Grant Park* (landbirds); *Jackson Park* (waterfowl and migrating warblers); *Powder Horn Swamp* (waterbirds and marshbirds); and *Wolf Lake* (waterfowl and shorebirds). These parks lie, mainly, along Lake Michigan between I-80 and I-90.

In general, caution should be exercised while visiting these parks. It is best not to go alone nor to stray too far from marked paths.

Lincoln Park, Decatur. To reach the park, go south on SR 48 through Decatur to Lake Shore Drive; turn right (west) at the dam; go for a mile to South Edward Street, which adjoins the park.

This 99-acre park consists of mixed hardwoods, gardens, and open fields; the Sangamon River runs along the southern end. Look for waterfowl along the river; hawks, owls, and passerines are also found here. Among the species seen in the spring are: Eared Grebe, Scarlet Tanager, Summer Tanager (rare), and 22 species of warblers.

Little Red Schoolhouse Nature Center, Willow Springs Road (104 Avenue), Palos Hills. The center is operated by the Cook Country Forest Preserve District. It is located near Longjohn, Saganashkee, and McGinnis Sloughs. All 3 sloughs are now wildlife sanctuaries of the Cook County Forest

Preserve District. At the center, various educational and interpretive programs are offered.

This 400-acre area is characterized by open water, bogs, marshy areas, and some old orchards. These areas are particularly attractive to waterfowl since the vegetation around the sloughs offers much food. Around the center, look for Common Redpoll, Pine Siskin, and other wintering finches. Around Longjohn Slough look for ducks, herons, and swallows; Saganashkee Slough is good for marshbirds, ducks, and Tree Sparrows; McGinnis Slough (900 acres, and the largest of the 3) is best for waterbirds and marshbirds, especially Pied-billed Grebe, American Coot, Canada Goose, Marsh Hawk, Little Blue Heron, Green Heron, Belted Kingfisher, Eastern Meadowlark, and various species of woodpeckers.

Lodge Park, Monticello. Entrance to the park is from an unmarked road (formerly SR 47) at a point just over a mile northeast of the junction of SR 105 and (new) SR 47. The park is located on the Sangamon River and is a county forest preserve. *Caution:* the Chicago-St. Louis line of the Wabash RR cuts through Lodge Park. Although there are only a few trains a day, extreme caution should be exercised when crossing the tracks.

This is largely a wooded area, mostly oak-hickory, with bottomlands of ash, silver maple, walnut, and cottonwood. The western part has been heavily planted with conifers. There are 2 small lakes in the park; one of which dries up in the summer, making it ideal for shorebirds and waders. A system of roads and trails winds through the park. Less common birds seen here include Horned Grebe, Little Blue Heron, Semipalmated Plover, Barred Owl, Yellow-breasted Chat, and Purple Finch.

Loud Thunder Forest Preserve, Andalusia. To reach the preserve, take SR 92 west from Andalusia for about 5 miles; look for sign indicating the preserve entrance on the right.

Loud Thunder Preserve is a wooded area with some open fields; a large lake has been impounded in a former creek bottom. This is a good area for waterfowl. The best time for birding here is early June. Look for Whip-poor-will, Pileated Woodpecker, Willow Flycatcher, Blue-gray Gnatcatcher, Yellow-throated Vireo, Prothonotary Warbler, Blue-winged Warbler, Kentucky Warbler, and Lark Sparrow among many other woodland birds.

Mark Twain National Wildlife Refuge, P. O. Box 225, Quincy 62301; (217) 224-0901, ext. 44. Headquarters are located in the post office building at Quincy. Mark Twain Refuge is a complex of 12 divisions located along the Mississippi and Illinois rivers; Clarence Cannon NWR is one of these divisions. Camping is not permitted at the refuge; however, facilities are available at nearby Siloam Springs State Park.

The refuge was established in 1947 and now totals over 30,000 acres. Principal objectives of the refuge include waterfowl management programs. This entails, in part, planting supplemental waterfowl food, such as corn, buckwheat, millet, and clover. Where water control is possible, impoundments are drained so that buckwheat and millet can be planted on the exposed mud flats. Mark Twain Refuge is a link in the chain of refuges that are located along the Mississippi Flyway. The principal species using the refuge is the Mallard — concentrations of over 100,000 on a single division are not unusual. Other birds seen in great numbers include Canada Goose, Snow (Blue) Goose, Pintail, Black Duck, American Wigeon and Blue- and Green-winged Teals. One of the largest wintering concentrations of Bald Eagles is found along the Mississippi River near the refuge. Wood Ducks are common except during the winter months. Hiking trails and self-guiding automobile trails are maintained throughout the refuge. In addition, fishing and boating are permitted at some of the districts. It is advisable to make arrangements with the refuge manager in advance. There have been 221 species of birds (84 nesting) recorded on the refuge. Among these are: Double-crested Cormorant, Whistling Swan, White-fronted Goose, Northern Shoveler, Bufflehead, Oldsquaw, Ruddy Duck, Red-breasted Merganser, Sharp-shinned Hawk, Harlan's Hawk (rare), Golden Eagle (rare), Marsh Hawk, Osprey, Peregrine Falcon, Ring-necked Pheasant, Yellow- and Black-crowned Night Herons, Least Bittern, Sora, American Avocet (rare), Black-bellied Plover, Common Snipe, Pectoral Sandpiper, Wilson's Phalarope, Franklin's Gull, Caspian Tern, Screech Owl, Chimney Swift, Pileated Woodpecker, Red-headed Woodpecker, Yellow-bellied Flycatcher, Cliff Swallow, Winter Wren, Swainson's Thrush, Loggerhead Shrike, Warbling Vireo, Prothonotary Warbler, Golden-winged Warbler, Worm-eating Warbler, Cerulean Warbler, Louisiana Waterthrush, Bobolink, Orchard Oriole, Scarlet Tanager, Rose-breasted Grosbeak, Indigo Bunting, Evening Grosbeak (rare), and Lark Sparrow. Checklist available.

The Morton Arboretum, Route 53, Lisle 60532; (312) 968-0074. The arboretum center and the Thornhill Building are open 9-5 Mondays through Saturdays; 1-5 on Sundays. The center is located 25 miles west of downtown Chicago, a mile north of Lisle. It is on SR 53, a mile south of Butterfield Road (SR 56). A variety of educational and interpretive programs is offered at the arboretum.

Morton Arboretum totals over 1500 acres and is graced with extensive plantings of trees, shrubs, vines, and flowers. The wooded hills are dotted with open meadows and small freshwater marshes; there are four lakes. Among the many birds to be seen here are: Snow Goose, Cooper's Hawk, Long-eared Owl, Saw-whet Owl, Tufted Titmouse, Red-breasted Nuthatch, Brown Creeper, Wood Thrush, Golden-crowned Kinglet, Philadelphia Vireo, Cedar Waxwing, Scarlet Tanager, Pine Grosbeak, Pine Siskin, and various species of warblers including Golden-winged, Magnolia, Blackburnian, Wilson's Chestnut-sided, and Bay-breasted.

Pilcher Park Nature Museum. The museum is operated by the Joliet Park District; it adjoins Bird Haven — both are on the east side of Joliet. When approaching from the east, drive through the city on US 30 and turn right just after passing through the Rock Island railroad underpass.

The parks cover 400 acres of varied habitat — oak-hickory forest, marshes, creek, and open meadows interspersed with shrubs and thickets. At the nature museum there are exhibits; various interpretive and educational programs are offered. Trails are maintained; there are also roads with turnoffs and parking areas. Over 130 species of birds (50 nesting) have been recorded here. Among them are: Pied-billed Grebe, Wood Duck, Red-tailed Hawk, Bobwhite, Great Blue Heron, American Woodcock, Yellow- and Black-billed Cuckoos, Hairy Woodpecker, Least Flycatcher, Brown Creeper, Red-breasted Nuthatch, Eastern Bluebird, Wood Thrush, Warbling Vireo, Northern (Baltimore) Oriole, American Goldfinch, Song Sparrow, and 20 species of warblers.

Prairie Chicken Sanctuaries, Botota (Jasper County) and Farina (Marion County). These areas total over 1300 acres and are managed by the Illinois Department of Conservation, the Prairie Chicken Foundation of Illinois, and The Nature Conservancy. Permits are needed for entry. Contact: Ron Westemeier, Research Manager, 304 Poplar Drive, Effingham 62401; (217) 342-6075. Stephen A. Forbes State Park is nearby and offers camping facilities.

The sanctuaries are abandoned farmlands that have been planted with crops to support these native upland birds. Late March and early April are the best times to observe the courtship dance and "booming" of the Prairie Chicken. Since many people want to use the observation blinds, arrangements to visit should be made well in advance. While here, also look for Upland Sandpipers (Plovers), Short-billed Marsh Wrens, and Henslow's Sparrows.

Robert Allerton Park, Monticello. The park is located 4 miles southwest of Monticello about halfway between Decatur and Champaign off SR 47. Turn south just west of Monticello off SR 47 and follow marked county roads. The park is owned by the University of Illinois, and is open from 10 AM to dark every day.

The 1685-acre park consists of mixed upland forests, formal gardens, open fields, and ponds. There are more than 20 miles of trails. Over 150 species of birds (73 nesting) have been recorded at Allerton. Among these are: Wood Duck, Green Heron, Barred Owl, Whip-poor-will, Eastern Bluebird, Bell's Vireo, Prothonotary Warbler, and Henslow's Sparrow.

Sand Ridge Nature Center, Paxton Avenue, South Holland. The center is owned and maintained by the Cook County Forest Preserve District. To reach the center from Chicago, take the Calumet Expressway south to the 159 Street Exit, turn east and go for about a mile to Paxton Avenue; there is a sign on the left. A naturalist is on staff. Various educational and interpretive programs are offered. The center is open 9-4, Mondays through Thursdays; Saturdays, Sundays, and holidays from 9-5; and is closed on Fridays. The parking area is open every day. Trails are maintained. Occasionally they are difficult to find in swampy or brushy areas.

The 235-acre center comprises marsh, mixed woodlands, and open water. Spring and fall are good times to observe ducks; shorebirds; and migrating flycatchers, thrushes, vireos, and warblers. Hawks and owls can be seen throughout the year.

Shawnee National Forest, 317 East Poplar Street, Harrisburg 62946. Shawnee is located in the southern portion of the state. To reach the Forest from Harrisburg, use US 45, SR 34/145, or SR 13. Public facilities at Shawnee include camping, hiking, fishing, swimming, boating, and picnicking. Of special interest are: nearby Crab Orchard NWR, which borders on the northwestern area of the Forest; the Oakwood Bottoms greentree reservoir; the Iron Furnace; the Indian mounds and prehistoric stone forts; and the Garden of the Gods, an area formed about 200 million years ago.

Shawnee Forest covers 241,000 acres. It is bordered by 2 major rivers: the Ohio on the east and the Mississippi on the west. The plant and animal life of the Forest is as varied as its habitat. There have been 237 species of birds identified at Shawnee. Among these are: Red-throated Loon, Gadwall, American Wigeon, Wood Duck, Canvasback, Hooded Merganser, Mississippi Kite, Sharp-shinned Hawk, Cooper's Hawk, Rough-legged Hawk, Ferruginous Hawk, Bald Eagle, Ruffed Grouse, Great Blue Heron, Least Bittern, Common Gallinule, American Golden Plover, Wilson's Phalarope, Short-billed Dowitcher, Bonaparte's Gull, Caspian Tern, Yellow- and Black-billed Cuckoos, Long- and Short-eared Owls, Whip-poor-will, Pileated Woodpecker, Yellow-bellied Flycatcher, Rough-winged Swallow, Brown Creeper, Bewick's Wren, Eastern Bluebird, Logger-head Shrike, Bell's Vireo, Prothonotary Warbler, Worm-eating Warbler, Golden-winged Warbler, Cerulean Warbler, Black-throated Green Warbler, Connecticut Warbler, Swainson's Warbler, Mourning Warbler, Boblink, Brewer's Blackbird, Dickcissel, and Bachman's Sparrow. Checklist available.

Shelbyville Wildlife Management Area. For information, contact: Illinois Department of Conservation, Division of Wildlife Resources, State Office Building, Springfield 62706. The area is located in central Illinois, near Sullivan, south of Decatur. Lake Shelbyville is an impoundment of the Kaskaskia River between Shelbyville and Sullivan. The 16,000-acre lake averages about 16 feet in depth; the several islands and many inlets and coves provide over 250 miles of shoreline. Public facilities include camping, fishing, boating, swimming, horseback riding, hiking, and picnicking. In addition there are 2 nearby state parks that also offer a variety of recreational activities. Common animals include rabbit and deer. Birdlife is abundant, especially during spring and fall migration periods. Among the birds likely to be seen are: Ring-necked Pheasant, Bobwhite, American Woodcock, Common Snipe, many passerine birds, and migrating waterfowl.

Sinnissippi Park, Sterling. To reach the park, drive to the eastern edge of Sterling on Alt. US 30, turn south (right) at Riverview Cemetery, and continue to the park; the entrance is on the right.

Covering about 125 acres, Sinnissippi Park is on a bayou. There are wooded hillsides, pine plantings, and a mature oak-hickory forest. Along the eastern side of the park there is a creek with wet, marshy areas, mud flats, and some dense undergrowth. Trails traverse the park. The diverse habitat supports a variety of plant and animal life. Among the many species of birds to be found here are: grebes, cormorants, long-legged waders, ducks, hawks, swallows, flycatchers, thrushes, warblers, orioles, and sparrows. During spring migration, look for Whistling Swan, American Woodcock, Connecticut Warbler, and sandpipers. Located nearby is the 2000-acre Sinnissippi Lake Wildlife Management Area.

Union County Conservation Area, Ware. The area is between Shawnee National Forest and the Mississippi River, north of Horseshoe Lake Wildlife Refuge. This conservation area covers 1500 acres of mixed woodlands, 3150 acres of croplands, and 1600 acres of water. The refuge extends along the east side of SR 3 about 5 miles south of Ware. There is one main road that runs through the area. Look for waterfowl, wading birds, and passerines. Birdlife here is much the same as at Crab Orchard NWR (see page 242), except that there are not as many diving ducks to be found at Union.

Washington Park, Springfield. The park is located nearly 2 miles southwest of City Square. The main entrance is 4 blocks west of the intersection of South Grand Avenue and MacArthur Boulevard.

This 120-acre municipal park is hilly and wooded, mostly with oak, hickory, and some conifers. There are scenic drives and paths throughout the park. The area around the pond is one of the better birdfinding places. Look for Ring-necked Duck, Bufflehead, Red-headed Woodpecker, Carolina Wren, Wood Thrush, Swainson's Thrush, Prothonotary Warbler, Black-throated Green Warbler, and Rose-breasted Grosbeak.

NATURE CENTERS

In addition to the many preserves, refuges, and parks discussed above, there are a large number of nature centers located throughout Illinois. Most of these offer a wide range of educational programs to schoolchildren, college students, and the general public. A variety of interpretive programs is also usually available.

Aldeen Nature Trail, 623 North Alpine Road, Rockford 61107; (815) 965-2707. The center is operated by the Rockford Park District. It covers 88 acres. Guided tours are offered. Trails are maintained. The center is open all year.

Chicago Commons Camping Services — Camp Reinberg, P.O. Box 218, Palatine 60067; (312) 359-0010. The camp covers 75 acres and is open all year, closed in December.

Crystal Lake Outdoor Education Center, 330 North Main Street, Crystal Lake 60014; (815) 459-5557. The center is operated by the Crystal Lake Park District. It covers 150 acres and is open on weekdays from 15 August to 15 June.

Environmental Education Department, 201 South Madison Street, Rockford 61101; (815) 968-0871. The center is operated by the Rockford Public Schools. It covers 340 acres. Guided tours are offered; trails are maintained. The center is open on weekdays all year, closed on weekends and school holidays.

Forest Park Nature Center, 5809 Forest Park Drive, Peoria 61614; (309) 688-6413. The center is operated by the Peoria Park District. It is located about 5 miles north of Peoria. The park consists of 800 acres of mixed hardwood forest and some open fields. There are five miles of trails. Look for woodland birds.

Fort Massic State Park, Nature Center, Metropolis 62960; (618) 695-2339. The center is operated by the Illinois Department of Conservation. The park totals 1380 acres; trails are maintained. The park is open all year; the center is closed on Mondays and Tuesdays.

Giant City State Park, Nature Center, Makanda 62958; (618) 457-4836. The center is operated by the Illinois Department of Conservation. The park is located in Shawnee National Forest. It totals 1960 acres. Guided tours are offered; trails are maintained. The park is open all year; the center is closed on Mondays and Tuesdays.

Illinois Beach State Park, Nature Center, Zion 60099; (312) 622-4811. The center is operated by the Illinois Department of Conservation. The park totals 2054 acres. Guided tours are offered; trails are maintained. The park is open all year; the center is closed on Mondays and Tuesdays.

The Landing, 881 West St. Charles Road, Lombard 60148; (312) 323-0389. The center is operated by the Forest Preserve District of DuPage County. It covers 132 acres. Trails are maintained; guided tours are available. The center is open all year.

Lombard Park District, 120 West Maple Street, Lombard 60148; (213) 627-1281. The park covers 360 acres and is open all year, closed on weekends.

Mississippi Palisades State Park, Nature Center, P.O. Box 364, Savanna 61074; (815) 273-2731. The center is operated by the Illinois Department of Conservation. The park covers 1117 acres. Guided tours are offered; trails are maintained. The park is open all year; the center is closed on Mondays and Tuesdays. There have been 249 species of birds seen here including Hooded Merganser, Common Nighthawk, Swainson's Thrush, and Yellow Warbler.

Pere Marquette State Park, Nature Center, Grafton 62737; (618) 786-3785. The center is operated by the Illinois Department of Conservation. The park covers 6400 acres. Guided tours are offered; trails are maintained. The park is open all year; the center is closed on Mondays and Tuesdays. Look for Pileated Woodpecker, Warbling Vireo, and Prothonotary Warbler.

Pleasant Valley Farm, 13315 Pleasant Valley Road, Woodstock 60098; (312) 338-5080. The farm is operated by the Community Renewal Society. It covers 460 acres. Of special interest are the nursery, garden, and educational farm. Guided tours are by appointment only. The center is open all year.

Rock Cut State Park, Nature Center, R. R. 1, Caledonia 61011; (815) 885-3311. The center is operated by the Illinois Department of Conservation. The park covers 2676 acres. Guided tours are offered; trails are maintained. The park is open all year; the center is closed on Mondays and Tuesdays.

Southern Illinois University Outdoor Laboratory, Department of Conservation and Outdoor Education, 606½ South Marion, Carbondale 62901; (618) 453-3192. The center covers 6000 acres. Guided tours are available by appointment.

Starved Rock State Park, Nature Center, Utica 61373; (815) 667-4906. The center is operated by the Illinois Department of Conservation. The park totals 2366 acres. Guided tours are offered; trails are maintained. The park is open all year; the center is closed on Mondays and Tuesdays.

Trailside Museum, Thatcher and Chicago Avenues, River Forest. The museum is operated by the Cook County Forest Preserve District. It covers 35 acres. Guided tours are offered; trails are maintained. The museum is open all year; closed on Thursdays and holidays.

Willow Shores Nature Center, Forest Glen Preserve, R. R. 1, Georgetown 61846; (217) 662-6284. The center is operated by the Vermilion County Conservation District, 703 Kimber Street, Danville. The center covers 1800 acres. Guided tours are offered; trails are maintained. The center is open all year. There have been nearly 200 species of birds recorded here. Among them are: Great Horned Owl, Pileated Woodpecker, Whip-poor-will, Great Crested Flycatcher, Bell's Vireo, Orchard Oriole, Summer Tanager, Scarlet Tanager, Eastern Bluebird, and various species of warblers and sparrows.

STATE PARKS

Illinois has a comprehensive system of state parks, state conservation areas, and state forests. Most of these allow camping in addition to providing facilities for a wide range of public recreational activities. Some of the larger parks have naturalists on duty and offer interpretive programs. The conservation areas are less developed than the parks; the emphasis is on protection of wildlife. Those parks and areas that are well-known birdwatching places are indicated by an asterisk (*). For additional information concerning these areas, contact the Illinois Department of Conservation, Division of Parks and Memorials, 605 State Office Building, Springfield 62706.

STATE PARKS

*Apple River Canyon, Apple River 61001; 296 acres.

Argyle Lake, Colchester 62326; 1052 acres.

Beaver Dam, Box 128, Plainview 62676; 737 acres.

Black Hawk, 1500-47th Avenue, Rock Island 61201; 206 acres; day use only.

Buffalo Rock, Ottawa 61350; 43 acres; day use only.

*Cahokia Mounds, 7850 Collinsville Road, East St. Louis 62201; 650 acres.

Cave-in-Rock, Cave-in-Rock 62919; 64 acres.

Chain-O-Lakes, 725 East State Park Road, Spring Grove 60081; 4892 acres.

Delabar, Oquawka 61469; 89 acres.

Dixon Springs, Brownfield 62911; 496 acres.

Douglas County, Oakland 61943; 464 acres; day use only.

Eagle Creek, 103 West South 2nd Street, Findlay 62534; 2173 acres.

Eldon Hazlett, 1351 Ridge Street, Carlyle 62231; 3000 acres.

*Ferne Clyffe, Box 125, Goreville 62939; 1073 acres.

Fort de Chartres, Prairie Du Rocher 62277; 1100 acres; day use only.

Fort Creve Coeur, Creve Coeur 61611; 86 acres; day use only.

Fort Defiance, Box 77, Miller City 62962; 38 acres; day use only.

*Fort Kaskaskia, Ellis Grove 62241; 250 acres.

Fort Massac, Box 708, Metropolis 62960; 1380 acres; nature center.

Fox Ridge, Charleston 61920; 751 acres.

*Frank Holten, 4500 Pockett Road, East St. Louis 62205; 1125 acres.

Gebhard Woods, Box 292, Morris 60450; 30 acres; day use only.

*Giant City, Makanda 62958; 3100 acres; nature center.

*Goose Lake Prairie, Morris 60450; 2292 acres; day use only.

Hennepin Canal Parkway, Box 458, Sheffield 61361; 5921 acres; day use only.

Illini, Box 60, Marseilles 61341; 510 acres.

*Illinois Beach, Zion 60099; 2746 acres; nature center.

Johnson Sauk Trail, Kewanee 61443; 857 acres.

Jubilee College, Box 72, Brimfield 61517; 1528 acres.

Kankakee River, Bourbonnais 60914; 2700 acres.

Kickapoo, Oakwood 61858; 1684 acres.

Lake Le-Aqua-Na, Lena 61048; 715 acres.

Lake Murphysboro, Murphysboro 62966; 904 acres.

Lewis and Clark, 223 St. Louis Road, Collinsville 62234; 168 acres; day use only.

Lincoln Log Cabin, Lerna 62440; 86 acres.

Lincoln Trail, Marshall 62441; 974 acres.

Lincoln Trail Homestead, Box 126, Mt. Zion 62549; 162 acres.

*Lincoln's New Salem, New Salem 62659; 522 acres.

Lowden Memorial, Oregon 61061; 207 acres.

McHenry Dam, 914 South River Road, McHenry 60050; 94 acres; day use only.

*Matthiessen, Box 381, Utica 61373; 1531 acres; day use only.

*Mississippi Palisades, Box 364, Savanna 61074; 1716 acres; nature center.

Morrison-Rockwood, 205 East High, Morrison 61270; 1152 acres.

Nauvoo, Box 337, Nauvoo 62354; 148 acres.

*Pere Marquette, Box 325, Grafton 62037; 8000 acres; nature center.

Prophetstown, 205 East High, Morrison 61270; 54 acres.

Pyramid, Box 115-A, Pickneyville 62274; 2524 acres; day use only.

Railsplitter, Lincoln 62656; 748 acres; day use only.

Ramsey Lake, Box 433, Ramsey 62080; 1880 acres.

Red Hills, Sumner 62466; 9218 acres.

Rock Cut, Box A-49, Caledonia 61011; 2400 acres; nature center.

Sam Parr, Newton 62448; 1063 acres; day use only.

Sangchris Lake, Rochester 62563; 4200 acres.

Siloam Springs, Clayton 62324; 3026 acres.

Silver Springs, Box 238, Yorkville 60560; 1314 acres.

South Shore, 1351 Ridge Street, Carlyle 62231; 850 acres; day use only.

Spitler Woods, Box 705 Spitler Park Drive, Mt. Zion 62549; 202 acres.

*Starved Rock, Box 116, Utica 61373; 2366 acres; nature center.

Stephen A. Forbes; Kinmundy 62854; 3019 acres.

Wayne Fitzgerrell, Box D, Benton 62812; 3010 acres.

Weingerg-King, Box 203, Augusta 62311; 772 acres; day use only.

Weldon Springs, Clinton 61727; 370 acres.

White Pines Forest, Mt. Morris 61054; 385 acres.

William G. Stratton, Morris 60450; 6 acres; day use only.

Wolf Creek, 103 West South 2nd Street, Findlay 62534; 1966 acres.

STATE CONSERVATION AREAS

Anderson Lake, Astoria 61501; 1364 acres.

Baldwin Lake, Baldwin 62217; 2200 acres; day use only.

*Beall Woods, Mt. Carmel 62863; 635 acres; day use only.

Des Plaines, Box 167, Wilmington 60481; 273 acres; day use only.

Hamilton County, McLeansboro 62859; 1603 acres.

Henderson County, Oquawka 61469; 87 acres.

*Horseshoe Lake, Box 77, Miller City 62962; 7901 acres.

Iroquois County, near Beaverville 60912; 1920 acres; day use only.

Lee County (Green River), Box 56, Harmon 61042; 480 acres; day use only.

McLean County, LeRoy 61752; 1616 acres.

Marshall County, Box 292, Lacon 61540; 2270 acres.

Mermet Lake, Belknap 62908; 10 acres; day use only.

Montebello, Box 337, Nauvoo 62354, 3 acres.

Randolph County, Box 346, Chester 62233; 1031 acres.

Rice Lake, Canton 61520; 2370 acres.

Saline County, Equality 62934; 1208 acres.

Sam Dale Lake, Johnsonville 62850; 1301 acres; day use only.

Sanganois, Box 35, Browning 62624; 3162 acres; day use only.

Sparland, near Sparland 61565; 1280 acres; day use only.

*Spring Lake, Manito 61456; 1946 acres.

Union County, Jonesboro 62952; 40 acres; day use only.

Washington County, Nashville 62263; 1378 acres.

William W. Powers, 12800 Avenue O, Chicago 60633; 580 acres; day use only.

Woodford County, Low Point 61545; 2462 acres.

STATE FORESTS

Big River, Keighsburg 61442; 1047 acres.

Hidden Springs, Box 110, Strasburg 62465; 314 acres.

*Sand Ridge, Box 82, Forest City 61532; 5504 acres.

Trail of Tears, Jonesboro 62952; 3558 acres.

In addition to the above-mentioned areas, there is a network of nature preserves throughout the state. These are administered by the Illinois Nature Preserves Commission, 819 North Main Street, Rockford 61103. There are also hundreds of acres of public lands that are used for hunting and fishing. These are known, variously, as conservation areas and/or wildlife management areas. For specific information regarding these areas, contact the Division of Wildlife Resources, 100 East Washington, Springfield 62701; or Department of Conservation, Chicago Office, State of Illinois Building, 160 North LaSalle Street, Chicago 60601.

INDIANA

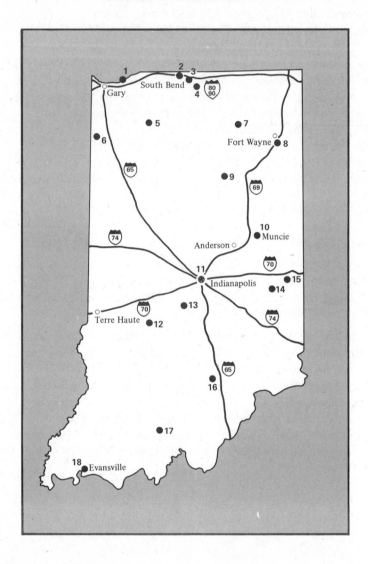

1. Indiana Dunes National Lakeshore
2. Bendix Woods County Park
3. South Bend Audubon Bird Sanctuary
4. Audubon Wildlife Sanctuary
5. Jasper-Pulaski Fish and Wildlife Area
6. Willow Slough State Game Preserve
7. Merry Lea Environmental Center
8. Franke Park
9. Honeywell Gardens
10. Christy Woods

11. Eagle Creek Park Nature Preserve
12. McCormick's Creek State Park NC
13. Bradford Woods Outdoor Education
    Center
14. Mary Gray Bird Sanctuary
15. Hays Regional Arboretum
16. Muscatatuck NWR
17. Hoosier National Forest
18. Wesselman Park NC

From the sand dunes along Lake Michigan to the Ohio River, Indiana's forests, open fields, ponds, and streams all contribute to support a complex wildlife community. Although heavily industrial, the state also has a good deal of agricultural production. Lakes and marshes characterize northeastern Indiana; central Indiana is flat; southern Indiana is wooded and scenic. The northern swamps were made famous by Gene Stratton Porter's writings, most notably *A Girl of the Limberlost*.

Well over 200 species of birds can be seen regularly in Indiana. The flights of Sandhill Cranes at Jasper-Pulaski Fish and Wildlife Area are a most exciting spectacle. The state owns and maintains several thousand acres of land as game areas. These are intended primarily as hunting areas, but are also rewarding birdwatching spots. Among the better areas are: *Hovey Lake* — 4400 acres in Mount Vernon, look for Wood Duck, Pileated Woodpecker, and Prothonotary Warbler; *Jasper-Pulaski* — 7585 acres in Medaryville, look for Sandhill Cranes; *Kankakee* — 2302 acres in Knox; *Pigeon River* — 11,100 acres in Howe; and *Willow Slough* — 9274 acres in Morocco. Although not listed individually (many are privately owned), all the small lakes in the northeastern corner of the state are likely to be good birdwatching spots. So, also, is the Geist Reservoir outside Indianapolis. The Mesker Park Zoo in Evansville is well known for its extensive bird collection.

For further information contact: Department of Natural Resources, 616 State Office Building, Indianapolis 46204.

Hoosier National Forest, 1615 J Street, Bedford 47421. Hoosier is divided into 2 major districts: Brownstown in the north and Tell City in the south. The Brownstown district is located just southeast of Bloomington; use SR 446. The Tell City district is near Paoli; use US 50, US 460, and US 130 and/or SR 37, SR 60, and SR 64. Public facilities include camping, picnicking, swimming, boating, fishing, and hiking. Of special interest are: the Pioneer Mothers Memorial Forest, containing an outstanding specimen of black walnut trees; the final outlet of the Lost River; and the scenic drives among spring flowers (dogwood and redbud) and fall coloring.

The Muscatatuck NWR is nearby, as are the mineral springs at French Lick and the Marengo Cave. The many overlooks, ponds, streams, and wooded areas provide excellent opportunities for birdwatching. Among the many species of birds likely to be found here are: Pied-billed Grebe, Snow Goose, Pintail, Wood Duck, Turkey Vulture, Red-tailed Hawk, Bald Eagle, Bobwhite, American Kestrel (Sparrow Hawk), Green Heron, Cattle Egret, Black-crowned Night Heron, American Coot, Killdeer, Black Tern, Barn Owl, Hairy Woodpecker, Pileated Woodpecker, Eastern Wood Pewee, Bank Swallow, Cliff Swallow, Tufted Titmouse, Winter Wren, Gray Catbird, Wood Thrush, Water Pipit, Cedar Waxwing, Bell's Vireo, Magnolia Warbler, Chestnut-sided Warbler, Blackpoll Warbler, Mourning Warbler, Northern (Baltimore) Oriole, Red Crossbill, Vesper Sparrow, and Snow Bunting.

Indiana Dunes National Lakeshore, Route 2, Box 139 A, Chesterton 46304; (219) 926-7561. Indiana Dunes is on the southern shore of Lake Michigan, just east of Gary. The visitors' center is located at the southwest corner of the intersection of US 12 and Kemil Road, 3 miles east of SR 49. Camping is not permitted; however, Indiana Dunes State Park, which is nearby, does have facilities.

Indiana Dunes National Lakeshore was established in 1966. When acquisition is complete, it will embrace 8200 acres of shoreline, dunes, bogs, and marshes. Facilities at the Lakeshore include beaches, a horseback riding trail, several self-guiding hiking and biking trails, ranger-guided interpretive hikes, and other naturalist programs. There are 5 areas that are open for the ranger-escorted hikes. One of them, the Mount Baldy Area, is dominated by a huge live or moving dune that slowly moving southward due to wind and wave action. It is burying an oak woodland in its path. From the dune's bare plateau, the dynamic interaction of Lake Michigan winds and waves on the dunes and beach can be seen. Indiana Dunes National Lakeshore also encompasses forested areas, marshes, and swamps. These all combine to support a varied wildlife community. Geese, ducks, hawks, herons, thrushes, and warblers all use the area.

Muscatatuck National Wildlife Refuge, P.O. Box 631, Seymour 47274; (812) 522-4352. The refuge office is located 4 miles east of Seymour, off US 50; turn south and continue for ½ mile down Entrance Road. Camping is not permitted on the refuge; however, facilities are available at nearby Hoosier National Forest.

Muscatatuck Refuge was established in 1966. It now comprises over 6000 acres. The primary species of the refuge is the Wood Duck. Management focuses on encouraging Wood Duck production and on developing suitable habitat for migrating waterfowl. A network of hiking trails and secondary roads increases visitors' opportunities for birdwatching. Marshes, ponds, and hardwood forests provide habitat for a wide variety of wildlife. There have been over 200 species of birds recorded on the refuge. Among these are: Horned Grebe, Whistling Swan, Canada Goose, Cinnamon Teal, Northern Shoveler, Canvasback, Bufflehead, Common Goldeneye, Hooded Merganser, Sharp-shinned Hawk, Golden Eagle, Bald Eagle, Osprey, Great Blue Heron, Little Blue Heron, Black- and Yellow-crowned Night Herons, American Bittern, Sandhill Crane, Sora, Pectoral Sandpiper, Yellow- and Black-billed Cuckoos, Barn Owl, Saw-whet Owl, Common Nighthawk, Pileated Woodpecker, Northern Three-toed Wood- pecker, Least Flycatcher, Cliff Swallow, Brown Creeper, Long- and Short-billed Marsh Wrens, Loggerhead Shrike, Bell's Vireo, Philadelphia Vireo, Prothono- tary Warbler, Cerulean Warbler, Blue-winged Warbler, Mourning Warbler, Orchard Oriole, Summer Tanager, Rose-breasted Grosbeak, Common Redpoll, Red Crossbill, Lapland Longspur, and Snow Bunting.

Willow Slough State Game Preserve, Morocco 47963. It is advisable to arrange visits in advance; permission *must* be obtained from the refuge manager in order to use the dike road. Do not use the road during waterfowl hunting season. The 7877-acre preserve is located about 70 miles south of Chicago, between US 41 and the Illinois border. The administration buildings are on SR 14, four miles west of Enos.

Much of the preserve has been impounded; the rest consists mostly of overgrown farmland, mixed woodlands, and a large pond. The chief attractions here are the Greater Prairie Chicken and Smith's Longspur. The spring and fall waterfowl migrations are particularly noteworthy. The Prairie Chicken is a permanent resident but is best seen when on its booming grounds — from the end of March to the middle of April. Smith's Longspur is only seen here during the spring. Among the other birds seen here are: Snow Geese, Little Blue Herons, and Bald Eagles.

STATE NATURE PRESERVES

The state of Indiana has set aside over 6200 acres as nature preserves. These are located throughout the state and are of varying habitats — from peat bogs to pine forests to dunes on Lake Michigan. Many of these preserves are good birdwatching places. The division of Nature Preserves, under whose direction these lands are acquired, was established in 1967. Conservation in Indiana continues, and more preserves are sure to be added in future years. The preserves that are currently open to the public are described below. These preserves are not shown on the map, owing to a lack of space.

Acres Along the Wabash, Murray. The preserve is located about 1½ miles northwest of Murray on the southwest side of SR 116. It is managed by Acres, Inc. This 27-acre preserve borders the north bank of the Wabash River for nearly a mile; it is characterized by a mixed hardwood forest. Chipmunks, fox squirrels, raccoons, and woodchucks are common mammals. Wood Ducks reside in the pools.

Beaver Lake, Enos. The preserve is located near the Illinois border. Permission to enter the preserve must be obtained from the area manager at the nearby Willow Slough Fish and Wildlife Area (see above). To reach the preserve from Enos, go 3 miles north on US 41, then turn one mile east, then one mile north. The preserve covers 640 acres. There are ponds and dry flatlands. Management programs include controlled burning to maintain prairie grass areas. Goldenrods, milkweed, blazing star, pasture rose, pasture thistle, and little bluestem characterize the dry areas; cattails and sedges are found in the swampy area.

Beechwood, Angola. The preserve is located north of the entrance to Pokagon State Park, on the west side of US 27/I-69. It is managed by Acres, Inc. Beechwood totals 19 acres and includes streams, a small lake, and swampy areas. There are foot bridges and trails that traverse the preserve. Cattail, black willow, pussy willow, and swamp dogwood are characteristic of the pond areas. Look for warblers and other passerines.

Bendix Woods, Rolling Prairie. The preserve is located 10 miles west of South Bend, on the south side of SR 2. It is managed by St. Joseph County. This 175-acre preserve is used for many types of recreation. One 27-acre section is a woodland consisting of sugar maple, red elm, basswood, and large beech. This area has been set aside for walking and nature study only. A naturalist conducts tours and a nature center is maintained; interpretive exhibits are on display at the center. The moist areas of the woods give rise to Solomon's seal, wild ginger, running euonymous, and a wide variety of ferns.

Blue Bluff, Centerton. The preserve is located in the central part of Indiana. To reach the preserve from Centerton (about 12 miles north of Martinsville), go southwest 1½ miles from the junction of CR 150 East and CR 600 North. The preserve is owned by The Nature Conservancy and is maintained by the Indiana Chapter. It is characterized by the Blue Bluff, one of a range of hills bordering the West Fork of the White River. It totals 32 acres. Because of its steepness, the east side of the preserve cannot support much vegetation. Thus the blue siltstone, for which it is named, is exposed. The forested area is dominated by red oak mixed with hickory, beech, tulip, sugar maple, and ash.

Dogwood, Versailles. The preserve is located in the southern section of Versailles State Park. This 20-acre preserve is dominated by flowering dogwood (hence its name). The forest is composed largely of beech and maple with hickory, tulip, white ash, and red oak. Ferns and wildflowers grow in the established areas.

Donaldson's Woods, Mitchell. The preserve is located in the southeastern corner of Spring Mill State Park. Twin Caves is nearby. An unusual feature of this mixed forest is the high percentage of white oaks. Donaldson's Woods preserve totals 67 acres.

Dunes Nature Preserve, Chesterton. The preserve is administered by the Division of State Parks. It is located 3 miles north of Chesterton on US 20, and abuts the Indiana Dunes National Lakeshore (see page 258). The preserve totals 1530 acres and includes the eastern section of Indiana Dunes State Park. Bearberry, sumacs, cottonwood, and prostrate juniper typify the vegetation here; a few stands of jack pine still persist on the slopes. The highest point is Mt. Tom — 186 feet above Lake Michigan. The forested areas of the back dunes are covered with black and white oaks with an understory of blueberry, bracken fern, and greenbrier.

Edna W. Spurgeon, Ligonier. The preserve is maintained by Acres, Inc. It is located about 3 miles northeast of Ligonier off SR 5. Locally known as "The Knobs," this preserve covers 60 acres of open fields, rolling uplands, and mixed forests. There are marked trails. The woods consist of beech, maple, ash, tulip, oak, and basswood. Trilliums, Solomon's seal, and other wildflowers grow in the understory.

Eunice Hamilton Bryan, Frankfort. The preserve is managed by the Division of Nature Preserves. It is located 7 miles northwest of Frankfort. Surrounded by farmland, this 30-acre woodland is a refuge for wildlife. Huge white oak, beech, basswood, and shagbark hickory are typical hardwoods found here. Spring wildflowers include Dutchman's breeches, spring beauty, yellow troutlily, wild phlox, and Virginia waterleaf.

Fox Island, 7324 Yohne Road, Fort Wayne. The preserve lies southwest of Fort Wayne. It is owned and maintained by the Allen County Park and Recreation Board. A resident naturalist oversees the property. Marshes, swamps, old fields, and mixed woodlands cover this 381-acre preserve. Various interpretive and educational programs are offered. Nature trails are maintained. The diversified habitat provides food and shelter for a wide variety of animal life. There have been 83 species of birds recorded here.

Grider's Woods. This 10-acre preserve is located in Turkey Creek Township on the Tri-County State Fish and Wildlife Area. There is a self-guiding nature trail that traverses the woodland.

Hemmer Woods, Buckskin. The preserve is located 2 miles east of Buckskin; to reach it, take CR 900 South to CR 1050 East. The preserve is managed by the Division of Natural Preserves. This is an old-growth, mixed forest totaling 72 acres and is representative of the original forests of southwestern Indiana. The upland portion is largely oak-hickory. The area is a registered national natural landmark.

Hornbeam, Liberty. The preserve is located in Whitewater State Park; it is 37 acres on the west side of Whitewater Lake. This is a mixed woodland consisting mainly of beech, maple, red oak, green ash, and hickory. Large ironwood and blue beech dominate the understory. Among the many spring wildflowers are Dutchman's breeches, bloodroot, trillium, Solomon's seal, and Jack-in-the-pulpit.

Laughery Bluff, Versailles. The preserve is located about a mile southeast of Versailles on US 50. It covers 81 acres of mixed woodlands. The bluff overlooks the valley made by Laughery Creek in Versailles State Park.

Lloyd W. Bender, Albion. The preserve is located 2 miles southwest of Albion; take River Road to the entrance sign and follow the trail into the woods. This 60-acre preserve is managed by Acres, Inc. It is characterized by swamp forest, ponds, reverting fields, and upland ridges. The diversity of habitat provides for a wide variety of plant and animal life.

Ogle Hollow, Nashville. The preserve is located in Brown County State Park, near the park office. This 41-acre preserve features the rare yellowwood tree. Brown County is the only place in Indiana where these trees are known to exist in the wild. The woodlands are truly mixed, containing a variety of trees: red oak, chestnut oak, shagbark hickory, butternut hickory, basswood, green ash, sycamore, and many others. Flowering dogwood, redbud, witch hazel, and wild hydranga are to be found in the understory. Typical wildflowers include bellwort, May apple, bloodroot, reflexed trillium, rue anemone, and Solomon's seal. On the slopes, maidenhair fern, Christmas fern, and narrowleaf spleenwort are to be found. A self-guiding trail is maintained.

Orangeville Rise of the Lost River, Orangeville. The preserve is located about 7 miles west of Orleans. It is owned by The Nature Conservancy. This 3-acre preserve is one of the 2 rises of the Lost River. It is a registered national natural landmark. The preserve is of geologic interest, primarily. This limestone region is well known for its caves, sinkholes, underground streams, and blind fish.

Pedestal Rock, Alamo. The preserve is located in Shades State Park, along the north side of Sugar Creek. This preserve totals 730 acres of deep canyons, high escarpments, uplands, and mixed hardwood forests. The steep slopes are covered with hemlock; Canada yew and partridge berry carpet the forest floor.

Pine Hills, Alamo. The preserve is located in Shades State Park, also bordering Sugar Creek. Pine Hills is a registered national natural landmark. This 470-acre preserve is characterized by scattered stands of conifers interspersed with mixed hardwoods. Two creeks flow through the property.

Portland Arch, Fountain. To reach the preserve from Attica, take US 41 south for about 5 miles, turn west on CR 650 North and continue for 5 miles to Fountain. Portland Arch adjoins the south side of this village. Portland Arch is a registered national natural landmark. This preserve comprises 247 acres. The stone arch and rugged canyon (of Bear Creek) are the main attractions. Oak, pine, and hickory characterize the woodlands. Marked hiking trails are maintained.

Post Oak-Cedar, White Cloud. The preserve is located in Harrison-Crawford State Forest, about 12 miles west of Corydon on US 460. This area totals 42 acres of mixed woodlands, swampy areas, and open hill prairies. Look for Ruffed Grouse and Turkey, both of which have been reintroduced.

Potawatomi, Angola. The preserve is located in Pokagon State Park. It totals 208 acres that include a small lake, cattail marshes. uplands, and mixed hardwood forest. Waterfowl nest in the swampy areas.

Rocky Hollow-Falls Canyon, Marshall. The preserve is located in Turkey Run State Park on the north side of Sugar Creek. It totals 404 acres and consists of gorges, waterfalls, sandstone cliffs, uplands, and mixed woodlands. Ferns, wildflowers, and flowering shrubs are indicative of the diversified plant community supported here.

Ropchan Memorial, Orland. The preserve is located in the northeast corner of the state. To reach it from Orland, take SR 120 east for 2 miles, then north on CR 750 West to the parking area. This 77-acre preserve is under the stewardship of Acres, Inc., a private preservation organization. The area is characterized by a diversity of geological features: kettle holes, morainal ridges, and swamps and bogs. Hickory and oak are interspersed with aspen; tamaracks are found in the peaty areas; the understory is largely composed of dogwood, Virginia creeper, mapleleaf viburnum, and bittersweet.

Sand Hill, Winamac. The preserve is located in Tippecanoe State Park, near Winamac, off US 35. Open fields, sandy ridges, and mixed woodlands characterize this 60-acre preserve. Pine oak, jack oak, and black gum are typical of the loamy, fine, sandy areas; black oak and white oak are found on the higher ridges.

Scout Ridge, Martinsville. The preserve is located in Morgan-Monroe State Forest. This 15-acre preserve is dominated by a beech-maple forest. Mapleleaf viburnum, spicebush, and pawpaw are characteristic of the understory. A self-guiding nature trail traverses the preserve.

Shrader-Weaver Woods, Bentonville. To reach the preserve from Connersville, take SR 1 north, turn left on a county road to Bentonville; then go a mile east on CR 700 North, continue for almost 2 miles south on CR 450 West. The 108-acre preserve is managed by the Division of Nature Preserves and is a registered national natural landmark. A self-guiding nature trail winds through the preserve, which consists mostly of open fields and mixed woodlands. There is also a pioneer homestead. Among the many species of birds to be found here are Pileated Woodpeckers.

Swamp Rose, North Liberty. The preserve is located in the extreme northeast corner of Potato Creek State Recreational Area. It is operated by the Division of State Parks. Named for the beautiful swamp rose flower, this 100-acre preserve supports a mixed woodland characterized by silver maple, red maple, red elm, green ash, beech, wild cherry, tulip, and red oak. Raccoons and white-tailed deer are among the resident mammals. Among the birds to be found here are: American Woodcock, flycatchers, and warblers.

Tamarack Bog, Mongo. The preserve is located in the northeast corner of the state, a mile east of Mongo. It is managed by the Division of Fish and Wildlife. This 100-acre nature preserve is located on the Pigeon River State Fish and Wildlife Area. Here is found the largest remaining stand of tamarack (American larch) in Indiana. The area is diversified — from small fields in the early stages of forest reversion to mixed hardwoods. There is a small stream which is bordered by clumps of royal fern, cinnamon fern, and skunk cabbage. White-tailed deer, fox, squirrels, and cottontails inhabit the upland areas; Beavers and muskrats live in the thickets and swamps. Look for American Woodcock, ducks, waterbirds, and songbirds.

White Oak, Scottsburg. The preserve is located in Clark State Forest. The entrance to the preserve is by Franke Lake. A self-guiding nature trail is maintained. The dominant tree is the white oak; hickory, red oak, and black oak are also supported. The understory is largely composed of flowering dogwood, Virginia creeper, and greenbrier. Wildflowers and ferns vary in accordance with soil moisture and exposure.

Wolf Cave, Spencer. The preserve is located in McCormick's Creek State Park. This 214-acre preserve is situated in the northcentral portion of the park. There are streams, waterfalls, large sinkholes, mixed woodlands, uplands, and caves. There is also a natural bridge. Typical of the woodlands are red oak, white ash, black walnut, and tulip. Mosses, liverworts, and ferns grow in the moist, woody areas. Trails are maintained throughout the area.

Woodland Bog, Angola. The preserve is located 3½ miles northeast of Angola. The entrance to the preserve is a stile, located ½ mile east of the intersection of CR 100 North and CR 200 East. This stile crosses a fence that follows a right-of-way to the southeastern corner of the tract. Look for signs at the stile entrance. This 20-acre preserve is managed by Acres, Inc. It is a former peat bog and is now a swamp forest characterized by pin oak, wild cherry, red elm, and largetooth aspen. Ferns and wildflowers cover the ground, growing on tussocks formed by the roots of fallen trees.

NATURE CENTERS

There are many nature centers, bird sanctuaries, parks, and arboretums located throughout Indiana. These centers usually offer a wide range of educational and interpretive programs, for school children, college students, and the general public. These centers are described briefly below.

Audubon Wildlife Sanctuary, 59395 Clover Road, Mishawaka 46544; (219) 255-7854. The sanctuary covers 30 acres. It includes a museum and outdoor laboratory. In addition there is a bird banding program. The sanctuary is open on Saturdays and Sundays, on weekdays by appointment.

Bendix Woods County Park, Route #2, Box 72 A, New Carlisle 46552; (219) 654-7658. The park and nature center are operated by St. Joseph County Parks and Recreation Department. The park totals 193 acres. Guided tours are offered. Trails, some self-guiding, are maintained. The park is open all year.

Bradford Woods Outdoor Education Center, Martinsville 46151; (317) 342-2035. The center is operated by Indiana University Department of Recreation and Park Administration. The center totals 2300 acres and includes 5 children's camps (one of which is for handicapped children). Also located here are the headquarters of the American Camping Association. Guided tours are offered. The center is open all year.

Christy Woods, Ball State University, Muncie 47306; (317) 285-5341. The preserve is owned and maintained by Ball State University. It is open all year.

Eagle Creek Park Nature Preserve and Outdoor Education Center, 6164 Reed Road, Indianapolis 46254; (317) 293-4827. The center is operated by the Division of Outdoor Education, Indianapolis Department of Parks and Recreation. It covers 3000 acres. Visitors may take guided tours through this park which surrounds a reservoir. Self-guiding trails are also maintained. The park is open all year. Look for flycatchers, warblers, and other landbirds.

Franke Park, 100 East Main Street, City-County Building, Fort Wayne 46802; (219) 423-7015. The park is operated by the Board of Park Commissioners. It covers 523 acres. Guided tours are offered; trails, some self-guiding, are maintained. The center is open on weekdays during the summer, at other times by appointment.

Hays Regional Arboretum, 801 Elks Road, Richmond 47374; (317) 962-3745. The arboretum is operated by the Stanley W. Hays Research Foundation. It covers 3000 acres. Guided tours are available. Trails are maintained, including a self-guiding automobile tour. The arboretum is open all year, closed on Mondays, Christmas Day, New Year's Day, and 1-15 September. Look for Pileated Woodpecker, Red-headed Woodpecker, Connecticut Warbler, Worm-eating Warbler, and Henslow's Sparrow among other birds.

Honey Gardens, R. R. #2, Box 585, Wabash 46992; (219) 563-3546. The gardens are operated by the Honeywell Foundation. They are located on SR 15, 2 miles north of Wabash. The Honeywell Gardens total 125 acres. Evergreen plantation, rose gardens, and a walnut experimental area are featured. The gardens are open all year.

Mary Gray Bird Sanctuary, Route 6, Connersville 47331; (317) 825-9788. The sanctuary is operated by the Indiana Audubon Society. It consists of nearly 700 acres of mixed woodlands, pastures, and fields with shrubbery. Guided tours are offered. Trails, some self-guiding, are maintained. The sanctuary is open all year. Look for Red-bellied Woodpecker, Great Crested Flycatcher, Carolina Chickadee, Bewick's Wren, White-eyed Vireo, Kentucky Warbler, and other landbirds.

McCormick's Creek State Park, Nature Center, Box 28, Spencer 47460. The nature center is located in a 1753-acre park. The park is characterized by mixed woodlands, thickets, a creek, and a gorge. There have been 85 species of birds recorded here.

Merry Lea Environmental Center, P. O. Box 263, Wolflake 46796; (219) 799-5869. The center is operated by the Merry Lea Nature and Religious Foundation, Inc. It covers 800 acres and is open all year.

South Bend Audubon Bird Sanctuary, South Bend 46600. The sanctuary is operated by the South Bend Audubon Society. It is open by appointment only.

Wesselman Park Nature Center, 551 North Boeke Road, Evansville 47711; (812) 426-5429. The center is operated by the Evansville Park Department. It totals 210 acres. Guided and self-guiding tours are available. The center is open all year.

STATE PARKS AND FORESTS

Indiana has many state parks and forests located all over the state. All have camping facilities, although many are primitive. Pets are permitted but must be leashed. While not intended primarily as nature preserves or bird sanctuaries, many state parks and forests are known as good birdwatching areas. These are marked with an asterisk (*). Interpretive programs are offered at some parks in addition to a variety of recreational activities. For further information about Indiana's state parks, contact: Department of Natural Resources, Division of State Parks, 616 State Office Building, Indianapolis 46204.

STATE PARKS

Bass Lake, Knox 46534; (219) 772-3382; 22 acres.
*Brown County, Nashville 47448; (812) 988-2825; 15,428 acres.
*Chain O' Lakes, Albion 46701; (219) 636-2654; 2678 acres.
*Clifty Falls, Madison 47250; (812) 265-3536; 1200 acres.
*Indiana Dunes, Chesterton 46304; (219) 926-1215; 2182 acres.
Harmonie, New Harmony 47631; (812) 682-4821; 3192 acres.
Lieber, Cloverdale 46120; (317) 795-4576; 8283 acres.
Lincoln, Lincoln City 47552; (812) 937-4710; 1731 acres.
*McCormick's Creek, Spencer 47460; (812) 829-2235; 1753 acres.
Mounds, Anderson 46014; (317) 642-6627; 254 acres.
Ouabache, Bluffton 46714; (219) 824-0926; 1037 acres.
*Pokagon, Angola 46703; (219) 665-9613; 1173 acres.
Potato Creek, North Liberty 46554; (219) 656-3490; 3840 acres.
Raccoon Lake, Rockville 47872; (317) 569-3792; 3938 acres.
*Shades, Waveland 47989; (317) 435-2810; 2960 acres.

Shakamak, Jasonville 47438; (812) 665-2158; 1766 acres.

Spring Mill, Mitchell 47446; (812) 849-4129; 1319 acres.

*Tippecanoe River, Winamac 46996; (219) 946-3213; 2761 acres.

*Turkey Run, Marshall 47859; (317) 597-2635; 2182 acres.

Versailles, Versailles 47042; (812) 689-6424; 5897 acres.

Whitewater, Liberty 47353; (317) 458-5565; 1515 acres.

STATE FORESTS

Clark, Henryville 47126; (812) 294-4306; 22,871 acres.

Ferdinand, Ferdinand 47532; (812) 367-1524; 7873 acres.

Greene-Sullivan, Carlisle 47838; (812) 648-2810; 5220 acres.

Harrison-Crawford, Corydon 47112; (812) 738-2722; 24,330 acres.

Jackson-Washington, Brownstown 47220; (812) 358-2160; 15,181 acres.

Martin, Shoals 47581; (812) 247-3491; 6124 acres.

Morgan-Monroe, Martinsville 46151; (317) 342-4026; 23,916 acres.

Pike, Winslow 47598; (812) 789-3251; 2858 acres.

Salamonie River, Largo 46941; (219) 782-2349; 621 acres.

Yellowwood, Nashville 47448; (812) 988-7945; 22,451 acres.

STATE LAKES / RECREATION AREAS / RESERVOIRS

Brookville, Brookville 47012; (317) 647-6557; 16,455 acres.

Hardy Lake, Scottsburg 47170; (812) 794-3800; 2062 acres.

Huntington Lake, Huntington 46750; (219) 356-3709; 8322; includes Little Turtle Recreation Area.

Mississinewa, Peru 46970; (317) 473-6528; 14,386 acres; includes Miami Recreation Area and Red Bridge Recreation Area.

Monroe, Bloomington 47401; (812) 837-9950; 23,592 acres; includes Fairfax Recreation Area and Paynetown Recreation Area.

Salamonie, Huntington 46750; (219) 468-2125; 11,506 acres; includes Lost Bridge Recreation Area.

MICHIGAN

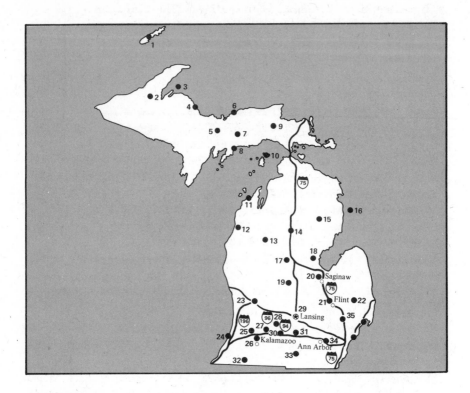

Michigan's unique position and diversity of habitat combine to make it one of the best states for birdwatching. There are thousands of lakes, hundreds of acres of uninterrupted forest, and lakeshores totaling over 3000 miles. The state owns and maintains several thousand acres of public land as game areas, wildlife research areas, and wildlife refuges. For information regarding these areas, contact the Department of Natural Resources, Stevens T. Mason Building, Lansing 48926. The best game areas for birdwatching include *Erie* and *Pointe Mouille,* near Monroe; *Tobico Marsh,* near Saginaw; and *Grand Mere,* near Stevensville.

The Great Lakes support large numbers of wintering seabirds such as Oldsquaws; even such rarities as phalaropes, jaegers, and Black-legged Kittiwakes occasionally appear. The Black-backed Three-toed Woodpecker, Gray Jay, and Boreal Chickadee find suitable nesting habitat in the cold, northern spruce bogs. Further south, in the deciduous forests, Red-bellied Woodpeckers, Prothonotary Warblers, and Louisiana Waterthrushes breed.

But Michigan's special bird is the Kirtland's Warbler, also known as the Jack-pine Warbler. A member of the wood warbler family (Parulidae), Kirtland's Warbler requires very specific nesting conditions. They will nest only in young jack pines that are in stands of over 80 acres. The birds nest in such stands when the trees are from 5 to 20 feet tall. The type of soil (the birds nest on the ground between the trees) on which the nests are built is Grayling sand. In addition to its restrictive habitat requirements, Kirtland's Warblers are plagued by the Brown-headed Cowbird, a parasitic bird. The cowbirds lay their eggs in the warblers' nests. A newly hatched cowbird is larger than a new-born Kirtland's Warbler and thus gets more food. Part of the Kirtland's Warbler management program is the removal of cowbird eggs from warblers' nests. The Kirtland's Warbler can be found at Huron National Forest (see page 271). Visitors are requested not to disturb the birds in any way — this includes photographing them. Photographs have been prepared and may be purchased.

Migration time is always a rewarding time for the birdwatcher. Shorebirds start appearing in Michigan in early April; waterfowl migration reaches its peak in mid-April; fall migration is well under way by mid-September. Snow Buntings, Lapland Longspurs, and other winter birds reach Michigan in October. Over 350 species of birds are known to occur in Michigan. For additional information about birdwatching in Michigan contact: Michigan Audubon Society, 7000 North Westnedge Avenue, Kalamazoo 49007; (616) 381-1574. They publish a booklet, "Enjoying Birds in Michigan." They also sponsor various trips and interpretive activities.

Baker Sanctuary, Convis Township, Calhoun County. The sanctuary is owned and operated by the Michigan Audubon Society. To reach the sanctuary from Battle Creek, take I-94 east to the intersection with I-69; turn north and go to N Drive North Exit; then go west to Walnut Point and turn north on 16 Mile

Road; continue to the intersection of Garfield and Junction Roads, which is the entrance to the sanctuary.

Baker Sanctuary was established in 1941 as a refuge for the endangered Sandhill Cranes. It is located on former government swamp land known as the Big Marsh. Baker Sanctuary now totals nearly 900 acres, including a 200-acre farm. The farm will be the site of an environmental center. There is also a small lodge. A self-guiding trail of 1½ miles winds its way through many differing habitats. Look for Marsh Hawk, American Bittern, Least Bittern, Virginia Rail, Sora, Common Snipe, American Woodcock, and various species of ducks and sparrows.

Grayling Wilderness Preserve, Grayling. The preserve is owned and managed by Trout Unlimited, 700 Fisher Building, Detroit 48202. The Nature Conservancy has a reversionary interest. The preserve consists of 2 tracts: the Guide's Rest area — 394 acres located about 5½ miles east of Grayling; and the Knight property — 150 acres located about 9 miles east of Grayling. The preserve is characterized by stands of jack pine and is crossed by the AuSable River, one of the finest trout streams in the east. State forests surround the preserve; Huron National Forest is nearby. The Kirtland's Warbler's major nesting area is located about 4 miles from the Guide's Rest area.

Nearly 300 species of birds can be seen at Grayling preserve during the year. They include: Mallard, Red-shouldered Hawk, Bald Eagle, Great Blue Heron, Great Horned Owl, Belted Kingfisher, Yellow-bellied Sapsucker, Pileated Woodpecker, Least Flycatcher, Purple Martin, Brown Creeper, House Wren, Wood Thrush, Eastern Bluebird, Cedar Waxwing, Red-eyed Vireo, Magnolia Warbler, Pine Warbler, Canada Warbler, Northern (Baltimore) Oriole, Evening Grosbeak, and Chipping Sparrow.

Hiawatha National Forest, Escanaba 49829. Hiawatha is divided into 2 major sections: the eastern one is located south of Sault Ste. Marie — use US 2, SR 28, and/or SR 123; the western division is just north of Escanaba — use US 2, US 41, and/or SR 28. Camping facilities are available at the Forest. Seney NWR is located between the divisions, see page 277.

Established in 1931, Hiawatha National Forest today totals 855,000 acres. The eastern division features an interpretive trail, a fish hatchery, a scenic area on the Straits of Mackinac, and miles of sandy Lake Superior shoreline. The western division has a self-guiding auto-walking tour, with short interpretive trails that loop off the Forest road. This area is characterized by dense, mixed evergreen and hardwood forests interspersed with many small lakes. Almost all of the area between the units is state forest land. The varied landscape provides habitat for a wide variety of birds. Over 220 species have been reported at Hiawatha. Among these are: Red-necked Grebe, Pintail, Canvasback, Hooded Merganser, Goshawk, Merlin (Pigeon Hawk), Sharp-tailed Grouse, Spruce Grouse, Great Blue Heron, Least Bittern, Sandhill Crane, Sora, American Golden Plover,

Whimbrel, Hudsonian Godwit (western unit only), Upland Sandpiper (Plover), Ruddy Turnstone, Snowy Owl, Black-backed Three-toed Woodpecker, Northern Three-toed Woodpecker, Boreal Chickadee, Swainson's Thrush, Bohemian Waxwing, Warbling Vireo, Golden-winged Warbler, Nashville Warbler, Blackburnian Warbler, Yellow-headed Blackbird (western unit only), Hoary Redpoll, Sharp-tailed Sparrow, and Lapland Longspur. Checklist available.

Huron Islands National Wildlife Refuge. Administered by Seney NWR. Access is by boat only. Huron Islands NWR is located in Lake Superior, 3 miles offshore, about 40 miles east of Houghton. The refuge is composed of 8 islands totaling 147 acres and was established in 1905. Only West Huron Island (Lighthouse Island) is open to public use, during daylight hours, for hiking and nature study.

The Huron Islands are composed of gray and pink granite upthrusts that are covered with trees — mostly red and white pine, balsam fir, white birch, and white cedar. The exposed rock frequently shows evidence of glacial activity. The rocks rise nearly 200 feet above Lake Superior offering steep cliffs on the south side. Many rocks are covered with lichens or reindeer moss. The small, nearly barren rocky islands on the eastern extremities of the group support nesting colonies of gulls, cormorants, and terns. Other species common to the islands are snowshoe hare, woodland deer mouse, Common Raven, Blue Jay, and Tree Swallow.

Huron National Forest, Cadillac 49601. Huron is located near Tawas City and East Tawas on the shore of Lake Huron; use SR 18, SR 33, SR 65, and/or SR 72 — all traverse the Forest. Huron is located near Manistee National Forest, Michigan Islands Wilderness, and numerous state parks and forests. Public facilities include camping, picnicking, swimming, and boating. In addition there are numerous hiking trails, including a section of the famous 220-mile shore-to-shore trail, and a self-guiding automobile forest trail. Huron National Forest totals 420,000 acres of ponds, forests, and streams. It was established in 1909 to protect both water and timber resources. Of special interest at Huron is the Tuttle Marsh Wildlife Area — an all-weather road has been constructed through this area.

The most significant and fascinating management program of Huron National Forest is in regard to the Kirtland's Warbler. A 4000-acre area has been set aside for this rare and endangered (only 438 individuals in 1977) songbird. It is the rarest wood warbler in the United States. Kirtland's Warbler is only found here and in the Bahamas, where it winters; rarely has it been seen in migration. It has very restrictive habitat requirements: young jack pine stands that are over 80 acres in size. To provide nesting sites for Kirtland's Warblers, an intensive management program — including nest protection and regulated burnings — is in force at Huron and at the neighboring state forests. All nesting areas are closed to public entry from 1 May to 15 August *except* by guided tours led by authorized

272 THE NORTH CENTRAL

U.S. Forest Service personnel. Tours are conducted daily. For information regarding Kirtland's Warbler management programs and/or the tours, contact the district forest ranger at Mio or the forest supervisor at Cadillac. Other birds likely to be seen at Huron National Forest include: Blue- and Green-winged Teals, Wood Duck, Common Goldeneye, Bufflehead, Goshawk, Ruffed Grouse, Killdeer, Black-billed Cuckoo, Barn Owl, Whip-poor-will, Belted Kingfisher, Red-headed Woodpecker, Alder Flycatcher, Tree Swallow, Gray Jay, Boreal Chickadee, Winter Wren, Wood Thrush, Cedar Waxwing, Northern Shrike, Warbling Vireo, Black-and-white Warbler, Blackburnian Warbler, Canada Warbler, Northern (Baltimore) Oriole, Evening Grosbeak, Common Redpoll, White-crowned Sparrow, Lapland Longspur, and Snow Bunting.

Isle Royale National Park, 87 North Ripley Street, Houghton 49931. Isle Royale is located in Lake Superior, 73 miles northwest of Houghton; 44 miles south of Thunder Bay, Ontario. The park is open to visitors from 15 May to 15 October; park sessions and schedules vary slightly from year to year. Contact the park prior to your visit for current information. The park is accessible by boat and plane; reservations are recommended. There are many seaplane and boating services that operate regularly between various cities and Isle Royale. There are no professional medical services available at the park. All campers, hikers, and boaters should carry a first-aid kit. Camping facilities are available; there are also lodge and housekeeping facilities available from June to Labor Day. All camping parties must register at a ranger station. Temperatures, even at midsummer, rarely exceed 80°; prolonged fog, rain, cold, and high winds are not unusual.

Forests dominate the island. The interior and upland portions of the park have pure hardwood stands; the cool, moist shores and lake borders have mixed evergreen forests. Despite the very short growing season, Isle Royale has several hundred species of wildflowers. Park rangers conduct various interpretive programs; in addition there are exhibits and self-guiding trails to further your understanding and enjoyment of the park. Over 160 miles of hiking trails traverse the park. Among the animals common to the island are moose, wolves, red foxes, and snowshoe hares. In addition, over 200 species of birds have been identified at the park. Among them are: Red-throated Loon, Red-necked Grebe, Snow Goose, Green-winged Teal, Wood Duck, Canvasback, Greater Scaup, Bufflehead, White-winged Scoter, Hooded Merganser, Goshawk, Sharp-shinned Hawk, Bald Eagle, Gryfalcon (rare), Peregrine Falcon (rare), Sharp-tailed Grouse, American Bittern, Black-bellied Plover, Caspian Tern, Snowy Owl, Hawk Owl, Long- and Short-eared Owls, Pileated Woodpecker, Black-backed Three-toed Woodpecker, Northern Three-toed Woodpecker, Olive-sided Flycatcher, Gray (Canadian) Jay, Common Raven, Red- and White-breasted Nuthatches, Winter Wren, Swainson's Thrush, Loggerhead Shrike, Northern Shrike, Red-eyed Vireo, Nashville Warbler, Blackburnian Warbler, Blackpoll Warbler, Connecticut Warbler, Mourning Warbler, Wilson's Warbler,

Bobolink, Common Redpoll, Pine Siskin, Red Crossbill, White-winged Crossbill, Clay-colored Sparrow, Lapland Longspur, and Snow Bunting. Checklist available.

Lew Sarett Sanctuary, Route 2, Box 217, Benton Center Road, Benton Center 49022; (616) 927-4832. The sanctuary is owned by the Michigan Audubon Society. To reach the sanctuary from St. Joseph, take I-94 east to the South Haven Exit; turn north on I-96 and go to the Red Arrow Highway Exit; turn west and proceed to Twelve Corners, the Benton Center Road; take that north to Duncan Road; the sanctuary is on Duncan Road. It is about 3 miles from the South Haven Exit to the sanctuary.

Lew Sarett Sanctuary is located along the Paw Paw River and totals 170 acres. It was established in 1964 and provides a diversified habitat for a wide community of plant and animal life. An interpretive center, boardwalks, and trails are maintained. There is also a wildlife pond. Look for waterbirds, shorebirds, and warblers, including the Prothonotary.

Manistee National Forest, Cadillac 49601. Manistee is located on the shore of Lake Michigan, just south of Sleeping Bear Dunes National Lakeshore; it is bordered on the east by numerous state parks and forests. To reach Manistee from Cadillac, use SR 55; other major routes that traverse the Forest are US 10 from Ludington; US 31 from Manistee, SR 20 from Big Rapids; and SR 37 from Traverse City. As in most national forests, camping facilities are available. Other public recreational facilities include canoeing, swimming, boating, and picnicking. In addition there are interpretive trails and a self-guiding automobile forest tour. Among the numerous hiking trails is a section of the famous 220-mile shore-to-shore trail.

Manistee Forest was established in 1938. It covers 500,000 acres of lakeshore, dunes, hardwood forests, lakes, and streams. The Pere Marquette River, which runs through the center of Manistee, is being considered for inclusion in the National System of Scenic and Wild Rivers. Management programs at Manistee include experimental forests, waterfowl areas, and timber management — harvesting and planting. The vast, uncivilized areas and varied landscape provide habitat for a wide variety of birds. Among the species likely to be seen here during the summer are: Common Loon, Canada Goose, Mallard, Blue-winged Teal, Wood Duck, Hooded Merganser, Red-tailed Hawk, Ruffed Grouse, American Bittern, Sora, Common Gallinule, Killdeer, Herring Gull, Great Horned Owl, Common Nighthawk, Belted Kingfisher, Pileated Woodpecker, Red-headed Woodpecker, Eastern Kingbird, Olive-sided Flycatcher, Purple Martin, Tree Swallow, White-breasted Nuthatch, Wood Thrush, Cedar Waxwing, Philadelphia Vireo (rare), Golden-winged Warbler, Yellow Warbler, Northern Parula, Pine Warbler, Rose-breasted Grosbeak, Indigo Bunting, and Vesper Sparrow.

Martha Mott Preserve, Almena Township, Van Buren County. The preserve is owned and maintained by the Michigan Audubon Society. To reach the preserve from Kalamazoo, take Michigan Avenue west, crossing US 131, to 24th Street; turn north (right) and continue to the preserve, which is at the corner of 24th and 44th Streets.

This 80-acre preserve was established in 1971. It consists mainly of sandy areas and varied habitats crossed by a small stream. Look for migrating landbirds.

Michigan Islands National Wildlife Refuge/Wilderness. Administered by Shiawassee NWR. For information about visiting the islands, contact the refuge manager at Shiawassee. The Michigan Islands were established as a refuge in 1947 and total over 12 acres. They are composed of Pismire, Shoe, and Scarecrow islands. The former are located in the northern part of Lake Michigan, near Beaver; Scarecrow is located in Lake Huron, off the south point of Thunder Bay. There is a ferry from Charlevoix to Beaver. The islands are generally made up of glacial boulders, sand, and gravel. They support minimal vegetation, although there are some trees and a rich growth of herbs on Pismire. Among the nesting birds on the islands are: Red-breasted Merganser, Mallard, Great Blue Heron, Herring Gull, Ring-billed Gull, Common Tern, and Caspian Tern. The islands are also used as a feeding and loafing place by cormorants, ducks, and other shorebirds and waterfowl.

Ottawa National Forest, Ironwood 49938. Ottawa Forest is located east of Ironwood; use US 2, US 45, and/or SR 28 — they all (plus numerous other local roads) traverse the area. Public facilities include camping, boating, and skiing. In addition, there are several historical sites. A network of hiking trails is maintained throughout Ottawa and there is also a self-guiding automobile trail.

Ottawa National Forest, on the shore of Lake Superior, totals 910,000 acres of forests, lakes, and streams. Attractions include numerous waterfalls, a Forest Service nursery, a state fish hatchery, Porcupine Mountain State Park, and various forest plantations. Ottawa Forest borders Nicolet National Forest (in Wisconsin) as well as many state parks and forests; it is near Huron Islands NWR. The abundance of open water, freshwater marshes, woodland ponds, grasslands, and dense forests provide food and shelter for many birds. Among the 238 species of birds (138 nesting) that have been seen here are: Common Loon, Horned Grebe, Whistling Swan, Snow Goose (white and blue morphs), Pintail, Northern Shoveler, Ring-necked Duck, Bufflehead, Oldsquaw (rare), Hooded Merganser, Goshawk, Broad-winged Hawk, Golden Eagle (rare), Bald Eagle, Spruce Grouse, Sharp-tailed Grouse, Green Heron, Sandhill Crane (rare), Sora, Ruddy Turnstone (rare), Dunlin, Wilson's Phalarope (rare), Black Tern, Black-billed Cuckoo, Snowy Owl, Saw-whet Owl (rare), Common Nighthawk, Pileated Woodpecker, Black-backed Three-toed Woodpecker, Olive-sided Flycatcher, Horned Lark, Bank Swallow, Common Raven, Gray Jay, Boreal

Chickadee, White- and Red-breasted Nuthatches, Long- and Short-billed Marsh Wrens, Eastern Bluebird, Northern Shrike, Philadelphia Vireo, Golden-winged Warbler, Mourning Warbler, Connecticut Warbler, Wilson's Warbler, Eastern and Western Meadowlarks, Yellow-headed Blackbird, Rusty Blackbird, Scarlet Tanager, Rose-breasted Grosbeak, Common Redpoll, Sharp-tailed Sparrow, Lapland Longspur, and Snow Bunting. Checklist available.

Phyllis Haehnle Memorial Sanctuary, Leoni Township, Jackson County. The sanctuary is owned and maintained by the Michigan Audubon Society. To reach it from Jackson, take I-94 east to Race Road Exit; turn north and continue to Seymour Road; turn left (west) and continue to the sanctuary entrance. It is about 3½ miles from the Race Road Exit to the sanctuary.

Phyllis Haehnle Memorial Sanctuary was established in 1955 and totals nearly 700 acres. Mud Lake and Mud Lake Marsh make up a large part of the sanctuary; there is also another lake, Eagle Lake. In addition there are some upland areas. Look for Sandhill Cranes and waterbirds.

Pictured Rocks National Lakeshore, Munising 49862. Pictured Rocks is on Lake Superior's southern shore; it is located near the western division of Hiawatha National Forest. The visitors' center is just northeast of Munising. Camping is permitted at Pictured Rocks; however, some of the areas within park boundaries are still privately owned. Visitors are requested to respect the rights of the owners. The park rangers conduct nature walks and campfire programs during the summer. There are hiking trails and gravel and sand roads that are passable, except in winter.

The lakeshore takes its name from the 200-foot high cliffs of multicolored sandstone that rise abruptly from Lake Superior. Most of these formations are visible only from a boat. Privately operated scenic cruises are conducted daily in the summer from Munising. The inland areas of the park consist of lakes, streams, waterfalls, and bogs. The beaches, freshwater ponds, and mixed hardwood forests provide ideal habitat for a great variety of animal life. Black bear, bobcat, muskrat, coyote, porcupine, beaver, and woodchuck are among the mammals of the area. There have been 220 species of birds (84 nesting) sighted at Pictured Rocks National Lakeshore. Among these are: Red-necked Grebe, Snow (Blue) Goose, Pintail, Northern Shoveler, Wood Duck, Bufflehead, Goshawk, Marsh Hawk, Sharp-shinned Hawk, Sharp-tailed Grouse, Great Blue Heron, Sandhill Crane, Yellow Rail, Piping Plover, Ruddy Turnstone, Baird's Sandpiper (rare), Marbled Godwit, Northern Phalarope, Black Tern, Short-eared Owl, Saw-whet Owl, Pileated Woodpecker, Red-headed Woodpecker, Olive-sided Flycatcher, Horned Lark, Tree Swallow, Common Raven, Winter Wren, Swainson's Thrush, Eastern Bluebird, Loggerhead Shrike, Northern Parula, Mourning Warbler, Black-throated Blue Warbler, Brewer's Blackbird, Indigo Bunting, Harris' Sparrow, and Lapland Longspur. (*Note:* Birds sighted here in the *winter only* are not listed.)

Prairie Chicken Management Area, Marion. The area is owned and maintained by the state. Information about visiting the area can be obtained by contacting the Department of Natural Resources, Paris 49338; (616) 832-2281. The area is posted against entry to minimize disturbances during the birds' mating and nesting seasons. An observation blind has been set up for visitors. Use of the blind is scheduled by the biologist in charge; it accommodates about 15 people.

The Prairie Chicken Management Area was established in 1970. Management programs include maintenance of nesting sites; controlled burns; mowing; and planting of corn, buckwheat, millet, and oats. Trees and brush are removed wherever possible to maintain a prairielike habitat. Male Greater Prairie Chickens begin to gather on the booming ground in February. Courtship activity continues into May, with the peak of activity occurring about mid-April. The observation blind is located about 150 yards from the booming ground and gives visitors a fine view of this unique spectacle.

Riverbank Sanctuary, Hiawatha Township, Schoolcraft County. The sanctuary is owned and maintained by the Michigan Audubon Society. To reach the sanctuary from Manistique, take SR 94 north to P 440, turn west (left) and continue to the sanctuary. Riverbank is located on the Indian River, near Hiawatha National Forest. Some of the schools in the area use the sanctuary for biological studies. There are no facilities.

The sanctuary was established in 1949; it totals 23 acres. Riverbank is characterized by a spruce-hemlock forest. Among the many birds likely to be seen here are: Pied-billed Grebe, Canada Goose, Blue-winged Teal, Least Bittern, Common (Yellow-shafted) Flicker, Least Flycatcher, Tree Swallow, Red- and White-breasted Nuthatches, Brown Thrasher, Hermit Thrush, Black-throated Blue Warbler, Canada Warbler, American Redstart, Brown-headed Cowbird, and Lincoln's Sparrow.

Rose Lake Wildlife Research Area, 8562 E. Stoll Road, Rt. #1, East Lansing 48823; (517) 339-8638. The area is owned by the state. A variety of interpretive and educational programs is available. Since hunting is permitted at Rose Lake, certain areas may be closed during some times of the year. Rose Lake is a research area, and therefore any use of the area may come under special restrictions or regulations. Appropriate signs are posted; if in doubt, ask at the office.

This 3300-acre area consists of moderately rolling farmland, abandoned fields, oak and swamp woods, marsh, and ponds. Management programs include flooding, tree and shrub planting, soil conservation, and planting supplemental wildlife food. A wildlife pathology laboratory is on the premises. There have been nearly 200 species of birds (34 nesting) recorded at Rose Lake. Among them are: Common Loon, Snow (Blue) Goose, Green- and Blue-winged Teals, Redhead, Sharp-shinned Hawk, Cooper's Hawk, Black-crowned Night Heron,

Sandhill Crane, Sora, Willet, Bonaparte's Gull, Long-eared Owl, Whip-poor-will, Belted Kingfisher, Yellow-bellied Sapsucker, Eastern Kingbird, Olive-sided Flycatcher, Cliff Swallow, Brown Creeper, Carolina Wren, Long- and Short-billed Marsh Wrens, Mockingbird, Veery, Golden- and Ruby-crowned Kinglets, Water Pipit, Cedar Waxwing, Loggerhead Shrike, Warbling Vireo, Brewster's Warbler (rare), Lawrence's Warbler (rare), Orange-crowned Warbler, Chestnut-sided Warbler, Mourning Warbler, Eastern and Western Meadowlarks, Scarlet Tanager, Common Redpoll, and Fox Sparrow. Checklist available.

St. Clair Flats Wildlife Area, Sans Souci, St. Clair County (near Algonac); (313) 748-9504. The land is owned by the state. To reach the flats from Algonac, take SR 29 south to the ferry, which crosses North Channel; then continue on SR 154 to Sans Souci. There are various state and local roads (some gravel) that enter the area at different points; SR 154 (Bates Highway) follows the perimeter of the area. This is basically a game area and is open to hunting, although there are some sections that have been set aside as waterfowl and/or wildlife refuges.

The area is characterized by mud flats, bays, marshes, and small islands — at the mouth of the St. Clair River. The St. Clair Flats are a well-known stopping point for large numbers of migrating waterfowl. Management programs include diking, in order to stabilize water levels, and planting supplemental food for waterfowl. There are some upland areas, fields and woods, on Harsens and Dickinson islands. In the low-lying areas, look for Pied-billed Grebe, Mallard, Black Duck, Wood Duck, Canvasback, Redhead, Greater Scaup, Common Goldeneye, American Bittern, Sora, Long-billed Marsh Wren, and other waterfowl.

Seney National Wildlife Refuge, Star Route, Seney 49883; (906) 586-6504. To reach the refuge from Escanaba, take US 2 east to Blaney Park, then turn north on SR 77, and continue to refuge headquarters, which are just north of Germfask. Seney is located between the eastern and western units of Hiawatha National Forest and amid several Michigan state forests. Public facilities include guided tours, self-guiding auto trails, and a nature trail with an observation tower. In addition there are environmental exhibits and dioramas at the visitors' center. Camping is not permitted on the refuge; however facilities are available at nearby state forests.

Seney Refuge was established in 1935 and consists of nearly 95,500 acres in the Great Manistique Swamp. It is a vast, open marsh with shallow pools interspersed between sand ridges that support stands of red and jack pine. Management programs on the refuge include farming to provide supplemental food for wildlife. Among the primary species at Seney are otter, deer, and bear. There have been 201 species of birds (120 nesting) sighted at Seney. Among these are: Red-necked Grebe (rare), Whistling Swan, Canada Goose, American

Wigeon, Wood Duck, Hooded Merganser, Goshawk, Marsh Hawk, Bald Eagle, Peregrine Falcon (rare), Spruce Grouse, Sharp-tailed Grouse, Great Blue Heron, Sandhill Crane, Yellow Rail (rare), Black-bellied Plover, Pectoral Sandpiper, Black Tern, Snowy Owl, Saw-whet Owl, Whip-poor-will, Black-backed Three-toed Woodpecker, Least Flycatcher, Rough-winged Swallow, Gray Jay, Boreal Chickadee (rare), Winter Wren, Wood Thrush, Bohemian Waxwing, Northern Shrike, Cape May Warbler, Black-throated Green Warbler, Bay-breasted Warbler, Connecticut Warbler, Brewer's Blackbird, Indigo Bunting, Common Redpoll, Red Crossbill, White-winged Crossbill, Clay-colored Sparrow, Le Conte's Sparrow (rare), Harris' Sparrow, Lapland Longspur, and Snow Bunting. Checklist available.

Seven Ponds Nature Center, 3854 Crawford Road, Dryden 48428; (313) 796-3419. The center is owned and operated by the Michigan Audubon Society. It is located between Port Huron and Flint. To reach the center from Flint, take SR 21 east to Imlay City, turn south on SR 53, and go for about 5 miles to Dryden Road, turn west (right) and go through Dryden to Lake George Road, turn south (left) and continue to the entrance.

The center was established in 1966 and now covers 243 acres of uplands, fields, mixed woodlands, and bog-lakes. A variety of educational and interpretive programs is offered at the center. Trails, some self-guiding, are maintained. Look for thrushes, flycatchers, warblers, and finches.

Shiawassee National Wildlife Refuge, 6975 Mower Road, Route 1, Saginaw 48601; (517) 793-2340; ext. 431. Refuge headquarters are 6 miles south of Saginaw; ½ mile west of SR 12 at the intersection of Mower Road and Curtis Road. The refuge is bordered on the west by the Shiawassee State Game Area. Camping is not permitted at the refuge; however, facilities are available at nearby Bay City State Park.

The 9000-acre refuge was established in 1953 and is another link in the system of wildlife refuges along the Mississippi Flyway. The primary objective of the refuge is to provide food and shelter for migrating waterfowl; management programs include farming to provide supplemental waterfowl food. The Shiawassee, Tittabawassee, and four other rivers converge in the refuge to form the Saginaw River, which flows into nearby Saginaw Bay. The refuge also contains vast areas of marshlands, greentree reservoirs, and open water. The Shiawassee flats support a wide variety of wildlife. Commonly seen animals include white-tailed deer, red fox, muskrat; other species such as beaver and racoon are encountered occasionally. Bird populations on the refuge vary greatly depending on the season. Spring and fall are the best times to observe large congregations of ducks, geese, and swans. During the summer many species of passerines may be seen. There have been 187 species of birds identified at Shiawassee Refuge. Among them are: Common Loon, Horned Grebe, Whistling Swan, Snow Goose, Gadwall, Pintail, Northern Shoveler, Wood Duck,

Canvasback, Common Goldeneye, Bufflehead, Ruddy Duck, Sharp-shinned Hawk, Golden Eagle (rare), Bald Eagle, Osprey (rare), Ring-necked Pheasant, Green Heron, Black-crowned Night Heron, American Bittern, Sandhill Crane, King Rail, American Golden Plover, Ruddy Turnstone, Caspian Tern, Long- and Short-eared Owls, Snowy Owl, Red-headed Woodpecker, Least Flycatcher, Horned Lark, Rough-winged Swallow, Black-capped Chickadee, White- and Red-breasted Nuthatches, Long-billed Marsh Wren, Eastern Bluebird, Northern Shrike, Black-throated Blue Warbler, Ovenbird, American Redstart, Bobolink, Scarlet Tanager, Rose-breasted Grosbeak, Common Redpoll, Pine Grosbeak, Vesper Sparrow, Lapland Longspur, and Snow Bunting. Checklist available.

Sleeping Bear Dunes National Lakeshore, 400½ Main Street, Frankfort 49635. Sleeping Bear Dunes is located on the shore of Lake Michigan, about 22 miles west of Traverse City on SR 72. To reach park headquarters, which are in Frankfort, turn south at Empire on SR 22, and continue for 22 miles. Sleeping Bear Dunes is just north of Manistee National Forest and is near many smaller state parks and forests. The Lakeshore, established in 1970, will total 67,000 acres when acquisition is completed. Much of the land within the boundaries is still privately owned. Visitors are requested to respect the rights of private owners. Public facilities include self-guiding nature trails, a scenic drive, overlooks, and hiking trails. In addition, there are camping facilities and interpretive programs.

The main attraction of the Lakeshore is, of course, the dunes themselves — 400 feet high. From the top one can see a magnificent panorama of Glen Lake and the surrounding countryside. The rivers and lakes, valleys and plains, and dunes and ridges support a richly diversified wildlife community. The sand dune deserts contrast sharply with the hardwood forests. There have been over 220 species of birds sighted here. Among the birds likely to be seen in the summer (150 species) are: Common Loon, Mute Swan, Wood Duck, Common Merganser (rare), Sharp-shinned Hawk, Marsh Hawk, Ruffed Grouse, Least Bittern, Virginia Rail, Piping Plover (rare), Caspian Tern, Black-billed Cuckoo, Great Horned Owl, Whip-poor-will, Common (Yellow-shafted) Flicker, Pileated Woodpecker, Eastern Phoebe, Purple Martin, Brown Creeper, Winter Wren, Eastern Bluebird, Cedar Waxwing, Western Kingbird (rare), Red-eyed Vireo, Golden-winged Warbler, Black-throated Green Warbler, Black-throated Blue Warbler, Mourning Warbler, Canada Warbler, Brewer's Blackbird, Scarlet Tanager, Rose-breasted Grosbeak, Red Crossbill (rare), and Chipping Sparrow.

Voorhees Brothers Wildlife Sanctuary, Lee Township, Calhoun County. The sanctuary is owned and maintained by the Michigan Audubon Society. To reach the sanctuary from Battle Creek, take I-94 to the Albion Exit; then take L Drive N to 24 Mile Road; turn north (right) and go to N Drive N; the sanctuary is on the corner.

Voorhees Sanctuary is located 9 miles from Baker Sanctuary (see page 269). From the exit off I-94 to the sanctuary is about 9 miles. This 40-acre sanctuary, established in 1948, is a fine example of a beech-maple forest. In the spring, the wildflowers here are specially delightful. Look for woodpeckers, thrushes, and warblers.

NATURE CENTERS

There are many privately and locally owned nature centers, parks, and sanctuaries located all over Michigan. Many of these offer a wide range of interpretive and educational programs. These centers are described briefly below.

Alma Outdoor Center, Alma 48801; (517) 463-1389. The center is operated by Alma Public Schools. It covers 53 acres. Trails are maintained. The center is open all year.

Belle Isle Nature Center, Inselruhe Road, Detroit; (313) 567-3911, ext. 22. This is an interpretive center located in a 1000-acre park. The center is open all year.

Blandford Nature Center of the Grand Rapids Public Museum, 1715 Hillburn Avenue, NW, Grand Rapids 49504; (616) 453-6192. The center is operated by the city of Grand Rapids. It covers 108 acres. Guided tours are offered; trails are maintained. The center is open all year, closed on Saturdays and holidays.

Carl G. Fenner Arboretum, 2020 East Mt. Hope Road, Lansing 48910; (517) 489-1686. The arboretum is operated by the city of Lansing. It totals 120 acres. Guided tours are offered; trails are maintained. The arboretum is open all year, closed on Mondays.

Chippewa Nature Center, 376 South Badour Road, Route #9, Midland 48640; (517) 631-0803. The 510-acre center has trails; guided tours are offered. It is open all year.

Civic Center Park Nature Area, 26000 Evergreen Road, Southfield 48076; (313) 356-1100. The area is operated by the Southfield Parks and Recreation Department. The park totals 180 acres; the nature area is 45 acres. It is open all year.

Cranbrook Institute of Science Nature Center, 500 Lone Pine Road, Bloomfield Hills 48013; (313) 644-1600, ext. 297. This is an 8-acre preserve. There is a trailside museum. The center is open all year, closed on Sundays and holidays.

Drayton Plains Nature Center, 2125 Denby Drive, Drayton Plains 48020; (313) 674-2119. The center totals 137 acres. Trails, some self-guiding, are maintained; guided tours are offered. The center is open all year, closed on Mondays and holidays in winter.

Fernwood, Inc., 1720 Rangeline Road, Niles 49120; (616) 695-6491. Fernwood covers 90 acres. It is open April through October, closed on Mondays.

For-Mar Nature Preserve and Arboretum and DeWaters Education Center, G-2252 North Genesee Road, Flint 48506; (313) 787-2575. The center is operated by the Genesee County Parks and Recreation Commission. The preserve covers 380 acres of open meadows and mixed woodlands. Trails are maintained; guided tours are available. The center is open all year, closed on weekends from 15 November to 15 March. There have been 125 species of birds identified here. Among them are: Green Heron, Red-bellied Woodpecker, Warbling Vireo, and Grasshopper Sparrow.

Hidden Lake Gardens, Tipton 49287; (313) 431-2060. The gardens are owned and maintained by Michigan State University. They cover 620 acres. There is a conservatory; trails are maintained. The gardens are open all year.

Huron-Clinton Metropolitan Authority, 600 Woodward Avenue, Detroit 48226. The authority operates 6 parks in the Detroit area. These do not have nature centers, however they do have trails and scenic drives. Write the authority for a guide to the parks.

Kalamazoo Nature Center, Inc., 7000 North Westnedge Avenue, Kalamazoo 49007; (616) 381-1574. The center serves as headquarters for the Michigan Audubon Society. Special features of the 512-acre preserve include a farmyard and an arboretum. Trails are maintained. The center is open all year, closed 1-15 September and on holidays. There have been 185 species of birds seen at Kalamazoo Center. Among them are: Wood Duck, Cooper's Hawk, Screech Owl, Gray-cheeked Thrush, and Clay-colored Sparrow.

Kellogg Bird Sanctuary (near Gull Lake), 12685 C Avenue East, Route 1, Box 339, Augusta 49012; (616) 671-5721. The sanctuary is operated by Michigan State University. It is located 13 miles northwest of Battle Creek. The sanctuary covers 540 acres and includes Wintergreen Lake, which is bordered by marshy areas. Trails traverse the area; a museum is maintained. Look for ducks, geese, and other waterfowl.

Kensington Metropolitan Park Nature Center, 2240 West Buno Road, Milford 48042; (313) 685-1561. The center is operated by the Huron-Clinton Metropolitan Authority. The center totals 700 acres within a 4300-acre park, which includes a 1200-acre lake. Kensington is located 33 miles from downtown Detroit; entrances are along I-96 near Brighton. The center is open all year, closed on Thanksgiving and Christmas.

Lower Huron Metro Park, Nature Center, Belleville; (313) 697-9181. The park is operated by the Huron-Clinton Metropolitan Authority and is located near Detroit. The center totals 50 acres and is in a 1000-acre park. Entrance to the center is on Hannon Road, ½ mile south of I-94. The center is open all year, closed on Thanksgiving and Christmas.

Nankin Mills Nature Center, 33175 Ann Arbor Trail, Westland 48185; (313) 261-1876. The center is operated by the Parks and Parkways Division of the Board of Wayne County Road Commissioners. It totals 500 acres and includes some historic buildings. Trails are maintained. The center is open all year, closed on Mondays and holidays.

Neithercut Interpretive Ecology Center, Mount Pleasant 48858; (517) 774-3009. The center is operated by Central Michigan University. It covers 252 acres. Trails are maintained. Guided tours are available by appointment. The center is open all year.

Nichols Arboretum, Ann Arbor. The arboretum totals over 100 acres and is hilly. Admission fee is charged. Look for warblers here. For additional information, contact the Ann Arbor Chamber of Commerce.

Oakwoods Metropark, The Nature Center, Flat Rock; (313) 782-1255. The park is operated by the Huron-Clinton Metropolitan Authority. It is located near Detroit. This 350-acre center is located in a 1700-acre park. There are exhibits and nature trails. Guided and self-guiding tours are available. The entrance is on Willow Road, about one mile southeast of its junction with Huron River Drive. The center is located about 4 miles northwest of the town of Flat Rock.

Presque Isle Park. The park is on the upper peninsula, just outside of Marquette. It consists of a wooded peninsula jutting into Lake Superior. Exhibits are on display at the Marquette County Historical Museum. Trails are maintained. The park is open all year.

Rouge Nature Center, 14250 West Outer Drive, Detroit; (313) 538-6088. The center is operated by the Detroit Department of Parks and Recreation. It covers 160 acres. There is a system of trails developed for visitors' use. The center is open all year, closed on holidays.

Stony Creek Metropark Nature Center, 4100 Inwood Road, Romeo 48065; (313) 781-4242. The center is operated by the Huron-Clinton Metropolitan Authority. This is a 770-acre center in a 4000-acre park. It is located 33 miles from downtown Detroit. Rolling hills surround a 600-acre lake; there are trails and a nature museum. The center is open all year. The entrance is along 26 Mile Road, 6 miles north of Utica.

Union City FFA Forest and Wildlife Area, Union City 49094; (517) 741-4221. The area is owned and maintained by the Union City Community Schools. It covers 15 acres. Trails are maintained. The center is open all year.

Willis C. and Mabel Lee Ward Nature Study Area, 4700 Pontiac Trail, Orchard Lake; (313) 644-1600, ext. 297. The area, located just outside of Detroit, is operated by the Cranbrook Institute of Science (see above). This center covers 36 acres and includes an outdoor laboratory. Guided tours are available by appointment only.

Whitehouse Nature Center, South Hanna Street, Albion 49224; (517) 629-5511. The center is operated by Albion College; it is located between Jackson and Battle Creek. It covers 87 acres. Trails are maintained. The center is open all year.

Woldumar Nature Center, 5539 Lansing Road, Lansing 48917; (517) 372-4991. The center is operated by Nature Way Association. It covers 188 acres. Trails are maintained; guided tours are offered. The center is open all year, closed on Sundays.

STATE PARKS AND FORESTS

There are numerous state parks and forests located throughout Michigan. Most of these parks offer camping in addition to a wide range of recreational activities, including boating, swimming, and hiking. Some parks have a naturalist on staff as well. Although not intended as nature sanctuaries, many of Michigan's state parks are known as good birdwatching places. These are marked as such with an asterisk (*). For further information about state parks and forests and/or camping in Michigan, contact: State Park Division, Department of Natural Resources, Lansing 48926. The state parks are listed below. They are in 3 groups: the southern lower peninsula, the northern lower peninsula, and the upper peninsula. Within each group they are arranged alphabetically.

PARKS IN THE SOUTHERN LOWER PENINSULA

Algonac, Algonac 48001; 981 acres.
Bald Mountain, Lake Orion 48035; 3100 acres.
Brighton, Howell 48843; 4706 acres.
Cambridge, Brooklyn 49230; 183 acres; day use only.
Dodge No. 4, Pontiac 48053; 136 acres; day use only.
Fort Custer, Augusta 49012; 2866 acres; day use only.
Grand Haven, Grand Haven 49417; 48 acres.
*Hayes, Onsted 49265; 210 acres.
Highland, Milford 48041; 5402 acres.
Hoffmaster, Muskegon 49440; 1030 acres.
Holland, Holland 49423; 142 acres.
Holly, Holly 48442; 6942 acres.
Ionia, Saranac 48881; 3826 acres.
Island Lake, Brighton 48116; 3420 acres.
Lakeport, Port Huron 48060; 565 acres.
Maybury, Northville 48167; 929 acres; day use only.
Metamora-Hadley, Metamora 48455; 683 acres.

*Muskegon, North Muskegon; 1125 acres.
 Ortonville, Ortonville 48462; 3996 acres.
 Pickney, Pickney 48169; 9613 acres.
 Pontiac Lake, Pontiac 48053; 3645 acres.
 Port Crescent, Port Austin 48467; 209 acres.
 Proud Lake, Milford 48042; 3434 acres.
 Rochester-Utica, Utica 48087; 862 acres; day use only.
 Sanilac, Port Austin 48467; 112 acres.
 Seven Lakes, Fenton 48430; 1378 acres; day use only.
 Sleeper, Caseville 48725; 963 acres.
 Sleepy Hollow, Lansing 48900; 2685 acres.
*Sterling, Monroe 48161; 997 acres.
 Van Buren, South Haven 49090; 326 acres.
*Warren Dunes, Sawyer 49125; 1499 acres.
*Warren Woods, Three Oaks 49128.
*Waterloo, Chelsea 48118; 17,053 acres.
 Yankee Springs, Middleville 49333; 4972 acres.

PARKS IN THE NORTHERN LOWER PENINSULA

 Aloha, Cheboygan 49721; 76 acres.
 Bay City, Bay City 48706; 196 acres.
 Benzie, Honor 49640; 2295 acres.
 Burt Lake, Indian River 49749; 406 acres.
 Cheboygan, Cheboygan 49721; 932 acres.
 Clear Lake, Atlanta 49709; 290 acres.
 D. H. Day, Glen Arbor 49636; 2002 acres.
 Gladwin, Gladwin 48624; 381 acres.
 Harrisville, Harrisville 48740; 94 acres.
*Hartwick Pines, Grayling 49738; 9138 acres.
*Hoeft, Rogers City 49779; 300 acres.
 Interlochen, Interlochen 49643; 187 acres.
*Ludington, Ludington 49431; 4156 acres.
 Mears, Pentwater 49449; 50 acres.
 Mitchell, Cadillac 49601; 32 acres.
 Newaygo, Newaygo 49337; 257 acres.
 North Higgins Lake, Roscocommon 48653; 429 acres.
 Onaway, Onaway 49765; 158 acres.
 Orchard Beach, Manistee 49660; 201 acres.
 Otsego Lake, Gaylord 49735; 62 acres.
 Petoskey, Petoskey 49770; 305 acres.
 Rifle River, Lupton 48635; 4329 acres.
 Silver Lake, Mears 49436; 2078 acres.
 South Higgins Lake, Roscocommon 48653; 305 acres.
*Tawas Point, East Tawas 48730; 175 acres.

Traverse City, Traverse City 49684; 39 acres.
White Cloud, White Cloud 49349; 89 acres.
*Wilderness, Carp Lake 49718; 6925 acres.
Wilson, Harrison 48625; 36 acres.
Young, Boyne City 49712; 563 acres.

PARKS IN THE UPPER PENINSULA

Baraga, Baraga 49908; 56 acres.
Bewabic, Crystal Falls 49920; 200 acres.
Brimley, Brimley 49715; 151 acres.
Detour, St. Ignace 49781; 403 acres.
Fayette, Fayette 49830; 357 acres.
Fort Wilkins, Copper Harbor 49918; 190 acres.
*Indian Lake, Manistique 49854; 567 acres.
Lake Gogebic, Marenisco 49947; 361 acres.
McLain, Hancock 49930; 401 acres.
*Muskallonge Lake, Newberry 49868; 172 acres.
Palms Brook, Manistique 49854; 308 acres; day use only.
*Porcupine Mountains, Ontonagon 49952; 58,327 acres.
Straits, St. Ignace 49781; 120 acres.
*Tahquamenon Falls, Paradise 49768; 19,244 acres.
Twin Lakes, Winona 49972; 175 acres.
Van Riper, Champion 49814; 1044 acres.
Wells, Cedar River 49813; 974 acres.

Kirtland's Warbler

OHIO

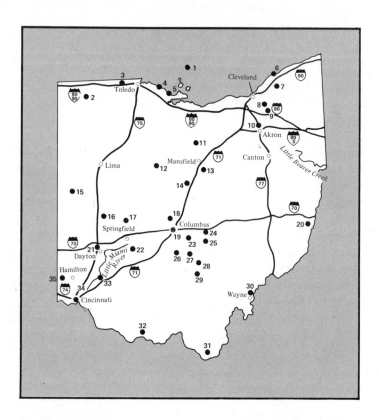

1. Point Pelee National Park
2. Goll Woods Nature Preserve
3. Irwin Prairie Nature
4. Magee Marsh Wildlife Area
5. Crane Creek Wildlife Experiment Station
6. Mentor Marsh
7. Chagrin River Forest Preserve
8. Tinkers Creek Nature Preserve
9. Eagle Creek Nature Preserve
10. Cuyahoga Valley National Recreation Area
11. Fowler Woods Nature Preserve
12. Killdeer Plains Wildlife Area
13. Clear Fork Gorge
14. Knox Woods Nature Preserve
15. Grand Lakes St. Marys Wildlife Area
16. Kiser Lake Wetlands Preserve
17. Cedar Bog State Memorial
18. Highbanks Nature Preserve
19. Edward Thomas Nature Preserve
   Gahanna Woods Nature Preserve
   Wahkeena Preserve

20. Dysart Woods
21. Aullwood Audubon Center/Farm
22. Clifton Gorge Nature Preserve
23. Blackbird Woods Nature Preserve
24. Blackhand Gorge Nature Preserve
25. Cranberry Bog Nature Preserve
26. Stage's Pond Nature Preserve
27. Shallenberger Nature Preserve
28. Christmas Rocks Nature Preserve
29. Little Rocky Hollow Sheick Hollow
30. Desonier Nature Preserve
   Wayne National Forest
31. Wayne National Forest
   Adams Lake Prairie Nature Preserve
32. Buzzardroost Rock
   Lynx Prairie
   The Wilderness
33. Caesar Creek Gorge Nature Preserve
34. Cincinnati Nature Center
35. Hueston Woods Nature Preserve

Ohio's forests and prairies, rivers and lakes all combine to provide interesting, varied habitats for avian life. There have been 288 species of birds recorded in Ohio, not counting accidentals, exotics, or hybrids.

Special birding areas in Ohio include the *Spring Grove Cemetery* in Cincinnati as well as several parks in that city. Among them are *Alms Park, Ault Park, Mt. Airy Forest, Mt. Echo Park,* and *Eden Park.* The latter houses the Irwin M. Krohn Conservatory and the Cincinnati Museum of Natural History. There are 3 county parks in the environs that are also rewarding birding places: *Sharon Woods* (740 acres), *Shawnee Lookout* (1010 acres), and *Miami-Whitewater* (2030 acres).

Just across Ohio's northern border in Ontario, is *Point Pelee National Park.* This park, which juts out into Lake Erie a few miles north of Sandusky, is a birdwatcher's paradise. On a spring morning, one can easily sight 100 to 150 species, perhaps 25 or 30 of these being warblers. Point Pelee has recorded 336 species of birds. It can be reached by car ferry from Sandusky.

For additional information about birdwatching in Ohio, contact: Ohio Department of Natural Resources, Fountain Square, Columbus 43224; or the Audubon Society, Aullwood Audubon Center, 1000 Aullwood Road, Dayton 45414. The *Ohio Journal of Science* has reprinted (Volume 68, Number 5; September 1968) the work of Milton B. and Mary A. Trautman: "Annotated List of the Birds of Ohio." This booklet is available from the bookstore at the Cincinnati Nature Center, 4949 Tealtown Road, Milford 45150. Up-to-date birding information for the Columbus area is available from *Dial-A-Bird:* (614) 299-7833.

Adams Lake Prairie Nature Preserve, West Union. The preserve is owned and managed by the Ohio Department of Natural Resources. It is located 2 miles north of West Union, off SR 41, near Adams Lake State Park.

Adams Lake Preserve totals over 22 acres and was established in 1973 to save perhaps the best stand of prairie-dock in the state. This preserve is surrounded by an oak forest. A system of nature trails has been developed. Among the many species of birds seen here are: Red-shouldered Hawk, Ruffed Grouse, Bobwhite, Killdeer, Yellow- and Black-billed Cuckoos, Great Horned Owl, Whip-poor-will, Hairy Woodpecker, Yellow-bellied Sapsucker, Eastern Phoebe, Purple Martin, Carolina Chickadee, Mockingbird, Hermit Thrush, Yellow-throated Vireo, Nashville Warbler, Pine Warbler, Common Yellowthroat, Orchard Oriole, Scarlet Tanager, Indigo Bunting, and Lark Sparrow.

Aullwood Audubon Center, 1000 Aullwood Road, Dayton 45414; (513) 890-7360. The center is operated by the National Audubon Society; for non-NAS members, there is an admission fee. To reach Aullwood Center from Dayton, take SR 48 north to US 40, turn right, pass the Englewood Dam, turn right again on Aullwood Road. The Aullwood Audubon Farm (see below) is located nearby on Frederick Road. The center is open from April to October,

7AM-8PM; from November to March, 9AM-5PM; and is closed on Sundays and holidays. A wide range of educational and interpretive programs is offered.

The 70-acre center includes marshland, fields, a tall grass prairie, ponds, a wet-wooded swamp, streams, and pine woods. This diverse environment provides habitat for a broad range of plant and animal life. Raccoons, skunks, foxes, opossums, and many smaller mammals live here. Turtles, frogs, and fish are found in the freshwater areas. There have been over 50 species of breeding birds recorded on the property. Among the birds likely to be seen here are: Wood Duck, Marsh Hawk, Bobwhite, Green Heron, Killdeer, Spotted Sandpiper, Black Tern, Barn Owl, Belted Kingfisher, Pileated Woodpecker, Yellow-bellied Sapsucker, Eastern Kingbird, Eastern Wood Pewee, Bank Swallow, White-breasted Nuthatch, Carolina Wren, Eastern Bluebird, Golden-crowned Kinglet, Red-eyed Vireo, Tennessee Warbler, Yellow-rumped (Myrtle) Warbler, Chestnut-sided Warbler, Common Yellowthroat, Northern (Baltimore) Oriole, Dickcissel, and Field Sparrow.

Aullwood Audubon Farm, 9101 Frederick Road, Dayton 45414; (513) 890-2963. The farm is operated by the National Audubon Society; it is located near Aullwood Audubon Center (see above).To reach the farm from Dayton, take SR 48 north to US 40, turn east (right) and continue to Frederick Road. An admission fee is charged to non-NAS members. The farm is open Tuesday through Saturday, 9-5; Sundays 1-5; and is closed on Mondays and holidays.

Aullwood is a 122-acre farm that is operated as a demonstration farm, conducted in a traditional fashion. A full range of interpretive and educational programs is offered. There are special farm activities such as maple syruping, sheep shearing, and candle dipping. Croplands, livestock, an herb garden, fruit orchard, and bee yard are all maintained.

Blackhand Gorge Nature Preserve, Tobosco. The preserve is owned and managed by the Ohio Department of Natural Resources. It is located 8 miles east of Newark. To reach the preserve from Newark, take SR 16 south to SR 146; turn west on SR 146 and continue along the Licking River to the preserve entrance (near Toboso). For additional information about the preserve, contact the preserve manager: Emliss Ricks, Route #4, Newark 43055.

This 732-acre preserve was established in 1975. Its prime feature is the narrow gorge cut by the Licking River. The topography is rugged. The hilltops are dominated by oak, hickory, Virginia pine, and mountain laurel. The area is also historically significant with remnants of the Ohio-Erie Canal being present.

Nearby is the *Hebron Fish Hatchery,* northwest of Buckeye Lake, where shorebirds can be found in early autumn. Look for Semipalmated Plover, Killdeer, and sandpipers. Hawks, owls, woodpeckers, and passerines can be seen in the vicinity of Buckeye Lake.

Blacklick Woods Nature Preserve, Reynoldsburg. The area is owned and managed by the Columbus and Franklin County Metropolitan Park District. The preserve is located in Reynoldsburg, a mile east of Brice Road on Livingston Avenue, within Blacklick Woods Metropolitan Park.

The 55-acre preserve is characterized by a beech-maple/elm-ash-oak swamp forest. It is considered to be one of the finest unspoiled woodlands in central Ohio. A wide variety of wildflowers is found here. Look for Great Horned Owl, Brown Creeper, and Black-throated Blue Warbler among other species of birds.

Buzzardroost Rock (The Christian and Emma Goetz Nature Preserve). The preserve is owned and maintained by the Cincinnati Museum of Natural History, 1720 Gilbert Avenue, Cincinnati 45202; (513) 621-3889. It is located on the east side of Ohio Brush Creek, about 7 miles southeast of West Union. To reach the preserve from Lynx, drive south on Tulip Road (CR 9) for nearly a mile to the first gravel road on the right, take it going west for almost 1½ miles to the community of Mahogany (look for the Mt. Armenia Church). Continue west for less than ¼ mile to a small parking area near the Copas' home.

The preserve totals 465 acres of mixed forest, stream with waterfalls, and prairie. It is mostly rocky and hilly. A booklet giving traveling directions, a brief history of the preserve, a description of the preserve's geology, and trail maps of the preserve is available from the Cincinnati Museum of Natural History. Among the many birds to be found here are: Pied-billed Grebe, Wood Duck, Marsh Hawk, Ruffed Grouse, Yellow- and Black-billed Cuckoos, Great Horned Owl, Chuck-will's-widow, Pileated Woodpecker, Eastern Kingbird, Tree Swallow, Tufted Titmouse, Winter Wren, Wood Thrush, Golden-crowned Kinglet, Warbling Vireo, Black-and-white Warbler, Chestnut-sided Warbler, and Evening Grosbeak.

Caesar Creek Gorge Nature Preserve, Oregonia. The preserve is owned and managed by the Ohio Department of Natural Resources. Access to the preserve is by written permission only. The preserve is located 2 miles north of Oregonia, along Caesar Creek between Corwin Road and O'Neall Road.

The preserve covers 470 acres. Caesar Creek is a tributary of the Little Miami River. In many places the gorge walls rise to 180 feet above the valley floor. Situated in a rural area, the gorge retains much of its wild character. The hillsides are heavily wooded with beech, maple, hickory, walnut, and oak.

Cedar Bog State Memorial. Owned and maintained by the Ohio Historical Society. The memorial is located 3½ miles south of Urbana, off US 68. Admission is by appointment only. Application for a permit to visit may be made to: Division of Natural History, The Ohio Historical Society, Columbus 43211. A naturalist is available, by appointment, to conduct guided tours through the area.

Cedar Bog, a national natural landmark, is the only alkaline bog remaining in Ohio. This delicate area now totals about 100 acres. It is hoped that an additional 500 acres will be added in order to include all of the remaining bog as well as a buffer zone to protect it. The area consists of a swamp forest and bog meadow surrounded by abandoned fields. It is located in the Mad River Valley, a rich agricultural area. There have been about 100 species of birds recorded at Cedar Bog. Among these are: Black Duck, Wood Duck, Marsh Hawk, American Bittern, Yellow-billed Cuckoo, Barred Owl, Chimney Swift, Red-headed Woodpecker, Eastern Kingbird, Eastern Wood Pewee, Tufted Titmouse, Brown Creeper, Winter Wren, Wood Thrush, Cedar Waxwing, Red-eyed Vireo, Blue-winged Warbler, Black-throated Blue Warbler, Cerulean Warbler, Hooded Warbler, Northern (Baltimore) Oriole, Rose-breasted Grosbeak, American Goldfinch, and Rufous-sided Towhee.

Chagrin River Forest Preserve, Hunting Valley. The preserve is located in the village of Hunting Valley, a suburb 15 miles east of Cleveland and 13 miles from Lake Erie. The preserve is on the south side of Fairmount Boulevard, on the east shore of the Chagrin River. To reach the preserve from I-271, exit in Lyndhurst at the Brainard-Cedar Road interchange; go east for 4 miles to River Road, than a mile south on River Road to Fairmount Boulevard, then east ½ mile to the preserve. The Cleveland Museum of Natural History manages the preserve. Parking at Chagrin River Preserve is with permission of the Hunting Valley police.

The 148-acre preserve is the wooded hillside of the Chagrin River Valley. This is a beech-maple-hemlock climax forest with tulip, oak, ash, hickory, sycamore, and cherry scattered throughout. Among the 118 species of birds sighted here are: Blue-winged Teal, Wood Duck, Common Goldeneye, Sharp-shinned Hawk, Marsh Hawk, Ruffed Grouse, Green Heron, Killdeer, American Woodcock, Solitary Sandpiper, Ring-billed Gull, Barred Owl, Common Nighthawk, Pileated Woodpecker, Great Crested Flycatcher, Tree Swallow, White-breasted Nuthatch, Swainson's Thrush, Veery, Eastern Bluebird, Ruby- and Golden Crowned Kinglets, Warbling Vireo, Blue-winged Warbler, Cape May Warbler, Cerulean Warbler, Palm Warbler, Canada Warbler, Scarlet Tanager, Rose-breasted Grosbeak, Common Redpoll, Pine Siskin, White-winged Crossbill, and Vesper Sparrow.

Christmas Rocks Nature Preserve, Hocking Township. The preserve is owned by the Ohio Youth Commission and is managed as a nature preserve by the Ohio Department of Natural Resources. Access to the preserve is by written permission only. For permits and additional information, contact: Ken Temple, preserve manager, 108½ Rosewood, Circleville 43113. The preserve is located off Christmas Rocks Road, 5 miles southwest of Lancaster in Hocking Township.

Christmas Rocks Preserve covers over 200 acres and was established in 1973. Its unusual geologic features — the Christmas Rocks — were formed when the Blackhand sandstone fractured along many lines. The individual blocks slowly moved downhill so that today the area is a maze of deep, narrow crevices. The area is composed of an oak-hickory forest. Wildflowers abound here, including several unusual species such as moccasin flower, nodding trillium, trailing arbutus, and lobed spleenwort.

Cincinnati Nature Center, 4949 Tealtown Road, Milford 45150; (513) 831-1711. To reach the center from Cincinnati, take US 50 east to Milford, then take Cleveland Road to Roundbottom Road, turn left on Roundbottom Road and continue for nearly 3 miles to the entrance.

The Cincinnati Nature Center was established in 1967 and now totals nearly 800 acres. The center also manages the 534-acre Long Branch Farm (located near Goshen). Long Branch Farm is a producing farm that specializes in registered Angus breeding cattle. The use of the grounds and trails at the center is open to the public Monday through Friday; restricted to members and their guests on weekends. The visitors' center houses exhibits, a members' library, and up-to-date birdwatching data. The Cincinnati Nature Center offers a comprehensive environmental education program to children; workshops, classes, and trips are available to members.

There are 6 miles of trails through woods, meadows, and along streams. Special plantings include an herb garden and several daffodil beds. There are over 70 varieties of wildflowers in bloom from February through November. Bird feeders are strategically located around the visitors' center. The habitat of the Cincinnati Nature Center supports a diversified wildlife community. Deer, squirrel, rabbit, and raccoon are among the common mammals. There are about 150 species of birds that are regularly seen. Among these are: Pied-billed Grebe, Wood Duck, American Kestrel (Sparrow Hawk), Bobwhite, Screech Owl, Barred Owl, Great Horned Owl, Pileated Woodpecker, Red-bellied Woodpecker, Cedar Waxwing, Carolina Wren, Wood Thrush, Brown Thrasher, Eastern Bluebird, Philadelphia Vireo, Prothonotary Warbler, Worm-eating Warbler, Golden-winged Warbler, Blue-winged Warbler, Kentucky Warbler, Black-throated Blue Warbler, Boblink, Indigo Bunting, and Henslow's Sparrow.

Clear Fork Gorge, Loudonville. The preserve is owned and managed by the Ohio Department of Natural Resources. It is located within Mohican State Forest and Park and is managed as part of the park-forest complex. A system of hiking trails in the gorge is available, but trails have not as yet been developed within the preserve. Access to the preserve itself is with written permission only. Contact the Ohio Department of Natural Resources for a permit.

The preserve covers over 51 acres and consists of a pine-hemlock forest along the gorge. The gorge itself is a registered national natural landmark. A variety of educational and interpretive facilities are available at the park.

Clifton Gorge Nature Preserve, Clifton. The preserve is owned by the Ohio Department of Natural Resources and managed by the Division of Parks and Recreation. It is located at the east end of John Bryan State Park, along SR 343, about ¼ mile west of Clifton.

This 255-acre preserve encompasses a 2-mile stretch of the Little Miami River. It has been designated as a national natural landmark. It is an outstanding example of interglacial and post-glacial canyon cutting. The physical features of the preserve create an unusual environment. The most outstanding plant community occurs along a narrow section of the gorge on the river's south side.

Cranberry Bog Nature Preserve, Buckeye Lake State Park. The preserve is owned and managed by the Ohio Department of Natural Resources. It is located off the north shore of Buckeye Lake in Buckeye State Park, 1½ miles southeast of the intersection of I-70 and SR 79. Owing to the extremely fragile condition of the island, access is restricted. Visitors must remain on the established boardwalk trail. Written permission to visit the island must be secured in advance. Contact the Division of Natural Areas and Preserves, Ohio Department of Natural Resources.

Cranberry Bog is a floating island; it is composed entirely of sphagnum moss and other compacted vegetation. The 9-acre island was established as a preserve in 1973. The central portions of the island are open bog meadow and provide habitat for such unusual plants as the pitcher plant, swamp-pink orchid, rose pagonia, and cranberry.

Crane Creek Wildlife Experiment Station, Division of Wildlife, 13229 West State Route 2, Oak Harbor 43449; (419) 897-3363. The station is operated by the state. It is located 10 miles north of Oak Harbor, the entrance is on SR 2, 17 miles west of Port Clinton. Public facilities include 2 nature trails and 27 miles of dikes that are available for walking. Guided tours can be arranged with the naturalist at the Sportsmen Migratory Bird Center. Camping is not permitted; however, facilities are available at nearby Crane Creek State Park.

Crane Creek Wildlife Experiment Station is the state center for research on wetlands wildlife. It was established in 1956. Headquarters are on the 2600-acre Magee Marsh Wildlife Area. Waterfowl flight lanes of both the Atlantic and Mississippi Flyways pass through Magee Marsh. Seventeen species of ducks and 4 species of geese occur during the year. Shorebirds are abundant in migration. Management programs include controlling water levels to produce greater harvests of waterfowl food plants. Artificial nesting structures have been effective in inducing geese to nest here. Among the 270 species of birds sighted here are: Whistling Swan, Snow Goose, Black Duck, American Wigeon, Blue-winged Teal, Bald Eagle, Osprey, Peregrine Falcon, Great Blue Heron, Snowy Egret, Least Bittern, American Bittern, Sandhill Crane, Sora, Common Gallinule, American Coot, and Great Horned Owl.

Cuyahoga Valley National Recreation Area, P. O. Box 158, Peninsula 44264. The Cuyahoga River runs between Akron and Cleveland; and this National Recreation Area preserves 30,000 acres of relatively open space, including 20 miles of the Cuyahoga River and Valley. It also includes sections of the valley rim, tributary ravines, and steep forested slopes. The area was established in 1975 and provides many opportunities for public recreation. About half the lands (13,000 acres) are maintained by the Cleveland Metroparks, the Akron Metropolitan Park District, or other organizations. Attractions include Hale Farm and Western Reserve Village, Blossom Music Center, Hudson Wildlife Park, and camps for Girl and Boy Scouts.

This area is biologically unique — a botanical crossroads situated in the transition zone between the central lowlands to the west and the Appalachian plateaus to the east. Here there are hemlock groves, upland meadows, and lowland bogs. This diversity of plant life provides a home for many animals including deer, fox, raccoon, as well as many species of birds. Among the birds sighted here are: Pied-billed Grebe, Pintail, Northern Shoveler, Wood Duck, Cooper's Hawk, Sharp-shinned Hawk, Marsh Hawk, Green Heron, Least Bittern, Virginia Rail, Ruddy Turnstone, Upland Sandpiper (Plover), Red Knot, Caspian Tern, Black-billed Cuckoo, Screech Owl, Saw-whet Owl, Whip-poor-will, Ruby-throated Hummingbird, Pileated Woodpecker, Alder Flycatcher, Rough-winged Swallow, Red-breasted Nuthatch, Carolina Wren, Brown Thrasher, Blue-gray Gnatcatcher, Cedar Waxwing, Loggerhead Shrike, White-eyed Vireo, Blue-winged Warbler, Brewster's Warbler (rare), Cape May Warbler, Hooded Warbler, Bobolink, Orchard Oriole, Rose-breasted Grosbeak, Common Redpoll, White-winged Crossbill, and Lapland Longspur.

Desonier Nature Preserve, Coolville. The preserve is owned and managed by the Ohio Department of Natural Resources. It is located along Jordan Run, 5 miles northwest of Coolville, near the intersection of US 50 and SR 144. Access to the preserve is with permission only; contact the Division of Natural Areas and Preserves, Ohio Department of Natural Resources for a permit.

This 301-acre preserve was established in 1975. It consists primarily of a mixed oak forest. The area is bisected by Jordan Run, a tributary of the Hocking River. Several waterfalls and rock outcroppings occur on the preserve. The area is diverse — the habitats range from abandoned fields to mature forests. Owing to this diversity, a large variety of plant and animal life is supported. This area is particularly good for songbirds.

Dysart Woods, Box 247, Belmont 43718. The preserve is owned by Ohio University. It is located nearly 2 miles west of Centerville in Belmont County. Information about the preserve can be obtained from: Ohio University, Athens 45701. To reach the preserve from St. Clairsville, take US 40 west to SR 149, turn south and continue to Belmont; in Belmont, take SR 147 for about five miles to Dysart Woods Laboratory. Visitors are requested to stay on the trails and to refrain from smoking. Guided tours are offered. Picnicking facilities are located at nearby Barkcamp State Park (east of Belmont).

This 456-acre forest is a national natural landmark. It is characterized by a 50-acre primeval oak forest, cutover forest lands, and mixed hardwoods. The largest tree is a tulip tree standing over 130 feet tall. A variety of ferns and wildflowers cover the forest floor. A small stream runs through the preserve. Among the many birds to be seen here are: Red-tailed Hawk, Screech Owl, Whip-poor-will, Pileated Woodpecker, Red-bellied Woodpecker, Acadian Flycatcher, White-breasted Nuthatch, Carolina Wren, Brown Thrasher, Red-eyed Vireo, Cerulean Warbler, Kentucky Warbler, Yellow-breasted Chat, Orchard Oriole, Summer Tanager, and Indigo Bunting.

Eagle Creek Nature Preserve, Garrettsville. The preserve is owned and managed by the Ohio Department of Natural Resources. It is located 1½ miles northeast of Garrettsville on SR 282. Access to the preserve is with permission only. Contact the preserve manager: Thomas Patrick, 11116 Center Road, Garrettsville 44231 or the Ohio Department of Natural Resources.

The preserve covers over 325 acres and was established in 1974. Eagle Creek Preserve contains the history of a glacial stream cutting through Mississippian rocks forming a south-facing slope that hosts an oak forest and a north-facing slope covered by a beech-maple forest. There is a small meandering floodplain with buttonbush swamp, several small peat bogs, and marshlands. Beaver lodges and ponds are established; fox dens are found on the hillsides. Among the more unusual plants found on the preserve are cotton sedge (common in the Arctic) and round-leaf yellow violets. Among the many species of birds likely to be seen here are: Wood Duck, Red-tailed Hawk, Green Heron, Killdeer, American Woodcock, Barred Owl, Pileated Woodpecker, Rough-winged Swallow, Red-breasted Nuthatch, House Wren, Gray Catbird, Hermit Thrush, Gray-cheeked Thrush, Golden-crowned Kinglet, Red-eyed Vireo, Blue-winged Warbler, Nashville Warbler, Cerulean Warbler, Bay-breasted Warbler, Common Yellowthroat, Cardinal, Indigo Bunting, American Goldfinch, and Rufous-sided Towhee.

Edward S. Thomas Nature Preserve, Columbus. The preserve is located in Sharon Woods Metropolitan Park, between Westerville and Worthington, 1¼ miles north of I-270, a mile west of Cleveland Avenue. It is owned and managed by Columbus and Franklin County Metropolitan Park District. The preserve is part of the Spring Hollow Outdoor Education Center, use of which is restricted to park district workshops and scheduled groups. The use of the trail and boardwalk, leading into the swamp, is restricted to scheduled groups. The park and preserve are open to the public.

The Edward S. Thomas Nature Preserve was established in 1975 and totals nearly 320 acres. It is a flat area containing two tracts of undisturbed woodland.

Of special interest is the spring wildflower display, including hepatica, ginseng, marsh marigold, showy orchids, and trilliums. Resident wildlife includes white-tailed deer, red fox, gray fox, mink, and many species of birds. Look for Great Horned Owl, Pileated Woodpecker, Hermit Thrush, and various species of warblers.

Fowler Woods Nature Preserve, Olivesburg. The preserve is owned and managed by the Ohio Department of Natural Resources. A system of hiking trails and boardwalks and a parking area are available for visitors. The preserve is located about 6 miles northwest of Olivesburg and a mile east of SR 13 on Noble Road, southwest of the intersection of Noble Road and Olivesburg-Fitchville Road.

Fowler Woods Preserve was established in 1973 and now totals 133 acres. It consists primarily of a beech-maple upland forest and a low-lying swamp forest; there are also marshy areas. Wildflowers, including marsh marigolds, and ferns, including the royal fern, abound. Wildlife in the preserve is also abundant. Look for Barred Owls, Wood and Hermit Thrushes, and many species of warblers.

Gahanna Woods Nature Preserve, Gahanna. The preserve is owned by the Ohio Department of Natural Resources and is managed by the City of Gahanna Parks. The preserve is located 2½ miles southeast of Gahanna, about ½ mile south of Havens Corners Road on the west side of Taylor Station Road.

This 50-acre preserve is in the immediate vicinity of Columbus. It was established in 1974. Trails traverse the preserve's gently rolling terrain. There are small, woodland ponds; a buttonbush swamp; upland forests of oak-maple, succeeded by oak-hickory, and finally beech-maple; and old fields. Numerous spring wildflowers can be found in the woods including Canada lily, wild hyacinth, and several species of trillium. Look for Pileated Woodpecker, Great Crested Flycatcher, Black-throated Blue Warbler, Mourning Warbler, and Pine Siskin.

Goll Woods Nature Preserve, Archbold. The preserve is owned and managed by the Ohio Department of Natural Resources. For additional information, contact the preserve manager: Robert Sanford, Route 3, Box 67, Archbold 43502. The preserve is located along the east bank of the Tiffin River, 3 miles northwest of Archbold. To reach the preserve from Archbold, take SR 66 north for 2½ miles, turn left (west) on Twp. Road F, proceed for nearly 3 miles to the third crossroad, turn left (south) on Twp. Road 26 and proceed about ¼ mile to the Goll Woods parking lot, which is on the east side of the road. Trails, including some self-guiding, are maintained.

This 320-acre swamp forest was established as a nature preserve in 1974. It is one of the finest remaining examples of the "black swamp" forest that once covered a vast area southwest of Lake Erie. A rich variety of native shrubs and wildflowers occur in the woods. Woodland ponds provide refuge for many animals. Look for Marsh Hawk, Great Horned Owl, Red-headed Woodpecker, House Wren, Veery, Prothonotary Warbler, Cerulean Warbler, and Henslow's Sparrow among other birds.

Grand Lake St. Marys Wildlife Area. The lake is located in western Ohio, near the town of St. Marys; the wildlife area is managed by the state. The Mercer County Waterfowl Refuge and the State Fish Farm are also located here. The lake is an artificial impoundment created by damming tributary streams of the Wabash and St. Marys rivers. It covers over 13,000 acres. Camping facilities are available at Grand Lake St. Marys State Park. Several highways surround the lake and many gravel roads connect the highways to the lake's shore.

There have been 290 species of birds recorded at Lake St. Marys. Among them are: Horned Grebe, Mute Swan, Snow Goose, Gadwall, Pintail, American Wigeon, Northern Shoveler, Redhead, Ring-necked Duck, Canvasback, Bufflehead, Oldsquaw, White-winged Scoter, Red-breasted Merganser, Sharp-shinned Hawk, Bald Eagle, Black-crowned Night Heron, American Bittern, Sora, American Golden Plover, Ruddy Turnstone, Spotted Sandpiper, Willet (rare), Red Knot, Baird's Sandpiper (rare), Wilson's Phalarope, Bonaparte's Gull, Forster's Tern, Snowy Owl, Long-eared Owl, Short-eared Owl, Downy Woodpecker, Least Flycatcher, Bank Swallow, Red-breasted Nuthatch, Bewick's Wren, Long-billed Marsh Wren, Veery, Eastern Bluebird, Loggerhead Shrike, Philadelphia Vireo (rare), Prothonotary Warbler, Orange-crowned Warbler, Blackpoll Warbler, Mourning Warbler (rare), Rusty Blackbird, Dickcissel, Vesper Sparrow, and Snow Bunting.

Highbanks Nature Preserve, Worthington. The preserve is located in Highbanks Metropolitan Park, west of US 23, 3½ miles north of SR 161 in Worthington, along the east bank of the Olentangy River. The area is owned and maintained by the Columbus and Franklin County Metropolitan Park District. Guided tours are available. Off-trail access is by permit only. For permits or for additional information, contact the Park District.

This 206-acre preserve was established in 1973. It consists of a massive bluff of shale over 100 feet high which overlooks the Olentangy River. An oak-hickory forest dominates the dry ridges; beech forests predominate in the moist ravines; while sycamore, elm, willow, and maple characterize the floodplain along the river. Look for woodpeckers, flycatchers, thrushes, and warblers in this area.

Hueston Woods Nature Preserve, Oxford. The preserve is owned and managed by the Ohio Department of Natural Resources. It is located 5 miles north of Oxford, within Hueston Woods State Park. There is a nature center in the park which offers a variety of educational and interpretive programs. A system of trails is maintained. Camping facilities are available.

This 200-acre preserve was established in 1973. It consists primarily of a beech-maple climax forest. Pawpaw, sassafras and spicebush characterize the understory. Wildflowers, including bloodroot, May apple, large-flowered trillium, and Dutchman's breeches, flourish on the forest floor. The area has been designated as a national natural landmark.

Irwin Prairie Nature Preserve, Berkey. The preserve is owned and maintained by the Ohio Department of Natural Resources. It is located 13 miles west of Toledo at the intersection of Irwin Road and Dorr Street, near Berkey. Access to the preserve is with written permission only. For permits, contact the Ohio Department of Natural Resources, Division of Natural Areas and Preserves.

Irwin Prairie Preserve was established in 1974 and now totals 142 acres. It is considered to be the finest wet prairie in the state and is a vestige of the "black swamp" that once covered this part of the state. Many rare plants grow in the low-lying wetlands; among them are: blazing stars, gentians, cardinal flower, scarlet painted cup, and several species of orchids. The prairie is also the habitat of the rare Spotted Bog Turtle. The area offers an excellent opportunity to study a wide spectrum of birdlife.

Killdeer Plains Wildlife Area, Harpster. The area is owned and managed by the state. It is located 14 miles northwest of Marion, near Marseilles, off SR 67. For further information, contact the Sportsmen's Service Center, Killdeer Plains Wildlife Area, R. R. #1, Box 105, Harpster 43323; (614) 496-2254.

The wildlife area covers 8622 acres and is quite flat. About two-thirds of the area is cropland and meadow, the remaining third is divided almost equally between woods and water areas. These latter areas include more than 800 acres of marsh, a 285-acre reservoir, and 16 ponds. Since hunting and fishing are permitted here, the area (or certain portions of it) may be closed during some seasons. It is advisable to inquire in advance. Public facilities include hiking trails, observation mounds, and a 14-mile self-guided auto tour.

Among the rare and unusual birds that have been seen here are: White Pelican, Mute Swan, Whistling Swan, Fulvous Tree Duck, Peregrine Falcon, Bald Eagle, Golden Eagle, and Sandhill Crane. Other, more common, species include: Canada Goose, Wood Duck, Mallard, Blue-winged Teal, Black Duck, Red-tailed Hawk, American Coot, Black-bellied Plover, American Golden Plover, and Short-eared Owl.

Kiser Lake Wetlands Nature Preserve, St. Paris. The preserve is located 3½ miles north of St. Paris, within Kiser Lake State Park. It is owned and managed by the Ohio Department of Natural Resources. Access to the preserve is with written permission only. Contact the Division of Natural Areas and Preserves, Ohio Department of Natural Resources for permits and additional information.

The preserve covers 50 acres and was established in 1975. It consists of 2 separate areas on the south side of Kiser Lake State Park. The areas are vestiges of an area known as Mosquito Lake Bog. The 2 areas have flora typical of bogs, including such species as shrubby cinquefoil, fringed gentian, swamp loosestrife, and marsh bellflower.

Knox Woods Nature Preserve, Mt. Vernon. The preserve is owned and managed by the Knox County Commissioners. It is located 3 miles northeast of Mt. Vernon on the south side of US 36, east of the former Knox County Children's Home.

The preserve totals nearly 30 acres and was established in 1973. Trails traverse the preserve. This is a hardwood forest, dominated by sugar maple, black oak, red oak, black walnut, and shagbark hickory. The understory is characterized by dogwood, sour gum, and saplings of ash, beech, and maple. Wildflowers flourish at Knox, including bloodroot, hepatica, Jack-in-the-pulpit, and large-flowered trillium.

Little Rocky Hollow, South Bloomingville. The preserve is owned and managed by the Ohio Department of Natural Resources. Access to the preserve is with written permission only. Contact the Ohio Department of Natural Resources, Division of Natural Areas and Preserves for permits. Little Rocky Hollow is the first hollow west of Kreachbaum Road (CR 9), and north of Big Pine Road (CR 11). The preserve is located near Hocking Hills State Park, which is well known as a good birdwatching area.

The chief feature of this 135-acre preserve is its narrow gorge, which terminates forming a large cove with beautiful waterfalls. Glacial relic vegetation of hemlock, yew, and birch is found in the cool, moist canyon and ravines; the ridges and cliff tops are covered with forests of white and black oak, shagbark hickory, and Virginia pine. Trailing arbutus, mountain laurel, and a variety of ferns are common to the area. Among the species of birds likely to be seen here are: Broad-winged Hawk, American Woodcock, Screech Owl, Red-bellied Woodpecker, Acadian Flycatcher, Brown Thrasher, White-eyed Vireo, and many species of warblers. No trails are maintained on the preserve.

Lynx Prairie (The E. Lucy Braun Preserve). The preserve is owned and managed by the Cincinnati Museum of Natural History, 1720 Gilbert Avenue, Cincinnati 45202; (513) 621-3889. Lynx Prairie is located near West Union, near Buzzardroost Rock Preserve. From Lynx, take CR 9 south for ½ mile to the East Liberty Church and cemetery. The entrance to the preserve is just there; look for the national landmark plaque. There are 4 marked trails traversing the preserve.

Lynx Praire consists of 53 acres of open prairie, swamp, upland meadow, mixed woodland, and streams with waterfalls. Among the many species of birds to be found here are: Mallard, Red-tailed Hawk, American Kestrel (Sparrow Hawk), Bobwhite, Barred Owl, Chimney Swift, Hairy Woodpecker, Eastern

Phoebe, Purple Martin, Carolina Chickadee, Carolina Wren, Eastern Bluebird, Red-eyed Vireo, Tennessee Warbler, Blackburnian Warbler, Prairie Warbler, American Goldfinch, and Lark Sparrow.

Magee Marsh Wildlife Area, Oak Harbor. The area is owned and maintained by the state. It abuts Ottawa NWR (see below). To reach the wildlife area from Port Clinton, take SR 2 west for 14 miles to Crane Creek Road, turn north (right) on Crane Creek Road, and continue to the wildlife office and checking station.

Magee Marsh is a 2131-acre area located on the shore of Lake Erie. It consists primarily of marshland with some grassy and wooded areas. A birding trail traverses the woodland. Since controlled waterfowl hunting is permitted at Magee Marsh, certain portions of the area may be closed to visitors during some times of the year. It is advisable to inquire in advance. Among the many species of birds to be seen here are: Double-crested Cormorant, Whistling Swan, Canada Goose, Blue-winged Teal, Green-winged Teal, Pintail, Gadwall, Wood Duck, Canvasback, Redhead, Black Duck, American Wigeon, Great Blue Heron, Black-crowned Night Heron, American Bittern, and various other shorebirds.

Mentor Marsh, 5185 Corduroy Road, Grand River. The preserve is a unit of the Cleveland Museum of Natural History and is owned and maintained by the Museum (10600 East Boulevard, Cleveland 44106). It is located about 30 miles northeast of Cleveland. To reach Mentor Marsh from Cleveland, take SR 22 (Shoreway) to SR 44 north exit (Headlands-Grand River Exit); go north on SR 44 for about ½ mile to Lake Shore Boulevard (SR 283); turn west on Lake Shore Boulevard and go to Corduroy Road (first light); turn right onto Corduroy Road and proceed for ¼ mile to the preserve entrance. Camping is not permitted at Mentor Marsh; however facilities are available at Punderson State Park (about 20 miles to the south). A variety of educational and interpretive programs is offered at Mentor Marsh; a network of trails is maintained.

Mentor Marsh, a national natural landmark, was established as an interpretive nature preserve in 1971. It covers 860 acres consisting of sand dunes, swamp forest, upland forest, open fields, and open marsh. It is located on the shore of Lake Erie, near the mouth of the Grand River. Owing to the variety of habitat, many species of birds can be seen at Mentor Marsh. Among them are: Common Loon, Horned Grebe, Gadwall, Green-winged Teal, Wood Duck, Bufflehead, Ruddy Duck, Hooded Merganser, Cooper's Hawk, Black-crowned Night Heron, American Bittern, Black-bellied Plover, Ruddy Turnstone, Upland Sandpiper (Plover), Pectoral Sandpiper, Baird's Sandpiper, Glaucous Gull, Bonaparte's Gull, Caspian Tern, Black- and Yellow-billed Cuckoos, Barred Owl, Belted Kingfisher, Pileated Woodpecker, Eastern Kingbird, Horned Lark, Purple Martin, Red-breasted Nuthatch, Winter Wren, Hermit Thrush, Cedar Waxwing, Loggerhead Shrike (rare), Philadelphia Vireo, Prothonotary Warbler, Worm-eating Warbler (rare), Blue-winged Warbler, Nashville Warbler, Black-throated

Green Warbler, Bay-breasted Warbler, Louisiana Waterthrush, Wilson's Warbler, Bobolink, Western Meadowlark (rare), Scarlet Tanager, Indigo Bunting, Common Redpoll, Red Crossbill (rare), Grasshopper Sparrow, Lapland Longspur (rare), and Snow Bunting.

Ottawa National Wildlife Refuge, 14000 W. State Route 2, Oak Harbor 43449; (419) 897-0211. The refuge is administered by Shiawassee NWR (in Michigan). Camping is not permitted at the refuge; however, facilities are available at nearby Crane Creek State Park. The refuge is located 15 miles east of Toledo on SR 2.

Ottawa Refuge was established in 1961. It is adjacent to Crane Creek Wildlife Area (a state-administered area, see page 292). Ottawa and its satellite refuges — Darby Marsh, Navarre Marsh, and Cedar Point — all border Lake Erie. West Sister Island (82 acres) is also a satellite refuge. It is located 9 miles offshore and supports an important Black-crowned Night Heron rookery. These refuges, totaling 8000 acres of marshes, meadows, and croplands combine to support a varied and abundant wildlife community. To enhance birdwatching opportunities on the refuge, several foot trails are maintained. Spring and fall migration periods are the best times for birdwatching here. Although managed primarily for waterfowl, there are many species of birds to be seen. There have been 288 species of birds (134 nesting) sighted at Ottawa NWR. Among them are: Eared Grebe (rare), Whistling Swan, Snow (Blue) Goose, Pintail, Northern Shoveler, Wood Duck, Bufflehead, Surf Scoter, Rough-legged Hawk, Bald Eagle, Marsh Hawk, Green Heron, Least Bittern, Glossy Ibis, Virginia Rail, Common Gallinule, Killdeer, Common Snipe, Whimbrel (rare), Greater Yellowlegs, Red Knot, Dunlin, Buff-breasted Sandpiper (rare), Wilson's Phalarope, Glaucous Gull (rare), Iceland Gull (rare), Forster's Tern, Barn Owl, Snowy Owl, Long-eared Owl, Red-headed Woodpecker, Olive-sided Flycatcher, Cliff Swallow, Red-breasted Nuthatch, Winter Wren, Cedar Waxwing, Philadelphia Vireo, Blue-winged Warbler, Magnolia Warbler, Black-throated Blue Warbler, Hooded Warbler (rare), Scarlet Tanager, Common Redpoll, Dark-eyed (Oregon) Junco, and Lapland Longspur. Checklist available.

Shallenberger Natural Preserve, Lancaster. The preserve is owned and maintained by the Ohio Department of Natural Resources. For additional information about the preserve, contact the preserve manager: Ken Temple, 108½ Rosewood, Circleville 43113. The preserve is located 3 miles southwest of Lancaster off US 22, on Beck Knob Road.

Shallenberger Preserve was established in 1973 and totals nearly 90 acres. The main feature of the preserve is Allen Knob, a sandstone promontory. Chestnut oak and mountain laurel cover the knob; a mixed hardwood forest characterizes the lower slopes. The forest floor is rich in wildflowers and ferns. A variety of songbirds common to the region abounds within the preserve.

Sheick Hollow, South Bloomingville. The preserve is owned and managed by the Ohio Department of Natural Resources. Access to the preserve is with written permission only. Permits are available from the Division of Natural Areas and Preserves, Ohio Department of Natural Resources. Sheick Hollow is the second hollow west of Kreachbaum Road (CR 9), east of Hockman Road Twp. Road 238, on the north side of Big Pine Road (CR 11). It is located near Little Rocky Hollow. There are no trails.

This 84-acre preserve consists of a narrow gorge with vertical sandstone cliffs — 100 feet or more in height. Several waterfalls cascade over the vertical walls. Black and white oaks, shagbark hickory, and Virginia pine characterize the ridges and cliff tops, while hemlock, yew, and birch are found in the cool, moist ravines. A wide variety of wildflowers and ferns grow here including trailing arbutus, pink moccasin flower, spinulose wood fern, and common polypody.

Stage's Pond Nature Preserve, Circleville. The preserve is owned and managed by the Ohio Department of Natural Resources. Additional information about the preserve can be obtained from the preserve manager: Ken Temple, 108½ Rosewood, Circleville 43113. Visitors are requested to stay on the trails. The preserve is located 5 miles north of Circleville off US 23, 1¼ miles east on Red Bridge-East Ringold Road, immediately northeast of the intersection with Ward Road.

Stage's Pond Preserve totals 178 acres and was established in 1974. The preserve is a kettle hole lake; about 30 acres at the northern end are all that now remain of the ancient 70-acre lake. Stage's Pond consists of woodlands, open fields, and marshes. It is known as a fine birdwatching area. The pond and marshy areas attract a wide range of migratory waterfowl as well as a summer resident community of Great Blue Herons and other shorebirds. Hawks, Ring-necked Pheasants, and Bobwhites are found in the fields; warblers and thrushes live in the woodlands.

Tinkers Creek Nature Preserve, Aurora. The preserve is located within Tinkers Creek State Park, about 4 miles southwest of the intersection of SR 306 and SR 82. It is owned and maintained by the Ohio Department of Natural Resources. A system of hiking trails traverses the area. A parking lot is located just east of the railroad on the north side of Davis Road. Camping facilities are available at the park.

This 786-acre preserve was established in 1974. The prime feature of the preserve is its extensive marsh, characterized by cattail, willow, buttonbush, and alder. In addition to the marshlands, several spring-fed lakes, bottomland forests, and old fields are to be found. The diversity of habitat supports a diverse wildlife community. Among the many species of birds likely to be seen here are: Wood Duck, Green Heron, Least Bittern, Killdeer, American Woodcock, Screech Owl, Great Crested Flycatcher, Hermit Thrush, and various species of warblers.

Wahkeena Preserve. The preserve is owned and maintained by the Ohio Historical Society, Columbus 43211; (614) 469-2915. The preserve is located south of Columbus. To reach it from Lancaster, take US 33 south for about six miles, turn west (right) on CR 86 and go to Pumping Station Road (CR 274), continue to preserve entrance. Although the preserve is open to the public, advance permission to visit it should be secured. A naturalist is available to lead groups of ten or more providing there have been arrangements made in advance. The preserve is open from April to October, Wednesday through Sunday, 8-5; during winter months, Monday through Friday, 8-5.

The 150-acre preserve consists of mixed woodlands, hemlock groves, old fields, gardens, a cattail swamp, and a pond. A network of paths and trails is maintained. A variety of educational and interpretive programs is offered at Wahkeena. Among the 53 species of breeding birds are: Wood Duck, Broad-winged Hawk, Spotted Sandpiper, Screech Owl, Yellow- and Black-billed Cuckoos, Pileated Woodpecker, Carolina Chickadee, Carolina Wren, Gray Catbird, Wood Thrush, Cedar Waxwing, Black-and-white Warbler, Blue-winged Warbler, Worm-eating Warbler, Kentucky Warbler, Summer Tanager, Rose-breasted Grosbeak, Indigo Bunting, and Rufous-sided Towhee.

Wayne National Forest. There are two district ranger offices; Ironton Ranger District, Ironton 45638 and Athens Ranger District, Athens 45701. The Forest Supervisor's office is at: 1615 J Street, Bedford, Indiana 47421. To reach the Forest, use US 33, US 50, and US 35 and/or SR 75, SR 141, SR 7, and SR 26. Among the public recreational facilities offered are camping, swimming, boating, and hiking.

Wayne National Forest totals 160,000 acres of woodlands, streams, and meadows. The easternmost section of the Forest (in the Athens district) is bordered by the Ohio River. Among the species of birds likely to be seen here are: Common Goldeneye, Broad-winged Hawk, Ruffed Grouse, American Woodcock, Yellow-billed Cuckoo, Screech Owl, Whip-poor-will, Belted Kingfisher, Pileated Woodpecker, Red-bellied Woodpecker, Acadian Fly-catcher, Barn Swallow, Tufted Titmouse, White-breasted Nuthatch, Carolina Wren, Gray Catbird, Brown Thrasher, Wood Thrush, Blue-gray Gnatcatcher, Ruby-crowned Kinglet, Yellow-throated Vireo, Tennessee Warbler, Orange-crowned Warbler, Nashville Warbler, Black-throated Green Warbler, Scarlet Tanager, Indigo Bunting, and Fox Sparrow.

The Wilderness (The Charles A. Eulett Preserve). The preserve is owned and maintained by the Cincinnati Museum of Natural History, 1720 Gilbert Avenue, Cincinnati 45202; (513) 621-3889. The Wilderness is located off SR 125 near the town of Lynx. It is very near Buzzardroost Rock (see page 289). The main entrance to the preserve is off Shivener Road, which turns north from the west end of Lynx. A network of trails traverses the preserve.

The Wilderness is a 567-acre tract of mixed woodlands, abandoned fields, prairie, streams, cliffs, and a gorge. There have been about 130 species of birds recorded at The Wilderness. Among them are: Pied-billed Grebe, Wood Duck, Cooper's Hawk, Marsh Hawk, Sandhill Crane, Killdeer, Screech Owl, Chuck-will's-widow, Pileated Woodpecker, Least Flycatcher, Barn Swallow, Long-billed Marsh Wren, Hermit Thrush, Gray-cheeked Thrush, Eastern Bluebird, Philadelphia Vireo, Worm-eating Warbler, Black-throated Green Warbler, Prairie Warbler, Orchard Oriole, Evening Grosbeak, and Lark Sparrow. The Wilderness is a registered national natural landmark.

In addition, the museum manages two other preserves in the area: *Red Rock* (92 acres of mixed woodlands) and *Abner Hollow* (200 acres of woodlands). These preserves are also located in Adams County. For information about them, contact the museum at the address given above.

NATURE CENTERS

There are many nature centers, arboretums, city parks, and preserves located throughout Ohio. At many of these centers, a variety of educational and interpretive programs is offered. They can all be rewarding birdwatching areas. Brief descriptions of these centers follow. Owing to a lack of space, these are not shown on the map.

Alfred K. Nippert Nature Museum, Sharon Woods, Sharonville. The park and museum are operated by the Hamilton County Park District, 10245 Winton Road, Cincinnati 45231; (513) 521-9866. Sharon Woods is located on US 42, north of Sharonville. It contains 740 acres of mixed woodlands, rolling meadows, streams, waterfalls, and gorges. There are scenic overlooks and trails; guided tours are available. The museum and park are open all year. Look for Pied-billed Grebe, Black Duck, Wood Duck, Carolina Chickadee, Acadian Flycatcher, Cedar Waxwing, Cerulean Warbler, Kentucky Warbler, Canada Warbler, and various species of sparrows.

Avon Woods Outdoor Education Center, 4135 Paddock Road, Cincinnati 45229; (513) 861-3435. The center is operated by the Cincinnati Recreation Commission. It covers 15 acres. Guided tours are available. The center is open all year; closed on weekends.

California Woods Outdoor Education Center, 5400 Kellogg Avenue, Cincinnati 45220; (513) 231-8678. The center is operated by the Cincinnati Recreation Commission and covers 100 acres. Guided tours, only, are offered. The center is open all year; closed on weekends. Look for Goshawk, Worm-eating Warbler, Louisiana Waterthrush, and Scarlet Tanager here.

Camp Tippecanoe, 405 Second Street, NW, Canton 44702; (216) 456-7141. The camp is operated by the Canton District YMCA. It totals 1100 acres and is open all year.

Cleveland Metropolitan Park District, 2000 Standard Building, Cleveland 44113; (216) 621-1054. The district operates 3 areas totaling 18,000 acres: (1) Brecksville Trailside Interpretive Center; (2) North Chagrin Trailside Interpretive Center; and (3) Rocky River Trailside Interpretive Center. Guided and self-guiding tours are available. The centers are open all year. At *Brecksville,* look for Great Crested Flycatcher, Yellow-throated Vireo, Cerulean Warbler, and Rose-breasted Grosbeak, among other species; at *North Chagrin* look for Wood Duck, Pileated Woodpecker, Wood Thrush, Red-eyed Vireo, Hooded Warbler, and Rose-breasted Grosbeak; at *Rocky River,* look for Broad-winged Hawk, Green Heron, Killdeer, Belted Kingfisher, Barred Owl, Carolina Wren, Brown Creeper, Indigo Bunting, and various species of ducks.

Cleveland Museum of Natural History, Wade Oval, University Circle, Cleveland 44106; (216) 231-4600. The museum operates Mentor Marsh, see page 299.

Columbus Metropolitan Park District, 999 Park Road, P.O. Box 72, Westerville 43081; (614) 891-0700. The district operates 4 areas: (1) *Blacklick Woods Nature Center* — trailside museum, trail for the handicapped; look for Pileated Woodpecker, Brown Creeper, Mourning Warbler, and Pine Siskin here (see also page 289); (2) *Sharon Woods Reservation* — Spring Hollow Outdoor Education Center, nature preserve and outdoor laboratory; (3) *Darby Creek Reservation;* and (4) *Walden Wildlife Refuge.*

Community Camps, Inc., 4965 North High Street, Columbus 43214; (614) 846-6600. The 1500-acre center is operated by Community Camp of Columbus and Franklin County, Inc. Guided and self-guiding tours are offered; the center is open March through November.

Davis Nature Preserve, Peebles. The preserve is owned and maintained by the Ohio Historical Society, Interstate 71 and 17 Avenue, Columbus 43211. It is located 3½ miles southeast of Peebles near SR 41. The preserve consists of mixed woodlands and open meadows. A system of trails is maintained. The preserve is open all year.

The Dawes Arboretum, Route 5, Newark 43055; (614) 345-2355. The arboretum is privately owned. It covers 325 acres and is open all year. Guided and self-guiding tours are available. The arboretum is well known as a fine birdwatching location.

F. A. Seiberling Nature Center, Sand Run Metropolitan Park, 1828 Smith Road, Akron. Mailing address: 975 Treatyline Road, Akron 44313; (216) 733-4900. The center is operated by Akron Metropolitan Park District. It covers 100 acres in a 1039-acre park. Guided tours are offered; trails, some self-guiding, are maintained. The center is open all year, closed on holidays.

Ford Nature Education Center, Old Furnace Road, 816 Glenwood Avenue, Youngstown 44502; (216) 743-5868. The center is located in Mill

Creek Park and is operated by the Youngstown Township Park District. The center totals 6 acres in a 2389-acre park. Guided tours are available. Trails, some self-guiding are maintained. The center is open all year, closed on Mondays. Look for American Woodcock, Pileated Woodpecker, Scarlet Tanager, and migrating landbirds.

George P. Crosby Park Gardens, 5403 Elmer Drive, Toledo 43624; (419) 536-1031. The gardens are operated by the city. They cover 50 acres and are open all year. Guided and self-guiding tours are available.

Glen Helen Nature Reserve, Antioch College, Yellow Springs, 45387; (513) 767-7331. The reserve is operated by Antioch College. It covers 930 acres and is open all year. Guided and self-guiding tours are available.

Glen Helen Outdoor Education Center, Antioch College; (513) 767-7648. The center is operated by Antioch College and is located on the grounds of the Glen Helen Reserve. It is open all year, closed on holidays and during August.

The Holden Arboretum, Sperry Road, Mentor 44060; (216) 946-4400. The arboretum covers 2400 acres. It includes ponds, woodlands, lawns, and wildflower gardens. There is an observation center; trails are maintained. Guided and self-guiding tours are offered. Look for Whistling Swan, Black Duck, Bald Eagle, Osprey (rare), Cedar Waxwing, Pine Grosbeak, and various species of warblers.

Hueston Woods Nature Center, Hueston Woods State Park, Route 1, College Corner 45003; (513) 523-6347 (see page 296). The center is operated by the Ohio Department of Natural Resources. Guided and self-guiding tours are available. The center is open all year, closed in December. Look for passerines, especially warblers.

Independence School and Community Land Laboratory, 7733 Stone Road, Independence 44131; (216) 524-4124. The laboratory covers 35 acres.

Laboiteaux Woods Outdoor Education Center, 5400 Lanius Lane, Cincinnati 45224; (513) 542-2909. The center is operated by the Cincinnati Recreation Commission. It covers 60 acres; is open all year and closed on weekends. Guided tours only are offered.

Lake Erie Junior Nature and Science Center, 28728 Wolf Road, Bay Village 44140; (216) 871-2600. The center covers 825 acres. Guided and self-guiding tours are available. Of special interest is the planetarium. The center is open all year; closed on Sundays, holidays, and weekdays in August.

Lake Hope State Park Nature Center, Zaleski 45698; (614) 596-4300. The center is operated by the Ohio Department of Natural Resources. The park covers 3103 acres. Guided and self-guiding tours are available; the center is open all year.

Mohican State Park, Box 211 A, Route 2, Loundonville 44842; (419) 994-4290. The center is operated by the Ohio Department of Natural Resources. The park covers 1294 acres. Guided and self-guiding tours are available. The park is open all year.

Rouff Family Farm, 9579 Brehm Road, Cincinnati 45247; (513) 385-6295. The farm is open by appointment only; call between 8 and 10 in the morning. Guided tours are given through this 73-acre farm, which is open every day from March through November.

Shaker Lakes Regional Nature Center, 2600 South Park Boulevard, Shaker Heights 44120; (216) 321-5935. The center totals 300 acres. Guided and self-guiding tours are offered. The center is open all year, closed 15 August to Labor Day. Look for Pied-billed Grebe, Common Redpoll, herons, ducks, and migrating songbirds, especially warblers in May.

Stark Wilderness Center, Box 38, Wilmot 44689; (216) 359-5117. The center covers 409 acres. Guided and self-guiding tours are offered. The center is open all year.

Swinging Bridge Nature Preserve, Bluffton College, Bluffton 45817; (219) 358-1186. The preserve is operated by the college. It covers 100 acres and is open all year. Guided and self-guiding tours are offered.

Toledo Metropolitan Park District, 911 Madison Avenue, Toledo 43624; (419) 255-1400. The district operates 3 areas: (1) *Oak Openings Metropark* — 3300 acres; swamp woodlands, bogs, wet and dry prairies, oak forests; look for Great Crested Flycatcher, Blue-gray Gnatcatcher, Veery, Golden-winged Warbler, Scarlet Tanager, and Lark Sparrow; (2) *Secor Metropark Nature Center,* Route 1, Berkey 43504; (419) 882-1010 — 500 acres, 250-acre arboretum, guided and self-guided tours, open all year; and (3) *Swan Creek Metropark,* Glendale Center, 4102 Glendale Avenue, Toledo 43614; (419) 385-6736 — 412 acres; open all year, guided and self-guiding tours.

Trailside Nature Center, Burnet Woods Park, P. O. Box 27, Cincinnati 45220; (513) 281-0190. The center is operated by the Cincinnati Park Board. It is located off Clifton Avenue. The center makes use of 3783 acres of various park lands. Guided tours are offered. Trails are maintained. The center is open all year. Look for warbler waves during spring migration.

Warder-Perkins Audubon Sanctuary, 8575 Bridgetown Road, Cincinnati. The sanctuary is owned and operated by the Audubon Society of Ohio. It covers 26 acres and is open by appointment. Contact: Robert Borosch, 5393 Karen Avenue, Cincinnati 45211; (513) 574-3698 for information on visiting the sanctuary. Warder-Perkins is a hilly woodland divided into 2 parts by a grassy strip. The best time for birding here is during spring and fall migration.

West Branch State Park, Route 5, 5708 Esworthy Road, Ravenna 44244; (216) 296-3239. The nature center is operated by the Ohio Department of Natural Resources. The park totals 8456 acres. Guided tours are offered. Trails, some self-guiding, are maintained. The park and center are open all year.

STATE PARKS AND FORESTS

The Ohio Department of Natural Resources maintains numerous parks and forests that are located throughout the state. Most of these offer camping in addition to many other recreational facilities such as swimming, boating, hiking, and nature study. While not intended primarily as bird sanctuaries, some of these parks and forests are known as good birdwatching areas. These are marked with an asterisk (*). For additional information about parks and forests in Ohio, contact: Department of Natural Resources, Division of Parks and Recreation, Fountain Square, Columbus 4324.

STATE PARKS

Adams Lake, West Union 45693; 94 acres; day use only.
Alum Creek, Delaware 43015; 8600 acres; day use only.
A. W. Marion, Circleville 43113; 412 acres.
Barkcamp, Belmont 43718; 1121 acres.
*Beaver Creek, Lisbon 44432; 2450 acres; Little Beaver Creek, a part of the National Wild and Scenic River system, runs through the park.
Blue Rock, Duncan Falls 43734; 337 acres.
Buck Creek, Springfield 45500; 3778 acres; day use only.
*Buckeye Lake, Hebron 43025; 3310 acres; day use only.
Burr Oak, Glouster 45732; (614) 767-2112; 3256 acres.
*Catawba Island, Port Clinton 43452; 9 acres; day use only; access by boat only.
Cowan Lake, Wilmington 45177; (513) 289-2105; 1775 acres.
*Crane Creek, Port Clinton 43452; 72 acres.
Deer Creek, Mt. Sterling 43143; (614) 869-3124; 7007 acres.
Delaware, Delaware 43015; 7411 acres.
Dillon, Nashport 43830; (614) 453-4377; 7548 acres.
East Fork, Batavia 45103; under development.
*East Harbor, Port Clinton 43452; 1829 acres.
Findley, Wellington 44090; 931 acres.
Forked Run, Reedsville 45772; 817 acres.
Geneva, Geneva 44043; (216) 466-8400; 695 acres.
*Grand Lake St. Marys, St. Marys 45885; 13,851 acres.
*Guilford Lake, Lisbon 44432; 489 acres.
Harrison, Fayette 43521; 247 acres.
*Headlands Beach, Mentor 44040; 120 acres; day use only.

*Hocking Hills, Logan 43138; (614) 385-6841; 1943 acres.

*Hueston Woods, College Corner 45003; 3584 acres.

*Independence Dam, Defiance 43512; 622 acres.

Indian Lake, Bellefontaine 43311; 6448 acres.

Jefferson Lake, Richmond 43944; 933 acres.

*John Bryan, Yellow Springs 45387; 881 acres; Little Miami River, a national scenic and wild river, flows through the park.

*Kelleys Island, Port Clinton 43452; 659 acres; access by boat only.

Kiser Lake, Quincey 43343; 864 acres.

Lake Alma, Wellston 45692; 231 acres; day use only.

Lake Hope, Zaleski 45698; (614) 596-5253; 3103 acres.

Lake Logan, Logan 43138; 717 acres; day use only.

Lake Loramie, Minster 45865; 2005 acres.

*Lake White, Waverly 45690; 328 acres.

Madison Lake, London 43140; 183 acres; day use only.

Malabar Farm, Mansfield 44900; 661 acres; guided tours only; home of Aldo Leopold.

Mary Jane Thruston, Grand Rapids 43522; 105 acres.

*Mohican, Loudonville 44842; 2669 acres.

*Mosquito Creek, Warren 44481; 11,843 acres.

Mount Gilead, Mount Gilead 43338; 172 acres.

Muskingum River. The 120-acre park runs from Marietta to Zanesville. There are several camping and boating areas along the river.

Nelson-Kennedy Ledges, Garrettsville 44231; 167 acres; day use only.

Paint Creek, Hillsboro 45133; 10,200 acres.

*Pike Lake, Bainbridge 45612; (614) 493-4201; 600 acres.

Portage Lakes, Akron 44300; 2441 acres; day use only.

Punderson, Middlefield 44062; 890 acres.

*Pymatuning, Andover 44003; (216) 293-6329; 8500 acres.

Rocky Fork, Hillsboro 45133; 3464 acres.

Salt Fork, Cambridge 43725; 20,143 acres.

Scioto Trail, Chillicothe 45601; 248 acres.

*Shawnee, Portsmouth 45662; 1165 acres.

*South Bass Island, Port Clinton 43452; 35 acres; access by boat only.

Stonelick, Edenton 45117; 1210 acres.

Strouds Run, Athens 45701; 2602 acres.

Tar Hollow, Laurelville 43135; (614) 887-4818; 540 acres.

Tinkers Creek, Twinsburg 44087; 1143 acres; day use only.

Van Buren, Van Buren 45889; 296 acres.

West Branch, Ravenna 44266; 8002 acres.

Wolf Run, Belle Valley 43717; 1266 acres.

STATE FORESTS

Blue Rock, Blue Rock 43720; 4573 acres; day use only.
Brush Creek, Peebles 45660; 11,760 acres; day use only.
Chapin, Willoughby 44094; 362 acres; day use only.
Dean, Pedro 45659; 1798 acres; day use only.
Fernwood, Bloomingdale 43910; 2107 acres.
Gifford, Chesterhill 43728; 320 acres.
*Hocking, Rockbridge 43149; 8854 acres.
*Maumee, Swanton 43558; 3068 acres.
*Mohican-Memorial, Perrysville 44864; 4091 acres.
*Pike, Latham 45646; 10,586 acres.
Richland Furnace, Byer; 2343 acres.
Scioto Trail, Chillicothe 45601; 9151 acres.
Shade River, Reedsville 45772; 2409 acres.
*Shawnee, Friendship 45630; 58,788 acres.
Sunfish Creek, Clarington 43915; 638 acres.
Tar Hollow, Londonderry 45647; 16,126 acres.
Yellow Creek, Wellsville 43968; 756 acres.
Zaleski, Zaleski 45698; 25,937 acres.

In addition, there are 2 "reclamation areas": *Harrison* in Bloomingdale (1344 acres) and *Perry* in New Lexington (4400 acres). Camping facilities are available at Harrison.

Canada Geese

WISCONSIN

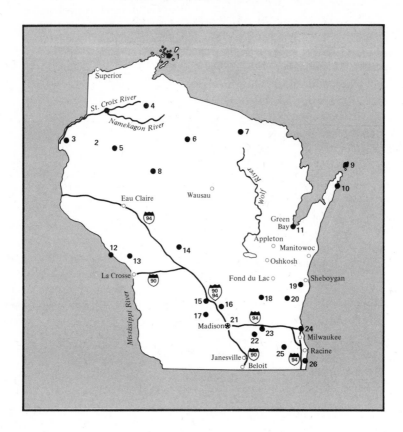

1. Apostle Islands National Lakeshore
2. St. Croix National Scenic Riverway
3. Crex Meadows Wildlife Area
4. Chequamagon National Forest
5. Hunt Hill Sanctuary
6. Chequamagon National Forest
7. Nicolet National Forest
8. Chequamagon National Forest
9. Gravel Island NWR/Green Bay NWR
10. Ridges Sanctuary
11. Green Bay Wildlife Sanctuary
12. Upper Mississippi River Wild Life and
    Fish Refuge
13. Trempealeau NWR
14. Necedah NWR
15. Camp Upham Woods
16. MacKenzie Environmental Center
17. Devil's Lake State Park NC
18. Horicon NWR/Four Mile Island Rookery
19. Sheboygan County Arboretum
20. Riveredge NC
21. Audubon Wildlife Refuge
    Cherokee Marsh
    Jackson School Forest
    Madison Arboretum
22. Palmyra Camp
23. Oak Ridge Demonstration Farm
24. ⎰ Boerner Botanical Gardens
    ⎪ Hawthorne Glen Outdoor Education
    ⎪   Center
    ⎨ Milwaukee Arboretum
    ⎪ Mitchell Park Conservatory
    ⎪ Schlitz Audubon Center
    ⎩ Todd Wehr NC
25. Howard Greene Scientific Preserve
26. Hawthorne Hollow Arboretum & Wildlife
    Sanctuary
    Kenosha Botanical Gardens

Owing to its relationship to large bodies of water, Wisconsin is very attractive to waterfowl. Canada Geese gather by the hundreds of thousands at Horicon Marsh each year; Whistling Swans collect in vast numbers on Lake Winnebago; ducks congregate along Lake Michigan. Lakes Superior and Michigan combine to give the state a 500-mile shoreline. In addition, there are about 8000 lakes; hundreds of marshes; several large rivers — the Mississippi, the Wisconsin, and the St. Croix — and countless smaller ones. The northern part of the state is heavily wooded, mostly aspen and birch mixed with conifers. Wisconsin lies along the Mississippi Flyway and has 2 prominent migration routes: the Lake Michigan shore and the Mississippi and Wisconsin Rivers. About 300 species of birds occur regularly in Wisconsin.

Of special interest in Wisconsin is the Ice Age National Scientific Reserve. This reserve consists of nine separate units across the state from Lake Michigan to the St. Croix River. Each unit possesses features that are significant in the story of Wisconsin glaciation. Four of these units are situated in state parks or forests. Glacial formations and topography — such as kames, eskers, and kettles — can be seen at these units. The Wisconsinian glacial stage, named for its most southerly advance, covered much of the northern United States from the Atlantic Coast to the Rocky Mountains as recently as 12,000 years ago. Nowhere is the evidence of the glaciers better preserved than across Wisconsin. The reserve is a division of the National Park Service, but is administered by the state. For additional information regarding Ice Age NSR, contact: State Bureau of Parks, Pyare Square Building, 4610 University Avenue, Box 450, Madison 53701.

The Department of Natural Resources maintains several thousand acres of preserves as scientific areas. There are 124 of these preserves located throughout the state. Many of these have been acquired with the assistance of The Nature Conservancy. Several adjoin other preserves, sanctuaries, or refuges. Among the most noteworthy are *Four Mile Island Rookery*, at Horicon Marsh (see page 313); *The Ridges Sanctuary*, near Sturgeon Bay (see pages 316 and 325); *Crex Meadows Wildlife Area*, along the St. Croix River (see page 317); and *Cedarburg Bog*, which adjoins the Milwaukee Arboretum (see page 315). Cedarburg Bog totals over 1000 acres of open water, floating mat, shrubs and thickets, tamarack-white cedar forests, and lowland elm-maple-ash woods. It is very wet which makes hiking difficult. There have been about 200 species of birds seen at Cedarburg Bog, including waterfowl, shorebirds, woodpeckers, thrushes, warblers, finches, buntings, and sparrows. The Department of Natural Resources also maintains several thousand acres of state game lands. Many of these wildlife areas are rewarding birdwatching places. Information about wildlife management areas and scientific areas can be obtained from the Department of Natural Resources, Box 450, Madison 53701.

The Wisconsin Society for Ornithology has published *Wisconsin's Favorite Bird Haunts*. This helpful book is available from: WSO Supply Department, Harold Kruse, Hickory Hill Farm, Loganville 53943.

Apostle Islands National Lakeshore, 1972 Centennial Drive, Rural Route, Bayfield 54814. The islands are located in Lake Superior, 10 miles off the coast near Bayfield. Access is by boat only. Transportation is available through the park concessioner, Apostle Islands Outfitters, Inc.; the Apostle Islands Cruise Service; and other charter companies. Some of the islands are privately owned; visitors are requested to respect the rights of the owners. Check at headquarters for information about which areas are open to the public. Primitive camping sites are available. A variety of interpretive programs is offered by the park service. During the summer, a daily excursion is run out of Bayfield; this is a 5-hour boat trip. Hikers and campers are warned of deer flies during July and August — wear long pants and long-sleeved shirts.

Eventually, 20 of the 22 islands in the archipelago plus 10 miles of mainland shoreline will be included in the park. The islands range in size from 3-acre Gull Island to 10,000-acre Stockton Island. They are mostly heavily wooded; some have rocky cliffs plunging to the lake. The woodlands are mostly maple, birch, and aspen with occasional pine groves. The secluded, boggy lakes are surrounded by stands of spruce. Owing to the wilderness nature of the islands and the varied habitat — hills, valleys, shoreline, and diverse plant life — a wide variety of birds can be seen on the islands. Summer birds include: Common Loon, Gadwall, Blue- and Green-winged Teals, Wood Duck, Red-breasted Merganser, Goshawk, Sharp-shinned Hawk, Bald Eagle, Osprey, Great Blue Heron, Sandhill Crane, Killdeer, Common Snipe, Ring-billed Gull, Black-billed Cuckoo, Long-eared Owl, Saw-whet Owl, Belted Kingfisher, Yellow-bellied Sapsucker, Black-backed Three-toed Woodpecker, Yellow-bellied Flycatcher, Cliff Swallow, Common Raven, Red- and White-breasted Nuthatches, Short-billed Marsh Wren, Gray-cheeked Thrush, Cedar Waxwing, Red-eyed Vireo, Golden-winged Warbler, Palm Warbler, Black-throated Blue Warbler, Chestnut-sided Warbler, Black-throated Green Warbler, Common Yellowthroat, Mourning Warbler, Scarlet Tanager, Rose-breasted Grosbeak, and Tree Sparrow.

Chequamegon National Forest, Park Falls 54552. Chequamegon encompasses 837,000 acres in northern Wisconsin. There are several districts, the largest is located near Ashland; from Ashland, take US 2, US 63, SR 13, and/or SR 77 to the Forest; from Park Falls, use SR 70 or SR 182. Much of the area around Chequamegon is state forest land. The Namekagon Scenic River flows through part of the Forest (see St. Croix National Scenic River, page 316). Chequamegon is located near the Chippewa Moraine Unit of the Ice Age National Scientific Reserve. As in most national forests, camping and picnicking facilities are available. There is also a winter sports area located near Washburn.

Attractions include hundreds of large and small lakes; pine, spruce, and balsam forests; and extensive jack pine plantations. Miles of logging trails provide birdwatching opportunities. The vegetation is varied — from swamps to climax forests. The numerous plant communities provide habitat for a wide variety of birdlife. Two good birding spots are the areas around Clam Lake and Teal Lake. At least 218 species of birds (118 nesting) use the Forest each year. Among these are: Common Loon, Eared Grebe (rare), Snow (Blue) Goose, Northern Shoveler, Wood Duck, Redhead, Lesser and Greater Scaups, Oldsquaw, Hooded Merganser, Goshawk, Marsh Hawk, Bald Eagle, Peregrine Falcon (rare), Sharp-tailed Grouse, Green Heron, Sandhill Crane (rare), Yellow Rail, Upland Sandpiper (Plover), Black Tern, Snowy Owl, Hawk Owl, Long- and Short-eared Owls, Boreal Owl, Great Gray Owl, Pileated Woodpecker, Black-backed Three-toed Woodpecker, Purple Martin, Gray Jay, Common Raven, Boreal Chickadee, Long- and Short-billed Marsh Wrens, Northern Shrike, Loggerhead Shrike, Philadelphia Vireo, Golden-winged Warbler, Northern Parula, Cerulean Warbler (rare), Mourning Warbler, Bobolink, Yellow-headed Blackbird (rare), Common Redpoll, Le Conte's Sparrow, and Snow Bunting. Checklist available.

Gravel Island National Wildlife Refuge and Green Bay National Wildlife Refuge. Both refuges are administered by Horicon NWR. These refuges are composed of islands in Lake Michigan. Gravel Island comprises 2 islands totaling 27 acres; Green Bay Island totals 2 acres. They were established as refuges in 1913 and 1912, respectively, and are nesting areas for herons, gulls, terns, and other waterfowl. Access is by boat only. Arrangements to visit the islands must be made in advance; permission can be obtained from the refuge manager at Horicon.

The islands are a mile offshore. They are geologically similar, varying chiefly in size and elevation. Gravel Island is treeless; while Spider Island has dogwood, wild currant, raspberry brush, and remnants of white birch, white cedar, and white spruce. The historical success of the ground-nesting birds on these islands may be largely due to the solid limestone base, which, because of the lack of burrowing opportunities, discourages use by mammalian predators.

Horicon National Wildlife Refuge, Route 2, Mayville 53050; (414) 387-2658. To reach the refuge, take SR 49 east from Waupun for 6½ miles; then take CR Z south for 4 miles. Horicon Refuge is located near several state forests and parks where camping facilities are available. Also located nearby is the Ice Age National Scientific Reserve. Adjacent to the refuge is the Horicon Marsh Wildlife Area which is state-owned. The roads around the refuge are open all year; some of the interior roads are closed during hunting season or in inclement weather.

Horicon Refuge was established in 1941 primarily as a migration stopover point for Canada Geese. Peak concentrations in the fall reach as many as 200,000 geese. Management programs on the refuge include wetland restoration, water level controls, and farming to provide supplemental waterfowl food. Horicon is characterized by cattail marshes, open shallow water, and brushy marsh borders. In the center of the marsh (the state-owned section) is a rookery known as Four Mile Island. Abundant summer birds to be seen are ducks, egrets, herons, and gallinules. Deer, fox, opossum, and raccoon also benefit from the management of the refuge. There have been 197 species of birds (plus 42 accidentals) observed at Horicon. Among these are: Double-crested Cormorant, Whistling Swan, American Wigeon, Northern Shoveler, Wood Duck, Canvasback, Bufflehead, Common Goldeneye, Sharp-shinned Hawk, Golden Eagle, Bald Eagle, Gray Partridge, Ring-necked Pheasant, Green Heron, Black-crowned Night Heron, Sandhill Crane, King Rail, American Golden Plover, Upland Sandpiper (Plover), Wilson's Phalarope, Short-eared Owl, Common Nighthawk, Yellow-bellied Sapsucker, Eastern Wood Pewee, Rough-winged Swallow, Brown Creeper, Long- and Short-billed Marsh Wrens, Philadelphia Vireo, Golden- and Blue-winged Warblers, Cape May Warbler, Bay-breasted Warbler, Mourning Warbler, Wilson's Warbler, Bobolink, Brewer's Blackbird, Cardinal, Rose-breasted Grosbeak, Common Redpoll, Henslow's Sparrow, Lark Sparrow, Harris' Sparrow, Lapland Longspur, and Snow Bunting. Checklist available.

Howard T. Greene Scientific Preserve, Genesee. The preserve is owned and maintained by Carroll College, Waukesha 53186; (414) 547-1211. Permission to visit the preserve must be obtained from the college's biology department; contact John Batha, preserve director, for permits. The preserve is located near the junction of SR 83 and SR 59, outside of the town of Genesee. It covers 39 acres and consists of wetlands, a trout stream, fen, marsh, and a prairie restoration. Among the many birds sighted here are: Blue-winged Teal, Mallard, Wood Duck, Great Blue Heron, Green Heron, Black-crowned Night Heron, Sora, Virginia Rail, Belted Kingfisher, Blue Jay, Red-winged Blackbird, and White-throated Sparrow. Warblers and other migratory songbirds are also seen here.

Hunt Hill Sanctuary, Sarona 54870; (715) 635-3379. The sanctuary is owned by the National Audubon Society. A full-time naturalist is on duty. Visits to the sanctuary must be arranged in advance. This 342-acre preserve in northwestern Wisconsin is the site of the Audubon Workshop of Wisconsin — adult courses in ecology are offered during the summer. The workshop is located on the south shore of Devil's Lake, 4 miles east of Sarona off Highway D, which is between Spooner and Rice Lake on US 53. The area is typical of the northern transition zone; there are lakes, bogs, open meadows, and mixed forests. Among the many species of birds to be found here are: Common Loon, Osprey, American Bittern, Sora, Red-headed Woodpecker, Cliff Swallow, Cerulean Warbler, and Bobolink.

Nearby is *Dory's Bog Sanctuary,* which is also owned by National Audubon. It is patrolled by the Hunt Hill warden. This 40-acre preserve is a sphagnum bog. Arrangements to visit it must be made in advance. Dory's Bog is occasionally used for field trips by the Audubon Workshop.

Milwaukee Arboretum, University of Wisconsin at Milwaukee Field Station, 3095 Blue Goose Road, Saukville 53080; (414) 675-6844. The arboretum is owned and operated by the university. Permission to visit must be obtained in advance. To reach the arboretum from Milwaukee, take US 141 north to SR 33, turn left and go west about 5 miles to Blue Goose Road, turn left again and go about 2 miles further to the field station. Adjacent to the field station is the state-owned *Cedarburg Bog,* which is open to the public for birdwatching.

The field station totals 225 acres and consists of mixed woodlands; open fields; and plantings of trees, shrubs, and herbaceous plants used for scientific study. Among the many birds seen here are: Common Loon, Horned Grebe, Snow Goose, Pintail, Green- and Blue-winged Teals, Wood Duck, Redhead, Canvasback, Bufflehead, Ruddy Duck, Goshawk, Cooper's Hawk, Sharp-shinned Hawk, Osprey, Black-crowned Night Heron, Least Bittern, Sora, Common Gallinule, Common Snipe, Forster's Tern, Snowy Owl, Short-eared Owl, Red-bellied Woodpecker, Eastern Wood Pewee, Barn Swallow, Long-billed Marsh Wren, Brown Creeper, Swainson's Thrush, Golden-crowned Kinglet, Warbling Vireo, Philadelphia Vireo, Tennessee Warbler, Blue-winged Warbler, Black-throated Green Warbler, Mourning Warbler, Wilson's Warbler, Red Crossbill, Evening Grosbeak, and Henslow's Sparrow.

Necedah National Wildlife Refuge, Star Route, Necedah 54646; (608) 565-2551. The refuge is located 6 miles from the town of Necedah. To reach the refuge, take SR 21 west for 4 miles, then turn north on Entrance Road. Necedah maintains a nature trail with an observation tower, a self-guiding automobile trail, and a visitors' center. In addition, there are town roads that border and traverse the refuge. Birdwatching is permitted on the interior of the refuge during July, from 1 December to 15 March, and during fishing and hunting seasons; from the town roads, it is encouraged all year round. Camping is not permitted at the refuge; a state campground is adjoining.

Necedah was established in 1939 as a refuge for waterfowl. The 39,500-acre refuge is characterized by many marshes and ponds separated by sandy ridges and islands. The forested areas consist mainly of jack pine, aspen, oak, red pine, and white pine. There is also a 6000-acre prairie that is maintained by controlled burning. Another of the management programs is providing supplemental food for migratory birds. The diversified habitat provides food and shelter for many forms of animal life; red fox, coyote, badger, raccoon, skunk, muskrat, mink, otter, and beaver are residents here. Necedah is on the Mississippi Flyway, making spring and fall migration periods the most spectacular for birdwatching. There have been 227 species of birds sighted at Necedah. Among these are: Pied-billed Grebe, Snow Goose, Blue- and Green-winged Teals, Ruddy Duck, Bufflehead, Hooded Merganser, Goshawk, Sharp-shinned Hawk, Bald Eagle, Golden Eagle, Sharp-tailed Grouse (rare), Ruffed Grouse, Great Blue Heron, Sandhill Crane, Sora, American Woodcock, Pectoral Sandpiper, Baird's

Sandpiper (rare), Wilson's Phalarope, Black Tern, Snowy Owl, Saw-whet Owl, Red-headed Woodpecker, Purple Martin, Common Raven, Winter Wren, Gray Catbird, Northern Shrike, Golden-winged Warbler, Nashville Warbler, Chestnut-sided Warbler, Mourning Warbler, Wilson's Warbler, Bobolink, Yellow-headed Blackbird (rare), Brewer's Blackbird, Scarlet Tanager, Common Redpoll, Henslow's Sparrow, and Snow Bunting. Checklist available.

Nicolet National Forest, Rhinelander 54501. The Forest is located east of Rhinelander; use US 8/47, SR 17, SR 70, and/or SR 139. Nicolet borders on Ottawa National Forest (Michigan, see page 274). Camping facilities are available.

Attractions in the 650,000-acre Forest include trout streams and scenic rivers; pine, hardwood, and cedar-spruce forests; interpretive trails; whitewater canoeing on the many rivers; and birdwatching. The entire Forest is managed for wildlife habitat. Among the many birds that can be seen here are: Common Loon, Whistling Swan, Canvasback, White-winged Scoter, Hooded Merganser, Goshawk, Osprey, Sharp-tailed Grouse, American Bittern, Sora, Spotted Sandpiper, Black Tern, Short- and Long-eared Owls, Black-backed Three-toed Woodpecker, Yellow-bellied Flycatcher, Bank Swallow, Gray Jay, Common Raven, Boreal Chickadee, Winter Wren, Eastern Bluebird, Northern Shrike, Blackburnian Warbler, Connecticut Warbler, Eastern and Western Meadow-larks, Rusty Blackbird, Evening Grosbeak, Common Redpoll, Harris' Sparrow, and Snow Bunting.

Ridges Sanctuary, Box 152, Baileys Harbor 54202. Ridges is located about 20 miles north of Sturgeon Bay, adjacent to SR 57. It is owned by The Ridges Sanctuary, Inc. The sanctuary is open to the public year round. An educational program is offered during the summer. The nature center at Ridges is open from 15 May to 15 October.

Ridges Sanctuary totals 10 acres. Among the many birds seen here are: Sharp-shinned Hawk, Ruffed Grouse, Green Heron, American Bittern, Caspian Tern, Pileated Woodpecker, Olive-sided Flycatcher, Wood Thrush, Veery, Chestnut-sided Warbler, Black-throated Green Warbler, Ovenbird, American Redstart, Rose-breasted Grosbeak, Purple Finch, and Chipping Sparrow. Many of the above birds nest at the Sanctuary.

St. Croix National Scenic Riverway, P. O. Box 579, St. Croix Falls 54024. Park headquarters are located just outside of the town of St. Croix Falls, on the Minnesota border. The river runs from there, along the border to Danbury, where it turns and continues north through Wisconsin until it reaches Gordon Dam. The 102-mile St. Croix River is met at Riverside by the 101-mile Namekagon River. A variety of canoe trips along the rivers is possible. Camping is permitted at specific sites. Much of the land along the rivers has not yet been acquired and remains in private ownership. Visitors are requested to respect the rights of private owners.

The mixed hardwood-conifer forest adjacent to the riverway supports an abundance of wildlife. Most common mammals include white-tailed deer, black bear, red fox, gray fox, and coyote. Beaver, muskrat, mink, and otter are also present. The many swamp and marsh areas, small lakes and ponds, and small islands provide food and shelter for a wide variety of birds. Nearly 100 species have been observed along the riverway. Among the birds most likely to be seen (excluding winter birds) are: Horned Grebe, Snow (Blue) Goose, Ruddy Duck, Bufflehead, Osprey, Bald Eagle, Cooper's Hawk, Sharp-tailed Grouse, Green Heron, Sandhill Crane, Virginia Rail, Black Tern, Short-eared Owl, Whip-poor-will, Pileated Woodpecker, Cliff Swallow, House Wren, Gray Catbird, Wood Thrush, Cedar Waxwing, Black-and-white Warbler, Nashville Warbler, Northern (Baltimore) Oriole, Scarlet Tanager, Rose-breasted Grosbeak, Indigo Bunting, and Sharp-tailed Sparrow. Winter residents include: Golden Eagle, Goshawk, Snowy Owl, Northern Shrike, Pine Grosbeak, and Hoary Redpoll.

Near Grantsburg is the 20,000 *Crex Meadows Wildlife Area*. To reach the area from the intersection of SR 48 and SR 70, take CR F north for about a mile. The area is made up of lakes and marshes and is an important stopover point for waterfowl in both spring and fall. Look for ducks, herons, bitterns, rails, Yellow-headed Blackbirds, and sparrows. Sandhill Cranes can often be seen from the West Refuge Road.

Schlitz Audubon Center, 1111 East Brown Deer Road, Milwaukee 53217; (414) 352-2880. The center is operated by the National Audubon Society. This 185-acre sanctuary fronts on Lake Michigan. To reach it from downtown Milwaukee, take US 141 north to Brown Deer Road Exit (SR 100), exit east and continue along Brown Deer Road to the sanctuary. The center is open all year, during daylight hours, closed on Sundays, Mondays, and holidays. An admission fee is charged to non-NAS members. Various educational and interpretive programs are offered at the center. Brochures are available for the self-guiding trails.

The center was established in 1971 and preserves a large area of undeveloped land. The marshes, open fields, mixed woodlands, ponds, ravines, and bluffs, and beach are laced with a system of trails. The variety of habitat at the center supports a diversified wildlife community. Resident animals include deer, fox, squirrel, woodchuck, skunk, and opossum. Look for Common Loon, Red-throated Loon, Horned Grebe, Mallard, Ring-necked Duck, Canvasback, Gadwall, Forster's Tern, Ruddy Turnstone, Red Knot, and sandpipers and plovers along the lake. Landbirds — especially woodpeckers, thrushes, and warblers — are to be found in the wooded areas and open fields.

Also along Lake Michigan, just south of Schlitz Audubon Center, are 3 city parks: *Lake, Juneau,* and *McKinley* — all are good for birdwatching. Look for ducks and shorebirds.

Sheboygan County Arboretum, Wilson 54027. The arboretum is owned and maintained by the University of Wisconsin, Sheboygan County Campus, P.O. Box 719, Sheboygan 53081. It is located south of Sheboygan on County OK, about a mile west of I-43 (US 141) along the railroad tracks. The arboretum is open to the public, every day.

Sheboygan County Arboretum encompasses 34 acres of hardwood forest dominated by yellow birch, black ash, green ash, and red maple. There are also swampy areas. Among the many species of birds seen at the arboretum are: Red-tailed Hawk, Red-headed Woodpecker, Eastern Kingbird, Tree Swallow, Gray Catbird, Northern (Baltimore) Oriole, Common Grackle, and Cardinal. A variety of warblers also use the area.

Trempealeau National Wildlife Refuge, Route 1, Trempealeau 54661; (608) 539-3620. Trempealeau is administered by Upper Mississippi Wild Life and Fish Refuge. The 707-acre refuge is located along the Mississippi River, just north of LaCrosse. To reach it from LaCrosse, take US 53 north to SR 35/54; turn west and continue to Centerville; 3 miles west of Centerville is a turnoff to the left that leads to the refuge. No camping is permitted at Trempealeau; however, facilities are available at nearby Perrot State Park. Various educational and interpretive programs are offered at the refuge; guided tours are available by appointment. Trails are maintained, and there is a self-guiding automobile tour.

The refuge consists of marshland, mixed woodlands, prairie, and ponds. Trempealeau's diverse habitat provides for a varied wildlife community. Among the many species of birds to be found here are: Pied-billed Grebe, Mallard, Hooded Merganser, Sharp-shinned Hawk, American Kestrel (Sparrow Hawk), Ruffed Grouse, Green Heron, Black-crowned Night Heron, Killdeer, Barred Owl, Great Horned Owl, Whip-poor-will, Hairy Woodpecker, Red-bellied Woodpecker, Willow (Traill's) Flycatcher, Least Flycatcher, Barn Swallow, Brown Creeper, House Wren, Brown Thrasher, Cedar Waxwing, Warbling Vireo, Black-and-white Warbler, Yellow-rumped (Myrtle) Warbler, Common Yellowthroat, American Redstart, Eastern and Western Meadowlarks, Indigo Bunting, and Fox Sparrow.

Upper Mississippi River Wild Life and Fish Refuge, P. O. Box 226, Winona, Minnesota 55987. There are several district offices located throughout the refuge: at Trempealeau, LaCrosse, and Cassville in Wisconsin; at Lansing in Iowa; and at Savanna in Illinois. This is one of the oldest refuges in the region; it was established in 1924. The 195,000-acre refuge extends from Wabasha (Minnesota) along both sides of the Mississippi River for 280 miles to Rock Island (Illinois). There are many public access points. Contact the refuge manager at the above address for specific information. A continuous system of highways, known as the Great River Road, closely follows the refuge boundaries. Bluffs along the way afford superb views. Limited camping on refuge islands is permitted.

Because it is so long, the refuge maintains several differing climactic conditions. The wooded islands, waters, marshes, and river bottoms combine to form a habitat conducive to many forms of plant and animal life: 113 species of fish, 45 species of amphibians and reptiles, and 50 species of mammals are found on the refuge. Checklists for all of these are available from the refuge manager.

Although particularly noted for its waterfowl population, the refuge is host to many other birds. There have been 291 species of birds (125 nesting) sighted on the refuge. Among these are: Common Loon, White Pelican, Green Heron, Whistling Swan, Snow Goose (both white and blue morphs), Wood Duck, Canvasback, Ruddy Duck, Red-breasted Merganser, Turkey Vulture, Cooper's Hawk, Rough-legged Hawk, Bald Eagle, Peregrine Falcon, Ruffed Grouse, Gray Partridge, Sora, American Avocet (rare), American Golden Plover, Black-bellied Plover, Ruddy Turnstone (rare), Baird's Sandpiper, Wilson's Phalarope, Bonaparte's Gull, Caspian Tern, Snowy Owl, Long- and Short-eared Owls, Saw-whet Owl, Pileated Woodpecker, Willow (Traill's) Flycatcher, Red-breasted Nuthatch, Winter Wren, Brown Thrasher, Loggerhead Shrike, Bell's Vireo, Philadelphia Vireo, Prothonotary Warbler, Blue-winged Warbler, Cerulean Warbler, Louisiana Waterthrush, Mourning Warbler, Canada Warbler, Eastern and Western Meadowlarks, Indigo Bunting, Hoary Redpoll (rare), Common Redpoll, White-winged Crossbill (rare), Henslow's Sparrow, Lark Sparrow, Harris' Sparrow, and Snow Bunting. Checklist available.

NATURE CENTERS

In addition to the sanctuaries, refuges, and preserves discussed above, there are several privately or locally owned nature centers, sanctuaries, and arboretums in Wisconsin. At most of these areas, a wide range of interpretive and educational programs is available. These centers are described below, in brief.

Audubon Wildlife Refuge, Madison. This 62-acre refuge is owned and maintained by the Madison Audubon Society. It is open every day. For additional information, contact the Madison Audubon Society.

Boerner Botanical Gardens, Milwaukee. The gardens are open all year; an admission fee is charged.

Camp Upham Woods, Route #1, Box 292, Wisconsin Dells 53965; (608) 254-8077. The preserve is operated by the Youth Development Department, University of Wisconsin. It covers 318 acres. Trails are maintained; guided tours are offered. The center is open every day.

Cherokee Marsh Outdoor Education Area, Madison. The area is operated by the Board of Park Comissioners, 704 East Gorham Street, Madison 53703.

Devil's Lake State Park, Nature Center, Route 4, Box 36, Baraboo 53913; (608) 356-8301. The park is operated by the Wisconsin Department of Natural Resources; it covers 5759 acres and is open all year.

Green Bay Wildlife Sanctuary, 1660 East Shore Drive, Green Bay 54302; (414) 468-7926. The sanctuary is operated by the Green Bay Park and Recreation Department. It covers 276 acres. Guided tours are available by appointment. The sanctuary is open all year. Among the birds to be seen here are: Canada Goose, Mallard, Black Duck, Downy Woodpecker, Hairy Woodpecker, Yellow-throated Vireo, and Hoary Redpoll.

Hawthorne Glen Outdoor Education Center, 1130 North 60 Street, Milwaukee 53208; (414) 475-8613. The center is operated by the Milwaukee Public Schools. It covers 25 acres. Guided tours only are available. The center is open all year.

Hawthorne Hollow Arboretum and Wildlife Sanctuary, Somers (Kenosha County); (414) 633-7124. The sanctuary is operated by the Hyslop Foundation, Inc. It covers 40 acres. Trails are maintained; guided tours are offered. The sanctuary is open all year, Wednesday through Friday; every day by appointment.

Jackson School Forest, 502 Caromar Drive, Madison 53711; (608) 233-5314. The Forest is operated by the Madison Public Schools. It covers 300 acres. Trails are maintained. Guided tours are offered. The forest is open all year.

Kenosha Botanical Gardens, Kenosha. The gardens are open all year; an admission fee is charged.

MacKenzie Environmental Center, Route 1, Poynette 53955; (608) 635-4498. The center is located 1½ miles east of Poynette, on County Q. It is operated by the Wisconsin Department of Natural Resources. The center covers 250 acres. Special features include a logging museum, an arboretum, and a display of native animals. Guided tours are offered. Trails, some self-guiding, are maintained. The center is open every day from April through October, and on weekdays from November through March. There have been 131 species of birds sighted here.

Madison Arboretum, University of Wisconsin, 1207 Seminole Highway, Madison 53711; (608) 262-2746. The arboretum is owned and maintained by the university. It covers 1240 acres. Guided tours are offered. Trails are maintained. The arboretum is open all year. Among the 90 species of birds that nest here are: Green Heron, Least Bittern, American Woodcock, Common Gallinule, Black-billed Cuckoo, Red-headed Woodpecker, Alder Flycatcher, White-breasted Nuthatch, Long- and Short-billed Marsh Wrens, Blue-gray Gnatcatcher, Wood Thrush, Yellow-throated Vireo, Eastern and Western Meadowlarks, and Savannah Sparrow.

Mitchell Park Conservatory, Mitchell Park, Milwaukee. The conservatory is open all year.

Oak Ridge Demonstration Farm, Dousman 53118; (414) 475-8192. The farm is operated by the Milwaukee Public Schools in cooperation with the Wisconsin Department of Natural Resources. It covers 100 acres. Only guided tours are available. The farm is open all year.

Palmyra Camp, Bluff Road, Palmyra 53119; (414) 475-8192. The camp is located in Kettle Moraine State Forest-South. It is operated by the Milwaukee Public Schools and covers 90 acres. Guided tours only are offered. The camp is open all year.

Riveredge Nature Center, P. O. Box 92, 4311 West Hawthorne Drive, Newberg 53060. The center covers 250 acres. Trails are maintained. Guided tours are offered. The center is open all year, closed during August.

Todd Wehr Nature Center, Whitenall Park, 5879 South 92 Street, Hales Corner (Milwaukee) 53130; (414) 425-1133. The center is operated by the Milwaukee County Park Commission. It covers 655 acres. Guided tours are offered; trails are maintained. The center is open all year, closed on weekends in the winter except for special events.

NATURE CONSERVANCY PRESERVES

The Wisconsin Chapter of The Nature Conservancy owns and maintains many preserves located throughout the state. Some of these preserves have been deeded to the University of Wisconsin or to the state. They vary greatly in size and habitat. For the exact location, traveling directions, and more information about these preserves, contact: Wisconsin Chapter, The Nature Conservancy, 2809 Sylvan Avenue, Madison 53705 or the preserve manager in charge. Most of the preserves are described briefly below; they are not shown on the map.

Ableman's Gorge, Rock Springs. The preserve totals nearly 7 acres and features a 200-foot notch cut by the Baraboo River. It consists mainly of a mixed woodland with patches of prairie. Ableman's Gorge is owned by the University of Wisconsin; contact: Robert Dott, Madison; (608) 262-1856.

Abraham's Woods, Albany. This 40-acre preserve is characterized by a maple-basswood forest. The understory features many beautiful spring wildflowers including spring beauty, trillium, trout lily, and Dutchman's breeches. The preserve is owned by the University of Wisconsin; contact: Katherine Bradley, Madison; (608) 262-2746.

Anderson Bottomlands. This tract runs along the Wisconsin River in Iowa County. It totals 119 acres and contains black oak barrens, lowland forest, and a freshwater slough. It is owned by the University of Wisconsin; contact: Katherine Bradley, Madison; (608) 262-2746.

Baxter's Hollow, Baraboo Hills, Sauk County. This 289-acre preserve is highlighted by Otter Creek. It consists of mixed woodlands. Winter Wrens nest here. The preserve is owned by The Nature Conservancy; contact: Donald Kindschi, 2554 Kendall Avenue, Madison; (608) 256-1901.

Benedict Prairie, Woodworth. The preserve totals 6 acres and features many rare plants. It is owned by the University of Wisconsin; contact: Philip Whitford, Milwaukee; (414) 228-4213.

Beulah Bog, East Troy. This 62-acre preserve is the most outstanding sphagnum bog in the region. It is surrounded by a tamarack swamp forest. The preserve is owned by the Department of Natural Resources; contact: Cliff Germain, Madison; (608) 266-8916.

Chiwaukee Prairie, Kenosha. The preserve covers 81 acres and is the best remaining example of a Lake Michigan shore low prairie. The low ridges permit both wet and dry prairie plants to coexist. The preserve is a registered national natural landmark. It is owned by the University of Wisconsin-Parkside; contact: Eugene Gasiorkiewicz, Kenosha; (414) 553-2206.

Comstock Marsh, Montello. This 240-acre preserve is a complex of sedge bog and open marsh with a small area of tamaracks. It is a resting place for migrating Sandhill Cranes. The preserve is owned by the Department of Natural Resources; contact: Cliff Germain, Madison; (608) 266-8916.

Decorah Mound, Galesville. This 30-acre preserve consists of a wooded bluff. On the south the slopes are characterized by oak-hickory; on the north by maple, basswood, and beech. The preserve is owned by The Nature Conservancy; contact: Winston Elkins, Trempealeau; (608) 534-6423.

Durst Rockshelter, Baraboo Hills (Sauk County). This 40-acre preserve is best known as an archeological site. It is owned by The Nature Conservancy; contact: Harold Kruse, Loganville; (608) 727-2289.

Fairy Chasm, Mequon. The preserve totals 19 acres. It consists of mixed woodlands. The forest floor is covered with wildflowers in springtime, including trailing arbutus, lady's slipper, and Jack-in-the-pulpit. Look for songbirds here. The preserve is owned by The Nature Conservancy; contact: Lorrie Otto, Milwaukee; (414) 352-0734.

Falk Woods, Waukesha County. The preserve covers 58 acres and consists of woodlands, open fields, and wetlands. Tamarack and aspen groves and cattail marsh characterize the wetlands. It is owned by The Nature Conservancy; contact: Peter Salamun, Milwaukee; (414) 228-4213.

Ferry Bluff, Sauk City. This 37-acre preserve is a high, wooded bluff that overlooks the Wisconsin River. It consists of mixed woodlands and a dry, limey prairie. The preserve is owned by the Head Foundation; contact: Frank Tervilcox, Baraboo; (608) 356-6208.

Fried-Sarona Forest, Washburn County. This 160-acre preserve is made up of mixed northern hardwoods. It fronts on Sunfish Lake. The preserve is owned by the University of Wisconsin-Eau Claire; contact: Marcus Fay, Eau Claire; (715) 836-4166.

Fried Sunfish Lake Forest, Washburn County. The 79-acre tract consists of a pine barrens that is quite level and has extremely sandy soil. The forest is composed of oak and jack pine. The preserve is owned by the University of Wisconsin-Eau Claire; contact: Marcus Fay, Eau Claire; (715) 836-4166.

Harris Tract, Paddock Lake (Kenosha County). This 257-acre preserve is composed of oak woods and cattail marsh. There are also open fields and small ponds. The preserve is owned by the University of Wisconsin-Parkside; contact: Eugene Gasiorkiewicz, Kenosha; (414) 553-2206.

Hemlock Draw, Baraboo Hills (Sauk County). This preserve is a long east-west canyon with mixed northern hardwood forests, stands of hemlock, upland oak forests, sandstone cliffs overlooking a brook, and small marshy areas. The preserve covers 540 acres and provides habitat for many nesting birds. It is owned by The Nature Conservancy; contact Harold Kruse, Loganville; (608) 727-2289.

Heritage Sanctuary, Madison. This sanctuary totals nearly 10 acres. It consists of an oak-hickory forest with many wildflowers growing on the forest floor. The preserve is owned by the Madison Parks Department; (608) 266-4711.

High Trestle Woods, Oshkosh. This 12-acre preserve features the rare Kentucky coffee tree. It is a floodplain forest with a wide variety of spring wildflowers. The preserve is owned by the University of Wisconsin-Oshkosh; contact: William Sloey, Oshkosh; (414) 424-5111.

Holmboe Preserve, Rhinelander. This preserve totals 32 acres of mixed woodlands located on the south side of the Pelican River. Walking is difficult in some areas because of steep slopes. A wide variety of spring wildflowers, including a number of orchids, bloom here. The preserve is owned by The Nature Conservancy; contact: John Thomson, Madison; (608) 262-2690.

Hub City Bog, Hub City. This preserve is a 55-acre tamarack bog. It is owned by the University of Wisconsin; contact: Robert Hirschy, Richland Center; (608) 647-6186.

Jackson Harbor Ridges, Washington Island. This 39-acre preserve consists of beach, dunes, and upland woods. It is a nesting area for hawks and warblers. For additional information, contact: Washington Island Natural Area Board, Washington Island 54246.

Jung Hemlocks, Shawano. This 80-acre preserve consists of a northern hardwood forest characterized by hemlock, American beech, and sugar maple. It is owned by the Department of Natural Resources; contact: Cliff Germain, Madison; (608) 266-8916.

Kettle Pond, Madison. This 8-acre preserve consists of a 2-acre pond bordered by fields, marsh, and some woodlands. It is owned by the Madison Parks Department; (608) 266-4711.

Leopold Woods, Baraboo Hills (Sauk County). This 80-acre tract is characterized by mixed woodlands. It is owned by The Nature Conservancy; contact: Harold Kruse, Loganville; (608) 727-2289.

Lodde's Mill Bluff, Sauk City. The preserve totals 17 acres. It is a sandstone bluff overlooking the lower Wisconsin River. Mixed woodlands cover the slopes. It is owned by the University of Wisconsin; contact: Katherine Bradley, Madison (608) 262-2746.

Nelson Oak Woods, Waukesha County. This 66-acre preserve consists of oak-hickory woodlands and a marshy area along Scuppernong Creek. It is owned by the University of Wisconsin-Waukesha; contact: Marlin Johnson, Waukesha; (414) 542-8825.

Newark Road Prairie, Beloit. This 22-acre preserve consists of a wet prairie and sedge meadow. White-fringed orchid, bottle gentian, shooting star, blazing star, and cream false indigo bloom here. The preserve is owned by The Nature Conservancy; contact: Richard Newsome, Beloit; (608) 365-3391.

Peat Lake, Kenosha County. This 157-acre preserve is a small, shallow lake surrounded by cattail marsh and sedge meadow. Look for herons, rails, and waterfowl here. The preserve is owned by the Department of Natural Resources; contact the wildlife manager, Burlington; (414) 763-7637.

Pine Hollow, Baraboo Hills (Sauk County). This 183-acre preserve is a heavily wooded, north-south canyon. It is owned by The Nature Conservancy; contact: Harold Kruse, Loganville; (608) 727-2289.

Ranger Mac Fen, Burlington. This 30-acre fen consists of a limey wet meadow. It is owned by the University of Wisconsin-Parkside; contact: Eugene Gasiorkiewicz, Kenosha; (414) 553-2206.

Renack-Polak Woods, Caledonia Township (Racine County). The preserve covers 46 acres and consists of a maple-basswood forest with a small bottomland along an intermittent stream. A variety of wildflowers bloom in the spring. The preserve is owned by The Nature Conservancy; contact: Al Krampert, Kenosha; (414) 657-7940.

Sacia Memorial Ridge, Galesville. This preserve totals nearly 29 acres. It consists of oak-hickory woods surrounded by apple orchards and farmland. Look for Ruffed Grouse. The preserve is owned by The Nature Conservancy; contact: Winston Elkins, Trempealeau; (608) 534-6423.

Schluckebier Sand Prairie, Prairie du Sac. This 22-acre preserve is a sand prairie with rare plant life. It is owned by The Nature Conservancy; contact: Donald Kindschi, 2554 Kendall Avenue, Madison; (608) 256-1901.

Schmidt Woods, Stanley. This 80-acre preserve is a mixed hardwood forest. Ferns and wildflowers flourish on the forest floor. The preserve is owned by the University of Wisconsin-Eau Claire; contact: Marcus Fay, Eau Claire; (715) 836-4166.

Spring Green, Spring Green. This 260-acre preserve consists of dry, sandy plain with a steep, rocky slope. A number of plants found here are more characteristic of the dry western plains than of Wisconsin. An unusual number and variety of reptiles live here. The preserve is owned by The Nature Conservancy; contact: Frank Terbilcox, Baraboo; (608) 356-6208.

Summerton Bog, Endeavor. The 250-acre preserve is located in a 3000-acre sedge marsh — containing springs, several tamarack swamps, and a small sandy island supporting oaks and prairie plants. Of special interest is a small meadow between the oak island and tamaracks that has fen plants, wild lilies, and 9 species of wild orchids. Sandhill Crane, Veery, and Nashville Warbler are among the many birds to be seen here. The bog is a registered national natural landmark. It is owned by The Nature Conservancy; contact: Russell Morris, 2309 Chamberlain Avenue, Madison; (608) 233-1917.

Sumpter Bluffs, Baraboo Hills (Sauk County). The preserve covers 100 acres and is located in the Baraboo Hills, adjoining Ice Age NSR. There is a 10-acre red oak grove in the preserve. Ferns and wildflowers grow on the forest floor. The preserve is owned by The Nature Conservancy; contact: Donald Kindschi, 2554 Kendall Avenue, Madison; (608) 256-1901.

Thiemann Arboretum. This 7-acre preserve is chiefly of botanical interest. It is located near the University of Wisconsin-Milwaukee Field Station, in Washington County, and is owned by the university. For further information, contact: Peter Salamun, Milwaukee; (414) 228-4213.

Toft Point, Bailey's Harbor. The preserve totals over 600 acres, and is located adjacent to the Ridges Sanctuary (see page 316). It consists of mixed woodlands, Lake Michigan shoreline, white cedar swamplands, and a large marsh. The marsh is attractive to many species of waterfowl. Among the many birds seen here are: Olive-sided Flycatcher, Red-breasted Nuthatch, Winter Wren, Northern Parula, Nashville Warbler, and Black-throated Green Warbler. Toft Point is a registered national natural landmark. The preserve is owned by the University of Wisconsin-Green Bay; contact: Keith White, Green Bay; (414) 465-2270.

Two Creeks Forest Bed, Two Rivers. This 12-acre preserve is located within the Ice Age NSR. The preserved buried spruce forest reflects glaciation. The preserve is owned by the Department of Natural Resources; contact: Larry Ketchbaw, manager, Point Beach State Park; (414) 794-7480.

Waubesa Wetlands, Madison. This 80-acre preserve is located on the southwest corner of Lake Waubesa. It includes sedge meadows, several springs, floating mats, and a sizeable fen. An adjacent 127-acre tract of wetlands is owned by the Department of Natural Resources. Sandhill Cranes are among the nesting birds. The preserve is owned by The Nature Conservancy; contact: Cal DeWitt, Madison; (608) 266-8916.

STATE PARKS AND FORESTS

State parks and forests are to be found all over Wisconsin. Most of these areas offer camping in addition to a wide range of recreational activities including canoeing, swimming, and hiking. Although not intended as wildlife sanctuaries, some parks have nature centers, naturalists on duty, and interpretive programs. Much of this, however, is during the summer months only. Those parks that are likely to be good birdwatching places are marked with an asterisk (*).

STATE PARKS

Ahnapee Trail, Sturgeon Bay 54235; 203 acres; day use only.
Amnicon Falls, Brule 54820; 816 acres.
Aztalan, Stoughton 53589; 172 acres; day use only.
*Big Bay, Washburn 54891; 1690 acres.
Big Foot Beach, Lake Geneva 53147; 271 acres.
Blue Mound, Blue Mounds 53517; 1042 acres.
Brunet Island, Cornell 54732; 1032 acres.
Cadiz Springs, Monroe 53566; 18 acres; day use only.
Copper Falls, Mellen 54546; 2252 acres.
Council Grounds, Merrill 54452; 283 acres.
Cushing, Eagle 53119; 9 acres; day use only.
*Devil's Lake, Baraboo 53913; 5769 acres; nature center; part of Ice Age NSR.
Elroy Sparta Trail, Sparta 54656; 571 acres.
First Capitol, Dodgeville 53533; 195 acres; day use only.
*Governor Dodge, Dodgeville 53533; 5029 acres.
*Harrington Beach, Belgium 53004; 636 acres; day use only.
Hartman Creek, Waupaca 54981; 1005 acres.
*High Cliff, Menasha 54952; 1025 acres.
*Interstate, St. Croix Falls 54024; 1174 acres; nature center; part of Ice Age NSR.
*John M. Kohler, Sheboygan 53081; 544 acres; day use only; nature center.
Lake Kegonsa, Stoughton 53589; 343 acres.
Lake Wissota, Chippewa Falls 54729; 1044 acres.
Lizard Mound, Hartford 53027; 31 acres; day use only.
Lost Dauphin, Menasha 54952; 19 acres; day use only.
*Lucius Woods, Gordon 54838; 41 acres.
Merrick, Fountain City 54629; 325 acres.
*Mill Bluff, Tomah 54660; 747 acres; part of Ice Age NSR.

Mirror Lake, Baraboo 53913; 1990 acres.

Nelson Dewey, Cassville 53806; 744 acres; nature center.

New Glarus Woods, New Glarus 53574; 106 acres.

*Newport, Ellison Bay 54210; 1991 acres.

Ojibwa, Winter 54896; 365 acres.

Old Wade House, Greenbush 53026; 254 acres; day use only.

Pattison, Superior 54880; 1368 acres.

*Peninsula, Fish Creek 54212; 3763 acres; nature center.

*Perrot, Trempealeau 54661; 1393 acres; nature center.

Pike Lake, Hartford 53027; 678 acres.

*Potawatomi, Sturgeon Bay 54235; 1126 acres.

Rib Mountain, Mosinee 54455; 855 acres.

Roche A Cri, Friendship 53934; 411 acres.

*Rock Island, Washington Island 54246; 783 acres.

Rocky Arbor, Baraboo 53913; 225 acres.

Sugar River Trail, New Glarus 53574; 277 acres; day use only.

*Terry Andrae, Sheboygan 53081; 206 acres, nature center.

Tower Hill, Spring Green 53588; 108 acres.

Wildcat Mountain, Ontario 54651; 2907 acres.

Willow River, Hudson 54016; 2520 acres; nature center.

*Wyalusing, Bagley 53801; 2597 acres; nature center.

Yellowstone, Blanchardville 53516; 373 acres.

STATE FORESTS

*Apostle Islands, Washburn 54891; 16,609 acres.

*Black River, Black River Falls 54615; 64,584 acres.

*Brule River, Brule 54820; 33,790 acres.

*Flambeau River, Winter 54896; 86,385 acres.

*Kettle Moraine-North, Campbellsport 53010; 26,457 acres; nature center; part of Ice Age NSR.

*Kettle Moraine-South, Eagle 53119; 15,896 acres; nature center; part of Ice Age NSR.

*North Highland-American Legion, Boulder Junction 54512; 198,000 acres; nature center.

*Point Beach, Two Rivers 54241; 2770 acres; nature center.

For additional information concerning facilities and other features of Wisconsin state parks and forests, contact: State of Wisconsin, Department of Natural Resources, Box 440, Madison 53701.

Bibliography

The bibliography makes no attempt to be inclusive of all major books on ornithology. For excellent advice on this subject, the reader is referred to "Choosing a Basic Ornithological Library," *American Birds* 30:1009-16; "The Master List of Bird Books for North American Readers," *American Birds* 30:1016-18; and "An Annotated Selection of Regional Bird Books," *American Birds* 30:1018-23. A listing of national organizations and publications and journals related to birding follows this bibliography.

Albright, Priscilla and Rodney. *Short Walks on Long Island*. Chester, Connecticut: The Pequot Press, 1974.

Allen, Arthur. *The Book of Bird Life*, 2nd ed. New York: Van Nostrand Co., 1961.

———. *Stalking Birds with a Color Camera*. Washington, D.C.: National Geographic Society, 1951.

Anderson, Richard, and Richardson, Irving, ed. *Enjoying Maine Birds*, rev. ed. Portland: The Maine Audubon Society, 1972.

Arbib, Robert S., Jr.; Pettingill, Olin S., Jr.; and Spofford, Sally H. *Enjoying Birds Around New York City*. Boston: Houghton Mifflin Company, 1966.

Barbour, Roger W.; Peterson, Clell T.; Rust, Delbert; Shadowen, Herbert W; and Whitt, A.L., Jr. *Kentucky Birds; a Finding Guide*. Lexington: The University Press of Kentucky, 1973.

Berger, Andrew, Jr. *Bird Study*. 1961. Reprint. New York: Dover Publications, 1971.

Billard, Ruth Sawyer. *Places to Look for Birds*. Hartford: State of Connecticut Department of Environmental Protection, 1972.

Brady, Alan; Logan, W. Ronald; Miller, John C.; Reynold, George B.; and Sehl, Robert H. *A Field List of Birds of the Delaware Valley Region*. Philadelphia: Delaware Valley Ornithological Club, 1972.

Broun, Maurice. *Hawks Aloft*. New York: Dodd, Mead, and Co., 1948.

Bucklew, Albert R., Jr. "Birds of the West Virginia Northern Panhandle," *Redstart*, in press.

Bull, John. *Birds of the New York Area*. New York: Harper and Row, 1964.

Chapman, Frank. *Handbook of Birds of Eastern North America*. 1939. Reprint. New York: Dover Publications, 1966.

Comar, M.; Kibbe, D.; and McIlroy, D., eds. *Birding in the Cayuga Lake Basin*. Ithaca, New York: Laboratory of Ornithology, 1974.

Drennan, Susan Rodney. "National Directory of Rare Bird Alerts," *American Birds* 29:8-11.

Flugum, Charles, *Birding From a Tractor Seat*. New York: Thomas Y. Crowell, 1975.

Freeland, David B. *Where to Find Birds in Western Pennsylvania*. Pittsburgh: Audubon Society of Western Pennsylvania, 1975.

Green, Charlotte Hilton. *Birds of the South; Permanent and Winter Birds*. 1933. Reprint. New York: Dover Publications, 1975.

Green Mountain Audubon Society. *Birds of Vermont*. Burlington: Green Mountain Audubon Society, no date.

Hans, Daniel W., ed. *A Birder's Guide to Georgia*. Atlanta: Georgia Ornithological Society, no date.

Harwood, Michael. *The View from Hawk Mountain*. New York: Charles Scribner's Sons, 1973.

Hickey, Joseph J. *A Guide to Bird Watching*. 1943. Reprint. New York: Dover Publications, 1975.

Kaufmann, John, and Meng, Heinz. *Falcons Return*. New York: William Morrow and Company, 1975.

Kitching, Jessie. *Birdwatcher's Guide to Wildlife Sanctuaries*. New York: Arco Publishing Company, Inc., 1976.

Krutch, Joseph Wood, and Eriksson, Paul. *Treasury of Birdlore*. New York: Paul Eriksson, Inc. 1962.

Laycock, George. *The Bird Watcher's Bible*. Garden City, New York: Doubleday and Company, 1976.

Leahy, Christopher W. *An Introduction to Massachusetts Birds*. Lincoln: Massachusetts Audubon Society, 1975.

Leck, Charles. *Birds of New Jersey: Their Habits and Habitats*. New Brunswick: Rutgers University Press, 1975.

Lobik, Paul H., and Fawks, Elton. *Bird Finding in Illinois*. Downers Grove: The Illinois Audubon Society, 1975.

McElroy, Thomas, Jr. *The Habitat Guide to Birding*. New York: Alfred A. Knopf, 1974.

The Nature Conservancy. *Preserve Directory*. Arlington, Virginia: The Nature Conservancy, 1974.

National Audubon Society. *Directory of Nature Centers and Related Environmental Education Facilities*. New York: National Audubon Society, 1975.

Ogburn, Charlton. *The Adventure of Birds*. New York: William Morrow and Company, Inc., 1976.

Peterson, Roger Tory. *Bird Watchers Anthology*. New York: Harcourt Brace and Company, 1957.

————. *A Field Guide to the Birds; Eastern Land and Water Birds*, 2nd ed., Boston: Houghton Mifflin Company, 1947.

Pettingill, Olin Sewall, Jr., ed. *The Bird Watcher's America*. New York: Thomas Y. Crowell Company, 1965.

————. *A Guide to Bird Finding; East of the Mississippi*. New York: Oxford University Press, 1951. (Revised edition, 1977)

————, and Spofford, Sally Hoyt. *Enjoying Birds in Upstate New York,* 4th ed. Ithaca: Laboratory of Ornithology, 1974.

Piatt, Jean. *Adventures in Birding; Confessions of a Lister.* New York: Alfred A. Knopf, 1973.

Plough, Richard. *Audubon Guides: All the Birds of Eastern and Central North America.* Garden City, New York: Doubleday and Company, 1946-1951.

Robbins, Chandler S; Bruun, Bertel; and Zim, Herbert S. *A Guide to Field Identification; Birds of North America.* New York: Golden Press, 1966.

Rue, Leonard Lee III. *Pictorial Guide to the Birds of North America.* New York: Thomas Y. Crowell Company, 1970.

Sprunt, Alexander, Jr., and Chamberlain, E.B. *South Carolina Bird Life,* rev. ed. Columbia: University of South Carolina Press, 1970.

Steffee, Nina D., and Mason C. Russell, eds. *Where to Find Birds and Enjoy Natural History in Florida.* Maitland: Florida Audubon Society, 1971.

Stirling, David, and Woodford, Jim. *Where to go Birdwatching in Canada.* Saanichton, B.C.: Hancock House Publishers, Ltd., 1975.

Stone, Witmer. *Bird Studies at Old Cape May.* 2 vols. 1937. Reprint. New York: Dover Publications, 1965.

Stupka, Arthur. *Notes on the Birds of Great Smoky Mountain National Park.* Knoxville: University of Tennessee Press, 1963.

Sutton, Ann and Myron. *Wilderness Areas of North America.* New York: Funk & Wagnalls, 1974.

Tahoma Audubon Society. *Nature Guide.* Federal Way, Washington: Tahoma Audubon Society, 1976.

Tate, James, Jr., and Kibbe, Douglas P. "Update Your Field Guides," *American Birds* 28:747-53.

Thompson, William L., ed. *Enjoying Birds in Michigan,* 3rd ed. Kalamazoo: Michigan Audubon Society, 1973.

Trautman, Milton B., and Mary A., "Annotated List of the Birds of Ohio," reprinted from *The Ohio Journal of Science* 68 (1968):257-332.

Related Publications

Acres Quarterly. Acres, Inc., 1802 Chapman Road, Huntertown, Indiana 46748

Alabama Conservation. Alabama Department of Conservation, Administration Building, Montgomery, Alabama 36104

American Birds. National Audubon Society, 950 Third Avenue, New York, New York 10022

Atlantic Naturalist. Audubon Society of the Central Atlantic States, Inc., 8940 Jones Mill Road, Washington, D.C. 20015

Audubon. National Audubon Society, 950 Third Avenue, New York, New York 10022

Audubon Flyer. Chattanooga Audubon Society, P.O. Box 245, Chattanooga, Tennessee 37401

The Auk; Journal of Ornithology. American Ornithologists' Union, National Museum of Natural History, Smithsonian Institution, Washington, D.C. 20560

Bird Banding; a Journal of Ornithological Investigation. Northeastern Bird-Banding Association, Inc., c/o Lydia Kennard, Treasurer, RR 5, Box 150, Bedford, New Hampshire 03102

Birding. American Birding Association, Box 4335, Austin, Texas 78765

Call. National Birdwatching Society, 2519 Maryland Avenue, Baltimore, Maryland 21218

Chat. Carolina Bird Club, Box 1220, Tryon, North Carolina 28782

Condor. Cooper Ornithological Society, Inc. c/o Treasurer, Oakland Museum, Natural Sciences Division, 1000 Oak Street, Oakland, California 94670

Connecticut Conservation Reporter. Connecticut Conservation Association, Northrup Street, Bridgewater, Connecticut 06752

Conservationist. New York State Environmental Conservation Department, Wolf Road, Albany, New York 12201

Conserve. Western Pennsylvania Conservancy, 204 Fifth Avenue, Pittsburgh, Pennsylvania 15222

Defenders of Wildlife. Defenders of Wildlife, 2000 N Street, NW, Washington, D.C. 20036

Ducks Unlimited. Ducks Unlimited, Inc., Box 66300, Chicago, Illinois 60666

EBBA News. Eastern Bird Banding Association, 84-55 Daniels Street, Jamaica, New York 11435

Florida Naturalist. Florida Audubon Society, P.O. Drawer 7, Maitland, Florida 32751

Florida Wildlife. Florida Game and Fresh Water Fish Commission, Farris Bryant Building, 620 S. Meridian Street, Tallahassee, Florida 32304

Flower and Feather. Chattanooga Audubon Society, 1100 Lula Lake Road, Lookout Mountain, Tennessee 37350

Forest Notes; New Hampshire's Conservation Magazine. Society for the Protection of New Hampshire Forests, 5 S. State Street, Concord, New Hampshire 03301

Friend O'Wildlife. North Carolina Wildlife Federation, Inc., Box 10626, Raleigh, North Carolina 27605

Georgia Conservancy Newsletter. Georgia Conservancy, 3376 Peachtree Road, NE, Atlanta, Georgia 30326

Highlands Voice. West Virginia Highlands Conservancy, 206 Union Street, Webster Springs, West Virginia 26288

Illinois Audubon Bulletin. Illinois Audubon Society, 1017 Burlington, Downers Grove, Illinois 60515

Illinois Wildlife. Illinois Wildlife Federation, 13005 S. Western Avenue, Blue Island, Illinois 60406

Indiana Audubon Quarterly. Indiana Audubon Society, Inc., RR #6, Connersville Indiana 47331

Jack Pine Warbler. Michigan Audubon Society, 7000 N. Westnedge, Kalamazoo, Michigan 49001

Kingbird. Federation of New York Bird Clubs, Inc., 20 Parish Road, Honeoye Falls, New York 14472

Linnaean Newsletter. Linnaean Society of New York, American Museum of Natural History, Central Park West at 79th Street, New York, New York 10024

The Living Bird. Cornell Laboratory of Ornithology, Cornell University, Ithaca, New York 14850

The Living Wilderness. Wilderness Society, 1901 Pennsylvania Avenue, Washington, D.C. 20006.

Maryland Birdlife. Maryland Ornithological Society, Inc., Clyburn Mansion 4915 Greenspring Avene, Baltimore, Maryland 21209

Maryland Conservationist. Maryland Department of Natural Resources, Tawes State Office building, B-3, Annapolis, Maryland 21401

Manomet Bird Observatory Research Report. Manomet Bird Observatory, P.O. Box O, Manomet, Massachusetts 02345

Massachusetts Wildlife. Massachusetts Division of Fisheries and Game, Field Headquarters, Westboro, Massachusetts 01581

Michigan Natural Resources. Michigan Department of Natural Resources, Mason Building, Lansing, Michigan 48926

Michigan Out-of-Doors. Michigan United Conservation Clubs, Inc., Box 2235, Lansing, Michigan 48911

Migrant. Tennessee Ornithological Society, c/o Gary Wallace, Ed., Route 7, Sunrise Drive, Box 338, Elizabethton, Tennessee 37643

Mississippi Game and Fish. Mississippi Game and Fish Commission, Box 451, Jackson, Mississippi 39205

National Parks and Conservation Magazine. National Parks and Conservation Association, 1701 18 Street, N.W., Washington, D.C. 20009

National Wildlife. National Wildlife Federation, Inc., 1412 16 Street, N.W., Washington, D.C. 20036

Nature Conservancy News. The Nature Conservancy, 1800 N. Kent Street, Arlington, Virginia 22209

Nature Guide. Tahoma Audubon Society, 34915 4th Avenue South, Federal Way, Washington 98003

New Hampshire Audubon Quarterly. Audubon Society of New Hampshire, 3 Silk Farm Road, Concord, New Hampshire 03301

New Hampshire Audubon News. Audubon Society of New Hampshire.

New Hampshire Conservation Commission News. New Hampshire Association of Conservation Commissioners, 5 S. State Street, Concord, New Hampshire 03301

New Jersey Audubon. New Jersey Audubon Society, 790 Ewing Avenue, Franklin Lakes, New Jersey 07417

New York City Audubon Newsletter. National Audubon Society, 950 Third Avenue, New York, New York 10022

Oriole. Georgia Ornithological Society, c/o T. McRae Williams, 775 Ellsworth Drive, NW Atlanta, Georgia 30318

Passenger Pigeon; a Magazine of Wisconsin Bird Study. Wisconsin Society for Ornithology, Inc., 733 Maple Street, Chippewa Falls, Wisconsin 54729

Purple Martin News. Griggsville Wild Bird Society, Griggsville, Illinois 62340

Raptor Report. Society for the Preservation of Birds of Prey, Pacific Palisades, California 90272

Raven. Virginia Society of Ornithology, 115 Kennondale Lane, Richmond, Virginia 23226

Redstart. Brooks Bird Club, 707 Warwood Avenue, Wheeling, West Virginia 26003

Sierra Club Bulletin. Sierra Club, 1050 Mills Tower, San Francisco, California 94104

South Carolina Wildlife. South Carolina Wildlife Resources Department, Box 167, Columbia, South Carolina 29202

Tennessee Conservationist. Tennessee Department of Conservation, 2611 West End Avenue, Nashville, Tennessee 37203

Virginia Wildlife. Virginia Commission of Game and Inland Fisheries, Box 11104, Richmond, Virginia 23230

Wildlife in North Carolina. North Carolina Wildlife Resources Commission, Albemarle Building, 325 N. Salisbury Street, Raleigh, North Carolina 27611

Wildlife Society Bulletin. The Wildlife Society, Suite S-176, 3900 Wisconsin Avenue, N.W., Washington, D.C. 20016

Wilson Bulletin; a Quarterly Magazine of Ornithology. Wilson Ornithological Society, Department of Zoology, Mississippi State University, Mississippi State, Mississippi 39762

Wisconsin Conservation Bulletin. Wisconsin Department of Natural Resources, Madison, Wisconsin 53701

Related Organizations

The following organizations are national or regional. Statewide organizations are mentioned in chapter introductions.

American Birding Association, Box 4335, Austin, Texas 78765

American Land Trust, P.O. Box 2076, Arlington, Virginia 22202

American Ornithologists' Union, National Museum of Natural History, Smithsonian Institution, Washington, D.C. 20560

Appalachian Mountain Club, 5 Joy Street, Boston, Massachusetts 02101

Federation of New York State Bird Clubs, 20 Drumlins Terrace, Syracuse, New York 13224

Linnean Society, American Museum of Natural History, Central Park West at 79th Street, New York, New York 10024

National Audubon Society, 950 Third Avenue, New York, New York 10022

National Wildlife Federation, 1412 16th Street, N.W. Washington, D.C. 20036

The Nature Conservancy, Eastern Regional Office, 294 Washington Street, Room 850, Boston, Massachusetts 02180

The Nature Conservancy, Midwest Regional Office, 325 West 15 Street, Minneapolis, Minnesota 55403

The Nature Conservancy, National Office, 1800 N. Kent Street, Arlington, Virginia 22209

The Nature Conservancy, Southeast Regional Office, 148 International Boulevard, NE, Atlanta, Georgia 30303

Sierra Club, Atlantic Chapter, 50 West 40 Street, New York, New York 10018

Sierra Club, National Office, 1050 Mills Tower, San Francisco, California 94104

Wilderness Society, 1901 Pennsylvania Avenue, Washington, D.C. 20006

The Wildlife Society, S-176, 3900 Wisconsin Avenue, N.W., Washington, D.C. 20016

Index